poverty/
privilege

 Other titles in this
series include:

poverty/
privilege

A READER *for* WRITERS

Connie Snyder Mick

University of Notre Dame

New York   Oxford
Oxford University Press

Oxford University Press publishes works that further Oxford University's
objective of excellence in research, scholarship, and education.

Oxford   New York
Auckland   Cape Town   Dar es Salaam   Hong Kong   Karachi
Kuala Lumpur   Madrid   Melbourne   Mexico City   Nairobi
New Delhi   Shanghai   Taipei   Toronto

With offices in
Argentina   Austria   Brazil   Chile   Czech Republic   France   Greece
Guatemala   Hungary   Italy   Japan   Poland   Portugal   Singapore
South Korea   Switzerland   Thailand   Turkey   Ukraine   Vietnam

For titles covered by Section 112 of the US Higher Education
Opportunity Act, please visit www.oup.com/us/he for the
latest information about pricing and alternate formats.

Published by Oxford University Press
198 Madison Avenue, New York, New York 10016
http://www.oup.com

Oxford is a registered trademark of Oxford University Press

Library of Congress Cataloging-in-Publication Data
Poverty/privilege : a reader for writers / [edited by] Connie Snyder Mick.
    pages cm
  ISBN 978-0-19-936125-0
  1. Poverty. 2. Wealth. 3. Social stratification. I. Mick, Connie Snyder. II. Title:
Poverty, privilege.
  HC79.P6P687 2014
  305.5'12--dc23
                                                        2014033950

Printing number: 9 8 7 6 5 4 3 2 1

Printed in the United States of America
on acid-free paper

brief table of contents

contents

"[A]s the nation began to embrace the conviction that access to education
is the pathway to social and economic mobility, poor women were denied
access to education that could have positively altered the course of their
lives and those of their children."

"People in the U.S. experiencing poverty by the age of 65: roughly half."

"[T]he Census Bureau uses a set of money income thresholds that vary by
family size and composition to determine who is in poverty."

"The core premise of the capability approach is that well-being should be defined by people's real and actual opportunities to undertake the pursuits that
they desire . . . and through these freedoms, be whom they would like to be."

"When asked, most poor families stated they had sufficient funds during the
past year to meet all essential needs."

"[M]oving toward broader measures of poverty and deprivation than simply
income has a number of advantages."

"For all the real horrors of slum existence today, it still usually beats staying in
a village."

2 Causes: Why Are People Poor?   71

"We need to distinguish between someone who is poor because he cannot find work and someone who is poor because she is unwilling to work."

"Mutually reinforcing inequalities in health, environment, education, and wealth have created a large and growing opportunity divide that wages alone cannot bridge."

"No longer can we measure compassion by how much we spend on poverty, but how many people we help to rise out of poverty. Adding endlessly to the debt is not compassionate—it is destructive."

"In this respect, for-profit schools function less like traditional educational institutions and more like payday lenders, rent-to-own businesses, pawn shops and the like—they all offer products that churn customers through debt for years on end."

"Discrimination in virtually every aspect of political, economic, and social life is now perfectly legal, if you've been labeled a felon."

"In many ways, black men in America are a walking gut check; we learn from them a lot about ourselves, how far we've really come as a country, and how much further we have to go."

"I did not learn how to treat this in medical school. There was no medicine for grief, for the inevitability of urban violence. I felt powerless. I mumbled my sympathy and asked her to return in a month to recheck her blood pressure."

"These 100 research questions would, if answered, help to reduce or prevent poverty."

3 Consequences: Who Is Poor? 157

"[W]hen the temp office clerk announces that there's a job available, Harper leaps at it even though the gig starts at 2 a.m. and he knows he'll have to arrive at the work site in the early evening, thanks to Fresno's limited bus service. He shrugs off the six hours he'll waste 'twiddling his thumbs.'"

"The laws that protect these workers are grossly inadequate. More importantly, the workers' ability to enforce what protections they do have is generally nonexistent."

"Food insecurity may reflect a household's need to make trade-offs between important basic needs, such as housing or medical bills, and purchasing nutritionally adequate foods."

"When nearly everyone in the county is poor, the distinction between have and have-not becomes meaningless. There are have-very-little's, but even they wouldn't always call themselves poor. . . . As far as Sue was concerned, 'poor' was the word for giving up."

"[A]s bad as the current situation is with regard to poverty, it will likely get worse in the immediate future. . . . Millions of workers have lost their jobs and have slipped out of the middle class and into poverty. Poverty is increasing."

"I never tell my mother how much I hate it. I don't want to be seen as weak. I prefer to look greedy. . . ."

"I had slated my own lesson plan: to master a new language, no matter how bitter or foreign its flavor on my tongue."

"It sucks to be poor, and it sucks to feel that you somehow deserve to be poor. You start believing that you're poor because you're stupid and ugly, and then you start believing that you're stupid and ugly because you're Indian. And because you're Indian you start believing you're destined to be poor. It's an ugly circle and there's nothing you can do about it."

"What is it about this city—and other poor, African American cities across the nation—that leaves children with a disproportionate burden of respiratory disease? Is it the factories? The traffic exhaust? The substandard housing? . . . All of the above."

"For the millions of American women who live this way, the dream of 'having it all' has morphed into 'just hanging on.'"

"Emerging research in neuroscience and developmental psychology suggests that poverty early in a child's life may be particularly harmful because the astonishingly rapid development of young children's brains leaves them sensitive (and vulnerable) to environmental conditions."

"Attempting to maintain a robust national military without addressing domestic poverty is like building a house on sinking sand; no matter how solid the house is, it will fall without a solid foundation to support it."

"American rice subsidies [enable] the United States to dump its product in developing countries at depressed prices, making it difficult for small-scale farmers to export their own rice or compete in their local markets."

4   Privilege: Who Isn't Poor?   243

"The question is not just about what unearned privileges we have been walking around with but also about what it would take to change the systems that gave us these privileges in the first place."

"[T]here is much more to doing good work than 'making a difference.' There is the principle of first do no harm. There is the idea that those who are being helped ought to be consulted over the matters that concern them."

"I believe that everyone in this country has a chance to succeed. Still. In 2011. Even a poor black kid in West Philadelphia."

"There's more to getting a foot-hold in middle class than simply knowing how to use Google Scholar. There are a number of complex and tangle-ly mazes to maneuver when one is climbing up the socioeconomic ladder."

"Why do poor people . . . buy status symbols? . . . We want to belong . . . belonging to one group at the right time can mean the difference between employment and unemployment."

"[A] plethora of government-enforced diversity policies have marginalized many white workers. The time has come to cease the false arguments and allow every American the benefit of a fair chance at the future."

"I'm not uncomfortable with the government using its power to help poor people of any color, or people who are discriminated against. But to write about poverty of the South without acknowledging the decades of massive government effort geared exclusively toward aiding white people is rather astonishing."

"It is the poor, not the rich, who are inclined to charity."

"'I can't possibly be guilty of a crime, officer' you point out, if anything comes up. 'I have too much money.'"

because they are fixed in our minds through our associations with labels and descriptions repeatedly cycled through public discourse."

"That a campaign can be mounted to influence people's perceptions of women on welfare without providing any information about them, except through pictures and a few words, indicates how susceptible these women are to being cast and recast in any light that serves a political interest."

"One billion people still live in extreme poverty. More than one billion people lack access to safe drinking water. 6,000 people die of AIDS each day. 750 million adults cannot read. And those who carry almost zero responsibility for climate change are bearing the brunt of its effects, widening the gap between the haves and the have-nots."

"Sometimes, even when we have all the good intentions in the world, we don't find the most effective or most efficient way to act on them."

"It's what I would call 'conscience-laundering'—feeling better about accumulating more than any one person could possibly need to live on by sprinkling a little around as an act of charity."

"Never have so many people . . . [and] so much money been deployed to improve Africa—and yet the majority of the movers are part-timers, merely dropping in, setting up a scheme . . . then returning to their real lives."

"[T]he story of hunger . . . is far more complex than any one statistic or grand theory; it is a world where those without enough to eat may save up to buy a TV instead, where more money doesn't necessarily translate into more food. . . ."

"We have become a low-wage economy to a far greater extent than we realize."

"We need to make sure that the working poor have on-ramps to improving their lives: opportunities like workforce training and job development."

"[A] conservative poverty agenda ought to be seen as essential to building a democratic society that favors and rewards the industrious and the innovative, yet includes the poor."

"Social business is important because it addresses very vital concerns of mankind. It can change the lives of the bottom 60 percent of the world population and help them to get out of poverty."

"When people can personally identify with others in need, they respond far more generously than when they're presented with large-scale problems or abstract situations."

"To simply measure the value and quality of our work by the numbers, the performance levels, or the concrete investments of time, energy, and resources seems to neglect another invaluable, but often hidden, dimension of this work: the non-doing."

"Here are 10 questions to ask yourself when writing a solutions-oriented story."

rhetorical contents

academic research

analogy

argument and persuasion

cause-and-effect analysis

comparison and contrast

definition

description

division and classification

example and illustration

narration

rhetorical analysis

visual

preface

In 1964, President Lyndon B. Johnson used his State of the Union address to declare an "unconditional" war on poverty in America. Outlining vast plans to create federal social service programs like Social Security and the National Service Corps, Johnson argued that "[v]ery often a lack of jobs and money is not the cause of poverty, but the symptom. The cause may lie deeper in our failure to give our fellow citizens a fair chance to develop their own capacities, in a lack of education and training, in a lack of medical care and housing, in a lack of decent communities in which to live and bring up their children." Many people, filled with good intentions and compassion, agree with Johnson's argument that in a developed country with ample natural and financial resources, people should not suffer for want of basic necessities. And yet they do. In 1988, President Ronald Reagan quipped in his State of the Union Address: "The federal government declared a war on poverty, and poverty won." Census Bureau data show that in 2012, 15% of the U.S. population—46.5 million people—had an income below the poverty level. Clearly, poverty persists in the United States and throughout the world. According to the World Bank, almost half the world—over 3 billion people—live on less than $2.50 a day, and 1.22 billion people live on less than $1.25 a day. The scale of this problem and its connection as both the cause and effect of so many other social concerns can be daunting. Still, global institutions and individuals alike are proposing solutions. *Poverty/Privilege: A Reader for Writers* takes readers through the causes, consequences, and solutions to poverty, exploring how writing and rhetoric are critical factors for understanding and addressing poverty.

If we agree in general that the world would be a better place without poverty, we disagree fiercely about whether that is actually possible and what we could do to make it happen. Whose job is it to prevent poverty and create Johnson's "fair chance" for everyone? Is it up to individuals and/or society? And does everyone even deserve that help? Do some people deserve our help based on the uncontrollable circumstances of their poverty (e.g., war, natural disasters, old age, youth, mental illness) while others do not because they seem to have made bad choices (e.g., drug use, crime)? If we do want to help, how do we start? Should we work through the government to create policies and programs directing resources toward those in need, legislating fair chances and equal opportunity? And/or should we work outside government, empowering nonprofit and religious organizations to lead the way? We often find ourselves at war not with poverty but with other compassionate, well-intentioned people as we try to craft effective solutions. The readings in *Poverty/Privilege: A Reader for Writers* guide readers through key questions about poverty with authors who have different perspectives and answers. Prior knowledge about poverty is not needed to access these readings, but readers of this text can expect to gain an introduction to the field of poverty studies that can inform their thinking and action on this critical domestic and global issue.

To craft effective solutions, we have to understand the causes of the problem: Why are people poor? And before that, we need to share a common definition. What is poverty? Is poverty just a lack of money? In the United States, we have historically used an *absolute* measure of poverty, a monetary threshold—the poverty line—meant to tell us who is poor and who is not. In 2013, that number was $23,550 for a family of four. So, if you earn $23,551, you are *not* poor? Of course, it's not that simple, but the absolute measure gives each community a way to track its progress over time. We can also measure poverty in *relative* terms as most of Western Europe does, looking at the distribution among the top and bottom earners in a community. Does the spread reflect the level of poverty that a community accepts? Some measurements combine these approaches. But should we measure more than money? What is the nature of poverty?

Nobel Prize-winning economist Amartya Sen argues for a multidimensional view of poverty, a human development index that measures quality of life and not just income. His index focuses on the freedom individuals have to lead a life they value, where they have access to the resources necessary to develop their capabilities so that they can do what they want to do and become who they want to be. The majority of poverty-fighting institutions around the world—the World Bank, Oxfam, the World Food Programme, and others—have adopted some version of this definition that speaks to human needs that exceed monetary measures. Indeed, as quoted above, President Johnson argued that the U.S. should address well-being holistically, not just financially. He argued for expanding community capabilities through diverse approaches, and many of the programs that grew from the War on Poverty reflect that sensibility even though the U.S. measure has been income-based.

If you define and measure poverty more holistically, then your solutions might address such consequences as social exclusion and loneliness. Giving people money alone does not fix the problem if it is not enough to permanently improve their social circumstances as well. Instead, we must understand the dynamics of both poverty and privilege, asking which social forces make it easier for some people to gain wealth and some people to stay poor, for some people to live with both high risk (e.g., poor health, low education level, unstable work) and low resilience (e.g., a lack of safety nets such as insurance, savings, and people who can help in a crisis). Anthropologist and doctor to the poor Paul Farmer writes of the "structural violence" that preserves this inequality—the racism, sexism, and religious prejudices that reward dominant groups, compounding the power and influence of those who already have both.

People around the world, however, are both acting to make sustainable change and sharing what does and doesn't work so that others can learn from their efforts. For example, rigorous research using the gold standard of science—randomized controlled trials that compare a control group that receives an intervention with one that does not—helps people with good intentions prove whether their ideas actually work. Yet even these "randomistas" are critiqued for claiming scientific objectivity within the messiness of human trials that are neither perfectly random nor controlled. Good intentions are not enough anymore, and some people, such as philanthropist Peter Buffett, challenge giving that seems to consider the donor's desires more than the recipient's needs or measurable impacts.

Sharing that growing empirical knowledge is critical to understanding the rhetorics of poverty that shape our thinking about the nature of poverty and thus the appropriate responses to it. Some would argue that the media have underrepresented the poor at best and misrepresented them at worst. It was the "invisibility" of poverty in America that prompted a media frenzy in the Appalachian region of the United States in the 1960s. Responding to Johnson's battle cry, scores of writers, photographers, and filmmakers descended on the area. Their intent was to make the invisible visible, to show, as the title of Michael Harrington's famous 1962 book on the subject called it—*The Other America*—to the affluent and middle-class Americans who knew little or nothing of the poverty in their country. The plan worked in the sense that it did seem to change public sentiment to support social programs. But there were casualties. Some would argue that the intense attention in Appalachia exploited the residents even as it helped them. In 1967, Canadian filmmaker Hugh O'Connor went to Appalachia to make a documentary about poverty in America. As he finished an interview with a poor coal miner on the porch of his worn-down rented home, the owner of the property, Hobart Ison, arrived and demanded that the filmmaker leave. As O'Connor left, Ison shot him dead. Some in the community rallied around Ison, saying that it was the filmmaker who started the violence by exposing the community to unsympathetic outsiders, showing only their deprivation and not their strength, stripping them of dignity with each word and image that made their suffering visible. Others considered O'Connor's interviews an essential method for telling the story of poverty in a way that would foster social change.

The media have the power to raise awareness of poverty when they do attend to it, but they can also reinforce stereotypes and myths, complicating the rhetorics of poverty that shape our thinking and our actions. While the majority of Americans in poverty are white, for example, research shows that African Americans are overrepresented in media stories of poverty. Similarly, children are the poorest age group in the United States, and women are more likely than men to be in poverty, yet the media often depict poverty through images of homeless men living on the streets. The readings in *Poverty/Privilege: A Reader for Writers* help readers see those errors and understand the damage done when we misrepresent the causes, consequences, and solutions to poverty. This book also challenges readers to become part of the rhetorics of poverty and privilege, to write themselves into these important conversations through such genres as op-ed articles, position papers, policy briefs, interviews, public service announcements, and researched arguments that inform, entertain, and persuade, adding accurate and compelling arguments that take us beyond good intentions and move us toward effective action.

Poverty/Privilege: A Reader for Writers is part of a series of brief single-topic readers from Oxford University Press designed for today's college writing courses. Each reader in this series approaches a topic of contemporary conversation from multiple perspectives:

- **Timely:** Most selections were originally published in 2010 or later.
- **Global:** Sources and voices from around the world are included.
- **Diverse:** Selections come from a range of nontraditional and alternate print and online media, as well as representative mainstream sources.
- **Curated:** Every author of a volume in this series is a teacher-scholar whose experience in the writing classroom, as well as expertise in a volume's specific subject area, informs their choices of readings.

In addition to the rich array of perspectives on topical (even urgent) issues addressed in each reader, each volume features an abundance of different genres and styles—from the academic research paper to the pithy Twitter argument. Useful but non-intrusive pedagogy includes:

- **Chapter introductions** that provide a brief overview of the chapter's theme and a sense of how the chapter's selections relate to both the overarching theme and each other.
- **Headnotes** introduce each reading by providing concise information about its original publication and pose an open-ended question that encourages students to explore their prior knowledge of (or opinions about) some aspect of the selection's content.
- **"Analyze" and "Explore" questions** after each reading scaffold and support student reading for comprehension, as well as rhetorical considerations, providing prompts for reflection, classroom discussion, and brief writing assignments.
- **"Forging Connections" and "Looking Further" prompts** after each chapter encourage critical thinking by asking students to compare perspectives and strategies among readings both within the chapter and with readings in other chapters, suggesting writing assignments (many of which are multimodal) that engage students with larger conversations in the academy, the community, and the media.
- **An appendix on "Researching and Writing about Poverty/ Privilege"** guides student inquiry and research in a digital environment. Co-authored by a research librarian and a writing program director, this appendix provides real-world, transferable strategies for locating, assessing, synthesizing, and citing sources in support of an argument.

about the author

Connie Snyder Mick is an associate special professional faculty member at the University of Notre Dame. Dr. Mick is director of Community-Based Learning and co-director of the Poverty Studies Interdisciplinary Minor through the Center for Social Concerns. She teaches community-based courses on writing, rhetoric, poverty, gender, and ethical leadership. She presents nationally and publishes on a wide range of topics, such as teaching writing through technology, teaching poverty and privilege through writing, and the development of multiple literacies in English language learners through service learning and civic engagement. She directed university writing centers for ten years and designed and directs the Community Engagement Faculty Institute at the University of Notre Dame. Dr. Mick has an additional composition textbook forthcoming from Oxford University Press, a rhetoric and reader on writing for social change called *Good Writing*. For additional support teaching *Poverty/Privilege: A Reader for Writers*, visit http://blogs.nd.edu/connie-snyder-mick/povertyprivilege/.

acknowledgments

This textbook allowed me to combine two passions: teaching writing and teaching poverty studies. I am deeply grateful to colleagues in both areas who helped me locate this powerful intersection in my work.

At Notre Dame, I thank Kasey Swanke for her tireless support as a graduate research assistant. An outstanding teacher and scholar, Kasey challenged and supported me throughout. I thank Mary Beckman and Jennifer Warlick for welcoming me into the Poverty Studies Interdisciplinary Minor, and I thank Fr. Paul Kollman, Fr. Bill Lies, Jay Brandenberger, and all my colleagues at the Center for Social Concerns for supporting my attention in this area. Debbie Blasko and Karen Manier provided invaluable administrative support. Stuart Greene, John Duffy, Patrick Clauss, Nicole MacLaughlin, Matthew Capdevielle, Beth Capdevielle, and Erin Dietel-McLaughlin kept me close to and in awe of the University Writing Program at Notre Dame. The Poverty Studies students at Notre Dame, such as Rachel Ganson, Allison Behrndt, Erin Fessler, Emma Borne, and

Matthew Mazur, gave input on readings, as did the remarkable students in my "Rhetorics of Gender and Poverty" and "Poverty Studies Capstone" courses. Colleagues in the Shepherd Program Higher Education Consortium on Poverty inspired and informed me along the way, as did Joe Buttigieg and our sharp students in the Hesburgh-Yusko Scholars Program "Ethical Leadership through Service and Civic Engagement" course.

At Oxford, I owe Carrie Brandon thanks for seeing the light and determination in my eyes when I said they *had* to have a title on poverty and privilege. And thanks to Meg Botteon for enthusiastically supporting this project even while we were working on *Good Writing*. Thanks to Beth Keister, Diane Kohnen, Bev Kraus and their teams for support on permissions and editing.

My deepest thanks go to my immediate family who made this possible— Brad, Sophia, Harper, and Mom. You inspire my concern for the world and confirm my belief that change is possible.

Finally, the generous and in-depth feedback, suggestions, and critique from a group of outstanding reviewers helped me make significant improvements to *Poverty/Privilege: A Readers for Writers*. I thank Dana Aspinall, Alma College; Suparno Banerjee, Texas State University; Cheryl Cardoza, Truckee Meadows Community College; Maricela Garcia, South Texas College; Chandler Gilman, Lyndon State University; Vickie Melograno, Atlantic Community College; Michael Moghater, James Madison University; Marilee Rust; K. T. Shaver, CSU Long Beach; Susan Slavicz, Florida State College-Jacksonville; and Jenise Williamson, Bowie State University.

Definitions: What Is Poverty?

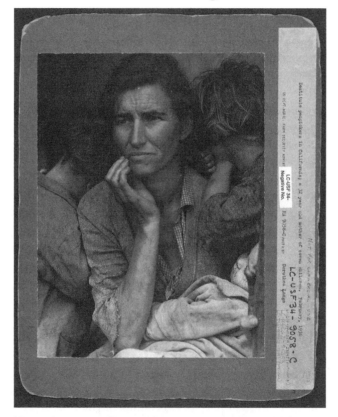

Migrant farmworker Florence Owens with her children (1936).
Photo by Dorothea Lange for the U.S. Resettlement Administration.
Photos record and thereby define poverty, but they also indicate
arguments about government and personal responsibility. Does
this photo frame the migrant mother and her children as the
deserving or the undeserving poor?

INTRODUCTION

Ask many people to define poverty and they will tell you pretty quickly that poverty is a lack of money. That's certainly true. But if you talk about *why* people lack money or how big that lack should be compared to others in the community to meet the poverty threshold, then you will often see that clear definition unravel just as quickly as it was constructed. Another way to think about poverty is that it isn't just about money or the things you own but about individual and community well-being. As Nobel Prize-winning economist Amartya Sen argues, well-being flourishes when *all* people have the capabilities and freedom to become who they want to be and do what they want to do. Understanding the nature of poverty—the social forces and structures that help people stay poor in money and capabilities—is the complicated but rewarding work we engage in this book.

The readings in this chapter will help you explore different definitions and measures of poverty across time and across the world so that you can articulate your own position on this issue. How you define a problem shapes how you attempt to solve it. Your definition guides your strategy, taking you toward particular tools and approaches and away from others, so it is important that you explore competing definitions of poverty and establish your own position among them before rushing to propose solutions.

In this chapter, John Iceland provides a historical overview of how American attitudes and policies regarding poverty have evolved, giving us a foundation for understanding what is at stake in those changing attitudes and policies. Barbara Ehrenreich argues that Americans still don't have a consensus about whether poverty is a cultural or governmental problem. *The Economist* presents research explaining that the concept of reducing poverty is new: Some early economic theories viewed poverty as a social necessity akin to slavery. Nonprofit CEO Ray Offenheiser argues that the government should do more to respond to the financial crisis that hit the most vulnerable Americans the hardest. In Vivyan Adair's testimony for the U.S. Senate hearing titled "Welfare Reform: A New Conversation on Women and Poverty," Adair cites examples of the harm done to women who lost opportunities for education after welfare reform. Greg Kaufmann represents poverty by the numbers, illustrating how much worse some of those numbers would be without certain public policies. The Census Bureau, which gathers most of the statistical data we use to study poverty in the U.S., offers its definition of key terms and concepts, sometimes giving usage advice and sometimes revealing its own uncertainty about key definitions. The Measure of America reading gives a defining framework for understanding the three core elements of human development: income, education, and health. Using survey research, Robert Rector and Rachel Sheffield offer a concrete picture of the material life of Americans in poverty—a picture, they argue, that challenges the images of extreme material deprivation often shown in the media. Economist Robert Haveman catalogs the available options for measuring national poverty levels, describes the American method, and proposes that we change our measurement system. Finally, Charles Kenny challenges popular thinking by sharing research that shows the many ways in which city slums are preferable to rural poverty.

John Iceland
"Early Views of Poverty in America"

John Iceland is a professor of sociology and demography at Pennsylvania State University, where he also chairs the Department of Sociology and Criminology. He has testified before Congress on measuring poverty in the U.S., and he has authored numerous academic articles and two books. In the following chapter from his book *Poverty in America*, Iceland explains that the definition of poverty has evolved over time, and that how policymakers distinguish between who is poor and who is not impacts their motivations for serving them.

What annual income would you set as the poverty line for a single adult in your community?

What is poverty? When I ask this question of my students, a common response is something like, "Being poor means not having a lot of money." This makes sense, but it is still rather vague. Although we commonly fumble about for a more precise answer, many of us nevertheless feel we can certainly recognize poverty when we see it. The historian James T. Patterson, for example, relates the following report from a social worker during the Great Depression: "Chicago, 1936: One woman wrote to a relief station as follows: 'I am without food for myself and child. I only got $6.26 to last me from the tenth to the twenty-fifth. That order is out and I haven't anything to eat. We go to bed hungry. Please give us something to eat. I cannot stand to see my child hungry.'" I venture that even the hardest-hearted would grudgingly agree that this is poverty. As one moves away from this kind of obvious example, however, it becomes more difficult to distinguish just what people mean when they refer to "the poor," as opposed to lower-income people more generally.

> "[W]hat people judge to constitute poverty varies across both time and place."

In 1993 the General Social Survey fielded the following question about poverty (they haven't asked it since): "People who have income below a certain level can be considered poor. That level is called the 'poverty line.' What amount of weekly income would you use as a poverty line for a family of four (husband, wife, and two children) in this community?" Answers ranged from as low as $38 to as high as $2,305 per week (all of these figures are in 2011 inflation-adjusted dollars). The average response was $524. Most families would find it difficult to live on $38 a week. At the other extreme, $2,305 per week seems excessive as a minimum standard. At what point does luxury become a necessity? More to the point, why did this question elicit such a wide variety of responses?

Although poverty is a concrete phenomenon for those who live it, what people judge to constitute poverty varies across both time and place. A working-class laborer in a developing country would likely be considered poor in Western Europe. In fact, the World Bank uses a poverty standard of $1.25 or $2 per person per day, or $1,369 to $2,190 per year, for a family of three in developing countries. In contrast, the average official poverty threshold for a family of three in the United States was $17,916 in 2011. It should be noted that this comparison is not altogether easy to make, as there are some poor regions around the world where people get by on subsistence farming and where relatively little money is exchanged.

As far back as 1776, Adam Smith noted the importance of social perceptions in determining what constitutes economic hardship. In the *Wealth of Nations* he defined the lack of "necessaries" as the experience of being unable to consume "not only the commodities which are indispensably necessary for the support of life, but whatever the custom of the country renders it indecent for creditable people, even of the lowest order, to be without." More recently, Peter Townsend observed that people are social beings who assume many roles in a community—worker, citizen, parent, friend, and so on. He maintained that poverty should be defined as the lack of sufficient income for people to "play the roles, participate in the relationships, and follow the customary behavior which is expected of them by virtue of their membership of society."

In order to understand who we, as a society, consider poor, therefore, we must begin by examining how our own views have evolved. This chapter begins by tracing views of poverty in America before 1900. I place these views in their economic, social, and political context, noting how these forces subsequently affected twentieth-century efforts to measure and understand poverty. I end by describing the emergence of the current official poverty measure in the 1960s.

Views of Poverty before 1900

Views of poverty reflect social conditions. A common assumption during the U.S. colonial period was that the roots of poverty lay primarily not in structural economic causes but in individual misbehavior. The poor were often categorized as either "deserving" or "undeserving" of public support. Voluntary idleness was regarded as a vice, and in early colonial times unemployed men were often either bound out as indentured servants, whipped and forced out of town, or put in jail. In 1619, the Virginia assembly ordered that idle able-bodied persons should be bound over to compulsory labor. Likewise, in 1633 the General Court of Massachusetts decreed harsh punishment for those who spent their time "idly or unprofitably." Yet hardship among the elderly and children was usually viewed more sympathetically, as many colonists recognized that poverty was widespread and sometimes unavoidable. Communities therefore often accepted responsibility for the well-being of the elderly in need.

By the early nineteenth century, many craftsmen and farmers displaced by the mechanization of agriculture and the mass production of goods struggled to earn a living, as did unskilled laborers. These groups constituted an economically insecure "floating proletariat," some of whom traveled extensively to find jobs. Some became "tramps," jobless men and, to a lesser extent, women who moved continuously from place to place in search of employment.

The distinction between the deserving and undeserving poor persisted through the nineteenth century. In 1834, for example, the Reverend Charles Burroughs spoke about the differences between poverty and pauperism: "The former is an unavoidable evil, to which many are brought from necessity, and in the wise and gracious Providence of God. It is the result, not of our faults, but of our misfortunes. . . . Pauperism is the consequence of willful error, of shameful indolence, of vicious habit."

The word *pauper* generally refers to someone receiving relief or assistance, usually from local or county governments. As illustrated in the quote above, the public has tended to have a dim view of people who seek assistance, and paupers have generally been considered as members of the "undeserving" poor. The poor were also sometimes stigmatized with other labels such as "dependent, defective, and delinquent."

10   The nineteenth century saw the growth of poorhouses, also known as "indoor relief," as a method for dealing with the poor. Starting in the 1830s, state governments began to write laws mandating that counties have a poor farm or poorhouse. Many of those who needed short-term aid nevertheless still received from local agencies or private charities "outdoor relief," which did not require those seeking help to enter institutions. The poorhouses were harsh; their purpose was to deter all but the most desperate from applying for help. Poorhouse inmates were expected to work as a form of punishment, moral training, education, and reform. It was not until the beginning of the twentieth century that poorhouses fell out of favor, as public officials and social professionals realized that such institutions did little to reduce poverty and sometimes even exacerbated family instability when family members were interned in these institutions.

Contemporary concerns about the geographical concentration of poverty echo fears voiced by many nineteenth- and early twentieth-century commentators. Indeed, in the middle decades of the nineteenth century, some middle-class and wealthy city residents began to build new homes in areas just outside cities such as New York and Boston in order to avoid the poor who lived in the cities themselves. Michael Katz recounts how, in an 1854 annual report, Charles Loring Brace, the head of New York City's

Children's Aid Society, argued that the "greatest danger" to America's future was the "existence of an ignorant, debased, and permanently poor class in the great cities. . . . The members of it come at length to form a separate population. They embody the lowest passions and the most thriftless habits of the community. They corrupt the lowest class of working-poor who are around them. The expenses of police, prisons, of charities and means of relief, arise mainly from them."

S. Humphreys Gurteen, a writer and preacher, also decried the problems of both poverty and pauperism in his 1882 description of poor city districts: "large families huddled together in tenements and shanties which barely afford protection from wind and storm; dwellings where the laws of health are defied, where the most ordinary sanitary arrangements are unknown, and where 'boards of health' fail to penetrate; . . . human forms, even those of children, shivering in rags; hunger written upon care-worn faces; and despair everywhere triumphant." He blamed these problems on the abandonment of the poor by the well-to-do, on immorality, and on the ineffectiveness of charity, which he believed fostered dependence.

Nevertheless, apart from these small, highly visible "slum" districts, cities were not nearly as segregated by class as they have been in recent decades. Urban working-class neighborhoods were in constant flux, with steadily employed workers sharing the same buildings, streets, and residential districts with those who were less steadily employed. This is a natural consequence of the fact that poverty was endemic in cities and rural areas across the country.

Katz ventures that perhaps half the population of typical nineteenth-century cities was poor, though this judgment is based more on contemporary notions of poverty than on the standards of the time. He does note, however, that the "working-class experience was a continuum; no clear line separated the respectable poor from paupers." According to another estimate, roughly 10 to 20 percent of late-nineteenth-century Americans lived in a family with a member who had "tramped" at some point, that is, moved from place to place in search of work. The receipt of government aid was far less common. According to an analysis of 1860 census data, 7.9 people in 1,000 received public relief. Robert Hunter, in his 1904 book *Poverty,* estimated that at least 10 million people were poor, which represented about 12 percent of the American population in that year. He noted that this was largely a guess and that the actual number was likely much higher. John Ryan, an advocate of a "living wage," used a less severe poverty standard and estimated that closer to 40 percent of wage earners were living in poverty at the time. As bad as some of the city slums were, the incidence of poverty was actually much higher in rural areas in general and in the South in particular. Sharecroppers and tenant farmers suffered from hard times after 1860, with some leaving for mill villages where working conditions were terrible and wages low.

15   Poverty among African Americans was likewise endemic. Largely concentrated in southern and rural areas, black sharecroppers struggled to earn a living. Blacks were barred by law or custom from a large range of full-time jobs, especially outside black communities, leaving agricultural wage labor as the most common occupation. As the new system of Jim Crow laws, disfranchisement, and racial violence escalated during the late nineteenth century, southern blacks began to migrate to northern cities in growing numbers. This migration north would swell in the following century. Most blacks who lived in cities were employed as common laborers or as domestic and personal servants. Opportunities for promotion and advancement were very uncommon for blacks in these and other occupations.

Because of their precarious economic position, African Americans were more likely to receive public assistance in some cities. W.E.B. DuBois, in his well-known study *The Philadelphia Negro,* estimated that about 9 percent of black families were very poor and another 10 percent were simply poor, earning less than $5 per week. As there was no official poverty measure at the time, DuBois's estimates of poverty are based on his own assessment, and his standard of poverty was meager compared with most other appraisals. Although African Americans made up about 4 percent of Philadelphia's population in the 1890s, they constituted about 8 percent of those either residing in the city's almshouses or receiving assistance from the county poor board or aid for orphans. DuBois believed that high levels of poverty among African Americans had a number of causes, including the legacy of slavery, white racial beliefs and discriminatory practices, low levels of skill and education, and, in industrial cities, competition from immigrants.

The United States continued its rapid industrialization and urbanization in the early twentieth century. Between 1860 and 1920 the nation's urban population increased from about 20 percent of the total U.S. population to over 50 percent. Immigrants from Europe poured into eastern and midwestern cities in growing numbers. And beginning in about 1915 and continuing for the next thirty years or so, the migration of blacks in search of better economic opportunities in northern cities accelerated. Corporations with large factories in industries such as steel and automobiles found a large pool of cheap and willing labor in the immigrant and black communities.

Industrialization was accompanied by economic growth, as real per capita income in 1929 was one and a half times greater than it was in 1900. Standards of living rose by several other measures as well, including size and quality of housing, the number of home appliances, and health. For example, in 1930 life expectancy at birth was sixty years, up from only forty-seven years in 1900. Nevertheless, a large part of the workforce, especially those in peripheral industries, remained vulnerable to periodic and often severe downturns in the economy. Sugrue describes the plight of these workers: "Trapped in insecure jobs with small companies increasingly marginal to a market dominated by large corporations, they shared with their nineteenth-century predecessors susceptibility to bouts of poverty."

The collapse of the stock market in October 1929 and the ensuing Great Depression, which stretched throughout the 1930s, brought economic hardship to nearly all corners of the country, though rural areas were often hit the hardest. In 1933 a full quarter of the labor force was unemployed. As one report from a social worker documented, "Massachusetts, 1934: About the unemployed themselves: this picture is so grim that whatever words I use will seem hysterical and exaggerated. And I find them all in the same shape—fear, fear driving them into a state of semi-collapse; cracking nerves; and an overpowering terror of the future. . . . They can't pay rent and are evicted. They . . . are watching their children grow thinner and thinner; fearing the cold for children who have neither coats nor shoes; wondering about coal."

Much of the economic progress of the previous decades had been dashed 20 and the natural optimism of the American people was shaken. Years passed with high unemployment and growth that was uneven at best. Just as the country seemed to be emerging from the depression, the economy again sputtered and sank in 1937. Despite Franklin D. Roosevelt's efforts to expand the safety net—bitterly opposed by free-market conservatives at every turn—only massive expenditures on the war effort in the early 1940s and the resurrection of associated industries brought back prosperity. Meanwhile, hardship flourished, and poverty could no longer be blamed solely on individual morality and misbehavior, for the role of larger economic forces was plain to see.

It was in this social and economic context—poverty, progress, and collapse—that an interest in studying and documenting poverty and other economic indicators blossomed. There was a growing recognition that in order to address economic problems, one had to have solid information about the economy with which to make informed decisions.

The Beginning of Poverty Measurement

It was not until the late nineteenth and early twentieth centuries that techniques to measure and study poverty began to be developed, in part because many social science disciplines and statistical methods themselves were only in youthful bloom. Sociology itself arose in the nineteenth century through the writings of such people as Auguste Comte, Herbert Spencer, and Karl Marx. Although economics has a longer history, the discipline's sophisticated quantitative methods are more recent in origin. In short, although there has long been an interest in issues related to poverty, the "science" of examining poverty began only in the last couple of centuries.

Concerned about working-class unrest that fed the revolutions of 1848, European statisticians began to study the incomes and expenses of working-class families in about 1850. This led to the development of "standard budgets," which basically refer to the cost of goods and services that families need to achieve a certain standard of living. Influenced by these studies, early efforts in the United States to develop standard budgets began between 1870 and 1895. Sometimes different budgets were constructed for people of different social classes or occupational groups. Although most were constructed to represent a minimum subsistence level, others were meant to represent minimum comfort levels.

Charles Booth came up with the term *line of poverty* in his well-known multivolume study of poverty and society in London. He defined poverty in the following way: "The 'poor' are those whose means . . . are barely sufficient for decent independent life; the 'very poor' those whose means are insufficient for this according to the usual standard of life in this country."

25   In fact, it was around the end of the nineteenth century when the word *poverty* became associated less with receiving public relief or private charity (i.e., "pauperism") and more with having insufficient income to live appropriately. This concept of poverty became widely accepted among the social workers, social scientists, and others who studied these issues more systematically in the first two decades of the twentieth century. It was also around

this time that people began to accept the view that poverty was also due to economic and other social factors rather than just individual weakness.

In a careful review of early poverty measurement efforts, Gordon Fisher suggests that these attempts to define poverty (or income inadequacy) inform us not only about economic deprivation but also about the social structure of the time and the social processes by which poverty lines are drawn. Illustrating the tendency of successive poverty lines to rise in real terms as the real income of the general population rises, early budgets and other measures of income inadequacy were quite low by recent standards (all comparisons below adjust for inflation). For example, Fisher notes that the 1890–91 report of the Iowa Bureau of Labor Statistics included a standard budget showing the "minimum cost" of "the necessary living expenses of laboring men with families" that was roughly equal to 52 percent of today's official poverty threshold for a family of five.

DuBois's 1896–97 poverty line (which was meant to be a standard budget rather than a bare-necessities demarcation line) of $5 a week, or $260 a year, represents only about 26 percent of the official poverty line for a family of five. This poverty line was markedly lower than every other contemporary American standard budget. In his classic 1904 volume *Poverty,* Robert Hunter used a poverty line of $460 a year for an averaged-size family in northern industrial areas, and $300 for such a family in the rural South. To live at the poverty line, he stated, was to use the "same standard that a man would demand for his horses or slaves." Other minimum subsistence budgets and poverty lines developed before World War I tended to represent from 43 to 54 percent of the current official poverty line.

Some Progressive Era advocates of the poor recognized that the standard budget methodology could be misused in ways that were unfair to working-class families. In 1918 William Ogburn, a University of Washington professor who had gone to work for the National War Labor Board, noted in a discussion of standard budgets, "We can not go on the assumption that the housewife can purchase food value with the skill of a domestic-science expert, or that she has the will power of a Puritan, or that no allowance would be made to the man for drinks and tobacco." Indeed, Fisher notes:

> Lower-income homemakers were consistently being expected to show a skill in food buying that would have actually been greater than that of most middle-class homemakers—and were being stigmatized as "ignorant" and having "poor buying habits" when they

failed to exhibit such impossible talents. Scott Nearing's trenchant analysis was correct: any "superwoman" who could live up to the expectations of such budgets would not have to be subjected to them in the first place, as she would already be earning almost twice the poverty level in private industry.

Into the 1940s there was still no consensus in the literature regarding "poverty" or "poverty lines." Federal government employees, labor union personnel, advocates for income redistribution and greater economic growth, and a handful of academics tried to develop or revise poverty lines during the 1946–65 period, but many were unaware of the work being done by others in different organizations.

30   Between 1949 and 1958 a common low-income line that was often cited, originally proposed by the congressional Subcommittee on Low-Income Families (SLIF), was equal in constant dollars to 81 percent of today's official poverty threshold for a family of four. The poverty lines offered after 1958 and before the official poverty line was introduced in 1965 tended to be even higher, again reflecting growing standards of living of the time.

The Development of the Official Poverty Measure

The late 1950s and early 1960s saw the publication of several books and reports that drew people's attention to poverty. One was John Kenneth Galbraith's *The Affluent Society*. Galbraith argued that, while rising standards of living reduced hardship, the materialism of American consumer culture contributed to inequality and that poverty remained entrenched in many parts of the country. He also discussed the relative nature of poverty: "In part [poverty] is a physical matter. . . . But . . . it is wrong to rest everything on absolutes. People are poverty-stricken when their income, even if adequate for survival, falls markedly behind that of the community. Then they cannot have what the larger community regards as the minimum necessary for decency: and they cannot wholly escape, therefore, the judgment of the larger community that they are indecent."

In 1962 Michael Harrington's *The Other America: Poverty in the United States* was published; reviews of this book and other contemporary reports caught the eye of the Kennedy administration and influenced its views and policies on poverty issues. Harrington's basic aim in the book was to draw attention to the poverty that persisted despite the plenty that many Americans enjoyed. He argued that the poor, black and white alike, were subjected to a chronic suppression of their living standards. This led to a culture of poverty that was perpetuated by an endless cycle of neglect and injustice.

Within the Kennedy administration, the economist Walter Heller, chairman of the Council of Economic Advisors (CEA), wanted to "launch a Kennedy offensive against poverty." The CEA favored doing so within the framework of the broader economic agenda they had been pursuing since 1961, which aimed at faster economic growth and full employment by means of tax cuts. Robert Lampman, a CEA economist at the time, also sought to devise a politically acceptable definition of poverty that would focus less on income inequality and more on the amount needed to achieve a minimum living standard. A narrower income definition would lend itself to the growth-centered economic policy (as opposed to income redistribution policies) the CEA was advocating.

After Kennedy's assassination in 1963, President Lyndon Johnson decided to adopt Kennedy's emerging plan as his own, and in fact to make it a centerpiece of his domestic agenda. Johnson announced his ambitious War on Poverty in his January 1964 State of the Union address. In 1965 Mollie Orshansky independently published an article in the *Social Security Bulletin* in which she presented two sets of poverty thresholds, "economy level" and "low-cost level." These were a refined and extended version of thresholds that she had described in a July 1963 *Social Security Bulletin* article.

At that time, poverty measurement had been a major item on the research agenda of the Office of Economic Opportunity (OEO). Influenced by views on the political feasibility and desirability of defining poverty as a lack of income, the OEO adopted the lower of Mollie Orshansky's two sets of poverty thresholds—the set based on the economy food plan—as a working definition of poverty for statistical, planning, and budget purposes. In 1969 the U.S. Bureau of the Budget (now the Office of Management and Budget) designated the thresholds as the federal government's official statistical definition of poverty. The weighted-average nonfarm poverty threshold for a family of four was $3,128 for the base year, 1963. In the following chapter I discuss this measure, as well as other types of poverty measures, in more detail.

Analyze

1. In the colonial U.S., the poor were often described as either the "deserving" or the "undeserving" poor. Who typically fell into each category? What were possible consequences of being considered "undeserving"?

2. In the 19th century, how were "poverty" and "pauperism" distinguished? What does that distinction tell us about public views of poverty at that time?

3. According to W. E. B. DuBois, what caused the high level of poverty among African Americans in the 19th century?

4. What developments made the scientific study of poverty possible? What shift in the definition of poverty begins to happen around the end of the 19th century?

5. What inspired the Kennedy administration to launch a war on poverty?

Explore

1. What can we gain from understanding the history of poverty in certain contexts? Is Iceland's history of poverty an argument? Explain.

2. What do "social perceptions" or "community standards" have to do with poverty historically and today? Should our measurement of the poverty line consider community/social standards of living?

3. The "poorhouse" was an actual place in the 19th century where those who needed long-term support went to live and work for the government. Iceland writes, "The poorhouses were harsh; their purpose was to deter all but the most desperate from applying for help. Poorhouse inmates were expected to work as a form of punishment, moral training, education, and reform." What do these goals tell us about the perception of poverty then? Compare and contrast the mission statement of at least two social service agencies that serve the poor today (e.g., a homeless shelter and a food bank). What does this suggest about current definitions of poverty?

Barbara Ehrenreich
"How We Cured 'The Culture of Poverty,' Not Poverty Itself"

A self-professed "myth-buster by trade," Barbara Ehrenreich is a widely read writer on far-reaching social issues, including poverty. She has authored several books, including *Nickel and Dimed: On (Not) Getting By in America*, and numerous essays, earning various awards and the title "Veteran Muckraker" by *The New Yorker* magazine. In the following essay, Ehrenreich argues that some antipoverty policies wrongly aim to fix people's character flaws, not their financial flow.

Do people choose poverty?

It's been exactly 50 years since Americans, or at least the non-poor among them, "discovered" poverty, thanks to Michael Harrington's engaging book *The Other America*. If this discovery now seems a little overstated, like Columbus's "discovery" of America, it was because the poor, according to Harrington, were so "hidden" and "invisible" that it took a crusading left-wing journalist to ferret them out.

Harrington's book jolted a nation that then prided itself on its classlessness and even fretted about the spirit-sapping effects of "too much affluence." He estimated that one quarter of the population lived in poverty—inner-city blacks, Appalachian whites, farm workers, and elderly Americans among them. We could no longer boast, as President Nixon had done in his "kitchen debate" with Soviet Premier Nikita Khrushchev in Moscow just three years earlier, about the splendors of American capitalism.

At the same time that it delivered its gut punch, *The Other America* also offered a view of poverty that seemed designed to comfort the already comfortable. The poor were different from the rest of us, it argued, radically different, and not just in the sense that they were deprived, disadvantaged, poorly housed, or poorly fed. They *felt* different, too, thought differently, and pursued lifestyles characterized by shortsightedness and intemperance. As Harrington wrote, "There is . . . a language of the poor, a psychology of the poor, a worldview of the poor. To be impoverished is to be an internal alien, to grow up in a culture that is radically different from the one that dominates the society."

Harrington did such a good job of making the poor seem "other" that when I read his book in 1963, I did not recognize my own forbears and extended family in it. All right, some of them did lead disorderly lives by middle class standards, involving drinking, brawling, and out-of-wedlock babies. But they were also hardworking and in some cases fiercely ambitious—qualities that Harrington seemed to reserve for the economically privileged.

5   According to him, what distinguished the poor was their unique "culture of poverty," a concept he borrowed from anthropologist Oscar Lewis, who had derived it from his study of Mexican slum-dwellers. The culture of poverty gave *The Other America* a trendy academic twist, but it also gave the book a conflicted double message: "We"—the always presumptively affluent readers—needed to find some way to help the poor, but we also needed to understand that there was *something wrong with them*, something that could not be cured by a straightforward redistribution of wealth. Think of the earnest liberal who encounters a panhandler, is moved to pity by the man's obvious destitution, but refrains from offering a quarter—since the hobo might, after all, spend the money on booze.

In his defense, Harrington did not mean that poverty was *caused* by what he called the "twisted" proclivities of the poor. But he certainly opened the floodgates to that interpretation. In 1965, Daniel Patrick Moynihan—a sometime-liberal and one of Harrington's drinking companions at the famed White Horse Tavern in Greenwich Village—blamed inner-city poverty on what he saw as the shaky structure of the "Negro family," clearing the way for decades of victim-blaming. A few years after The Moynihan Report, Harvard urbanologist Edward C. Banfield, who was to go on to serve as an advisor to Ronald Reagan, felt free to claim that:

> "The lower-class individual lives from moment to moment.... Impulse governs his behavior.... He is therefore radically improvident: whatever he cannot consume immediately he considers valueless.... [He] has a feeble, attenuated sense of self."

In the "hardest cases," Banfield opined, the poor might need to be cared for in "semi-institutions . . . and to accept a certain amount of surveillance and supervision from a semi-social-worker-semi-policeman."

By the Reagan era, the "culture of poverty" had become a cornerstone of conservative ideology: poverty was caused, not by low wages or a lack of jobs, but by bad attitudes and faulty lifestyles. The poor were dissolute, promiscuous, prone to addiction and crime, unable to "defer gratification," or possibly even set an alarm clock. The last thing they could be trusted with was money. In fact, Charles Murray argued in his 1984 book *Losing Ground*, any attempt to help the poor with their material circumstances would only have the unexpected consequence of deepening their depravity.

So it was in a spirit of righteousness and even compassion that Democrats and Republicans joined together to reconfigure social programs to cure, not poverty, but the "culture of poverty." In 1996, the Clinton administration enacted the "One Strike" rule banning anyone who committed a felony from public housing. A few months later, welfare was replaced by Temporary Assistance to Needy Families (TANF), which in its current form makes cash assistance available only to those who have jobs or are able to participate in government-imposed "workfare."

In a further nod to "culture of poverty" theory, the original welfare reform bill appropriated $250 million over five years for "chastity training" for poor single mothers. (This bill, it should be pointed out, was signed by Bill Clinton.)

Even today, more than a decade later and four years into a severe economic downturn, as people continue to slide into poverty from the middle classes, the theory maintains its grip. If you're needy, you must be in need of correction, the assumption goes, so TANF recipients are routinely instructed in how to improve their attitudes and applicants for a growing number of safety-net programs are subjected to drug-testing. Lawmakers in 23 states are considering testing people who apply for such programs as job training, food stamps, public housing, welfare, and home heating assistance. And on the theory that the poor are likely to harbor criminal tendencies, applicants for safety-net programs are increasingly subjected to finger-printing and computerized searches for outstanding warrants.

Unemployment, with its ample opportunities for slacking off, is another obviously suspect condition, and last year 12 states considered requiring pee tests as a condition for receiving unemployment benefits. Both Mitt Romney and Newt Gingrich have suggested drug testing as a condition for *all* government benefits, presumably including Social Security. If granny insists on handling her arthritis with marijuana, she may have to starve.

What would Michael Harrington make of the current uses of the "culture of poverty" theory he did so much to popularize? I worked with him in the 1980s, when we were co-chairs of Democratic Socialists of America, and I suspect he'd have the decency to be chagrined, if not mortified. In all the discussions and debates I had with him, he never said a disparaging word about the down-and-out or, for that matter, uttered the phrase "the culture of poverty." Maurice Isserman, Harrington's biographer, told me that he'd probably latched onto it in the first place only because "he didn't want to come off in the book sounding like a stereotypical Marxist agitator stuck-in-the-thirties."

The ruse—if you could call it that—worked. Michael Harrington wasn't red-baited into obscurity. In fact, his book became a bestseller and an inspiration for President Lyndon Johnson's War on Poverty. But he had fatally botched the "discovery" of poverty. What affluent Americans found in his book, and in all the crude conservative diatribes that followed it, was not the poor, but a flattering new way to think about themselves—disciplined, law-abiding, sober, and focused. In other words, not poor.

15   Fifty years later, a new discovery of poverty is long overdue. This time, we'll have to take account not only of stereotypical Skid Row residents and Appalachians, but of foreclosed-upon suburbanites, laid-off tech workers, and America's ever-growing army of the "working poor." And if we look closely enough, we'll have to conclude that poverty is not, after all, a cultural aberration or a character flaw. Poverty is a shortage of money.

Analyze

1. Ehrenreich claims that Michael Harrington's 1962 book *The Other America: Poverty in the United States* "seemed designed to comfort the already comfortable." Explain.

2. Note all the references to politics and politicians in the text. What word choices suggest Ehrenreich's attitude about them? What can you tell about her political views based on the language she uses in this text?

3. What examples does Ehrenreich give to show that public policy since Harrington's book has often been designed to "cure, not poverty, but the 'culture of poverty'"?

Explore

1. Ehrenreich claims that Harrington's book shocked non-poor Americans into seeing a social concern that had been invisible to them. What other books, films, or writings have shocked society—or just you personally—into recognizing a social problem that had seemed invisible? What do these types of consciousness-raising texts have in common? How do they get your attention and get you to care about an issue?

2. What does it mean to believe in a "culture of poverty"? Why does Ehrenreich say that Harrington's book cleared the way for "decades of victim-blaming"? Where do you hear support or challenges to this viewpoint in governmental, religious, private, or personal domains? Do you see camps of people in these domains believing one way or the other based on those affiliations? Explain your observations.

3. Ehrenreich concludes: "a new discovery of poverty is long overdue." Imagine whom we might find in that new discovery. Think of examples from your reading or from your own experience that challenge the profile of people in poverty as having "bad attitudes and faulty lifestyles." Consider senior citizens who rely on social security, children who receive free or reduced lunches, etc. What external events, circumstances, or policies contributed to their poverty? Write a profile in which you make an invisible (or hidden) aspect of poverty visible. Consider writing this as an op-ed piece or letter to the editor.

The Economist
"Penury Portrait: The Consensus on Raising People Out of Poverty Is Relatively Recent"

The Economist is a weekly news magazine that offers reporting and commentary on news, world politics, business, science, and technology. To ensure uniformity in its voice and to reflect the collaboration of many writers, *The Economist* preserves the anonymity of its authors. This piece offers a historical account of theorizing about poverty and its consequences for economics on the whole, explaining why policymakers and the rich were invested in keeping poor people in their economies.

Who would want the poor to stay poor?

On July 17th India released its latest poverty figures. They tell an encouraging tale: just under 22% of Indians were below the poverty line in 2011–12, down from over 37% in 2004–05. With an election not far off, these statistics will not go unchallenged. Naysayers are already grumbling that the numbers have been released early to make the government look good. But even as political opponents slug it out, it is worth noting what they are not arguing about. Nobody is saying that a decline in poverty is a bad thing. Nor does anyone dispute that policymakers should try to help large numbers of poor people out of penury. This mirrors a worldwide consensus: whether the United Nations or the World Bank, sundry public officials or high-minded celebrities, everyone thinks that poverty alleviation is both desirable and possible. The debates are about the details.

That might sound wholly unsurprising. Yet in a new paper Martin Ravallion, an economics professor at Georgetown University and a former research director at the World Bank, charts the evolution of thinking on poverty over the past three centuries. He reckons that this consensus is of remarkably recent vintage. Not that long ago every element of the received wisdom—that poverty is a problem, that public policy should try to reduce the numbers of poor, and that there are good ways to try to do so without hurting the economy—would have been suspect.

According to the mercantilist thinking that dominated European thought between the 16th and 18th centuries, poverty was socially useful. True, it was miserable for the poor. But it also kept the economic engine humming by ensuring the availability of plentiful cheap labour. Bernard de Mandeville, an 18th-century economist and philosopher, thought it "manifest that in a free nation where slaves are not allow'd of, the surest wealth consists in a multitude of laborious poor." That attitude was the norm.

If poor people were regarded as instrumental in ensuring economic development, that explains why there was little appetite for policies to help them leave poverty behind. What action there was tended to be palliative in nature. In the 18th century changes to the Poor Laws were designed to stop adverse shocks like failed harvests or bereavements from making life even harder for already poor people. Such policies were designed to protect the poor from the worst deprivations, not to raise them up.

In the late 18th century attitudes towards the poor took on a moralising 5 tone. Thomas Malthus, a clergyman, blamed the plight of the poor on their own flaws. Technological change might drive wages above subsistence levels, but only temporarily because the fecundity of the poor would soon drive wages back down. His thinking inspired the introduction of a new Poor Law in 1834, which tried to make the workhouse their only option. "Outdoor relief"—giving the poor money—needed to be stopped.

Adam Smith took a more humane view. He saw the social and emotional toll poverty could take, and sought to increase support for the idea of redistributive taxation: "The rich should contribute to the public expence [sic], not only in proportion to their revenue, but something more than in that proportion." But even the father of economics did not provide a coherent strategy for moving people permanently out of poverty.

By the 20th century the research of Charles Booth and Seebohm Rowntree had brought the issue of poverty firmly into the public consciousness. This in turn encouraged new thinking about the economic rationale for reducing penury. The classical school believed that the real constraint on growth was aggregate savings. Given that the rich saved more than the poor, this implied that less poverty would mean lower growth. John Maynard Keynes disputed this view, arguing that it was aggregate consumption that mattered, in which case reducing poverty could actually aid growth. But it was not until the 1990s that a coherent theoretical framework emerged to show how high levels of poverty stifled investment and innovation. For example, several models showed how unequal access to credit meant that the poor were less able to invest in their own education or businesses than was optimal, leading to lower growth for the economy as a whole. Scholars buttressed the theory with empirical evidence that high initial levels of poverty reduced subsequent growth in developing countries.

Poor Relations

New theories of poverty were also overturning received notions of why the poor stayed poor. The fault had long been placed at their door: the poor were variously lazy, prone to alcoholism and incapable of disciplined work. Such tropes are still occasionally heard today, but the horrors of the

Depression in the 1930s led many to re-evaluate the idea that poverty was mainly the result of people's own actions. Advances in economic models meanwhile allowed policymakers to see how low levels of education, health and nutrition could keep people stuck in penury. Policies to subsidise education or health care were desirable not merely for their own sake but also because they would help people break out of poverty.

The growth of "conditional cash transfers," schemes like Brazil's *Bolsa Familia* that give poor people money as long as they send their children to school or have them vaccinated, are logical developments of these ideas. The notion of schooling the poor to a better life seemed absurd in the era of de Mandeville: "Going to school in comparison to working is idleness, and the longer boys continue in this easy sort of life, the more unfit they'll be when grown up for downright labour." Such poverty of thinking may sound archaic, but it persisted for longer than you might think.

Analyze

1. How does discussion of the release of the latest poverty figures in India introduce an article that is really about the history of public attitudes and policies on poverty?

2. Explain the claim that, from some economic perspectives, "poverty was socially useful."

3. What events and observations led to new theories of poverty that started to change public attitudes and policies, shifting blame away from individuals? How were these new approaches to addressing poverty different from earlier ones?

Explore

1. The article claims that we have a "worldwide consensus" in which "everyone thinks that poverty alleviation is both desirable and possible. The debates are about the details." First, what evidence supports or challenges this claim? What efforts worldwide—institutions, policies, programs, etc.—might indicate that the world *is* acting to reduce poverty? What examples suggest that we *don't* have a global consensus? Second, write a researched report on a "debate about the details" of a specific poverty policy or program in the U.S. or abroad, such as food stamps (SNAP) in the U.S. or *Bolsa Familia* in Brazil. Do the stakeholders agree on the causes of poverty?

2. How are the arguments about poverty presented in this article informed by practical and ethical understandings of how the world should work? Are people more motivated by the *practical* argument that everyone in society benefits economically and socially when we reduce poverty, or by the *ethical* argument that it's wrong to let some people live in misery? Write a strategy memo to an incoming politician in which you advise him or her to emphasize one of these two approaches.

3. The article states: "Not that long ago every element of the received wisdom—that poverty is a problem, that public policy should try to reduce the numbers of poor, and that there are good ways to try to do so without hurting the economy—would have been suspect." Name other examples where the "received" or popular wisdom on a significant social issue has changed over time. What other social issues are changing now? Who are the stakeholders? Are they motivated by practical or ethical arguments? What does the change in thinking about poverty teach us about other social changes?

Ray Offenheiser
"Poverty at Home"

Ray Offenheiser is the president of Oxfam America, a nonprofit organization devoted to international development. One initiative at Oxfam calls attention to U.S. poverty and low-wage work. Offenheiser is a frequent commentator in the media on issues including foreign aid, trade, human rights, and humanitarian crises. In this essay, he argues that income inequality is a public problem that governmental policies must alleviate.

How is poverty a threat to national and global security?

As Washington careens through one headline-grabbing, self-imposed fiscal crisis after another, one in three Americans faces a daily crisis of poverty or low-wage jobs that is barely a topic of conversation in Congress or the media.

The richest 1 percent of the US population has more aggregate wealth than the bottom 90 percent combined. Yet one in three of us is struggling just to make ends meet. We now have levels of inequality usually associated with countries like South Africa or Nigeria. While unchecked public debt could pose a future economic threat, unthinking 'across the board' budget cuts today will have an immediate impact on the working poor, the near poor, and countless others fighting to keep their heads above water.

The relationship between national budget priorities and poverty and inequality are both American issues and global ones.

Oxfam has fought against poverty and economic injustice for 70 years in the world's poorest nations. Currently we operate on the ground in more than 90 countries and see extreme dichotomies between wealthy elites and the desperately poor in places from Sudan and India to Cambodia and Mexico. We see the ravages of poverty and the corrosive effect that gross inequality has on civil society and democracy, as well as how it stalls economic growth.

5   Growing inequality is a global concern. It was a major theme of the 2012 World Economic Forum and is being increasingly seen as a threat to national and global security. At the heart of this debate is the paradox of middle and lower income families bearing the bulk of the social and economic costs of volatile economic growth, while wages stagnate or decline, pensions disappear, and investments to broaden economic opportunity like health, education and social insurance are slashed. More and more, countries are faced with choices of whether or how to make growth inclusive.

As a global development organization, Oxfam believes poverty is about power, not scarcity. As Americans, we believe that our nation must lead. Poverty and inequality, and the social exclusion they breed, are wrongs to be righted, whether they occur in sub-Saharan Africa, South Asia, or the United States. Our nation has long presented itself to the world as the model of successful, inclusive growth that lifts millions into the middle class. While that was true during the decades after World War II, since the 1970s, the story has been very different. That is simply not the case today.

America's poverty rate is now at its highest level in two generations. Contrary to the American Dream of broad-based upward mobility, the United States ranks 10th out of 12 OECD countries in social mobility.

In addition, our country has the highest proportion of low-wage workers of any developed country—people who work hard but earn less than $10.50 an hour and are barely able to make ends meet.

Poverty is the result of imbalances in power that privilege some and marginalize others. More than mere economics, poverty affects human rights. Because we believe that governments must protect and expand human rights, we further believe that while markets have a role to play in improving the livelihoods of marginalized populations, they must be guided by the public interest and held accountable by citizen oversight. Whether across the globe or here at home, nations and peoples must shape their own development.

Therefore, a government's budget, like all public policy, should not only reflect our values, but be means to an end. Fiscal policies—public spending and taxes—should focus on investments in broadly shared prosperity. That is why Oxfam—which already has on-the-ground programs with farmworkers and in poor, coastal areas—is becoming more deeply involved in addressing poverty, the working poor, low wage jobs and inequality at the national level.

We are engaging a wide range of Americans—economists, activists, journalists, faith leaders, and others—shine a spotlight on the injustice of America's inequalities. We are listening to the experiences and concerns of the poor, with the goal of bringing their voices to a national audience.   10

More than 100 million Americans—1 in 3 of us—live in or near poverty, struggling every day. We need a lively national conversation about how we can right this wrong.

Ending poverty must and will occur as a result of deliberate and equitable fiscal choices and policies—not blunt chopping instruments. This must be the overriding goal of our society and our budgets.

Analyze

1. What two situations does Offenheiser contrast in the introduction? What word choices reveal his attitude about how different stakeholders are attending to these situations?
2. What facts does Offenheiser provide about inequality and social mobility? How do those facts inform our sense of the American Dream?
3. How does Offenheiser refer to his connection with Oxfam to boost his ethos (character and credibility)?

Explore

1. Offenheiser writes that, "As a global development organization, Oxfam believes that poverty is about power, not scarcity." What does this mean? Explain why you agree or disagree with this claim.

2. If Oxfam is a global development organization, why does Offenheiser focus on the U.S. in this article?

3. If you were part of the Oxfam team charged with shining "a spotlight on the injustice of America's inequalities" by bringing the voices of the poor to a national audience, how would you do that? Which voices would you highlight? Where and how would you share them—in local or national newspapers, on a website, on television, in YouTube videos? Map a campaign strategy for getting those unheard voices to the public and explain your rationale. Next, create at least one profile for that campaign by conducting an interview with someone who has experienced poverty or who addresses poverty in his or her work.

Vivyan Adair
"Reclaiming the Promise of Higher Education: Poor Single Mothers in Academe"

Vivyan Adair is a professor of women's studies, the Elihu Root Peace Fund Chair, and the director of the ACCESS Project at Hamilton College, which aims to help single parents remain in college and finish their degrees. She has published various scholarly articles and authored two books: *Reclaiming Class: Women, Poverty, and the Promise of Higher Education in America*, and *From Good Ma to Welfare Queen: A Genealogy of the Poor Woman in American Literature, Photography, and Culture*. In the following testimony delivered before the U.S. Senate Committee on Finance, Adair argues that higher education should be an option for people on welfare because it helps them overcome long-term welfare dependence and make positive contributions to society.

Should single mothers on welfare be encouraged to seek higher education instead of working?

Testimony Submitted to the U.S. Senate Committee on Finance

Hearing on Welfare Reform: A New Conversation on Women and Poverty

Submitted by Vivyan Adair, The Elihu Root Peace Fund Chair, Associate Professor of Women's Studies at Hamilton College

September 21, 2010

As children, my siblings and I were marked by poverty, our lives punctuated by bouts of homelessness, hunger, lack of medical and dental care, fear and despair. My young mother, a single parent of four, was a hard worker and an intelligent and honest woman who did her best to bring order, grace, and dignity to our lives. Yet, she was trapped in dead-end and demeaning jobs with which she could not support, nurture, and provide security for the children she loved. Perhaps not too surprisingly, I followed suit as a young woman, dropping out of school and becoming a single mother involved with a string of men who neglected and abused me, leaving me hurt, frustrated, despondent, and profoundly impoverished.

I know the desperation and hopelessness that shape the lives of poor women in the United States today. Yet, I was fortunate to have been poor and broken and verging on irredeemable hopelessness in an era when education could provide a lifeline for poor single mothers, as it has historically done for so many in our country, but fails to do today. Because of my interaction with a pre-reform welfare system, with superb educational institutions, and with instructors who supported and guided me, I was able to transform my life and that of my child through the life-altering pathway of higher education.

Access to Higher Education Prior to Welfare Reform

I entered college in the summer of 1987, as a single mother and welfare recipient without the skills, self-esteem, or vision necessary to succeed in school. My passage was guided by patient and able teachers whose classrooms became places where I built bridges between my own knowledge of the world and crucial new knowledge, skills, and methodologies. Dedicated faculty created exciting and engaging exercises and orchestrated challenging discussions that enabled me to use my newfound skills to re-envision my gifts, strengths, and responsibilities to the world around me. Little by little the larger social, creative, political, and material world exposed itself to me in ways that were resonant and urgent, inviting me to analyze, negotiate, articulate, and reframe systems, histories, and pathways that had previously seemed inaccessible. The process was invigorating, restorative, and life altering.

As a result, today I have a PhD and am employed as a tenured faculty member at a wonderful college in central New York State. My life and experience are certainly not anomalous. In "Together We Are Getting Freedom," Noemy Vides recalls that her life as a poor immigrant welfare mother began anew when she was encouraged to seek an education. She confides that it was through higher education that she was "born as a new woman with visions, dreams, hopes, opportunities, and fulfillment," adding that a college education is "the key ingredient in poor women's struggles to survive."

5   One of my own former students—a young, Latina, single mother of three—now a chemical engineer in California, recently wrote of a similar transformation through higher education. Valuing both the products and the processes of higher education, she reflected:

> "School gave me the credentials to pull my three daughters and me permanently out of poverty. After being raised in dire and painful poverty and then watching my own children suffer as I worked for minimum wage [at a fast food restaurant], this is so important to me. Today we own a home, a car, and pay taxes. I have a great paying job, my children excel in school and I can afford to care for them properly. But what is really revolutionary is what education did to our heads. I think differently now, I act differently and my girls relate to our world differently. My mother died broke, an alcoholic living in public housing. My younger sister is in jail and her children in foster care. We have broken that cycle through education once and for all. We are so grateful for this journey."

Indeed, in 1987, the year that I entered college, around the nation almost half a million welfare recipients were similarly enrolled in institutions of higher education as a route out of poverty. Prior to welfare reform in 1996, tens of thousands of poor single mothers quietly accessed postsecondary education to become teachers, lawyers, social service providers, business and civic leaders, and medical professionals. While education is important to all citizens, my experience and my research convinces me that it is essential for those who will face the continued obstacles of racism, classism, sexism, and homophobia; to those who have been distanced and disenfranchised from U.S. mainstream culture; and to those who have suffered generations of oppression and marginalization.

Closing Education's Doors to Women on Welfare

Despite a large number of reputable studies confirming the relationship between higher education and increased earnings (and thus financial stability), in 1996, Congress enacted the Personal Responsibility and Work Opportunity and Reconciliation Act (PRWORA) as a part of welfare reform. This act was composed of a broad tangle of legislation that "devolved" responsibility for assistance to the poor from the federal to the state level, and through a range of block grants, sanctions, and rewards, encouraged states to reduce their welfare rolls by developing stringent work requirements, imposing strict time limits, discouraging "illegitimacy," and reducing the numbers of applicants eligible for services. The act also promoted the development of programs and requirements that had the effect of discouraging—and in many cases prohibiting—welfare recipients from entering into or completing educational programs, mandating instead that they engage in "work first."

Specifically, the Temporary Assistance for Needy Families (TANF) work requirements, part of the 1996 PRWORA, drastically limited poor women's opportunities to participate in postsecondary education programs while receiving state support. Unlike previous provisions in Aid to Families with Dependent Children (AFDC) and JOBS, education training programs in existence when I first went to college, TANF restrictions from 1996 did not allow higher education to be counted as "work" and required a larger proportion of welfare recipients to engage in full-time recognized work activities. This work-first philosophy emphasized rapid entry into the labor force and penalized states for allowing long-term access to either education or training.

As a result of the dramatic overhaul of welfare policy in 1996, welfare recipient students left college for low-wage jobs in record numbers. Even as the nation began to embrace the conviction that access to education is the pathway to social and economic mobility, poor women were denied access to education that could have positively altered the course of their lives and those of their children. According to the Center on Budget and Policy

Priorities, in the first year of welfare reform, tens of thousands of poor women were forced to drop out of school. Across the nation, the decrease in enrollments among welfare recipients ranged from 29 percent to 82 percent.

10   In 1998, the Center for Law and Social Policy (CLASP) conducted a preliminary survey of key policy advocates in the fifty states and Washington, D.C., regarding welfare recipients' abilities to enter into and complete educational degrees. The study found that in 1995, almost 649,000 students across the nation were receiving AFDC benefits while enrolled in full-time educational programs; by the 1998–1999 school year, that figure had dropped by 47.6 percent, to fewer than 340,000 students. Today the number is estimated to have been reduced again by over 93 percent, with a national enrollment of less than 35,000 students.

The Personal Cost of Work-First Policies

A few years later, the prospects for these students remain dismal. One former computer science major with a ten-year-old son now earns $7.90 per hour. Recently she described changes in her family's quality of life as a result of the 1996 reform: "I call it welfare deform. Things are so much harder now. We can barely pay our rent. My son is alone all the time when I work. I just don't see a future anymore. With school there was hope. I was on my way to making a decent living for us. Now it is just impossible to survive day to day. Usually I can't pay my rent. I don't have a cent saved for emergencies. I don't know what I'm [going to] do."

A second student, who was a gifted and dedicated education major, returned to welfare after being forced to leave the university and then losing several minimum-wage jobs because she could not afford reliable childcare and was denied child-care assistance from the state for failing to name her child's father. She described the nightmare of losing job after minimum-wage job in order to care for her child, emphasizing that this was a "choice no mother should be forced to make." She added:

> It came down to, if I want to keep this job at [the fast-food restaurant] I have to leave my three-year-old daughter alone or maybe with a senile neighbor. And I couldn't even really afford that! Or we could go back to her dad who is a drunk. If I don't do that, we could both end up hungry or homeless. The choice they are making me make is to either abandon or hurt my daughter, and for what?

Similarly, Tonya Mitchell, the single mother of twins and a very successful pre-nursing major committed to providing health care for low-income and minority populations, was forced to drop out of a nursing program and assigned a "work first position" in a nursing home. She reminds us, "All I wanted was to be a nurse and help care for people. I had a very high grade point average and was on my way to a nursing degree with jobs that pay over $25 an hour in addition to benefits." Today, after over six years as a nursing aid, Mitchell makes $8 per hour. In an interview she told me:

> "I still need help from the state with childcare and food stamps and life is so much harder for us now than it was before. Clearly welfare reform and the Personal Responsibility Act changed our lives. I do not have the money I need to pay my rent and bills, my twins are in an awful daycare for about ten hours a day while I work in a job I hate, and we have little hope. If we survive it will be despite welfare reform!"

The experiences of students who had worked diligently to become responsible workers, taxpayers, and parents capable of providing their families with financial security, and who were forced to drop out of school to live in perpetual poverty, illustrates one startling failure of 1996 "welfare reform." Certainly not all low-income single mothers are able or willing to go to college. However, to prevent women who can do so from completing postsecondary degrees is the mark of shortsighted and fiscally-irresponsible policy.

Analyze

1. What is PRWORA? What aspects of welfare reform concern Adair?
2. Name three facts from the testimony that interest you.
3. What does Adair want her audience to think or do based on her testimony?

Explore

1. How does Adair build her ethos (character or credibility)?
2. Who are the stakeholders on the issue of women and welfare? Who would argue for supporting education and not just work as a condition

for public support? Who would argue against this? Where is the common ground?

3. Research welfare reform and write your own testimony for a U.S. Senate hearing on an aspect of this topic. Follow the format for the genre (type) of testimony.

Greg Kaufmann
"By the Numbers: U.S. Poverty"

Greg Kaufmann writes for *The Nation* as a correspondent on poverty. He has also written for the *Washington Post* and *CBS News*. Additionally, he serves as an advisor for the Economic Hardship Reporting Project and the Half in Ten campaign, which aims to cut the poverty rate in half within ten years. Here, Kaufmann offers a summary of the number of Americans affected by poverty and aided by public assistance. Note that if you access this article online, the numbers are hyperlinked to original sources that explain the calculations.

Do you find numbers or narratives about poverty more compelling?

U.S. poverty (less than $17,916 for a family of three): 46.2 million people, 15.1 percent

Read the full report at the National Center for Children in Poverty website.

Children in poverty: 16.1 million, 22 percent of all children, including 39 percent of African-American children and 34 percent of Latino children. Poorest age group in country.

Deep poverty (less than $11,510 for a family of four): 20.4 million people, 1 in 15 Americans, including more than 15 million women and children

5   People who would have been in poverty if not for Social Security, 2011: 67.6 million (program kept 21.4 million people out of poverty)

People in the U.S. experiencing poverty by age 65: Roughly half

Children by family income, 2011

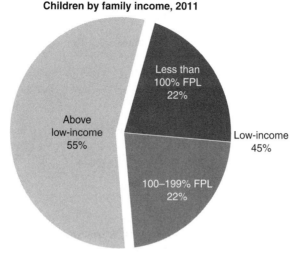

Percentages may not add to 100 due to rounding.

Figure 1.1

Gender gap, 2011: Women 34 percent more likely to be poor than men

Gender gap, 2010: Women 29 percent more likely to be poor than men

Twice the poverty level (less than $46,042 for a family of four): 106 million people, more than 1 in 3 Americans

Jobs in the U.S. paying less than $34,000 a year: 50 percent   10

Jobs in the U.S. paying below the poverty line for a family of four, less than $23,000 annually: 25 percent

Poverty-level wages, 2011: 28 percent of workers

Percentage of individuals and family members in poverty who either worked or lived with a working family member, 2011: 57 percent

Families receiving cash assistance, 1996: 68 for every 100 families living in poverty

Families receiving cash assistance, 2010: 27 for every 100 families living   15
in poverty

Impact of public policy, 2010: Without government assistance, poverty would have been twice as high—nearly 30 percent of population

Percentage of entitlement benefits going to elderly, disabled or working households: Over 90 percent.

Number of homeless children in U.S. public schools: 1,065,794

Annual cost of child poverty nationwide: $550 billion

20   Federal expenditures on home ownership mortgage deductions, 2012: $131 billion

Federal funding for low-income housing assistance programs, 2012: Less than $50 billion

Analyze

1. Which facts explicitly tell us something about the role of public policy in addressing poverty?
2. Which facts are most surprising to you? Why?

Explore

1. Are these neutral facts about poverty, or has Kaufmann structured an underlying argument into the facts he shares? If so, what is that argument?
2. Compare the facts in this piece with those shared by Rector and Sheffield later in this chapter. Are the two sets of facts compatible? Is one set more credible than the other? Write a letter to one of the authors in which you commend or challenge them for sharing this information, perhaps asking clarifying questions. Cite information from the other author(s) to support or challenge your position.
3. How can infographics help explain facts? Select some poverty facts at census.gov/hhes/www/poverty/ or gapminder.org and convert them into a compelling infographic by drawing them or using a digital visual-design program such as piktochart.com, infogr.am, or visual.ly.

Census Bureau
"Definition and Resources for Poverty"

The U.S. Census Bureau is a federal agency under the U.S. Department of Commerce that collects and organizes data about the American people and the economy. Its data are used to determine the number of congressional seats in the U.S. House and how much of the federal government's

$400 billion should go to each local community for improvements to public health, education, and much more. In the following list, the Bureau explains the different terms it uses to determine who lives in poverty.

What other factors, besides income dollars, could help determine whether one lives in poverty?

Absolute Poverty Thresholds vs. Relative Poverty Thresholds

As explained by a National Academy of Sciences panel, "Absolute thresholds are fixed at a point in time and updated solely for price changes. . . . In contrast, relative thresholds, as commonly defined, are developed by reference to the actual expenditures (or income) of the population." See Citro and Michael, eds., *Measuring Poverty: A New Approach* (National Academy Press, 1995), page 31, "Types of Poverty Thresholds."

Annual Poverty Rate

Percent of people who were in poverty in a calendar year. Annual poverty rates from the Current Population Survey and the decennial census long form are based on income reported at an annual figure. In the Survey of Income and Program Participation (SIPP), income is reported a few months at a time, several times a year. Therefore, in the SIPP, annual poverty rates are calculated using the sum of family income over the year divided by the sum of poverty thresholds that can change from month to month if one's family composition changes.

Average Monthly Poverty

Average percent of people poor per month in each year of a longitudinal survey panel. See also longitudinal survey data.

Chronic or Long-Term Poverty

Percent of people in poverty every month for the duration of a longitudinal survey panel (typically 3 to 4 years). See also longitudinal survey data.

Cross-Sectional Survey Data

5   Data from a survey in which a new group of respondents is sampled for each interview, instead of following the same group of respondents over time. The Current Population Survey Annual Social and Economic Supplement (CPS ASEC), the American Community Survey (ACS), and the decennial census long form are cross-sectional surveys. See also longitudinal survey data.

Entrance Rate

Percent of people who were not in poverty during the first year of a longitudinal survey but were in poverty in a subsequent year. Uses an annual poverty measure.

Episodic Poverty

Percent of people who were poor in 2 or more consecutive months in a given time period. Episodic poverty can only be computed using longitudinal survey data.

Equivalence Scale

The numerical relationship by which poverty thresholds vary for families of different sizes and compositions.

Federal Poverty Level (FPL)

According to the Department of Health and Human Services, "The poverty guidelines are sometimes loosely referred to as the 'federal poverty level' (FPL), but that phrase is ambiguous and should be avoided, especially in situations (e.g., legislative or administrative) where precision is important." [http://aspe.hhs.gov/poverty/05poverty.shtml, last accessed May 24, 2005.] See also HHS poverty guidelines.

Gini Ratio

10   The Gini ratio (or index of income concentration) is a statistical measure of income equality ranging from 0 to 1. A measure of 1 indicates perfect inequality; i.e., one person has all the income and rest have none. A measure of 0 indicates perfect equality; i.e., all people have equal shares of income.

The Census Bureau used grouped data to compute all Gini ratios. For a more detailed discussion, see Current Population Reports, Series P-60, No. 123.

Income Deficit/Income Surplus

Income deficit is the number of dollars that the income of a family in poverty (or unrelated individual) falls below its poverty threshold. If income is negative, the deficit equals the threshold. Income surplus is the difference in dollars between the income of a family or unrelated individual above the poverty level and its poverty threshold.

Income Surplus

Income surplus is the difference in dollars between the income of a family or unrelated individual above the poverty level and its poverty threshold.

Income-to-Poverty Ratio

See ratio of income to poverty.

Longitudinal Survey Data

Data from a survey in which the same respondents are interviewed multiple times, using the same set of questions, over a period of time (a panel). The Survey of Income and Program Participation (SIPP) is a longitudinal survey. While cross-sectional data have been compared to "snapshots" in that differences between two cross-sectional estimates are based on two different samples of people, longitudinal data instead allow the analyst to observe how the status of the same group of people changes over time—for instance, by observing the average number of months a person falls below the poverty level, or by observing the demographic characteristics of people who enter and leave poverty. In that sense, longitudinal data have been compared to "videos." See, for instance, Mary Naifeh, "Dynamics of Economic Well-Being, Poverty, 1993–94: Trap Door? Revolving Door? Or Both?"

Long-Term Poverty

See chronic or long-term poverty.

Median Income

Median income is the amount which divides the income distribution into two equal groups, half having incomes above the median, half having incomes below the median. The medians for households, families, and unrelated individuals are based on all households, families, and unrelated individuals, respectively. The medians for people are based on people 15 years old and over with income.

Monthly Poverty

See average monthly poverty.

National Academy of Sciences (NAS) Panel

The National Research Council's Panel on Poverty and Family Assistance: Concepts, Information Needs, and Measurement Methods. A group of scholars who co-authored a publication in 1995, *Measuring Poverty: A New Approach* (National Academy Press, 1995), that recommended alternative methods for measuring poverty. The Census Bureau has conducted research to refine some of the panel's measurement methods and to examine how its recommendations would affect the number in poverty and the poverty rate. (For further information, see Poverty Measurement Studies and Alternative Measures.)

Poverty Areas

Poverty areas are census tracts or block numbering areas (BNA's) where at least 20 percent of residents were below the poverty level.

Poverty Definition

20   Following the Office of Management and Budget's (OMB) Statistical Policy Directive 14, the Census Bureau uses a set of money income thresholds that vary by family size and composition to determine who is in poverty. If a family's total income is less than the family's threshold, then that family and every individual in it is considered in poverty. The official poverty thresholds do not vary geographically, but they are updated for inflation using Consumer Price Index (CPI-U). The official poverty definition uses money

income before taxes and does not include capital gains or noncash benefits (such as public housing, Medicaid, and food stamps).

Poverty in the Past 12 Months
The American Community Survey measures poverty in the previous 12 months instead of the previous calendar year. For more information, see ACS poverty definition.

Poverty Rate
The percentage of people (or families) who are below poverty.

Poverty Spell
Number of months in poverty as measured using panel data from a longitudinal survey (excluding spells underway in the first interview month of the panel). Minimum spell length is 2 months. Spells are separated by 2 or more months of not being in poverty. Individuals can have more than one spell.

Poverty Thresholds
Dollar amounts the Census Bureau uses to determine a family's or person's poverty status.

Poverty Universe
Persons for whom the Census Bureau can determine poverty status (either "in poverty" or "not in poverty"). For some persons, such as unrelated individuals under age 15, poverty status is not defined. Since Census Bureau surveys typically ask income questions to persons age 15 or older, if a child under age 15 is not related by birth, marriage, or adoption to a reference person within the household, we do not know the child's income and therefore cannot determine his or her poverty status. For the decennial censuses and the American Community Survey, poverty status is also undefined for people living in college dormitories and in institutional group quarters. People whose poverty status is undefined are excluded from Census Bureau poverty tabulations. Thus, the total population in poverty tables—the poverty universe—is slightly smaller than the overall population.

Ratio of Income to Poverty

People and families are classified as being in poverty if their income is less than their poverty threshold. If their income is less than half their poverty threshold, they are below 50% of poverty; less than the threshold itself, they are in poverty (below 100% of poverty); less than 1.25 times the threshold, below 125% of poverty, and so on. The greater the ratio of income to poverty, the more people fall under the category, because higher ratios include more people with higher incomes.

Relative Poverty Thresholds

See absolute poverty thresholds vs. relative poverty thresholds.

Small Area Income and Poverty Estimates

The Small Area Income and Poverty Estimates (SAIPE) program produces estimates of income and poverty for states and counties, and population and poverty for school districts. The estimates are provided for the administration of federal programs and the allocation of federal funds to local jurisdictions.

Spells of Poverty

See poverty spell.

Standard Error

30   A measure of an estimate's variability. The greater the standard error in relation to the size of the estimate, the less reliable the estimate.

Threshold

See poverty threshold.

Unrelated individual

Unrelated individuals are people of any age who are not members of families or subfamilies.

Working Poor

The Census Bureau does not use the term "working poor." The "working poor" may mean different things to different data users, based on the question they are trying to answer, such as:

- People who worked, but who, nevertheless, fell under the official definition of poverty. See table POV22 of our Detailed Poverty Tables. Table POV22 focuses on workers versus non-workers, age 16 and over.
- People who were in poverty and had at least one working family member. See table POV10 of our Detailed Poverty Tables. Table POV10 includes the children and other family members of workers (such as stay-at-home parents, retired family members, and others).
- People who may not necessarily be "in poverty" according to the official measure of poverty, but who fall below some percentage of the poverty level (for instance, 200 percent of poverty).
  - Percentages of the poverty level are referred to as "Ratio of income to poverty" in our Detailed Poverty Tables.
  - "Below 100% of poverty" is the same as "in poverty."
  - "Below 200% of poverty" includes all those described as "in poverty" under the official definition, plus some people who have income above poverty but less than 2 times their poverty threshold.

Analyze

1. Explain in your own words the difference between "absolute" and "relative" measures of poverty. What are the advantages and disadvantages of each type of measurement tool?
2. Read the entry on "Federal Poverty Level (FPL)" and comment on how it warns readers to avoid this phrase. What does this suggest about the changing rhetoric around poverty?
3. Which entry explains most fully how inequality is measured? Why is inequality discussed in relation to poverty?

Explore

1. Pick one entry to research further through a different site or source. How is the definition of that concept expanded or presented

differently? How does that different rhetorical situation—different author and different context—change the message? Which definition is most helpful and why?

2. Read the entry on the "Working Poor," which says that it "may mean different things to different data users, based on the question they are trying to answer." Have you heard this term before? What was the rhetorical situation where you heard this (place and speaker), and how was it defined? What connotation or feeling does this term evoke for you? In his book *The Working Poor: Invisible in America*, David Shipler vents his frustration with this term: "Most of the people I write about in this book do not have the luxury of rage. They are caught in exhausting struggles. Their wages do not lift them far enough from poverty to improve their lives, and their lives, in turn, hold them back. The term by which they are usually described, 'working poor,' should be an oxymoron. Nobody who works hard should be poor in America" (ix). Write a definitional argument in which you outline your own position on this contested term using examples for support.

3. Research the debate surrounding poverty measures referenced in the entry on the National Academy of Sciences (NAS) panel. Who are the stakeholders in this debate? What is at stake if the measurement stays the same or if it changes? What are the most recent developments on this issue? If you were a member of the NAS panel, what would you recommend?

Measure of America
"About Human Development"

Commonly, statistics such as the Gross Domestic Product help to provide analysts with an overall measure of well-being within a country. Measure of America, however, works to develop alternative statistical indicators that account for various concepts of well-being in addition to economic metrics. In particular, their American Human Development Index "is comprised of health, education, and income indicators and allows for well-being rankings of the 50 states, 435 congressional districts, county groups within states, women and men, and racial and ethnic groups" so that communities and groups can use this information to track progress over time. In this piece, they explain the components that are accounted for in their measure.

Why might a measure of opportunity be more helpful than a measure of Gross Domestic Product?

About Human Development

Human development is defined as the process of enlarging people's freedoms and opportunities and improving their well-being. Human development is about the real freedom ordinary people have to decide who to be, what to do, and how to live.

The human development concept was developed by economist Mahbub ul Haq. At the World Bank in the 1970s, and later as minister of finance in his own country, Pakistan, Dr. Haq argued that existing measures of human progress failed to account for the true purpose of development—to improve people's lives. In particular, he believed that the commonly used measure of Gross Domestic Product failed to adequately measure well-being. Working with Nobel Laureate Amartya Sen and other gifted economists, in 1990 Dr. Haq published the first Human Development Report, which was commissioned by the United Nations Development Programme.

Central to the human development approach is the concept of capabilities. Capabilities—what people can do and what they can become—are the equipment one has to pursue a life of value. Basic capabilities valued by virtually everyone include: good health, access to knowledge, and a decent material standard of living. Other capabilities central to a fulfilling life could include the ability to participate in the decisions that affect one's life, to have control over one's living environment, to enjoy freedom from violence, to have societal respect, and to relax and have fun.

Our capabilities are expanded (or constrained) by our own efforts and by the institutions and conditions of our society. People with extensive, well-developed capabilities have the tools they need to make their vision of "a good life" a reality. Those poor in capabilities are less able to chart their own course and to seize opportunities. Without basic capabilities, human potential remains unfulfilled.

5   The capability approach is a normative framework used for analyzing well-being, often employed to understand development problems. Although certain aspects of the approach can be linked to Aristotle and Adam Smith, it is philosopher-economist Amartya Sen and more recently, University of Chicago professor of law and ethics Martha Nussbaum, who are responsible for its development and proliferation.

The core premise of the capability approach is that well-being should be defined by people's real and actual opportunities to undertake the pursuits that they desire (often referred to as 'capabilities to function')—and through these freedoms, be whom they would like to be. One illustration of the difference between capabilities to function and formal freedoms is found in the area of educational opportunity. All U.S. citizens have the formal freedom to earn a college degree. However when comparing students from low-income neighborhoods with more affluent students, low-income students' real freedoms to attend college can be constrained by, among other things, low quality local high schools and financial considerations. Formal freedoms, in this and many cases, are necessary but not sufficient to provide true capabilities to function. The capability approach to well-being, which prioritizes the ability to actualize opportunity into 'beings and doings,' contrasts with other theories of well-being which focus on subjective measures, such as happiness, or on material means, such as income.

The Human Development Index

The state of the nation is often expressed through Gross National Product, daily stock market results, consumer spending levels, and national debt figures. But these numbers provide only a partial view of how people are faring.

The Human Development Index was developed as an alternative to simple money metrics. It is an easy-to-understand numerical measure made up of what most people believe are the very basic ingredients of human well-being: health, education, and income. The first Human Development Index was presented in 1990. It has been an annual feature of every Human Development Report since, ranking virtually every country in the world from number one (currently Iceland) to number 177 (currently Sierra Leone).

This composite index has become one of the most widely used indices of well-being around the world and has succeeded in broadening the measurement and discussion of well-being beyond the important, but nevertheless narrow, confines of income. In a number of countries, the Human

Development Index is now an official government statistic; its annual publication inaugurates serious political discussion and renewed efforts, nationally and regionally, to improve lives.

The American Human Development Index

The Measure of America presents a modified American Human Development Index. The American HD Index measures the same three basic dimensions as the standard HD Index, but it uses different indicators to better reflect the U.S. context and to maximize use of available data. For example, while the standard index measures access to knowledge using the average number of years that students spend in school, we have chosen instead to use educational attainment, a more demanding indicator. 10

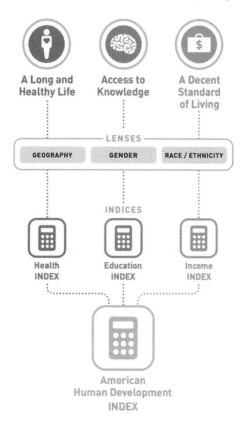

Figure 1.2

While data are plentiful on the extremes of affluence and deprivation in the United States, the American Human Development Index provides a single measure of well-being for all Americans, disaggregated by state and congressional district, as well as by gender, race, and ethnicity. All data used in the index come from official U.S. government sources—the American Community Survey of the U.S. Census Bureau and the Centers for Disease Control and Prevention.

The data included in the American Human Development Index will help us understand variations among regions and groups. It is a snapshot of America today. Moreover, the index will serve as a baseline for monitoring future progress.

Why Health, Education, and Income?

Most people would agree that a long and healthy life, access to knowledge, and a decent material standard of living are the basic building blocks of well-being and opportunity. They are also the building blocks of the American Human Development Index as well as the U.N. Human Development Index upon which it is modeled. These three core capabilities are universally valued around the world, and measurable, intuitively sensible, and reliable indicators exist to represent them—two critical considerations in the construction of a composite index.

A Long and Healthy Life

The most valuable capability people possess is to be alive. Advancing human development requires, first and foremost, expanding the real opportunities people have to avoid premature death by disease or injury, to enjoy protection from arbitrary denial of life, to live in a healthy environment, to maintain a healthy lifestyle, to receive quality medical care, and to attain the highest possible standard of physical and mental health.

15   In the American HD Index, life expectancy at birth stands as a proxy for the capability to live a long and healthy life. Life expectancy at birth is the average number of years a baby born today is expected to live if current mortality patterns continue throughout his or her lifetime. The most commonly used gauge of population health the world over, life expectancy at birth represents one-third of the overall American HD Index.

The American Human Development Project calculates life expectancy for the 50 states, the 435 congressional districts, women and men, and major racial and ethnic groups from mortality data from the Centers for Disease Control and Prevention, National Center for Health Statistics, and population data from the CDC WONDER database.

Access to Knowledge

Access to knowledge is a critical determinant of long-term well-being and is essential to individual freedom, self-determination, and self-sufficiency. Education is critical to people's real freedom to decide what to do and who to be. Education builds confidence, confers status and dignity, and broadens the horizons of the possible—as well as allowing for the acquisition of skills and credentials. Globalization and technological change have made it extraordinarily difficult for poorly educated Americans to achieve the economic self-sufficiency, peace of mind, and self-respect enabled by a secure livelihood.

Access to knowledge is measured using two indicators: school enrollment for the population age 3 and older, and educational degree attainment for the population 25 years and older. A one-third weight is applied to the enrollment indicator and a two-thirds weight is applied to the degree attainment indicator. Both indicators are from the American Community Survey, U.S. Census Bureau.

A Decent Standard of Living

Income is essential to meeting basic needs like food and shelter—and to moving beyond these necessities to a life of genuine choice and freedom. Income enables valuable options and alternatives, and its absence can limit life chances and restrict access to many opportunities. Income is a means to a host of critical ends, including a decent education; a safe, clean living environment; security in illness and old age; and a say in the decisions that affect one's life. Money isn't everything, but it's something quite important.

A decent standard of living is measured using median personal earnings 20 of all full- and part-time workers 16 years and older from the American Community Survey, U.S. Census Bureau.

Analyze

1. Why was the human development concept established?
2. In human development, what are "capabilities"? Give a definition and examples. What is the difference between "capabilities" and "formal freedoms"? Name the example given in this reading and add one of your own.
3. What three "basic ingredients" represent the core elements of human well-being in the Human Development Index? Why were these chosen?

Explore

1. This reading states: "Without basic capabilities, human potential remains unfulfilled." How would you respond to someone who reads that and says: "So what? I can only worry about fulfilling my own potential, not the potential of all humanity." Write a persuasive argument in response.
2. Choose one of the three core elements measured in the Human Development Index and write a persuasive argument in which you explain why this is the most important of the three elements. Explain why this element should receive top priority, garnering most of our resources, including time and financial support. Consider writing this to a political leader who has the ability to set the agenda in this area.
3. Research one of the key leaders mentioned in this text who redefined our approach to understanding human development. What did that leader write and do to help change our thinking? What were his/her unique contributions, and how was he/she recognized for that work? In your profile, highlight that person's definition of poverty and show how it informs his/her work.

Robert Rector and Rachel Sheffield
"Air Conditioning, Cable TV, and an Xbox: What Is Poverty in the United States Today?"

Robert Rector and Rachel Sheffield research and write for the Heritage Foundation, a think tank whose stated mission is to "formulate and promote conservative public policies." Rector focuses his work on poverty, welfare, immigration, and the collapse of marriage and families. His work impacted the

1996 federal welfare reform legislation, notable for its requirement that welfare recipients work or pursue job training in order to receive benefits. Sheffield researches and writes on family issues and religion in civil society. This reading is only the executive summary of a full research report on this topic.

Should people with modern amenities be considered "poor"?

E ach year for the past two decades, the U.S. Census Bureau has reported that over 30 million Americans were living in "poverty." In recent years, the Census has reported that one in seven Americans are poor. But what does it mean to be "poor" in America?

To the average American, the word "poverty" implies significant material deprivation, an inability to provide a family with adequate nutritious food, reasonable shelter, and clothing. Activists reinforce this view, declaring that being poor in the U.S. means being "unable to obtain the basic material necessities of life." The news media amplify this idea: Most news stories on poverty feature homeless families, people living in crumbling shacks, or lines of the downtrodden eating in soup kitchens.

The actual living conditions of America's poor are far different from these images. According to the government's own survey data, in 2005, the average household defined as poor by the government lived in a house or apartment equipped with air conditioning and cable TV. The family had a car (a third of the poor have two or more cars). For entertainment, the household had two color televisions, a DVD player, and a VCR. If there were children in the home (especially boys), the family had a game system, such as an Xbox or PlayStation. In the kitchen, the household had a microwave, refrigerator, and an oven and stove. Other household conveniences included a clothes washer, clothes dryer, ceiling fans, a cordless phone, and a coffee maker.

The home of the average poor family was in good repair and not overcrowded. In fact, the typical poor American had more living space than the average European. (Note: that's average European, not poor European.) The poor family was able to obtain medical care when needed. When asked, most poor families stated they had had sufficient funds during the past year to meet all essential needs.

5   By its own report, the family was not hungry. The average intake of protein, vitamins, and minerals by poor children is indistinguishable from children in the upper middle class, and, in most cases, is well above recommended norms. Poor boys today at ages 18 and 19 are actually taller and heavier than middle-class boys of similar age in the late 1950s, and are a full one inch taller and 10 pounds heavier than American soldiers who fought in World War II. The major dietary problem facing poor Americans is eating too much, not too little; the majority of poor adults, like most Americans, are overweight.

The living standards of the poor have improved steadily for many decades. In particular, as the prices of new consumer items fall, these conveniences become available throughout society, including poor households. Consumer items that were luxuries or significant purchases for the middle class a few decades ago have become commonplace among the poor. As a rule of thumb, poor households tend to obtain the latest conveniences about a dozen years after the middle class.

True, the average poor family, described above, does not represent every poor family. There is a range of living conditions among the poor. Some poor households fare better than the average household described above. Others are worse off.

Although the overwhelming majority of the poor are well housed, at any single point in time during the recession in 2009, around one in 70 poor persons was homeless. Although the majority of poor families have an adequate and reasonably steady supply of food, many worry about keeping food on the table, and one in five experienced temporary food shortages at various times in 2009. Those who are temporarily short on food or are homeless will find no comfort in the fact that their condition is relatively infrequent. Their distress is real and a serious concern.

Nonetheless, sound public policy cannot be based on faulty information or misunderstanding. Regrettably, most discussions of poverty in the U.S. rely on sensationalism, exaggeration, and misinformation. But an effective anti-poverty policy must be based on an accurate assessment of actual living conditions and the causes of deprivation. In the long term, grossly exaggerating the extent and severity of material deprivation in the U.S. will benefit neither the poor, the economy, nor society as a whole.

Analyze

1. Why are the words "poverty" and "poor" in quotation marks in the first paragraph? How does this affect the reader? Is this tactic successful?
2. According to Rector and Sheffield, what definition of poverty do most Americans use? Where does that idea come from? Does that fully represent your concept and definition of poverty? Explain.
3. What do the authors say is a more accurate description of the material conditions of poverty in the U.S.? Name three to five of the material goods a person living in poverty might have, particularly items that surprise you.

Explore

1. The authors argue that "sound public policy cannot be based on faulty information or misunderstanding." Most people would agree with that. The next sentence, however, might cause disagreement: "Regrettably, most discussions of poverty in the U.S. rely on sensationalism, exaggeration, and misinformation." Think of or find actual representations of poverty that the authors might classify as such (e.g., a photo of someone apparently living out of a shopping cart). How common are these representations? Do they, as the authors suggest, skew our sense of the actual poverty environment in the U.S.? What are the consequences if that is true?
2. The latter paragraphs include a "naysayer," the person who interrupts an argument to rebut it, saying, "Yes, but what about...." In this section, the authors almost speak directly to that naysayer, anticipating and tackling some objections: "True," this section begins as if conceding to another voice. What effect does this section have on the argument overall and on the ethos (character or credibility) of the authors? Does it represent opposing viewpoints successfully? Would you use this device? Explain.
3. Choose one of the material goods listed and write a letter to the authors explaining why that particular item, though it might have been a luxury a few decades ago, is a necessity today. In doing so, explain your own working definition of poverty (consult Haveman's article that follows or others that give expanded definitions of poverty). Or, write a letter to the authors explaining why their research successfully counters misleading reports of material conditions of poverty in the U.S. Cite misleading examples from the media and advocacy groups.

Robert Haveman
"What Does It Mean to Be Poor in a Rich Society?"

Robert Haveman is an emeritus professor of public affairs and economics at the University of Wisconsin–Madison where he also serves at the Institute for Research on Poverty. He has served as an expert economist for the U.S. Congress and published in many academic journals on the economics of poverty and social policy, environmental and natural resources policy, and public finance. In the following, Haveman focuses on how people, including policymakers, should conceive of poverty and deprivation beyond using measures of income.

What is at stake in defining and measuring poverty one way or another?

Introduction

Mollie Orshansky, whose contributions led to the nation's official poverty measure, passed away in 2007 after a notable career as an analyst for the federal government. In the early 1960s when she developed her poverty measure, Orshansky's proposal—based on family cash income and an absolute poverty threshold—made perfect sense. President Johnson had declared a War on Poverty in 1964, and the nation needed a statistical picture of the poor. Although Orshansky recognized the shortcomings of her measure, she also knew that it provided the first official gauge of poverty that could be analyzed across years.

Since Orshansky's proposal was adopted, the U.S. official poverty measure has stood nearly unchanged. This, in spite of extensive efforts designed to improve the measurement of both financial means (for example, extensions of the income concept to include the value of in-kind transfers and tax liabilities) and the poverty threshold (for example, alternative equivalence scales and revised needs standards).

Concepts of Poverty

Improving the well-being of deprived people is a nearly universal goal among policymakers in all nations. However, no commonly accepted way of identifying who is deprived or who has an unacceptably low level of well-being has emerged.

Economists tend to prefer a concept of hardship that reflects "economic position" or "economic well-being," which is typically measured by an indicator of *command over resources,* typically annual income. These economic poverty measures seek to identify families whose command over resources (income) falls below some minimally acceptable level. This approach requires precise definitions of both available economic resources and the minimum level of economic needs, both of which must be measured in the same units.

Such economic poverty measures allow for differentiation according to household size and composition. They also have the potential advantage of not imposing norms on people's preferences among goods or services (for example, their sense of necessities versus luxuries) or between work and leisure. However, by focusing on "command over resources," they ignore many noneconomic considerations that may affect individual utility or well-being. To the extent that such factors—for example, living in unsafe surroundings, being socially isolated, or experiencing adverse health or living arrangements not remediable by spending money—are neglected by these measures, policy efforts designed to reduce economic poverty may overlook important aspects of what it means to be poor.

Because of such concerns, income-based poverty measures are increasingly challenged, particularly in other western industrialized countries. Critics argue for a multidimensional poverty concept. For example, people deprived of social contacts (with friends, families, and neighbors) are described as socially isolated, and hence poor in this dimension; people living in squalid housing, as "housing poor"; and people with health deficits, as "health poor." However, those who prefer a broader approach to the measurement of poverty face a difficult task in changing the official U.S. measure. Dimensions of well-being beyond income need to be identified and agreed upon, indicators that accurately reflect these dimensions must be defined, data necessary to accurately measure them for individual living units must be collected, and the several indicators must be weighted to produce an index of the size of the poor population and its composition.

While debates over the appropriate concept of poverty seem unlikely to cease, a basic question lurks over the discussion: "Does the measure of poverty that is chosen matter?" Nearly all observers believe that it does. Different measures imply a different size and composition of the target poverty population, different patterns of change in the extent of poverty over time, and thus a different set of antipoverty policies. Policymakers and citizens react to information on these patterns. Changes in poverty over time lead to questions about the direction of the nation, the effectiveness of its social policies, and the level of equality or inequality in the distribution of income.

Measuring Economic Poverty

Even among those who prefer income-based or command-over-resources poverty measures, there are substantial differences of opinion regarding which is the best measure. For example, the official U.S. measure relies on the annual cash income of a family, and compares this to a minimum income standard or "poverty line." An alternative position is that annual consumption better reflects a family's level of living, or that some measure of a family's ability to secure income identifies a nation's truly needy population. Others advocate reliance on families' own assessment of their economic well-being. Once the measure of economic position has been chosen, poverty measures can still be either absolute or relative. The indicator is absolute if the definition of "needs" is fixed, so that the poverty threshold does not change with the standard of living of the society. A relative measure uses a poverty line that increases along with the general standard of living of the society.

The Official U.S. Measure of Absolute Income Poverty

The official U.S. poverty measure seeks to identify families whose annual cash income—from either government support or their own efforts—falls below the official poverty threshold. It compares two numbers for each living unit—the unit's annual cash income and the poverty threshold for a unit of its size and composition. It is an absolute measure because it is adjusted each year only for changes in prices, not for changes in living standards.

10   This official measure assumes that (1) money can buy those things the absence of which make people feel deprived, (2) cash income is a good proxy for welfare (or utility), and (3) a particular year's income is an acceptable indicator of longer-run income. Although people may experience hardship in many dimensions—education, housing, food, social contacts, security, environmental amenities—only a low level of cash income matters in determining who is poor.

The U.S. Census Bureau performs the official poverty measurement each year, and each year presents a public report on the level of poverty in the prior year and changes in the level and composition of the poor from year to year. All major news media carry the story and reflect on who is winning, who is losing, and how the nation is doing in fighting poverty.

This annual news story also provokes a barrage of commentary on the nature of the official measure, and whether or not the message it conveys is reliable. Although the cash income numerator of the measure may reflect the extent to which a family can meet its immediate needs, this value may fluctuate substantially from year to year due to unemployment, job changes, health considerations, and especially income flows from farming and self-employment. For this reason, some claim that the measure conveys an unreliable picture of who is poor over the longer run.

It is also argued that even as an indicator of a family's ability to meet its immediate needs, the measure is flawed. The income reported by families to census surveyors tends to be artificially low, and often income from various nonstandard sources is not reported at all. As a result, the overall poverty rate tends to be higher than it should. Moreover, the annual income measure reflects neither the value of in-kind transfers (for example, food stamps and Medicaid) nor taxes paid nor tax credits received, including the Earned Income Tax Credit. Indeed, virtually all major social policy reforms since the 1960s have been in the form of giving families benefits such as food, health care, and child care that don't count in the poverty statistics. Similarly, the assets available to families are not counted, nor is the value of leisure (or voluntary nonwork) time reflected in the measure. As a result the consumption spending of a family in any given year may differ substantially from the family's reported income. Although there are major differences in the needs of workers and nonworkers, those with and without serious medical care needs, or those living in high cost areas relative to those in low cost areas, none of these considerations are reflected in the official measure.

The denominator of the poverty ratio—the poverty line threshold—also comes under fire. Critics claim that this needs indicator has little conceptual basis and rests on empirical evidence about food consumption from the mid-1950s. The same criticism applies to the equivalence scales used to adjust needs for differences in family size.

In addition to these criticisms, conservative commentators also empha- 15 size that many of those who are poor by the official measure do not live in destitute circumstances; that they own color television sets, automobiles, refrigerators, stoves, and in some cases homes; and that they are not under-nourished. At the other end of the political spectrum, some liberal analysts find that in order to meet "basic needs," income must to be substantially greater than the current poverty thresholds; they find a much higher poverty rate than the official measure. These critiques highlight the complex nature of political sentiment about American poverty, and emphasize the need for improvements in the official poverty measure.

Some attempts have been made to improve the nation's official poverty measure. In 1995, the National Research Council of the National Academy of Sciences reported the results of a comprehensive study of the strengths and weaknesses of the official measure, and proposed a major revision designed to correct many of the criticisms that have been levied against it. The reform proposed would involve a new threshold based on budget studies of food, clothing, shelter (including utilities), and amounts that would allow for other needs to be met, such as household supplies, personal care, non-work-related transportation. The thresholds would reflect geographic differences in housing costs. The income measure would also be reworked to include the value of near-money benefits that are available to buy goods and services (for example, food stamps), and would subtract from income required expenses that cannot be used to buy goods and services (for example, income and payroll taxes, child care and other work-related expenses, child support payments to another household, and out-of-pocket medical care costs, including health insurance premiums).

Since that report, the Census Bureau and other governmental statistical agencies have developed a variety of improved poverty measures reflecting the recommendations of the 1995 report. Two extensive reports by the Census Bureau present estimates of these alternative measures since 1990; in addition, the Bureau has released a number of alternative poverty measure estimates in supplements that accompany the annual official poverty report. However, none of these alternatives has been adopted to replace the existing official poverty measure.

Alternative Measures of Economic Poverty

In addition to the official U.S. absolute income poverty measure (and extensions of it), a wide range of other indicators of economic poverty have been proposed and implemented. In this section, I briefly describe a few of these, and indicate some of their pros and cons.

Relative income poverty. Many accept the access to resources (income) basis for measuring poverty, but reject an absolute poverty threshold. Instead, relative income measures compare the income of a family to a norm reflecting the economic position of the overall society (say, the income of the median family), adjusted for price level changes. Because overall measures of social well-being, such as median income, tend to increase over time, the poverty standard will also tend to increase. Both the United Kingdom (UK) and countries in the European Union (EU) measure income poverty using such a relative definition.

Relative poverty measures have their weaknesses. Absolute poverty standards have the advantage of allowing citizens to judge the effectiveness of antipoverty programs by whether the programs move families above the fixed standard; in contrast, poverty will decline under relative measures only if the income of families in the bottom tail of the distribution increases more than that of the median family. 20

Consumption poverty. One of the main criticisms of measures of income poverty concerns the highly transitory nature of an annual income measure of resources. For many households, income may temporarily dip below the poverty line because of something that happened that year, such as unemployment or a bad harvest. An alternative is to use annual family consumption rather than annual income as a more permanent indicator of resources.

Although a consumption poverty measure probably does better reflect the "permanently poor" population, it is difficult to obtain the accurate and complete family expenditure data necessary to construct a consumption-based index. Furthermore, consumption may not fully reflect a family's true well-being; it is possible that simple frugality may be mistaken for poverty.

"Capability" poverty. Poverty indicators based on income or consumption presume that families should have actual resources to meet some minimum standard. An alternative objective would identify the poor as those who do not have the capability to secure a sufficient level of resources to meet this standard. To many analysts and policymakers, policy interventions should seek to provide a pathway to self-sufficiency. A capability measure of poverty focuses attention on policies that foster economic independence. Such measures are preferred by some to income-conditioned in-kind or cash support, which are viewed as encouraging dependence.

Haveman and Bershadker have proposed an "earnings capacity" self-sufficiency poverty measure based on a family's education level and other indicators of earnings capacity. Their measure of earnings capacity adjusted the full-time, full-year earnings of all adults in a family for health and other constraints on full-time work and for the required expenses (largely child care) associated with full-time work. The resulting net family earnings capacity value is compared to the official U.S. poverty line.

25   This measure rests on several norms and assumptions. First, it assumes that full-time, full-year work indicates the full (or capacity) use of human capital. Second, the adjustments to family earnings capacity reflecting constraints on and costs of working full time are assumed to be accurate. Finally, the measure captures only those capabilities that are reflected in market work and earnings; the potential services of other valuable, though nonmarketed, capabilities are neglected.

Asset poverty. There has been much interest recently in the role of asset (wealth) holdings in understanding the level and composition of poverty in the U.S. In the words of Oliver and Shapiro, "Wealth is . . . used to create opportunities, secure a desired stature and standard of living, or pass class status along to one's children. In this sense the command over resources that wealth entails is more encompassing than is income or education, and closer in meaning and theoretical significance to our traditional notions of economic well-being and access to life chances."

Haveman and Wolff estimated the level and composition of asset poverty in 2001, presuming that net worth equal to less than one-fourth of the official poverty line (reflecting the ability to live for 3 months at the poverty line by drawing down assets) indicates asset poverty. In 2001, one-fourth of American families were asset poor; among blacks and Hispanics, the asset poverty rate was 62 percent, among those with less than a high school degree it was 60 percent, and among non-aged female heads with children the asset poverty rate stood at 71 percent. From 1983 to 2001, the rate of asset poverty grew by over 9 percent, much faster than the growth of income poverty.

Subjective poverty. Some researchers have measured poverty by relying on the subjective responses of individuals to questions about their perceptions of economic position or well-being, relative to some norm. Because the norms applied by people are likely to change over time (as their incomes change), subjective poverty measures are relative poverty indicators. These measures survey households and ask them to specify the minimum level of income or consumption they consider to be "just sufficient" to allow them to live a minimally adequate lifestyle.

Establishing an overall poverty rate requires an assumption that individual perceptions of these notions reflect the same level of real welfare for all respondents. The effectiveness of subjective measures is limited by the small sample sizes on which they are based; most estimates show wide variation around the mean, impeding the setting of a reliable and generally accepted poverty threshold.

Measuring Other Dimensions of Deprivation

In both the U.S. and in Europe, social scientists and policymakers have 30 expressed concerns about using money-valued indicators to measure the well-being of citizens and to evaluate the effect of policy changes on various groups of people. In the 1960s, these concerns led to substantial efforts by U.S. and European government and university researchers to develop a wide variety of indicators both to measure the social and economic performance of society and to evaluate the effectiveness of policy efforts. These efforts resulted in a number of prominent government and other reports presenting a variety of social indicators.

In the context of measuring poverty, this interest in broader measures of well-being was the strongest in the European Union countries. A basic argument in support of a broader, multidimensional concept of poverty contends that markets fail and are incomplete so that cash income cannot always be readily transformed into fundamental goods and services necessary for the attainment of well-being. If this is the case, then the measure of poverty must explicitly recognize these shortfalls. A policy judgment provides a second argument in support of this approach; if one believes that antipoverty policies should target those with multiple disadvantages, it follows that the poverty measure should also be multidimensional.

Recently, the EU countries and the United Kingdom have emphasized this multidimensional nature of deprivation, and have developed supplementary indicators of poverty based on indicators of material hardship and a broad concept of "social exclusion." Some use the term "social exclusion" to refer to concepts such as "marginalization," "ghettoization," and "the underclass"; others use the term to refer to a broader concept of poverty, encompassing polarization, discrimination, and inequality.

Measuring Poverty and Social Exclusion in the UK

British social scientists have advanced this multidimensional approach to poverty measurement. Their writings implicitly accept the proposition that, because of lack of information and other market failures, important dimensions of well-being cannot be purchased in markets with money, and thus require independent measurement.

Even if this proposition is accepted, any proposal for including non-income aspects of well-being in a formal poverty measure has to confront difficult questions. One concerns how to deal with people with substantial amounts of cash income who voluntarily choose low levels of certain non-income dimensions of well-being (such as housing or vehicle access). A second concerns the selection of appropriate indicators and how to weight them.

35   Atkinson reflected these concerns in his analysis of the concept of social exclusion. In his view, there are three key issues in thinking about social exclusion—*relativity* (which element of society an individual is being excluded from); *agency* (being excluded requires an act, either by the person excluded or by others); and *dynamics* (being excluded implies a lack of long-term prospects).

In this framework, being long-term unemployed because of lack of aggregate demand or changing technology may classify as social exclusion, but being long-term unemployed because of unwillingness to accept an available job will not. Failure to receive public benefits for which one is eligible (due, say, to lack of information, the time costs of applying, or stigma associated with receipt) or failure to obtain certain goods and services such as housing, health care, credit, or insurance (through, say, explicit discriminatory practices by property owners or banks) may all classify as social exclusion. In these cases, it is the acts of others that lead to the exclusion of some from benefits, work, or consumption.

Political support in the UK for a multidimensional approach to poverty measurement. Efforts to include dimensions beyond income were supported by the government of Prime Minister Tony Blair, who described social exclusion as "the greatest social crisis of our time." In 1997, the New Labour government set up the Social Exclusion Unit as a Cabinet office headed by a Minister. Since 1999, reports presenting measures of social exclusion in the UK have been published under the title *Opportunity for All,* the most recent of which appeared in 2007. These reports indicate the government's commitment to annually monitor the state of poverty and social exclusion through a set of quantitative indicators.

**Measuring Poverty and Social Exclusion
in the European Union (EU)**

The European Commission recently developed a formal protocol for measuring poverty and social exclusion for the EU countries. The indicators, and their measurement, include those shown in the box on the next page.

Toward Measuring the Many Dimensions of Low Well-being in the U.S.: A Modest Proposal

Researchers and policymakers in the UK and the EU have adopted a broader concept of poverty than have their U.S. counterparts. The European developments reflect the view that rich societies require officially recognized measures that track progress in meeting many dimensions of needs and that income alone fails to capture the complex situation in which the most-deprived citizens find themselves. These developments also reflect the judgment that as societies become more affluent, the non-money aspects of well-being take on increased salience. While an income poverty measure served western nations well a half-century ago, today a variety of additional considerations—including the level of cognitive and non-cognitive skills, access to important social institutions (for example, the labor market), attaining minimum standards of food and shelter, sufficient available time for home production and child care—need to be taken into account.

The European developments also reflect the fact that rich societies possess vastly improved data sources on individual living units than in the 1960s. In the 1960s, when the first efforts to measure poverty were undertaken in the U.S., cash income was one of the few accurately recorded indicators of well-being available in survey or census-type data. Today, numerous continuing cross-section and longitudinal datasets with large and nationally representative samples are available. Many datasets reveal multiple aspects of the well-being of living units beyond their annual cash income.

U.S. academic and policy discussions should move beyond the concept of income poverty, and additional statistical measures of U.S. poverty and deprivation should be developed and published as supplements to an improved set of official income-poverty measures. Any proposal for additional, formal measures of "disadvantage" encounters the issue of whether or not to combine or weight these measures. Techniques are available for developing either a single measure based on the weighting of multiple

BOX 1.1 **PARTIAL LIST OF INDICATORS FOR MEASURING POVERTY AND SOCIAL EXCLUSION IN EUROPEAN UNION COUNTRIES**

- At-risk-of-poverty rate (share of persons aged 0+ with an equivalised disposable income below 60 percent of the national equivalised median income);
- Persistent-at-risk-of-poverty rate (share of persons aged 0+ with an equivalised disposable income below the at-risk-of-poverty threshold in the current year and in at least 2 of the preceding 3 years);
- Relative median poverty risk gap (difference between the median equivalised income of persons aged 0+ below the at-risk of poverty threshold and the threshold itself, expressed as a percentage of the at-risk of poverty threshold);
- Long-term unemployment rate (total long-term unemployed population ($\geq$12 months' unemployment; ILO definition) as a proportion of total active population aged 15 years or more);
- Population living in jobless households (proportion of people living in jobless households, expressed as a share of all people in the same age group);
- Early school leavers not in education or training (share of persons aged 18 to 24 who have only lower secondary education);
- Employment gap of immigrants (percentage point difference between the employment rate for non-immigrants and that for immigrants);
- Material deprivation (to be developed);
- Housing (to be developed);
- Unmet need for care (to be developed); and
- Child well-being (to be developed).

indicators of deprivation or describing deprivation by using counts of the presence of disadvantage in multiple dimensions.

To perform a multidimensional poverty measurement analysis, a large scale, detailed survey including information on a wide range of living conditions is needed; ideally, the survey would be longitudinal in nature. Currently, such information is not available for the U.S. population. What is possible, however, is to make use of annual survey data from the

U.S. Census Bureau's American Community Survey (ACS) to develop an illustrative multidimensional measure of deprivation in the U.S. The ACS includes many indicators of the living circumstances of American households in addition to income. Like the Current Population Survey on which the current official U.S. poverty measure rests, the ACS measures income, educational attainment, and labor force and employment status. The ACS also includes information on the quality of housing (such as the degree of crowding and the existence or lack of plumbing or kitchen facilities), health and disability status, vehicle availability, and linguistic isolation.

A research study that made use of the ACS data could illustrate the many-faceted nature of deprivation, and demonstrate the possibility of a U.S. poverty measure that reflected dimensions of disadvantage beyond cash income. Both researchers and policymakers would be well served by complementary measures of poverty that reveal the complexity and multi-faceted nature of deprivation. Such an illustration of the extent of multiple forms of deprivation in America would incorporate the income and threshold reforms proposed in 1995 and highlight the many other dimensions of what it means to be poor in a rich society. It would also accelerate debate on needed changes in the official poverty measure.

Conclusion

Any poverty measure is an indicator of a nation's performance in improving social conditions, and as such it serves many functions. The poverty measure documents the size and composition of the deprived population within a country and allows citizens and policymakers to assess the nation's progress against poverty. The measure also provides guidance for policymakers in assessing the potential of proposed measures for reducing poverty and for evaluating the impact of social policy measures in effect. I have argued that moving toward broader measures of poverty and deprivation has a number of advantages.

First, measures of material hardship or social exclusion capture intrinsic elements of the underlying deprivation that people face and complement income-based measures by providing "important insights into different dimensions of people's well-being." [45]

Moreover, because antipoverty policy measures are often directed at increasing access to particular goods, services, or environments, it is important to use measures of deprivation that reflect these needs. Ongoing reports detailing how many citizens of working age are excluded from health, disability, or unemployment insurance coverage; how many families fail to live in adequate housing; or how many families are excluded from employment because of health problems or disabling conditions, could be influential in policy discussions and choices.

Finally, measures that reflect the lack of access to various non-income dimensions of deprivation also indicate different patterns of hardship by particular sociodemographic groups than do measures of income poverty, making it possible to measure the effectiveness of targeting policies to these groups.

Some analysts emphasize the inherent difficulties in developing meaningful measures of material hardship or social exclusion. While these obstacles are formidable, they need to be weighed alongside the benefits of a more complete picture of deprivation in a rich society. Progress in addressing these issues would also advance the agenda for improving the current national measure of income poverty.

Analyze

1. What is Haveman's response to the lurking question: "Does the measure of poverty that is chosen matter?"
2. The U.S. currently uses an absolute measure of poverty. Why is it called "absolute"? Name at least two of the criticisms for using this type of measurement.
3. Name some of the other dimensions of deprivation, aside from money, that could be and often are measured.

Explore

1. What do we learn about being poor in a rich society from this text? How does Haveman's work help us think about Rector and Sheffield's work?
2. Haveman moves from describing various poverty measures to advocating that we should take a particular approach. Are you convinced by his argument? Do Haveman's references to the U.K. and the European Union's broader concept of poverty measures help or hurt his argument? Explain.

3. What does this article teach us about the importance of data collection and management in relation to setting public policy? If it's so important, why has the U.S. held on to an admittedly flawed measure of poverty developed in the early 1960s?

Charles Kenny
"In Praise of Slums"

A fellow at the Center for Global Development, Charles Kenny also serves as a contributing editor for *Foreign Policy* magazine, researching and writing on topics such as economic growth, technology as it impacts quality of life, and anticorruption. He has authored many articles and book chapters, and he wrote the book *Getting Better: Why Global Development is Succeeding and How We Can Improve the World Even More.* In this essay, Kenny considers the advantages of living in urban slums rather than rural villages.

How could slum growth be "a force for good"?

There is something viscerally repulsive about urban poverty: the stench of open sewers, the choking smoke of smoldering trash heaps, the pools of fetid drinking water filmed with the rainbow color of chemical spills. It makes poverty in the countryside seem almost Arcadian by comparison. The rural poor may lack nutrition, health care, education, and infrastructure; still, they do the backbreaking work of tending farms in settings that not only are more bucolic, but also represent the condition of most of humanity for most of history. With life so squalid in urban slums, why would anyone want to move there?

Because slums are better than the alternative. Most people who've experienced both rural and urban poverty choose to stay in slums rather than move back to the countryside. That includes hundreds of millions of people in the developing world over the past few decades—and 130 million migrant workers in China alone. They follow a well-trodden path of seeking a better life in the bright lights of the city—think of Dick Whittington, the 14th-century rural migrant who ended up lord mayor of London. The good news is that the odds of living that better life are better than ever. For all the real horrors of slum existence today, it still usually beats staying in a village.

Start with the simple reason that most people leave the countryside: money. Moving to cities makes economic sense—rich countries are urbanized countries, and rich people are predominantly town and city dwellers. Just 600 cities worldwide account for 60 percent of global economic output, according to the McKinsey Global Institute. Slum dwellers may be at the bottom of the urban heap, but most are better off than their rural counterparts. Although about half the world's population is urban, only a quarter of those living on less than a dollar a day live in urban areas. In Brazil, for example, where the word "poor" conjures images of both Rio's vertiginous *favelas* and indigenous Amazonian tribes living in rural privation, only 5 percent of the urban population is classified as extremely poor, compared with 25 percent of those living in rural areas.

But is it much of a life, eking out an existence in today's urban squalor? Our image of modern slums comes from films like *Slumdog Millionaire* and books like Katherine Boo's *Behind the Beautiful Forevers*, portraits of India's urban underclass not all that far removed from the horrifying picture of 19th-century industrialization in Charles Dickens's novels about the misery and violence of London's slum dwellers. A recent opinion article in the *New England Journal of Medicine* called urbanization "an emerging humanitarian disaster." And urban theorist Mike Davis writes in *Planet of Slums*, "[N]o one knows whether such gigantic concentrations of poverty are biologically or ecologically sustainable."

5   But slum living today, for all its failings, is markedly better than it was in Dickens's time.

For one thing, urban quality of life now involves a lot more actual living. Through most of history, death rates in cities were so high that urban areas only maintained population levels through constant migration from the countryside. In Dickensian Manchester, for instance, the average life expectancy was just 25 years, compared to 45 years in rural Surrey. Across the world today, thanks to vaccines and underground sewage systems, average life expectancies in big cities are considerably higher than those in the countryside; in sub-Saharan Africa, cities with a population over 1 million have had infant mortality rates one-third lower than those in rural areas.

In fact, most of today's urban population growth comes not from waves of villagers moving to the city, but city folks having kids and living longer.

In part, better quality of life is because of better access to services. Data from surveys across the developing world suggest that poor households in urban areas are more than twice as likely to have piped water as those in rural areas, and they're nearly four times more likely to have a flush toilet. In India, very poor urban women are about as likely to get prenatal care as the non-poor in rural areas. And in 70 percent of countries surveyed by MIT economists Abhijit Banerjee and Esther Duflo, school enrollment for girls ages 7 to 12 is higher among the urban poor than the rural poor.

That said, modern slum dwellers—about one-third of the urban population in developing countries—are some of the least likely to get vaccines or be connected to sewage systems. That means ill health in informal settlements is far more widespread than city averages would suggest. In the slums of Nairobi, for example, child mortality rates are more than twice the city average and higher, in fact, than mortality rates in Kenya's rural areas.

But Nairobi's slums are atypically awful, more an indicator of the Kenyan government's dysfunction than anything else. In most developing countries, even the poorest city dwellers do better than the average villager. Banerjee and Duflo found that, among people living on less than a dollar a day, infant mortality rates in urban areas were lower than rural rates in two-thirds of the countries for which they had data. In India, the death rate for babies in the first month of life is nearly one-quarter lower in urban areas than in rural villages. So significant is the difference in outcomes that population researcher Martin Brockerhoff concludes that "millions of children's lives may have been saved" in the 1980s alone as the result of mothers worldwide moving to urban areas.

Slum life remains grim. HIV prevalence rates are twice as high in urban areas of Zambia as they are in rural areas, for instance, and the story is worse with typhoid in Kenya. Slum residents are also at far greater risk from violence, outdoor air pollution, and traffic accidents than their rural counterparts. And the closer conditions in slum areas get to a state of anarchy mixed with kleptocracy, the more health and welfare outcomes tend to resemble those of Dickensian Manchester.

But all things considered, slum growth is a force for good. It could be an even stronger driver of development if leaders stopped treating slums as a problem to be cleared and started treating them as a population to be serviced, providing access to reliable land titles, security, paved roads, water

10

and sewer lines, schools, and clinics. As Harvard University economist Edward Glaeser puts it, slums don't make people poor—they attract poor people who want to be rich. So let's help them help themselves.

Analyze

1. Why do people leave the countryside to live in urban slums?
2. From where does Kenny claim most people get their image of urban slums? Where does your image of slums come from (i.e., is Kenny right?)?
3. Where does most of the urban population growth come from today? What specific advances helped make that possible?

Explore

1. "[S]lum growth is a force for good," writes Kenny. Name some of the most compelling reasons Kenny gives to support this argument. Does he exaggerate his argument to get attention? How might you frame the argument differently? Complete this sentence in your own words: "Slum growth is _____."
2. Although the purpose of Kenny's article is to help us think about the positive aspects of slums, he also acknowledges some of the problems. How well does he address opposing viewpoints? Name those problems and construct an argument in which you recommend to city officials which of them should be addressed first.
3. Gather and compare three to five images of poverty in urban slums with three to five images of rural poverty. Consider the rhetorical situation of those images, noting their place and purpose in order to analyze the messages they send. What themes emerge? Do they support or complicate any elements of Kenny's argument?

Forging Connections

1. The readings in this chapter explore our discernment over time about what it means to be poor. Societies have a practical reason to have a common definition of poverty: Having a fixed measure helps us know if poverty is growing or shrinking in our community and can teach us which programs, policies, and interventions do the best job of making positive change. But that practical reason is driven by an ethical reason:

Most societies want to reduce suffering in order to improve the well-being of individuals and society in general. Less poverty generally makes for a happier, safer community. Drawing insight from readings in this chapter, write an argument explaining your definition of poverty. Is poverty just about money, or are there other dimensions we should consider? If possible, interview people who have direct experience with poverty (e.g., people who have experienced poverty, people who work with those in poverty, or people who study poverty). Consider and cite their definitions as you compose your own.

2. Several of the readings in this chapter reference the role of the media in defining public conceptions of poverty (e.g., Ehrenreich, Iceland, Kenny, Rector and Sheffield). Others mention attitudes conveyed by people in power (e.g., Adair, Offenheiser). Think about your own experience understanding and defining poverty. When did you first realize that people have different levels of money and resources? How did poverty become visible to you? What sources or encounters influenced your thinking about this issue? How have you personally moved toward and/or away from poverty in your lifetime? Complete the Measure of America Well-O-Meter quiz to see your position relative to others (measureofamerica.org/well-o-meter/). You do not have to share your results. Write a narrative essay in which you trace your own encounters with the concept of poverty, whether in your family, in your community, or mediated through such sources as the news, films, and books. How were your views of poverty shaped? You may include all those encounters or highlight just the most formative one(s).

Looking Further

1. Readings in this chapter (e.g., Ehrenreich, Haveman, Offenheiser) and throughout this book (e.g., Alexander, Banerjee and Duflo, Bauer and Ramírez, Burd-Sharps and Lewis, DuBois, Duncan and Magnuson, Gammon, Haskins and Sawhill, O'Connor, Olson et al., Poo, Sanders, Sanders and Lehrer, Serwer, Webb, Zurcher) address the role of public policy in both *reflecting* public views on poverty and *shaping* them. Write a researched position paper explaining your position on a public issue related to poverty (e.g., local bus lines should be expanded to help low-income people get to work, the Earned Income Tax Credit should be expanded to give more incentives for people to work, the minimum wage should be raised).

2. Readings in this chapter (e.g., the *Economist*, Ehrenreich, Haveman, Iceland, Kenny, Rector and Sheffield) and throughout this book record a history of changes in the way we understand and respond to poverty. Research one of those fundamental changes, such as the move away from using poorhouses to punish and supposedly deter the poor from being poor, to more holistic centers for the homeless that address income, health, and educational needs onsite. Who were the leaders, and what were the arguments that helped shape that change? Was there a confrontational campaign for change with specific leaders or did it happen gradually? Create an educational website, video, or audio narrative in which you narrate and analyze this important turning point in the history of poverty. Identify a specific target audience, such as a high school civics class, and pitch your language and story to an appropriate level for that audience.

2

Causes: Why Are People Poor?

Boys heading to Texas on an "orphan train" (1904). Americans sent roughly 250,000 homeless or abandoned children from the East Coast to the Midwest for foster care between 1853–1929. What consequences might have been caused by this solution to child poverty?

INTRODUCTION

We can be born into poverty or fall into it later in life, but where does poverty come from? Is it something we bring onto ourselves? That's certainly not true of children or people harmed by natural disasters, disease, war, or global economic crises, circumstances out of their control. But are *external circumstances* the only dynamic controlling poverty? To what extent do our *personal choices* about such factors as education, health, employment, marriage, and parenthood determine our personal circumstances? And yet, do we all really have the same range of personal choices? Are we at the mercy of economic forces that expand or limit job opportunities just for some and social forces that expand or limit our choices based on race, ethnicity, and gender—factors beyond our control? Some are satisfied that if we offer equal opportunity, we need not worry about equal outcomes. Others argue that growing income inequality entrenches poverty and causes instability that isn't good for society. David Shipler, author of *The Working Poor: Invisible in America*, notes the elaborate interconnectedness of the causes and consequences of poverty: "Poverty is a peculiar, insidious thing: a cause whose effects then cause the original cause, or an effect whose causes are caused by the effect. It depends on where in the cycle the analysis begins" (53). The readings in this chapter explore these philosophical differences about the causes of poverty in practical ways. They examine how people move toward or away from poverty based on their environment, access to healthcare, education, employment, wealth, religious and cultural affiliations, and the public policies and programs that reinforce economic and social flourishing.

When we talk about the initial cause of poverty, we should also think about how long people stay there, their poverty "spell" in official terms, and how likely they are to return. When we talk about these issues, we need to think about a person's safety net, which includes a variety of capabilities that make it possible for that person to climb out of poverty and stay out. We all face risks in our lives—injury, illness, disease, divorce, unemployment, poor schooling, natural disasters, etc.—but some of us have more resilience, more capability to bounce back when those events happen. Our ability to rebound has a lot to do with both personal and societal conditions that strengthen our individual safety nets, such as:

1. family resources (e.g., inherited wealth that cushions us during job loss or medical insurance that prevents catastrophic debt);
2. social connections (e.g., neighbors or church members who boost our spirits, care for our children, and deepen our mental and spiritual resolve); and
3. government policies and programs that encourage economic opportunity for all (note that programs vary by state and city, so where you live matters).

Access to these resources has a lot to do with whether and for how long we stay out of poverty. Without a robust safety net, a crisis that is a temporary setback to some becomes a life-altering downturn into poverty for others. Imagine medical bills compounded by time off work and a lack of social connections or public programs to find better work overwhelming someone's resources and reducing their resilience. In other words, some people "play by the rules" and still can't make it. The readings in this chapter help us think about the initial and sustaining causes of poverty.

In this chapter, Ron Haskins and Isabel Sawhill analyze the general debate about what causes poverty, suggesting how public policy can create effective structures and incentives for change. Sarah Burd-Sharps and Kristen Lewis argue that the growing income inequality is just one area we should attend to: inequalities in health, environment, education, and wealth reinforce one another, weakening individuals' safety nets. In a memo to fellow Republicans, Senator Jeff Sessions of Alabama asks his colleagues to counter what he calls the "slanderous" accusations by Democrats that paint Republicans as lacking compassion for the poor because they want to limit spending. Challenging the adage that education is the path to prosperity, Kai Wright investigates how for-profit colleges often succeed not in increasing African Americans' job prospects but in increasing their debt. Michelle Alexander argues that unequal incarceration rates for black men have created a new Jim Crow era. Joshua DuBois explores the role of Alexander and other writers and activists who are fighting to overcome the legacy of slavery and discrimination despite the visible success of, for example, the election of a black president. In an interview and personal narrative, Dr. David Ansell reflects on his decades of experience as a doctor for the poor in Chicago, where he saw how poverty contributes to poor health and learned that compassion is critical medicine. The Rowntree Foundation offers readers 100 questions that identify research priories for poverty prevention and reduction, ranging from identifying effective housing solutions to asking who benefits from poverty, questions that help us identify the underlying causes of poverty.

Ron Haskins and Isabel Sawhill
"Perspectives on Poverty"

Ron Haskins and Isabel Sawhill serve as co-directors for the Center on Children and Families at the Brookings Institution, an organization devoted to analyzing national public policy issues. Haskins has served on a subcommittee for the U.S. House's Ways and Means Committee, providing welfare policy counsel to Republicans. In 2002, he served as President George W. Bush's senior advisor on welfare policy, and his research expertise spans the subjects of welfare reform, marriage, child support, and child protection. Sawhill researches and writes on such economic and social issues as welfare reform, the economic well-being of children, poverty and inequality, and changes in the family. The following chapter is from Haskins and Sawhill's 2009 book *Creating an Opportunity Society*, in which they argue that both of the competing explanations of poverty caused by unemployment are useful—some people are poor because they cannot find work, and some people are poor because they choose not to work.

Does the existence of poverty suggest that not all men and women are created equal?

"The core conservative truth is that culture matters . . . and the core liberal truth is that government can reshape culture."

—Senator Daniel Patrick Moynihan

Debates about what the rest of society owes the less fortunate are often based on underlying assumptions about why people are rich or poor, successful or unsuccessful. This chapter examines that debate. As chapter 2[25] notes, the public is divided in ranking personal effort or outside circumstances as the bigger cause of poverty.

Expert and political opinion on the issue is also equally divided. To many liberals it seems obvious that a large part of the problem is societal, that the very structure of a market economy, which offers low wages and uncertain job prospects for the least skilled, makes it impossible for many people to achieve economic success without robust government intervention. To many conservatives it seems equally obvious that anyone who is willing to obtain an education, work hard, and take advantage of the opportunities that exist in the United States will achieve a modicum of success—as many immigrants to this country have, in fact, done.

Our view—probably most people's view—is that it isn't either-or. On the one hand, low market wages and uncertain job prospects are a fact of life. In addition, and even more important, as emphasized in chapter 5, children don't get to pick their genes, their parents, or their early home environments. These can greatly affect later success yet are not a matter of personal choice. Still, individual choice matters. Decisions about how hard to study, how much to work, and what kind of family life to lead all ultimately contribute to individual success.

In this chapter we begin with a review of the debate between those who believe that poverty is a cultural phenomenon and those who believe it is structural in nature. In chapter 3 we review some of the key data and research that relates to this debate. However, that kind of factual evidence is far from dispositive, so in this chapter we focus primarily on the debate itself and some of the more qualitative evidence upon which researchers draw. Different people can honestly interpret the same facts quite differently. Nor does one explanation fit all segments of the poverty population, which after all is exceedingly diverse. We need to distinguish between someone who is poor because he can't find work and someone who is poor because she is unwilling to work. Statistical data on employment rates cannot distinguish one from the other. In the end, our view is that it is possible to find policies that recognize the importance of both culture and structure in explaining American poverty today.

Cultural Explanations

5   The debate about whether there is a culture of poverty began in the 1950s and 1960s, with scholars such as Oscar Lewis and Edward Banfield arguing that poverty stems at least in part from insufficient orientation to the future, little sense of self-efficacy, and a too-ready acceptance of life as it is.

Empirical data on these issues are hard to find and even harder to interpret. In a series of papers in the mid-1980s, researchers associated with the Institute for Social Research at the University of Michigan used a longitudinal survey (the Panel Study of Income Dynamics, or PSID) to study the attitudes of the poor. They found that the heads of poor families, when compared to the heads of more affluent families, had less-positive attitudes, greater fear of failure, less orientation to the future, and less confidence that they could affect their own lives. However, these attitudinal measures were, for the most part, not predictive of future economic mobility. Indeed, if anything, the causation ran in the other direction, from economic circumstances to attitudes. For example, in one paper the researchers conclude: "Poor people differ from others on some motivational and personality measures, but the differences appear to have been caused by the events they have experienced. There is virtually no consistent evidence that the motivational and psychological characteristics measured by the study affect subsequent achievement, either within or across generations."

Similarly, reviewing extensive qualitative research from the Urban Poverty and Family Life Study in the mid-1990s, William Julius Wilson finds that the attitudes and values of the poor were not different from those of the middle class and the wealthy in any basic way. If anything, motivation and action are driven by individual circumstance and location, rather than the reverse. According to Wilson,

> Our research reveals that the beliefs of inner-city residents bear little resemblance to the blanket media reports asserting that values have plummeted in impoverished inner-city neighborhoods or that people in the inner city have an entirely different value system. What is so striking is that despite the overwhelming joblessness and poverty, black residents in inner-city ghetto neighborhoods actually verbally endorse, rather than undermine, the basic American values concerning individual initiative.

This conclusion is echoed by Katherine Newman, based on her ethnographic study of inner-city fast-food workers:

> Given the divergence of experience, the stability of our respondents' views of opportunity and personal responsibility is notable. While one might expect that those who have done well would see the world through positive lenses and argue that everyone is the master of his or her own destiny, it is testimony to the power of mainstream values that even those who have had less positive trajectories generally subscribe to [those same] views. . . . The durability of these views is impressive for the way in which it displays the power of mainstream, middle-class morals. Conservative thought infuses the lives of the working-poor and their fellow job seekers in the inner city.

Although low-income families may accept mainstream values, what stands out in Newman's work is the difficulty many of them have in integrating these values into their own lives. 10

In contrast to Newman, the Harvard sociologist Orlando Patterson argues that cultural attributes—including the distinctive attitudes, values, and predispositions of a group and the effects such attitudes have on behavior—are critical to understanding why millions of young black males feel disconnected from the American mainstream. He is critical of social scientists who rely heavily on structural factors like low incomes and joblessness as explanations for self-destructive behavior out of fear of blaming the victim or implying that the behavior of certain subgroups is immutable. Instead, Patterson reasons that culture can be a powerful factor in explaining certain behaviors, such as failing to complete high school:

> The "cool-pose culture" of young black men was simply too gratifying to give up. For these young men, it was almost like a drug, hanging out on the street after school, shopping and dressing sharply, sexual conquests, party drugs, hip-hop music and culture, the fact that almost all the superstar athletes and a great many of the nations best entertainers were black. . . . Hip-hop, professional basketball and homeboy fashions are as American as cherry pie. Young white Americans are very much into these things, but selectively; they know when it is time to turn off Fifty Cent and get out the

SAT prep book. For young black men, however, that culture is all there is—or so they think.

Bill Cosby and Alvin Poussaint advance a similar view in their book, *Come on, People: On the Path from Victims to Victors*. They write:

> Too often the word *victim* shows up in our discussions. We have all driven through lower economic neighborhoods where there are three and four families living in a one-family house, and the music is loud enough to wake the dead. It seems as if the folks living there are trying to drown out their own feelings. This culture is sedating. It encourages people to see themselves as victims, as being incapable of helping themselves, of feeling anything but totally defeated.
>
> We know that there are forces that make the effort to escape poverty difficult. . . . [But] many people in these communities, who are trying to make it, find themselves struggling against their fellow African Americans who are so lost in self-destructive behaviors that they bring down other people as well as themselves.

A theme in much of this more observationally oriented literature is hopelessness—a sense of passivity or fatalism in the face of limited opportunity. Jason DeParle, a journalist with a distinguished record of covering social policy issues, picks up on this theme in his 2004 book, *American Dream: Three Women, Ten Kids, and a Nation's Drive to End Welfare*. Following the lives of three young women living in Milwaukee in the wake of the welfare reforms of the mid-1990s, DeParle observes that two of his subjects, Angie and Jewell

> offered no theory about what stood between them and conventional success. But one striking part of the story they told is what they left out. They didn't talk of thwarted aspirations, of things they had sought but couldn't achieve. They certainly didn't talk of subjugation; they had no sense of victimhood. The real theme of their early lives was profound alienation—not of hopes discarded but of hopes that never took shape.

A similar view is expressed by Kathryn Edin and Maria Kefalas in their book, *Promises I Can Keep: Why Poor Women Put Motherhood before*

Marriage, which is based on interviews with more than 150 low-income single mothers in Philadelphia and its suburbs. In examining how the women approach pregnancy, especially unintended pregnancy, the authors observe the complex and fatalistic view the women often take regarding their own life prospects. Without any defined plans or even dreams for the future, many of the women come to embrace pregnancy quickly, whether planned or not. Edin and Kefalas note that the women are often fatalistic about the challenges (and gifts) that life presents. Two of the subjects in the study, Jasmine and Susan, underscore this mentality when discussing the conception of their own children: Jasmine explains that "I never used anything [when] I got pregnant. *God* is in control. And [my kids] was *meant to be.* . . . I feel like, if it happens, it happens." Susan adds that "it wasn't like I could just *plan* things. Things happen, and so you just go ahead. Some things happen you just can't plan!"

In an in-depth and heroic attempt to sort out the relative influence of economic incentives, individual motivation, and culture on people's behavior, Mary Jo Bane and David Ellwood conclude that all three factors play a role, although the influence of each factor depends on the nature of the behavior in question and the circumstances. Economic incentives (or structure) seem to play a larger role in explaining work, and social norms (or culture) play a larger role in explaining family behavior. For example, economic models do a poor job of explaining the decline in marriage or the rise in nonmarital births.

Larry Mead suggests that another way to think about the intersection of culture and structure is to distinguish attitudes from behavior. He postulates that the chronically poor may have conventional values but be unable to convert those values into orthodox behavior. He contrasts this group to three other groups: members of the middle class, who have both conventional attitudes and conventional behavior; bohemians, who have unorthodox values and unorthodox behavior; and political radicals, who combine unorthodox values with more conventional behavior. 15

One problem in most of this literature is a tendency to paint with too broad a brush. As suggested in chapter 3, the poor are very diverse. Of the nonelderly poor, 60 percent of all people who begin a spell of poverty are only temporarily poor; the adults in these families may have lost a job, become ill, seen a business fail or a home foreclosed, and they will typically get back on their feet within a year or two. The remaining segment (about 40 percent) consists of chronically poor working-age adults and their children, with only about 12 percent of those entering poverty staying there ten years or more. However, precisely because those who are chronically poor have difficulty escaping poverty, the majority of the poor measured at any given time (for example, in an annual cross-sectional survey like that used for the official poverty measure) tends to be the chronically poor. Measured at a given point in time, over 80 percent of the poor have been poor for three or more years, and a little more than half have been poor for ten or more years. If there is a culture of poverty or an underclass in American society, it is drawn from this second group. Indeed, Ellwood concludes that ghetto poverty is hard to explain without reference to cultural variables. But how large a group is this?

In an attempt to answer this question, Isabel Sawhill, in collaboration with Errol Ricketts, earlier offered one possible definition of the American underclass:

> Behavioral norms are not invariant. But in American society . . . it is expected that children will attend school and delay parenthood until at least age eighteen, that adult males (who are not disabled or retired) will work at a regular job, that adult females will either work or marry, and that everyone will be law abiding. The underclass, in our definition, consists of people whose behavior departs from these norms and in the process creates significant social costs.

To estimate the size of this group, Sawhill and Ricketts used census data to identify "underclass areas," or neighborhoods in which the proportion of the residents who failed to achieve such norms was one standard deviation above the national norm for each of these four behaviors simultaneously. They find that in 1980 the proportion of the poor living in such neighborhoods was only 5 percent. Thus as troubling and costly as these behaviors are, the underclass, according to this definition, is very small.

Subsequent research by Paul Jargowsky and Sawhill, using the same definition, finds that the size of the underclass, after rising rapidly in the 1970s, rose only slightly in the 1980s and declined sharply in the 1990s. Four factors may have played a role in this decline.

20   First, the reform of welfare addressed some of the underlying behavioral problems associated with poverty, especially nonwork. By imposing work requirements on recipients and emphasizing the importance of marriage, the reforms attempted to link assistance to personal responsibility.

Second, changes in federal housing policy, which slowed the creation of high-rise housing projects in favor of vouchers and mixed-use housing, may have reduced the concentration of poverty in many urban neighborhoods.

Third, easier access to abortion reduced the number of unwanted births following the *Roe* v. *Wade* Supreme Court decision of 1973, leading to fewer disadvantaged teens or young adults and, thus, less crime or other antisocial behavior several decades later.

Fourth, in addition to policy changes, a strong economy in the late 1990s undoubtedly contributed to these positive trends.

Whatever the reasons behind these trends, the history of rising and falling numbers of the ghetto poor suggests that culture is malleable and that both societal expectations (such as a shift in welfare policy toward requiring work) and opportunity (such as a stronger economy and more supports for low-wage workers) matter.

Much of the literature on the culture of poverty focuses on the impor- 25
tance of family structure. Daniel Patrick Moynihan famously called attention to this issue in 1965, arguing that "a community that allows a large number of young men to grow up in broken homes, dominated by women, never acquiring any stable relationship to male authority, never acquiring any set of rational expectations about the future—that community asks for and gets chaos."

His message—that the growth in black single-parent households was damaging to children as well as to the entire black community—struck a harsh chord in the media and among many academics for its unequivocal tone. But the disappearance of marriage has continued apace. It has affected not just the African American community but virtually all Americans. The proportion of white children born out of wedlock is now higher than the proportion of black children in 1965, when Moynihan first raised a firestorm over the issue. Indeed by 2007 (the latest available data), almost two of every five children were born outside of marriage.

Subsequent research by several well-respected scholars has convinced most experts that growing up in a single-parent family leads to poor outcomes for children and that a substantial portion of the increase in poverty since the 1970s is the result of the decline of marriage and an increase in unwed childbearing. Some researchers, such as Harvard's William Julius Wilson, argue that the decline of marriage, especially in the black community, is the result of a lack of employed males; however, the empirical evidence in favor of this hypothesis is weak. A more likely explanation is a change in culture and social norms, perhaps exacerbated by the availability of welfare for single mothers and the lack of well-paid jobs for men. Whatever trends in economic conditions may have occurred over the past half century, they are not sufficient to explain the collapse of the two-parent family.

A similar debate swirls around the question of why more poor adults— especially minority men—don't work. Some researchers, such as Wilson and Harry Holzer, contend that the problem is lack of jobs; others, such as Larry Mead, emphasize the willingness to work. In his 1996 book, *When Work Disappears,* Wilson argues that, since the 1960s, the urban poor have largely fallen victim to fundamental and interrelated shifts in the American economy, including the greater use of technology in manufacturing, the rise of global trade, the weakening of unions, and the influx of poor immigrants. The transition away from manufacturing and toward a service economy has also led to a greater suburbanization of employment and an increase in demand for higher-skilled workers, further reducing the jobs available to the low-skill, minority workers living in urban areas.

Harry Holzer similarly argues that the retreat of young black men from the labor market is largely economic in nature, the product of weak employment opportunities and inadequate wages. In one review, Gordon Berlin notes that a 10 percent increase in wages among low-income workers could lead to a 2-to-10 percent boost in employment. Other evidence along these lines comes from programs that guarantee jobs to disadvantaged men, such as the New Hope Project of the 1990s.

30   In contrast to Wilson, Berlin, and Holzer, Mead argues that work norms among the poor explain much of the joblessness found among the chronically poor:

> Today's urban poverty arose chiefly because work discipline broke down in the mid-twentieth century among low-income people, especially blacks. Somehow, many parents lost their own discipline and thus their authority over children. Fathers failed to work and often disappeared. Their sons then became rootless, seeking to work but not knowing how. Paradoxically, the collapse came just as opportunities for blacks were expanding. To a cultural interpretation, poverty reflects social disorder more than deficient opportunity.

Observing that opportunities to find decent employment have actually been rising over the past several decades for blacks and other minorities in conjunction with civil rights reforms, Mead remains troubled by the number of individuals who continually fail to take advantage of what he sees as promising opportunities. He argues that, beyond providing a direct source of income, employment can represent an organizing principle in one's life and a way to achieve respect. Without this anchor, self-defeating and destructive behaviors like gang activity and nonmarital births flourish. Like Orlando Patterson, Mead points to an oppositional or rebellious culture among young minority men that undermines both their willingness to work and their ability to interact comfortably with supervisors and customers and thus retain the kinds of low-wage jobs for which they qualify. As we show in chapter 4, work is a powerful antidote to poverty. In fact only 3.5 percent of families with at least one full-time worker were poor in 2007.

Finally, the debate about structure versus culture also plays a role in explaining why so many youth fail to graduate from high school with the skills needed to survive in today's economy. A great deal of the education literature focuses on the failures of public schools. But schools cannot improve without the active cooperation of students and their families. When Hugh Price became the president of the Urban League in 1994, he focused on the large achievement gaps between black and white students as well as the fact that some black students resisted doing well academically because they believed it was tantamount to "acting white." He launched a campaign aimed at encouraging children, families, and communities to care more about achievement. As he explains, "I felt that families and communities had to step up and take responsibility for boosting student commitment to achievement rather than look to outsiders to do that job for them. If an academic culture is truly to take hold and endure, it must be embedded in the hearts and minds—and the belief systems and behaviors—of youngsters, their families, and the organizations that make up their communities."

Similarly, when he was speaking at the 2004 Democratic convention, Senator Barack Obama said, "Go into any inner-city neighborhood and folks will tell you that government alone can't teach our kids to learn; they know that parents have to teach, that children can't achieve unless we raise their expectations and turn off the television sets and eradicate the slander that says a black youth with a book is acting white." President Obama repeated this message in his February 2009 address to a joint session of Congress.

Although people may disagree about why the poor are less likely to finish school, more likely to be jobless, and more likely to form single-parent families, there is no question that these are the underlying causes of their poverty. In a 2003 analysis of census data, we show that if the poor complete high school, work full time, have no more than two kids, and marry as much as they did in the 1970s, the poverty rate would fall by slightly more than 70 percent (figure 2.1). These results parallel the more recent analysis presented in chapter 4.

35   Both our 2003 analysis and the more recent analysis presented in chapter 4 demonstrate that "playing by the rules" (finishing high school, working full-time, marrying before having children) can lead to large reductions in poverty; full-time work is shown to have a particularly large

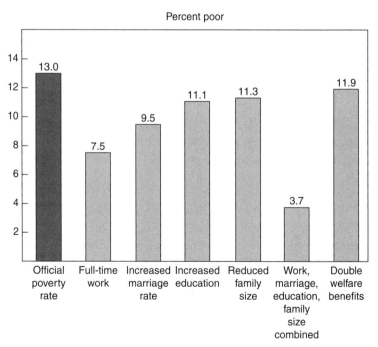

Percent poor

Figure 2.1 Poverty Rates, by *Influencing Factors*, 2001

Source: Ron Haskins and Isabel Sawhill, "Work and Marriage: The Way to End Poverty and Welfare," Policy Brief 28 (Brookings, Welfare Reform and Beyond 2003), figure 1.

effect. The bad news is that even full-time work leaves some people in poverty. And not everyone can find full-time work, especially in periods of high unemployment. With these facts in mind, we turn next to more structural explanations and, in particular, to how the labor market may restrict opportunities for the poor.

> "The bad news is that even full-time work leaves some people in poverty."

Structural Explanations

Conservatives often assume that markets deliver the best outcomes. While markets efficiently allocate resources most of the time, there are three important exceptions to this rule, all of which especially affect the poor. One exception occurs when the economy goes into a recession and produces too few jobs. A second exception occurs when the market distributes earnings and income inequitably. A third exception occurs when employers discriminate against certain classes of workers on noneconomic grounds, such as race or gender. In these three cases, some government intervention—fiscal and monetary policy to increase the number of jobs, wage supplements or other assistance for low-wage workers, and antidiscrimination laws—are in order. We consider these three cases of market failure and their effects on the poor below.

Lack of Jobs

It is natural to assume that all or most joblessness reflects a lack of jobs rather than a disinclination or inability of workers to fill the jobs that are available. Some joblessness surely does reflect a lack of jobs. We know, for example, that the poverty rate rises during periods of high unemployment. Examining the relationship between the macroeconomy and poverty from the 1960s through 2006, the labor economist Rebecca Blank estimates that a 1.00 percentage point rise in the unemployment rate leads to a 0.45 percentage point rise in the poverty rate. Blank also observes that less-skilled workers experience much higher rates of unemployment and are more affected by changes in the macroeconomy than other workers. We also know that local economic circumstances, such as the closing of a plant, can affect people's job opportunities and cause a sharp drop in their incomes, at least in the short run, and that unemployment rates can vary widely from one area to another. For example, in December 2008 the national unemployment rate stood at 7.2 percent, while state unemployment rates ranged from 3.2 percent in Wyoming to 10.2 percent in Michigan.

Job scarcity, though, is not the major issue among those who are chronically poor (although it is a very important reason for those who are temporarily poor). The U.S. labor market creates between 7 million and 8 million jobs every quarter, even in a year like 2008, when job loss was large and overall employment was declining. There are always some job openings, because people move frequently in and out of the labor market and also in and out of jobs, opening up slots for others. In periods of high unemployment, the ratio of such openings to the pool of those looking for work shrinks, and it becomes harder for those with the fewest skills to compete for the smaller number of available jobs.

Except in times of recession, then, the major problem is not so much a lack of jobs as it is the ability of less-skilled workers to compete for the jobs that are available. Even the poor themselves rarely mention a lack of jobs as their primary problem. When asked why they did not work in the previous year, only 11 percent of poor men and 4 percent of poor women ages eighteen through sixty-four said it was because they "could not find work." Much more important were such factors as being ill or disabled, going to school, retirement, or taking care of home or family (the last-mentioned being especially true for women). Problems with substance abuse, depression, or a prison record also make finding and keeping a job difficult.

40   These reasons for lack of employment should not blind us to the real difficulties that a period of high unemployment poses for the least-skilled members of the labor force. Because they are likely to be the hardest hit by a recession, countercyclical fiscal policies like those introduced in 2008 and 2009 should be designed to provide extra help to these workers. This help can take the form of greater spending on unemployment insurance, food stamps, Medicaid, cash assistance, and other programs targeting low-income families.

Inadequate Wages

A much more serious problem than a scarcity of jobs during normal economic times is the wages paid in jobs at the bottom of the skills ladder. In 2007, by one definition more than a quarter of the workforce earned poverty-level wages. Moreover, the United States has a higher proportion of workers in low-paying jobs than other rich countries; and differences in the incidence of low pay are correlated strongly with differences in poverty rates across these countries.

To see the effect of low wages on family well-being, consider a single parent with two children who earns $8.00 an hour (just a little above the current minimum wage of $7.25 an hour) and works full time (2,000 hours a year). This worker would earn only $16,000 a year—well below the poverty line of $16,705 for this family. On the other hand, such a family would be eligible for a number of government benefits, which can augment its income significantly (figure 2.2).

However, most poor families do not get all of these benefits. Eligibility requirements can be confusing, and working families may wrongly assume that they are not eligible, or they may be unable to spend the time it takes to secure these benefits. The multiplicity of programs and their different

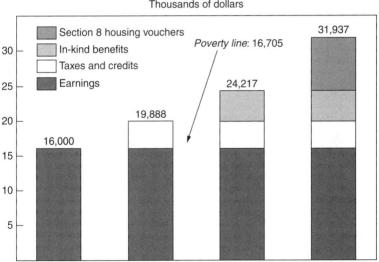

Figure 2.2 Estimated Annual Income, Including Taxes and Benefits, for a Low-Wage Household Head, 2007. [Household is composed of a single parent with two children. Hourly wage is $8.]

Source: Authors' calculations as follows: Tax liabilities and credits for tax year 2007 estimated using the NBER TAXSIM Model, Version 8.0; food stamp estimate based on data from Dorothy Rosenbaum, "Families' Food Stamp Benefits Purchase Less Food Each Year" (Center on Budget and Policy Priorities, 2007); lunch program estimate based on data from United States Department of Agriculture, Food and Nutrition Service, "National School Lunch Program Fact Sheet" (2007), housing assistance data from John Karl Scholz, Robert Moffitt, and Benjamin Cowan, "Trends in Income Support," paper prepared for conference, "Changing Poverty," Institute for Research on Poverty, May 29–30, 2008.

eligibility standards require applicants to visit different offices and complete different application forms for each program—a process that is especially burdensome for working parents.

Even if they do apply, there may be waiting lists for some programs—child care subsidies or housing assistance, for example. Housing assistance, in particular, can provide enormous help to a low-income family. Unfortunately, receiving such assistance is relatively uncommon. Currently, only one in four eligible households receives any housing help at all. Unlike tax credits, food stamps, and free school lunches, housing vouchers are not entitlements, for which the right to participate is based solely on a person's eligibility. Instead, housing vouchers are distributed largely on a first-come, first-served basis, and long and growing waiting lists exist. Many local housing agencies have even stopped accepting new applications because existing waiting periods are so long. Meanwhile, in 2005, 6.5 million low-income renter households that did not receive housing assistance faced "severe housing problems," defined as paying more than half their income for rent or living in severely substandard housing.

45   Even entitlements like food stamps do not achieve full participation, especially among working families. Evidence suggests that changes to welfare in the mid-1990s designed to move women from welfare to work dissuaded many women from collecting benefits from other government programs. In response, the food stamp program has implemented several important changes in eligibility rules and outreach efforts. Participation has improved substantially since the early 2000s: 67.3 percent of all persons eligible for food stamps received them in 2006 (the most recent data available), up from 53.8 percent in 2002. It is likely that food stamp applications and participation will rise sharply in coming years—as will participation in other benefit programs—as a result of the current economic downturn.

Another valuable form of government assistance not included in these calculations, but vital to low-income families, is Medicaid. Putting a dollar value on medical care for low-income families is difficult. Nevertheless, access to health care does have large benefits for low-income families, even if those benefits are less directly quantifiable than other forms of aid.

Ultimately, those families fortunate enough to qualify for all of this assistance, and that have the knowledge and the fortitude to navigate the system that provides it, will still have a difficult time living in any major American city and supporting several children on less than $31,937 a year.

Furthermore, in most programs, working reduces a poor family's benefits, creating a disincentive to work or to earn more.

While current spending on social services in the United States is not insignificant, a global perspective suggests that more could be done. A number of European nations and Canada report much higher spending (as a percent of GDP) on cash and near-cash assistance to the poor, and this spending is strongly correlated with relative poverty rates across countries. As Gary Burtless and Tim Smeeding conclude, "Simply put, the United States does not spend enough to make up for low levels of pay, and so we end up with a relatively higher poverty rate than do other nations." For all of the above reasons, we argue in chapter 9 that it makes sense to provide more assistance to low-income families than at present and to structure that assistance in a way that encourages work or at least does not discourage it.

Discrimination in the Labor Market

White men working full time and year round earned a median wage of roughly $51,000 in 2007, while their female counterparts earned about $38,000, or 74 percent of that amount. Black men earned 73 percent, and Hispanic men 61 percent, of what white men earned. Black women earned 62 percent and Hispanic women 54 percent of the typical earnings for a white man. Somewhat surprisingly, these gaps persist even among those with roughly similar levels of education. Given the extent of pay disparity across groups, it is worth asking what role discrimination may play in constraining labor market opportunity. [50]

The literature on discrimination has been summarized by a number of social scientists, including Devah Pager, Melissa Kearney, and Joseph Altonji and Rebecca Blank. The general consensus is that outright discrimination has declined sharply since the 1950s but that more subtle forms of bias may be playing an increasing role as more explicit forms of prejudice diminish. These more subtle judgments may include the tendency to assess a particular individual on the basis of group averages (statistical discrimination) or unconscious associations made between a subgroup and a given attribute (implicit bias). An example of statistical discrimination would be an employer assuming correctly that women, on average, are not as strong as men but then inferring that a particular woman who happens to be strong cannot be a baggage handler. An example of implicit bias would be an employer who chooses a male over an equally qualified female job applicant because of a deep seated but unconscious belief that women are less rational or more emotional than men.

Analysts who have used statistical techniques to explain the lower earnings of women find that differences in education and experience cannot explain the gaps noted above. Instead, most of these pay gaps appear to be due to the fact that women work in lower-paid occupations and industries, either out of choice or because of larger cultural forces.

Nearly all of the black-white gap can be explained by racial differences in education, experience, region of residence, measured aptitude, and as in the case of women, the kinds of jobs in which each racial group is found. In a seminal study, Derek Neal and William Johnson look at the black-white gap in test scores on the Armed Forces Qualifying Test (AFQT) and find that adding this proxy for skill explains all of the black-white wage gap for young women and much of the gap for men. Of course, skill or ability as measured by the AFQT may represent the product of earlier discrimination and its effects on opportunities for black children. Nevertheless, this and similar studies tend to indicate relatively low levels of labor market discrimination and high levels of premarket disadvantages associated with childhood experiences for blacks.

Other studies provide a more direct measure of discrimination by testing how employers or others respond to applications that differ by only one particular trait (such as gender, race, and age). These studies, called audit studies, consistently find evidence of bias against women and minorities. For example, in an audit study of high-priced restaurants in Philadelphia, the women in the study are about 40 percent less likely to receive a job offer for a waitstaff position than the men. Similarly, when symphony orchestras started using screens to conceal the identity of job candidates from the hiring team, women's chances of being selected improved sharply.

55   Harry Cross and colleagues observe similar results in a 1989 audit study of Chicago and San Diego with Hispanic and white job applicants, as do Margery Austin Turner and colleagues in a 1990 audit of black and white applicants in Washington and Chicago. Likewise, in a more recent study in Boston and Chicago, Marianne Bertrand and Sendhil Mullainathan find that resumes bearing white-sounding names received 50 percent more callbacks for interviews than resumes carrying black-sounding names. In light of their results, Bertrand and Mullainathan conclude "that African Americans face differential treatment when searching for jobs, and this may still be a factor in why they do poorly in the labor market. Job applicants

with African American names get far fewer callbacks for each resume they send out. Equally importantly, applicants with African American names find it hard to overcome this hurdle in callbacks by improving their observable skills or credentials."

Taken together, this evidence suggests that bias still exists. Indeed, the findings from audit studies are particularly striking. Still, it's hard to conclude that labor market discrimination is currently a major cause of disadvantage. To be sure, earlier discrimination in housing markets, in the education system, and in the criminal justice system may affect labor market participation and must also be taken into account. Still, we maintain that class (family background) is more important than race or gender per se, as are a person's education and training, their "people skills," and their motivation to succeed.

Toward a Synthesis of Conservative and Liberal Views

While one's behavior and one's circumstances are inextricably linked, it is not clear which is the chicken and which is the egg. Conservatives emphasize the fact that those who work hard and play by society's rules will usually get ahead. Liberals emphasize instead the effects of low wages, poor job prospects, and discrimination by race or gender on the ability and motivation to improve one's lot. Surely both are right, and the balance varies depending on each individual's circumstances. Not all poor people are the same.

The two authors of this volume do not always see eye to eye on these matters but we have benefited enormously from working together and have come to a common view that informs the policy proposals we offer in later chapters. Our view might be summarized as follows: We accept the idea that fundamental inequalities are large. As much as we might like to believe otherwise, not all men—or women—are created equal, and children's early environment and schooling as well as their genetic endowment have important effects on later attainments.

Low wages for those dealt a poor hand early in life are almost inevitable. But even low-wage workers can move out of poverty and into at least the lower middle class with the right motivations and the right kind of support. For these reasons, we argue that interventions early in life that compensate for the initial inequalities should be aggressively pursued. As for adults who are working to support their families and for whom such early interventions are too late, we think their struggle to achieve a decent standard of living should be rewarded by help from the public. But in our view, help means linking assistance to people's own efforts to improve their lives, not providing them with unconditional support. We do not argue that it is easy to make the right choices in life. Bad things happen to good people, and many of those from disadvantaged families do not have the cultural capital, the private safety nets, or the supportive peer networks available to their more privileged counterparts. Moreover, as we have noted, their economic opportunities, especially the wages they can earn, may be constrained.

60   If one accepts the premise that both behavior and circumstances matter, then policy should shore up wages at the bottom but in ways that encourage education, work, and stable families. Good policy should be designed to both encourage and reward behavior that is in people's own long-run self-interest. It should also recognize that there are limits to what good policy can accomplish. Not only will middle-class Americans likely rebel against transferring too much income to the poor, especially if the transfers are not conditional on behavior, but other strategies may actually do more good. For example, even a tripling of welfare benefits would accomplish less in reducing poverty than finding ways to keep most people fully employed. So thinking about how to help people make the right choices is important.

Should Policy Be More Paternalistic?

One reason we believe it's important to encourage people to make the right choices is because new research in economics and psychology suggests that people do not always act rationally. All of us need to be prodded to do things that will improve our long-term well-being, whether it is eating the right foods or setting aside funds for our own retirement. Low-income families are no different. This line of reasoning argues for using public policy as a kind of "soft paternalism" to encourage, or even require, people to do what is arguably in their own long-term self-interest.

If education, work, and family stability are the keys to success, as we believe, then how far should the nation go in encouraging or requiring such behaviors? The nation has compulsory school attendance laws, seat belt laws, airport security checkpoints, abundant restrictions on smoking, and a host of other laws that interfere with individual freedom but imposes such restrictions only when there is a compelling societal interest for doing so. In other areas, the nation may offer incentives for people to work harder, save for their retirement, smoke or drink less, get more education, give to charity, or buy an energy-efficient home or a more fuel-efficient car, but stop short of compelling such behavior. Finally, the nation may simply exhort people to do certain things, through social marketing campaigns, for example, and provide them with more information about the potential consequences of their actions (for example through food or drug labeling).

Individual freedom and civil liberties are highly valued in the United States and so is tolerance toward those whose behavior fails to conform to mainstream norms. But there are several reasons for accepting some restrictions on people's behavior. The first is because your right to do what you choose may affect me, in which case more than one person's freedom is at issue. If your behavior imposes costs on me, then I may have a right to impose some limits on what you can do. As a taxpayer who pays for welfare or other social programs, for example, I may want to require that you seek work or stay in school as a condition of receiving benefits, and I may want to provide additional benefits through the EITC only if you maintain your commitment to a job.

But quite apart from the rights of taxpayers or other members of society, there is another reason to justify a certain amount of paternalism in social policy; namely, that people often do not behave in ways consistent with their own self-interest. An increasing body of work in psychology, neuroscience, and behavioral economics calls into question the extent to which individuals act in ways that are rational, consistent, future-oriented, and self-interested.

In an important article that draws on this literature and spells out its   65 implications in a provocative way, Richard Thaler and Cass Sunstein argue that, because self-defeating behaviors are common, there is a role for government in steering behavior in more positive directions. They call this "libertarian paternalism" or "soft paternalism" because the steering preserves individual choice while making clear to the individual that not all choices are equally constructive, even from the standpoint of the individual's own long-run welfare. An example of such steering can be found in 401k plans. By making automatic participation in such plans the default option, but giving people the option of declining to participate—as opposed to the reverse—more people end up participating, and saving for retirement rises. These kinds of policies are nonetheless paternalistic because they involve the government intervening in people's lives even when there are no benefits or harms to others involved.

Another example of soft paternalism is the effort to reduce smoking through the use of media campaigns and health warnings on packaging. These efforts appear to have contributed to a marked decline in the incidence of smoking. The example of smoking may be particularly salient since it suggests that it is at least possible to change self-destructive behaviors by moving social norms in a new direction. As smoking has become less common and has acquired negative connotations, more people have been encouraged to quit and fewer and fewer people are taking up the habit. Such shifts in norms, once started, often turn into cascades. Other areas where fundamental changes in social norms have occurred—triggered by some combination of public and private action—are the greater acceptance of women in nontraditional roles, the greater use of helmets and seat belts, the growth of recycling, and lower rates of sexual activity among teenagers.

Attempts to use similar approaches to reduce poverty could include efforts to reduce nonmarital childbearing; efforts to reintroduce a marriage-friendly culture into low-income communities, where marriage as an institution has mostly disappeared; conditional cash transfers designed to encourage parents to get their children to school on time or to keep medical appointments; and programs that create a stronger work norm in low-income neighborhoods or housing projects by saturating them with employment-based programs.

Harder forms of paternalism, such as work requirements in welfare, tying college scholarships or tuition assistance to performance in high school, and wage subsides for full-time work, have also been tried with some success. Here we review the evidence from three demonstration programs that have had considerable success in encouraging work: the New Hope Project, operated in Milwaukee from 1994 to 1998; the Minnesota Family Investment Program (MFIP), which started as a pilot program in 1994 and became Minnesota's statewide welfare program in 1998; and the Canadian Self-Sufficiency Project (SSP), which operated from November 1992 to December 1999.

Each of these three programs provided earnings supplements that were contingent on full-time work. The Canadian SSP was a voluntary program available to individuals who had been living on Income Assistance (Canadian welfare) for at least one year. The program offered lucrative earnings supplements to participating workers, but to participate in SSP individuals were required to forgo their welfare benefits. A variant of SSP that yielded even stronger results, known as SSP Plus, offered employment services to its participants in addition to the standard earnings supplements.

The New Hope program offered broader financial supports than SSP, including child care and health care subsidies, along with earnings supplements. For individuals unable to secure employment, the program provided access to temporary community service positions. Participation in the program was voluntary and contingent on the individual working thirty hours a week. New Hope was available to all low-income people, including males and females, those without children, and those currently not receiving welfare benefits.

In contrast to the New Hope program, the MFIP primarily targeted long-term welfare recipients. Participants in MFIP who secured full-time employment saw their basic welfare benefits increased by 20 percent to offset work-related expenses. These participants also benefited from an increased "earned income disregard," which is the amount of income that is excluded in the calculation of a household's welfare benefit. Participation in MFIP was mandatory for long-term welfare recipients. Those who did not find employment totaling thirty or more hours per week were required to participate in employment-focused services aimed at assisting them in their search for a job.

All three experiments were rigorously evaluated by MDRC, a respected policy research organization. MDRC President Gordon Berlin observed that, across all three programs,

> the results were encouraging. The mostly single mothers who were offered earnings supplements in these large-scale, rigorous studies were more likely to work, earned more, had more income, and were less likely to be in poverty than those in control groups who were not offered supplements.... The pattern of results also suggests that income gains—and thus the poverty reduction—could be sustained by an ongoing program of supplements.

These programs demonstrate that promoting work through use of incentives or requirements plus incentives can stimulate significant employment and earnings gains among previously unemployed adults. Indeed, long-term welfare recipients, a population typically deemed unemployable, were the most successful at improving their employment rates as compared with similar recipients not offered the work incentives.

Conclusion

This brief review of different perspectives on poverty suggests four conclusions.

75   First, the debate about whether high rates of dropping out of school, joblessness, and unwed births reflect a failure of individuals to act responsibly or a failure of society to respond to poverty and inequality is hard to resolve. Our view is that it is some of both, with the balance between the two varying across individuals.

Second, the job market for those who don't have sufficient education is not good. It is hard to support oneself, much less a family, in today's economy if one is stuck in a low-skill job. Government benefits for the working poor do make a difference, but they could usefully be expanded in ways we address in chapter 9.

Third, discrimination against women and minorities has not disappeared, even though its role in constraining opportunities has diminished.

Fourth, social norms or culture matter, and a more authoritative or directive set of policies that nudge people in the right direction can make a difference. A little more paternalism in social policy is in order.

These conclusions have clear policy implications. They suggest that higher educational achievement depends not just on fixing schools but also on motivating students. They suggest that policies targeting less-advantaged adults should focus on work, providing greater assistance to those who work full time. They suggest that efforts to bring back the two-parent family would produce good results for adults and children. The principle in each case should be to help those who are "playing by the rules." This principle marries social and personal responsibility, structural and cultural perspectives. It also builds on the idea that we should nudge people to do what is in their own long-term interest. In subsequent chapters, we describe policies that build on this principle.

Analyze

1. Haskins and Sawhill open this chapter of their book by explaining that while much of their research focuses on creating and analyzing

quantitative or statistical data, they focus here on qualitative data. First, define quantitative and qualitative data. Second, explain why they think it's important to explore qualitative data.

2. Research shows that heads of households in poor families are less positive about the future than those in more affluent households. Does most research suggest that negative attitudes cause poverty or that poverty causes negative attitudes?

3. What behavioral or cultural norms related to poverty does the text say mark American culture? According to research in this reading, do the poor say they share those conventional values? What evidence does the reading provide that behavior can be nudged back toward that cultural norm? What two methods of nudging behavior do the authors explore?

Explore

1. Haskins and Sawhill claim their research shows that "'playing by the rules' (finishing high school, working full time, marrying before having children) can lead to large reductions in poverty; full-time work is shown to have a particularly large effect. The bad news is that even full-time work leaves some people in poverty." In other words, people who "play by the rules" have a better chance of success, but there's still no guarantee that "conventional" behavior will keep them out of poverty. What are some of the *structural* reasons given to explain why some people who "play by the rules" still struggle to get by?

2. Haskins and Sawhill conclude that "a little more paternalism in social policy is in order." First, define "paternalism" in this context and explain the two methods of expressing it. Second, give some current examples of paternalistic social policy. Finally, explain why you agree or disagree with the authors' conclusion. Give examples of current social policies that seem too paternalistic, or name an issue that we ought to be more paternalistic about to encourage behavior that reduces poverty.

3. Haskins and Sawhill write that Americans are divided on whether they think poverty is generally caused by "personal effort" or "outside circumstances." Later, the authors reveal that they personally don't always agree on this either, yet they were able to find a "common view" that informs their policy proposals. What effect does this revelation

have on their ethos (character and credibility) as authors? Write a letter seeking to find common ground with someone—a politician, academic, religious leader, or personal acquaintance—who views a poverty issue differently than you do.

Sarah Burd-Sharps and Kristen Lewis
"Inequality: Shifting the Spotlight from Wall Street to Your Street"

Sarah Burd-Sharps and Kristen Lewis are co-directors of Measure of America, a project with the Social Science Research Council that aims to "stimulate fact-based dialogue" about issues concerning health, education, and income. Both Burd-Sharps and Lewis have worked previously for the United Nations, and each publishes her writing in many popular media outlets. In the following article, they challenge the audience to widen their thinking about the causes of poverty beyond the growing income gap.

What non-income inequalities do you see in your community?

Income inequality, for years the great unmentionable in political discourse, is suddenly on everyone's lips. Thanks to the Great Recession, Occupy Wall Street, and the ensuing focus on the "1 percent," the gulf between the richest and the rest is now not only acknowledged, it is being cited by people across the political spectrum as an impediment to economic recovery.

While income inequality is enjoying its moment in the sun, other forms of inequality are getting far less attention. Just as we rely too heavily on economic metrics like Gross Domestic Product to gauge human progress, so too are we taking an overly narrow view of inequality. Mutually reinforcing inequalities in health, environment, education, and wealth have created a large and growing opportunity divide that wages alone cannot bridge. These inequalities have a particularly pernicious impact on disadvantaged children, limiting their life chances long before they cash their first pay-check. Ignoring the ways in which these non-income inequalities take root and multiply is a costly mistake for society. Here are some examples.

Let's start at the most basic level: being alive. Our research shows that a baby born today in southwest Louisiana can expect to outlive a baby born in parts of New Orleans by seven-and-a-half years. At the national level, Asian Americans can expect to outlive African Americans by a dozen years. Lifespan disparities like these are less about access to doctors and medicine—the focus of our national health care debate—than about the conditions of people's daily lives. Improving conditions in poor neighbor-hoods such that families have ready access to full-service grocery stores and parks where children can safely play and exercise can go a long way towards laying the foundation for long and healthy lives. Vigorous public health campaigns to raise awareness of the "fatal four" health risks of smoking, poor diet, physical inactivity, and excessive drinking have great potential for reducing both premature death and health care costs. And policies that increase job security can mitigate the health-eroding chronic stress that Americans living paycheck-to-paycheck experience. Communities where preventive efforts are strong boast some of the world's longest life expectan-cies. By contrast, other groups of Americans have lifespans on par with those that prevailed five decades ago.

The environments in which different groups of Americans live, right down to the air they breathe, is another sphere of stark inequality. New York City offers an illustrative example. Manhattan, with less than a fifth of New York City's population, produces over half of its garbage. But when it comes to waste disposal, Manhattan is spared consumption's downsides. The Bronx has nineteen facilities where garbage and recycling are trucked, sorted, and shipped out; Manhattan has none. With these large-scale gar-bage facilities come diesel truck pollution, vermin, and cockroaches, all known asthma triggers, making it no surprise that the South Bronx has one of the region's highest rates of asthma hospitalization. Asthma is a common childhood condition, but it plays out differently depending upon where you live. In some communities, a frantic trip to the emergency room with a life-threatening asthma attack is a mercifully rare occurrence; in others, like the Bronx neighborhoods of Tremont and Melrose, such a trip is all too common. No community welcomes garbage facilities. But the pattern, found across the country, of making poor communities society's dumping ground is unjust and demands a solution.

5   Our country has historically placed faith in education as the great lev-
eler, the answer to inequality. Today, that faith is largely misplaced; on the
whole, our educational system is doing more to widen than to narrow inequality. In our work in California, we found that the Los Angeles Unified
School District (LAUSD) has high schools with top-notch facilities, well-
stocked libraries, and advanced coursework options for most students. But
LAUSD also has schools with severe overcrowding, outdated facilities, and
few advanced courses. These latter schools also typically serve students
facing the greatest out-of-school challenges—low English-language profi-
ciency, poverty, gang recruitment, and more. These variations yield strikingly different results. Graduation rates range from above 97 percent in
some LAUSD schools to only 56 percent in others. Within the Los Angeles
system, and in districts across the nation, schools whose students have the
greatest needs tend to get the fewest resources. In an age when the pie is not
growing, greater equity in how it is sliced matters more than ever; our current approach of giving the biggest pieces to those who already have a lot
makes little sense. Also critical is getting it right from the start. Robust evidence shows that high-quality preschool for disadvantaged children has
benefits that last well into adulthood, with less grade repetition, less need
for special education, and a lower dropout rate during the school years as
well as less incarceration, higher earnings, and higher rates of homeownership later on.

       While income inequalities are large and growing, inequalities in
wealth—or net worth—are even larger, and arguably more consequential.
For example, while African American young people are 43 percent more
likely to get an MBA than their white counterparts, they are one-third as
likely to become business owners. Why? A key reason is that the typical
white household has twenty times the median wealth of the typical black
household. This means that African Americans have fewer savings to invest
directly in business and, without collateral, are far less successful securing
business loans. While other factors, including discrimination, also shape
the fortunes of these young people, greater racial equity in wealth would be
a game changer. Unfortunately, while incentives for wealthy families to
save and invest abound (think mortgage interest deductions and lower tax
rates on capital gains), programs for low-income families are few and far
between. Developing such mechanisms (including automatic savings accounts for every child at birth, the option to deposit state tax refunds directly into college savings plans, greater support for homeownership, and

others) would go a long way toward reducing the huge wealth inequalities that dampen mobility, stifle entrepreneurship, and limit the horizons of too many young Americans.

Fortunately, the leading causes of premature death are largely preventable, environmental equity can become a priority, educational opportunities can be more fairly distributed, and proven programs to increase asset-building and reduce wealth disparities can be brought to scale. Greater recognition of how inequalities in these four areas interact and reinforce one another is the first step, and concrete action in the form of strong policy measures must follow. Income inequality matters, but it's just one piece of the puzzle; addressing non-income inequalities as well is key to creating an infrastructure of opportunity that serves the next generation of Americans.

Analyze

1. According to Burd-Sharps and Lewis, which disadvantaged demographic group should prompt us to think beyond wage inequalities into other spheres?

2. Burd-Sharps and Lewis claim that while we often focus in the U.S. on income inequality, increased wages alone will not reduce the opportunity divide. What four areas should we pay attention to instead?

3. Highlight a sentence in the text that makes a key point regarding each of the four areas of inequality. Note how the paragraphs are organized to help you track those four areas.

Explore

1. Burd-Sharps and Lewis claim that these four areas of inequality (answer to number 2 above) are "mutually reinforcing." What does that mean, and why is that the case? Give your own examples that show how these categories are connected such that low quality in one area contributes to low quality in another.

2. Burd-Sharps and Lewis conclude that change is possible when we first recognize inequality in these four areas and then create strong policy measures. Identify either (1) a campaign for recognition of an issue in one of the four key areas (it can be local, national, or international; consider Public Service Announcements or nonprofit campaigns by

the United Way, for example), or (2) a policy proposed or passed to address an issue in one of those areas. Do a rhetorical analysis of that document, literally analyzing how the rhetoric (language choices) and organization of the text are constructed. Explain how it presents the issue in order to increase recognition or convince us that the policy will help address the issue.

3. Burd-Sharps and Lewis focus on public interventions to create change. Is that level of intervention necessary? How could low-income individuals improve their own well-being in each of the four categories? What challenges would they face initiating changes on their own?

Jeff Sessions
"Memo on FY14 Budget Process"

Jeff Sessions is a Republican senator from Alabama. Throughout his tenure in the U.S. Senate, Sessions has served on committees on the budget, armed services, the judiciary, the environment, and public works. In this memo to fellow Republicans dated February 11, 2013, he explains that Democrats often accuse Republicans of not caring about the plight of the poor. He urges Republicans to counter this false rhetoric with a plan for economic growth and opportunity.

Does poverty as an issue belong to one political party more than another?

February 11, 2013

To: Republican Members

From: Ranking Member Jeff Sessions

Senate Democrats, bowing to Republican pressure, have announced that they will finally relent and produce a budget this year as the law requires.

This week Chairman Murray is holding a hearing entitled "The Impact of Federal Budget Decisions on Families and Communities," in which we expect her to portray the fiscal debate in stark moral terms. She will describe Republicans as the enemy of the working class and the protectors of the rich. We can expect this to be Democrats' theme throughout the budget season. It is the narrative around which President Obama has framed virtually every fiscal debate and his own reelection campaign. He will no doubt repeat this fiction during his State of the Union address.

In her speech at Brookings last year, Chairman Murray declared that "I will not agree to a deal that throws middle class families under the bus and forces them to bear this burden alone. Unless Republicans end their commitment to protecting the rich above all else, our country is going to have to face the consequences of Republican intransigence . . . They pay lip-service to deficit reduction, but what they actually seem to be concerned about is cutting taxes for the rich and starving programs that help middle class families and the most vulnerable Americans."

Too often, Republicans have responded to this attack upon our morality by either ignoring it altogether or dismissing it as "class warfare." Other responses have usually included the suggestion that Democrats are failing to lead, that we are offering credible solutions while they are not, or that their policies will hurt job creators. These are all true and important points, but they fail to rebut the underlying slander. They also fail to cast the argument for conservative reform in the necessary moral dimension.

As we enter the first Senate budget process in four years, it is my intention as Ranking Member not to let these slanders go unanswered. But in order to fully respond to Democrats' charges, it is useful to consider the central premise upon which it is based: that every single penny the public sector extracts from the private sector is wisely spent and improves the quality of life of everyday citizens. Only if one accepts this ludicrous premise could one characterize even the slightest attempts to reduce the $47 trillion [that the] CBO estimates will be spent over the next 10 years as an assault on the middle class.

The White House has succeeded to an alarming degree in framing the fiscal debate as a choice between fiscal restraint and compassion. Reductions in government are, in the White House narrative, inherently harmful; therefore, any approach that mitigates spending cuts through tax hikes is always the morally preferable approach.

Consider the debate over welfare reform. We now spend a trillion dollars annually on federal welfare programs. Converted to cash, spending on federal poverty programs would equal $60,000 for each household living in poverty. Almost 1 in 6 Americans are now on food stamps. The Administration is aggressively working to boost these figures even more, and labels any attempt at reform as uncaring and heartless. They even awarded a food stamp recruiter for overcoming a community's "mountain pride."

Yet what has all this spending produced? More people are living in poverty, wages are flat, millions have completely exited the labor force, and fraud and abuse remain rampant. We will make the case that the time has come for another 1996-style welfare reform that reduces poverty, strengthens family, and helps more Americans transition from dependency to self-sufficiency. This is not merely a financial imperative; it is a moral imperative. No longer can we measure compassion by how much we spend on poverty, but how many people we help to rise out of poverty. Adding endlessly to the debt is not compassionate—it is destructive.

Compassion demands reform. We will confront the Majority directly with this argument. They will have to defend the social and economic harm their policies have afflicted on cities and communities across the country. And we believe the American people will be with us.

We will also explain how excessive taxation and debt is weakening growth today. Weaker growth translates to fewer job openings, smaller paychecks, and more people dependent upon the federal government. Balancing the federal budget is the only way to replace a future of weak growth and high taxes with strong growth and high wages. We have a moral obligation to taxpayers, and to our children, to balance the budget of the United States.

We hope to have a productive and cooperative budget process with the Majority this year. I have already expressed to the Chairman my willingness to work with her and her staff in an effort to balance the federal budget.

10   But, as demonstrated by their refusal to do a budget for nearly four years, the Majority has viewed the fiscal debate not as an exercise in problem-solving but an exercise in political combat. Their strategy has been to issue expertly crafted sound bites from their comfortable station in Washington while happily offering nothing to help those Americans trapped in a cycle of poverty and joblessness. Meanwhile, repeated good-faith Republican efforts to reform government have been rhetorically savaged by a Majority that refuses to contribute with a solution of their own. This pattern must end.

If the Democrat Majority accuses us of the same fictions I have listed earlier, we will reply: your policies are creating poverty, dependency, and chronic unemployment. Your policies are responsible for lost wages and lost jobs. Your policies have denied people access to quality health care. Your policies have shut down factories, surged energy costs, and brought economic growth to a standstill. And your policies are responsible for a nearing debt crisis that threatens each and every American family.

The budget process, carried out in the open light of day, is an opportunity to provide the nation with a bold contrast. The Majority offers a bleak future where millions of Americans are left behind, unable to find steady work, and where faceless government gradually erodes the human bonds of family and community. This will be contrasted against a confident vision of growth and opportunity where the central bonds in our lives are not with the government but with each other.

Our policies are rooted in our firm belief free people thrive most when a minimum burden is placed upon them. By capturing that spirit, and by defending working Americans from the surging federal colossus, our ideas will carry the day.

Analyze

1. Sessions rebuts what he calls the narrative fiction of Democrats who paint Republicans as "the enemy of the working class and protectors of the rich." He calls such characterizations "slander." What is the definition of slander? Is this slander?

2. What does Sessions say has been missing from the Republican response to these accusations so far? How does he claim his contribution to this debate offers something different?

3. Identify a *claim of fact* in the text—something concrete that most people would agree is true. Identify a *claim of value* in the text—something that expresses a personal judgment or sense of right and wrong about which people might disagree. Are these claims supported by evidence and examples? What is the effect of having or not having that support?

Explore

1. Sessions writes: "The White House has succeeded to an alarming degree in framing the fiscal debate as a choice between fiscal restraint and compassion. Reductions in government are, in the White House

narrative, inherently harmful; therefore, any approach that mitigates spending cuts through tax hikes is always the morally preferable approach." First, what does it mean to "frame" a debate? Name some common frames used in public policy debates. How does Sessions want to reframe the debate?

2. Sessions taps into a longstanding debate about poverty when he writes: "No longer can we measure compassion by how much we spend on poverty, but how many people we help to rise out of poverty. Adding endlessly to the debt is not compassionate—it is destructive." In general, some people see welfare programs as creating dependency on public funding at the expense of developing independence and self-sufficiency; others see such programs as a means toward stability and progress in a world full of uncertainties beyond individual control. How is compassion connected to our spending on social welfare programs?

3. Sessions concludes with a script outlining a response Republicans can use to counter the narrative Democrats tell about them. Each sentence begins: "Your policies . . . ," creating a refrain of reprisals. This type of parallelism (repetition of words or formats) is often an effective rhetorical strategy for helping an audience digest a list of like items. Is that strategy effective here? Imagine you are on the receiving end of this refrain: What type of response might it provoke?

Kai Wright
"Young, Black, and Buried in Debt: How For-Profit Colleges Prey on African-American Ambition"

Kai Wright is a professional writer and editor for *Colorlines* and *The Investigative Fund*. An investigative reporter and news commentator, he has also authored books and published in such periodicals as *The Nation* and *The American Prospect*. In the following article, Wright argues that for-profit educational institutions often prey upon black students, crippling them with student loan debt.

Should lenders and universities be responsible for providing loans that students can't afford to pay back?

There are a few dictums that have enjoyed pride of place in black American families alongside "Honor your parents" and "Do unto others" since at least Emancipation. One of them is this: The road to freedom passes through the schoolhouse doors.

After all, it was illegal even to teach an enslaved person to read in many states; under Jim Crow, literacy tests were used for decades to deny black voters their rights. So no surprise that from Reconstruction to the first black president, the consensus has been clear. The key to "winning the future," in one of President Obama's favorite phrases, is to get educated. "There is no surer path to success in the middle class than a good education," the president declared in his much-discussed speech on the roots of gun violence in black Chicago.

Rarely has that message resounded so much as now, with nearly one in seven black workers still jobless. Those who've found work have moved out of the manufacturing and public sectors, where good jobs were once available without a higher ed degree, and into the low-wage service sector, to which the uncredentialed are now relegated. So while it has become fashionable lately to speculate about middle-class kids abandoning elite colleges for adventures in entrepreneurship, an entirely different trend has been unfolding in black America—people are going back to school in droves.

It's true at all levels of education. Yes, black college enrollment shot up by nearly 35 percent between 2003 and 2009, nearly twice the rate at which white enrollment increased. But we're getting all manner of schooling as we seek either an advantage in or refuge from the collapsed job market. As I've reported on the twin housing and unemployment crises in black neighborhoods in recent years, I've heard the same refrain from struggling strivers up and down the educational ladder: "I'm getting my papers, maybe that'll help." GEDs, associates degrees, trade licenses, certifications, you name it, we're getting it. Hell, I even went and got certified in selling wine; journalism's a shrinking trade, after all.

5   But this headlong rush of black Americans to get schooled has also led too many down a depressingly familiar path. As with the mortgage market of the pre-crash era, those who are just entering in the higher ed game have found themselves ripe for the con man's picking. They've landed, disproportionately, at for-profit schools, rather than at far less expensive public community colleges, or at public universities. And that means they've found themselves loaded with unimaginable debt, with little to show for it, while a small group of financial players have made a great deal of easy money. Sound familiar? Two points if you hear troublesome echoes of the subprime mortgage crisis.

Between 2004 and 2010, black enrollment in for-profit bachelor's programs grew by a whopping 264 percent, compared to a 24 percent increase in black enrollment in public four-year programs. The two top producers of black baccalaureates in the class of 2011 were University of Phoenix and Ashford University, both for-profits.

These numbers mirror a simultaneous trend in eroding security among ambitious black Americans with shrinking access to middle-class jobs. It's true that the country's middle class is collapsing for everyone, but that trend is most profound among African-Americans. In 2008, as black folks flocked into higher ed, the Economic Policy Institute found that 45 percent of African-Americans born into the middle class were living at or near poverty as adults.

For too many, school has greased the downward slide. Nearly every single graduate of a for-profit school—96 percent, according to a 2008 Department of Education survey—leaves with debt. The industry ate 25 percent of federal student aid in the 2009–2010 school year. That's debt its students can't pay. The loan default rate among for-profit college students is more than double that of their peers in both public and nonprofit private schools, because the degrees and certificates the students are earning are trap doors to more poverty, not springboards to prosperity.

There's been growing, positive attention to this problem, and the Obama administration's ongoing efforts to rein in the excesses of for-profit schools are arguably among its most progressive policy goals. But few have understood the for-profit education boom as part of the larger economic challenge black America faces today. The black jobs crisis stretches way back to the 2001 recession, from which too many black neighborhoods never recovered. Workers and families have been scrambling ever since, trying to fix themselves such that they fit inside a broken economy. And it is that very effort at self-improvement, that same American spirit of personal re-creation and against-all-odds ambition that has so often led black people into the jaws of the 21st century's most predatory capitalists. From subprime credit cards through to subprime home loans and now on into subprime education, we've reached again and again for the trappings of middle-class life, only to find ourselves slipping further into debt and poverty.

Kiesha Whatley is an example. The 31-year-old mom in Queens, N.Y., has always done hair on the side to help make ends meet, so in 2006 she decided to go for her cosmetology certificate. She was in the city's welfare-to-work program, but was able to fill her work requirement by going to school. She figured what she needed most was to get a credential—to get legit. So she enrolled at a small, mom-and-pop for-profit in Brooklyn that her cousin had attended years before, but which had since changed ownership. Over what Whatley says was a seven-month program, she racked up more than $7,500 in debt, much of which she thought was actually a grant. She has still not passed the state cosmetology exam and she's back to doing hair on her own, now with debt she can't dream of paying back.

The subprime mortgage crisis was fueled by a similar mix of economic 10 desperation, financial illiteracy and aspirational ideology. For a generation, working-class people who hoped to achieve more permanent economic stability were told, loudly and repeatedly, that buying a home would validate them as legitimate participants in American life, not just as people with an asset, but as true neighbors and community members and citizens. Prosperity preachers and presidents alike sung the praises of the "ownership society," as George W. Bush so often called it, in which "more Americans than ever will be able to open up their door where they live and say, welcome to my house, welcome to my piece of property." Homeownership was understood then—just as higher education is now—as good no matter what. Just don't read the fine print.

All it took was one devastating downturn for those doors to slam shut, forcing millions of Americans into foreclosure. That still unfolding crisis has been particularly devastating for African-Americans, who have lost more than half of their collective assets after being targeted with subprime mortgage products. The black-white wealth gap is larger today than it's been since economists began recording it in 1984. And according to a recent analysis from the Alliance for a Just Society, ZIP codes with majority people of color populations saw 60 percent more foreclosures than white neighborhoods and these homeowners lost 69 percent more wealth.

Now, to make matters worse, expensive, nearly useless degrees may be to the bust years what expensive, totally useless refinance loans were to the boom: too-good-to-be-true golden tickets to the American Dream, sold in an unregulated market and targeted at the people for whom that dream is most elusive.

Last year, Garvin Gittens became a literal poster child for why that market is so dangerous. For several months, his face was plastered all over the New York City subway system as part of a city-led campaign to warn would-be students about debt scams. When we met last summer, Gittens laid out for me how he racked up more than $57,000 in public and private debt in pursuit of a two-year associate's degree in graphic design at the for-profit Katharine Gibbs School, in Midtown Manhattan. Like subprime mortgages, the debt didn't appear so intimidating at first, but just as balloon payments capsized so many tenuous family finances, a cascading series of loans, a few thousand dollars at a time, eventually caught up with Gittens. In the end, his degree proved as meaningless as it was expensive. When he went to apply for bachelor's programs, no legitimate college would recognize his credits because the school's shoddy performance had finally led the state to sanction it.

So Gittens has started over from scratch—but with tens of thousands of dollars in loans hanging over his head. As I listened to him recount his tale, just as he was about to once again begin his freshman year of college, what struck me most was how insistently the 27-year-old was holding on to his goal of getting credentialed. Even without a degree, he'd built a modestly successful graphic design business of his own. He'd landed fancy internships with hip-hop clothing designers and made smart choices like offsetting his design work with more reliable income from printing jobs. Yet a college degree remained such a coveted treasure for him that, even having [wasted] tens of thousands of dollars and two years of his life, he was prepared to do it all again.

"It's more of an emotional thing," Gittens explained, citing a graduate degree as his ultimate goal. "I'd like to say, 'I have a master's in design.' That would make me feel good." And the sky's the limit when you're buying self-worth.

Of course, the industry that's been turning fast profit off of ambitions like Gittens' is finally seeing tough times of its own. Take Gittens' alma mater, the now-closed Katharine Gibbs School. It was owned by Illinois-based Career Education Corp., a publicly traded firm that still runs dozens of schools across the country and in Europe, and which is among the industry's largest players. Career Ed booked $1.49 billion in revenue in 2012, but it faces steadily declining stock values as a series of investigations and scandals have limited its ability to pull in new students. Its "student starts"—as enrollment is called in the for-profit sector—dropped 23 percent last year. That comes after attorneys general in both New York and Florida launched probes in 2011 of the company for falsifying job placement rates. Career Ed has also had to answer to two national accrediting bodies for its job placement reporting in the past two years.

The company responded to these probes by launching its own investi   15 gation and revealing that barely a quarter of its health and design schools actually placed enough graduates in jobs to maintain accreditation. So Chairman Steve Lesnik, who also runs a company that develops golf facilities and athletic clubs, took over as CEO and overhauled the way Career Ed reports job placements, adding independent verification. He stresses Career Ed's newfound compliance with regulators and called 2012 a "year of renewal." "It's a simple thought: students first," he said last February, as he addressed investors for the first time as CEO and sought to calm nerves over the regulatory probes. "That idea permeates every action we take."

But while the company reassures regulators and investors that its education is sound, it's failing starkly by another blunt measure. Nearly 28 percent of students at Career Ed's health services school in New York City, the Sanford Brown Institute, default on their loans after three years. That rate's outstanding even among for-profits, and it is a sure sign that these degrees aren't leading to jobs with decent salaries—if they're leading to jobs at all.

Big for-profits like Career Ed—often run by financiers, not educators— are eager to differentiate themselves from small, independent trade schools like the one Whatley attended, where they argue the bad behavior is concentrated. But what all of the industry's players have in common is a business model that targets desperate people who have been pushed out of the workforce in overwhelming numbers over the past decade.

You needn't look further than these schools' ad campaigns to discover who's in their target demographic. They're a model of diversity. It's tough to find a marketing image that doesn't picture a happy person of color or a young woman, or both. One Sanford Brown online ad features a verbal montage of emotional touchstones that seem tailor-made to speak to working-class frustrations. "Before I contacted Sanford Brown I was working second shift," says one woman's voice. "I needed a career for myself and my family," says another woman. "They empowered me to be a better person," another declares. Watching the ads reminds me of one Atlanta woman's explanation when I asked her why she signed off on such a bad deal as the subprime refinance that put her home at risk of foreclosure. She talked about the "nice young man" who came and sold it to her. He was well-dressed and clean cut and black. He seemed successful. He seemed to remind her of her ambitions for the young black men in her own life. Then he stole from her on behalf of his bank.

In this respect, for-profit schools function less like traditional educational institutions and more like payday lenders, rent-to-own businesses, pawn shops and the like—they all offer products that churn customers through debt for years on end. And, like the rest of the subprime market, selling for-profit degrees is especially good business in the worst of times. Career Ed's previous CEO left his post just as the New York attorney general's probe sent the company's stock into free fall; he departed with a reported $5.1 million parachute. According to a Senate report last July, which used data from 2009, three-quarters of students at for-profit schools attended institutions that were owned by publicly traded corporations or private equity firms. The former had an average profit margin of nearly 20 percent—and their CEOs made an average of $7.3 million.

20   Regulators at both the federal and state level have begun working furiously to rein all of this in. Among other things, the Obama administration has tightened rules for schools to participate in the federal student aid program upon which for-profits depend. Last year, the Department of Education instituted a rule that disqualifies any school at which 30 percent of students or more have defaulted on their loans within three years of graduation. The first sanctions under the new rule won't come until next fall, but according to the department's tally, for-profits accounted for nearly three-quarters of the schools that would have been forced out in 2012.

There is significant evidence that schools were gaming the feds' previous system for monitoring default rates. The Senate report from last July revealed aggressive machinations to push struggling graduates into forbearance—a costly way to escape delinquency—just long enough to push their defaults beyond the oversight window. At Career Ed, for instance, employees called students with delinquent loans an average 46 times to nudge them to file for forbearance, regardless of whether that was in the students' best interest financially. Gittens, Whatley and thousands of other unemployed or underemployed African-American strivers have been told again and again—by elected officials, by community leaders, by their own optimistic families—that they hold their economic destiny in their own hands. That they must pick up new skills, get more training, earn more credentials, adapt or die. One day the jobs will come, we're told, and we'd all better be ready to fill them. They're earnestly heeding that message, but the only thing an awful lot of them are earning is another lesson in just how expensive it is to be both poor and ambitious in America.

Analyze

1. What was the difference in enrollment in public four-year schools and for-profit schools between black and white Americans? Explain the difference.

2. List Wright's references, including statistical data and personal interviews. Did he miss any important perspectives? What one part of this essay would you share with someone else? Why?

3. Referring to himself, Wright writes: "Hell, I even went and got certified in selling wine; journalism's a shrinking trade, after all." How do the self-references construct Wright's ethos (character and credibility)? Do his personal and professional references add to or detract from the argument?

Explore

1. Education has typically been viewed as a means for building resilience, a safety net that increases employment possibilities and earning potential over a lifetime. However, Wright claims: "For too many, school has greased the downward slide." He continues, "The loan default rate among for-profit college students is more than double that of their peers in both public and nonprofit private schools, because the degrees and certificates the students are earning are trap doors to more poverty, not springboards to prosperity." Cite cases you know that support or challenge this claim. Is any education worthwhile no matter the cost? Write a researched letter to a parent, child, or friend considering college in which you explain your view on the link between the cost of education and the potential return on that investment.

2. Wright uses analogy to sound the alarm about education debt: "From subprime credit cards through to subprime home loans and now on into subprime education, we've reached again and again for the trappings of middle-class life, only to find ourselves slipping further into debt and poverty." Is his analogy convincing? How is the education crisis he describes similar to or different from the subprime mortgage crisis that surfaced in 2008? What do illiteracy and aspiration have to do with both?

3. Wright does a rhetorical analysis of the ad campaign for a for-profit school, analyzing how, for example, race and aspiration are represented in their pictures and dialogue. Choose two post-secondary institutions and do a rhetorical analysis of their recruiting materials, attending carefully to how each institution taps into narratives of *hope* (aspiration toward the American Dream) and narratives of *fear* (e.g., escape from financial uncertainty). Do the approaches seem fair or manipulative?

Michelle Alexander
"The New Jim Crow: How the War on Drugs Gave Birth to a Permanent American Undercaste"

Michelle Alexander is a civil rights lawyer and a professor of law at Ohio State University. She also writes freelance pieces concerning the mass incarceration of black Americans. The following is an argument about the continued effects of racial discrimination caused by targeting black Americans as criminals. Her claims are based on her book *The New Jim Crow: Mass Incarceration in the Age of Colorblindness*, which has earned much critical acclaim and spent over a year on the *New York Times* best-seller list.

In what ways does incarceration increase the likelihood of future poverty?

Ever since Barack Obama lifted his right hand and took his oath of office, pledging to serve the United States as its 44th president, ordinary people and their leaders around the globe have been celebrating our nation's "triumph over race." Obama's election has been touted as the final nail in the coffin of Jim Crow, the bookend placed on the history of racial caste in America.

Obama's mere presence in the Oval Office is offered as proof that "the land of the free" has finally made good on its promise of equality. There's an implicit yet undeniable message embedded in his appearance on the world stage: this is what freedom looks like; this is what democracy can do for you. If you are poor, marginalized, or relegated to an inferior caste, there is hope for you. Trust us. Trust our rules, laws, customs, and wars. You, too, can get to the promised land.

Perhaps greater lies have been told in the past century, but they can be counted on one hand. Racial caste is alive and well in America.

Most people don't like it when I say this. It makes them angry. In the "era of colorblindness" there's a nearly fanatical desire to cling to the myth that we as a nation have "moved beyond" race. Here are a few facts that run counter to that triumphant racial narrative:

- There are more African American adults under correctional control today—in prison or jail, on probation or parole—than were enslaved in 1850, a decade before the Civil War began.
- As of 2004, more African American men were disenfranchised (due to felon disenfranchisement laws) than in 1870, the year the Fifteenth Amendment was ratified, prohibiting laws that explicitly deny the right to vote on the basis of race.
- A black child born today is less likely to be raised by both parents than a black child born during slavery. The recent disintegration of the African American family is due in large part to the mass imprisonment of black fathers.
- If you take into account prisoners, a large majority of African American men in some urban areas have been labeled felons for life. (In the Chicago area, the figure is nearly 80%.) These men are part of a growing undercaste—not class, caste—permanently relegated, by law, to a second-class status. They can be denied the right to vote, automatically excluded from juries, and legally discriminated against in

employment, housing, access to education, and public benefits, much as their grandparents and great-grandparents were during the Jim Crow era.

Excuses for the Lockdown

5   There is, of course, a colorblind explanation for all this: crime rates. Our prison population has exploded from about 300,000 to more than 2 million in a few short decades, it is said, because of rampant crime. We're told that the reason so many black and brown men find themselves behind bars and ushered into a permanent, second-class status is because they happen to be the bad guys.

The uncomfortable truth, however, is that crime rates do not explain the sudden and dramatic mass incarceration of African Americans during the past 30 years. Crime rates have fluctuated over the last few decades—they are currently at historical lows—but imprisonment rates have consistently soared. Quintupled, in fact. A main driver has been the War on Drugs. Drug offenses alone accounted for about two-thirds of the increase in the federal inmate population, and more than half of the increase in the state prison population between 1985 and 2000, the period of our prison system's most dramatic expansion.

The drug war has been brutal—complete with SWAT teams, tanks, bazookas, grenade launchers, and sweeps of entire neighborhoods—but those who live in white communities have little clue to the devastation wrought. This war has been waged almost exclusively in poor communities of color, even though studies consistently show that people of all colors use and sell illegal drugs at remarkably similar rates. In fact, some studies indicate that white youth are significantly more likely to engage in illegal drug dealing than black youth. Any notion that drug use among African Americans is more severe or dangerous is belied by the data. White youth, for example, have about three times the number of drug-related visits to the emergency room as their African American counterparts.

That is not what you would guess, though, when entering our nation's prisons and jails, overflowing as they are with black and brown drug offenders. Human Rights Watch reported in 2000 that, in some states, African Americans comprised 80%–90% of all drug offenders sent to prison. Rates of black imprisonment have fallen since then, but not by much.

This is the point at which I am typically interrupted and reminded that black men have higher rates of violent crime. *That's* why the drug war is waged in poor communities of color and not middle-class suburbs. Drug warriors are trying to get rid of those drug kingpins and violent offenders who make ghetto communities a living hell. It has nothing to do with race; it's all about violent crime.

Again, not so. President Ronald Reagan officially declared the current drug war in 1982, when drug crime was declining, not rising. President Richard Nixon was the first to coin the term "a war on drugs," but it was President Reagan who turned the rhetorical war into a literal one. From the outset, the war had relatively little to do with drug crime and much to do with racial politics. The drug war was part of a grand and highly successful Republican Party strategy of using racially coded political appeals on issues of crime and welfare to attract poor and working class white voters who were resentful of, and threatened by, desegregation, busing, and affirmative action. In the words of H. R. Haldeman, President Richard Nixon's White House Chief of Staff: "[T]he whole problem is really the blacks. The key is to devise a system that recognizes this while not appearing to."

A few years after the drug war was announced, crack cocaine hit the 10 streets of inner-city communities. The Reagan administration seized on this development with glee, hiring staff who were to be responsible for publicizing inner-city crack babies, crack mothers, crack whores, and drug-related violence. The goal was to make inner-city crack abuse and violence a media sensation, bolstering public support for the drug war which, it was hoped, would lead Congress to devote millions of dollars in additional funding to it.

The plan worked like a charm. For more than a decade, black drug dealers and users would be regulars in newspaper stories and would saturate the evening TV news. Congress and state legislatures nationwide would devote billions of dollars to the drug war and pass harsh mandatory minimum sentences for drug crimes—sentences longer than murderers receive in many countries.

Democrats began competing with Republicans to prove that they could be even tougher on the dark-skinned pariahs. In President Bill Clinton's boastful words, "I can be nicked a lot, but no one can say I'm soft on crime." The facts bear him out. Clinton's "tough on crime" policies resulted in the largest increase in federal and state prison inmates of any president in American history. But Clinton was not satisfied with exploding prison populations. He and the "New Democrats" championed legislation banning drug felons from public housing (no matter how minor the offense) and denying them basic public benefits, including food stamps, for life. Discrimination in virtually every aspect of political, economic, and social life is now perfectly legal, if you've been labeled a felon.

Facing Facts

But what about all those violent criminals and drug kingpins? Isn't the drug war waged in ghetto communities because that's where the violent offenders can be found? The answer is yes . . . in made-for-TV movies. In real life, the answer is no.

The drug war has never been focused on rooting out drug kingpins or violent offenders. Federal funding flows to those agencies that increase dramatically the volume of drug arrests, not the agencies most successful in bringing down the bosses. What has been rewarded in this war is sheer numbers of drug arrests. To make matters worse, federal drug forfeiture laws allow state and local law enforcement agencies to keep for their own use 80% of the cash, cars, and homes seized from drug suspects, thus granting law enforcement a direct monetary interest in the profitability of the drug market.

15   The results have been predictable: people of color rounded up en masse for relatively minor, non-violent drug offenses. In 2005, four out of five drug arrests were for possession, only one out of five for sales. Most people in state prison have no history of violence or even of significant selling activity. In fact, during the 1990s—the period of the most dramatic expansion of the drug war—nearly 80% of the increase in drug arrests was for marijuana possession, a drug generally considered less harmful than alcohol or tobacco and at least as prevalent in middle-class white communities as in the inner city.

In this way, a new racial undercaste has been created in an astonishingly short period of time—a new Jim Crow system. Millions of people of color are now saddled with criminal records and legally denied the very rights that their parents and grandparents fought for and, in some cases, died for.

Affirmative action, though, has put a happy face on this racial reality. Seeing black people graduate from Harvard and Yale and become CEOs or corporate lawyers—not to mention president of the United States—causes us all to marvel at what a long way we've come.

Recent data shows, though, that much of black progress is a myth. In many respects, African Americans are doing no better than they were when Martin Luther King, Jr. was assassinated and uprisings swept inner cities across America, particularly when it comes to the wealth gap and unemployment rates. Unemployment rates in many black communities rival those in Third World countries. And that's with affirmative action!

When we pull back the curtain and take a look at what our "colorblind" society creates without affirmative action, we see a familiar social, political, and economic structure: the structure of racial caste. The entrance into this new caste system can be found at the prison gate.

This is not Martin Luther King, Jr.'s dream. This is not the promised land. The cyclical rebirth of caste in America is a recurring racial nightmare.

Analyze

1. What is a "racial caste"?
2. Name at least two facts that counter the "triumphant racial narrative."
3. While crime rates have fluctuated over the past few decades, imprisonment rates have done what?

Explore

1. What do the data tell us about the disparities between white and black incarceration rates? Compare that to public perceptions.
2. How does Alexander describe the purpose and plan of the war on drugs? Find at least two outside sources that offer different perspectives. Compare and contrast those perspectives. Is there common ground on any facts, values, causes, or solutions?
3. Write a letter to Alexander in which you challenge and/or support her claim that we have a new Jim Crow. Research the original Jim Crow laws for support. Use your own examples of the presence or absence of colorblindness to support your perspective.

Joshua DuBois
"The Fight for Black Men"

Joshua DuBois was President Obama's former spiritual advisor and led many of the White House's faith-based initiatives. The author of *The President's Devotional: The Daily Readings that Inspired President Obama* and *Stories of Faith in the White House,* DuBois reaches beyond his focus on religion and spirituality in the following article to claim that the disproportionate rates of black incarceration and black unemployment require complex but attainable solutions. DuBois now serves as a weekly religion columnist for *Newsweek,* which published this article as its cover story in June 2013.

How is the fate of black men in the U.S. inextricably linked to every American's fate?

There is an easy way to meet Joe Jones, and a hard way. Let's start with the easy way. If you and I were at a cocktail party, I'd introduce you to a tall, bald, black man, standing a shoulder above most everybody else. Knowing Joe Jones, he'd probably be wearing a tan suit and muted tie. Joe's subdued, square-rimmed glasses fit nicely with his veiled intellect—he's the kind of guy who readily drops six-dollar words without a hint of pretense.

I'd probably ask Joe to tell you about the nonprofit he runs, the Center for Urban Families on Baltimore's West Side. CFUF is a national model for helping men and women who are confronting addiction, poverty, and despair turn their lives around, and teaching absent fathers how to reconnect with their kids. Joe's a modest guy, so I'd have to brag on his behalf, about the bigwigs who have dropped by his center, and all the awards the organization has won.

Finally, I'd say in passing: "You know, Joe has a powerful personal story himself. His own father wasn't around, he struggled in the streets for a while, and then pulled himself up, and made it out." Nice and neat. Joe would nod and smile. You'd nod and smile. I'd nod and smile. We'd all be smiling—appropriately inspired.

That's the easy way to meet Joe Jones. But there's also the hard way. The hard way is to grapple with the fact that Joe's family didn't just emerge from some unseen ghetto thousands of miles away. No, his grandfather migrated to Baltimore from North Carolina, and started a business—a waste-management facility, one of the city's more successful ones. His grandparents were "models of stability," Joe told me. A few generations before that, Joe's family were slaves.

It's hard to figure out what happened to Joe's dad, and thousands of other black fathers like him. Joe's dad was training to be a teacher, but one day in the mid-'60s he hopped into the driver side of a Ford Thunderbird, visibly angry, slung his duffel bag on the passenger side, and drove off for good. Joe saw the whole thing from his upstairs window in the Lafayette Court housing projects; he thought his dad was going to the laundromat, and sat waiting for him, for hours.

It's tough to stomach what happened later. How Joe, an adorable kid of 13—never a smoker, never a drinker—met a guy a couple years older than him. And this person put it into Joe's young head that maybe it wouldn't be a bad thing to stick a needle in his arm, and let a bit of heroin rush in. So, as a 13-year-old, he did. Joe's two cousins shared the needle with him— their dad wasn't around either—and his best friend, Barry, also fatherless, did too.

So now Joe's an adolescent junkie, hanging out on Edmonson Avenue in West Baltimore and shooting up wherever he can find a shadow long enough to hide himself: sometimes in a bowling alley bathroom, sometimes in his aunt's basement. He was 14 when he was busted for the first time for using drugs, along with his two cousins and Barry. The other boys' parents bailed them out, thank God, but the police suggested that Joe, the ringleader, should stew for a little while to learn his lesson—you know, "tough on crime."

Turns out, this wasn't the best move for Joe. During his few extra days in jail, in the throes of heroin withdrawal that his young system wasn't handling well, Joe met a local kingpin who taught him how to be a more efficient junkie, and a more effective criminal. Or as Joe puts it now (in his always-impeccable phrasing): "This man created a pathway for me to negotiate the street environment in a way that I hadn't anticipated. It was the worst thing that could've happened to me."

So in the span of a few years, Joe went from a stable household to a single-parent family. From a middle-school honor student to a street-corner addict. From the grandson of a businessman and great-great-great-grandson of slaves to the son of an absent father, and a future deadbeat dad himself.

It was a jumble of inputs—bad parenting and bad policy, misguided culture and tragic history—resulting in one clear output: a woefully lost kid.

10   There is a lot more to Joe Jones's story—more pain than most can bear; more beauty than you'd expect. We'll get to all of that, including his fateful encounter with the president of the United States.

But first, a few words about the world Joe comes from: the world of low-income black men. Why talk about this world? After all, it's simple enough to ignore. We can safely tuck these men away in our inner cities and allow them to interact largely among themselves. We can rush past them in front of the gas station, murmur silently when the nightly news tells us of a shooting across town, or smile when we meet a nice, inspiring man like Joe. We can keep them in these places. It's safe and easy for us.

Yet if we're honest, we'll have to admit that when one single group of people is conspicuously left behind, it never bodes well for society as a whole. In many ways, black men in America are a walking gut check; we learn from them a lot about ourselves, how far we've really come as a country, and how much further we have to go.

I spent the past few months talking to dozens of experts who are working to address the crisis among black men. It was clear from these conversations that the reasons for this crisis are complex—as are the solutions. But it was also clear that the fight for black men, which is currently being waged by activists, politicians, celebrities, and everyday people alike, can indeed be won.

As with Joe Jones, it starts by understanding their history, and their stories.

15   The earliest chapter in that story is a tough one. I'd rather skip it. You'd rather that I skip it. But as Ralph Ellison once remarked, channeling Faulkner, our complicated racial past is "a part of the living present"; it's a past that "speaks even when no one wills to listen."

The facts are a bit overwhelming, but not in much dispute. Africans were imported to the United States as purchased goods beginning around 1620. By 1770, when Crispus Attucks, a free black man, spilled the first drop of blood in the cause of the American Revolution, nearly 18 percent of the American population—almost 700,000 people—were slaves. By the time of the Emancipation Proclamation, that number had exploded to over 4 million.

Beneath these sterile facts lay a grisly reality. Blacks were systemically dehumanized for hundreds of years, a practice that had unique social and psychological effects on men. They were worked and whipped in fields like cattle. Any semblance of pride, any cry for justice, any measure of genuine manhood was tortured, beaten, or sold out of them. Marriage was strictly prohibited. Most were forbidden from learning to read and write. The wealth derived from their labor—the massive wealth derived from cotton, our chief export throughout much of the 19th and early 20th centuries—was channeled elsewhere.

But, because slavery ended 150 years ago, we often assume that this dehumanization is ancient history. It is not. As Douglas Blackmon of The Wall Street Journal meticulously documents in his Pulitzer Prize–winning book, *Slavery by Another Name*, blacks were kept in virtual bondage through Jim Crow laws, sharecropping, and, quite often, a form of quasi-slavery called peonage, which endured well into the middle of the 20th century.

Here's how it worked: black men (it was usually men) were arrested for petty crimes or no crimes at all; "selling cotton after sunset" was a favorite charge. They were then assessed a steep fine. If they could not pay, they were imprisoned for long sentences and forced to work for free. This allowed savvy industrialists to replace thousands of slaves with thousands of convicts.

While some whites were caught up in this system, the forced labor 20
camps were 80 to 90 percent populated by black men. This practice endured until 1948, when the federal criminal code was rewritten to helpfully clarify that the law forbade involuntary servitude.

Around that time, determined activists—from the Rev. Martin Luther King Jr. to Fannie Lou Hamer—organized to demand equal treatment. We know the civil rights story well: Brown v. Board of Education in 1954, which overturned the separate-but-equal doctrine; the Civil Rights Act of 1964, which outlawed various forms of discrimination; and the Voting Rights Act of 1965, which carved a clear path to the unfettered right to vote.

And that, we told black men, was that. Immediately following the civil rights movement, in the early 1970s, we assured these men, with fingers perhaps gently crossed behind our backs, that all the discrimination they had faced was behind them; that there would be no further barriers to opportunity, even unspoken ones; that it was time for them to wake up. Get a job. Get married, and start a family. Build wealth. Take hold of the American dream. We won't stop you—we promise.

We focused our social investments in this period—our brief War on Poverty—on women and children, because men were supposed to figure it out. But in the 1970s and 1980s, many of these black men didn't. Just like their great-grandfathers never fully figured out how to teach their sons about manhood while being lashed in a field. Just like their grandfathers never completely figured out how to pass on lessons about building wealth when theirs was stolen through peonage and sharecropping.

Their fathers tried to rally around Martin Luther King as a symbol of what they could be—but he was gunned down on the balcony of the Lorraine Motel. In the post–civil rights era, many of these black men, men like Joe Jones's father, weren't quite figuring it out either. And neither are many of their sons and grandsons, those bright if often scowling men we see on our streets.

25   Why not? The reasons are as complicated as the difficult history, and simple debates about government spending versus personal responsibility are woefully insufficient.

But one of the key reasons has to do with our criminal justice system. And it points the way toward one of the key solutions—perhaps the single most important thing government can do to help win the fight for black men.

No one has done more to shed light on this issue than Michelle Alexander. Alexander may be this century's Harriet Beecher Stowe, the storied author of *Uncle Tom's Cabin* about whom President Lincoln remarked, "So you're the little woman who wrote the book that made this Great War?" But instead of making a war, Alexander wrote a book to end one.

Alexander was a young civil rights attorney working for the ACLU of California and trying to find a model plaintiff for a civil rights case against the Oakland Police Department, which at the time was rife with corruption. One day, a 19-year-old black man walked into her office, and he looked like the perfect case to prove that the Oakland PD had gone bad.

The man had been stopped and released dozens of times, for no reason at all. He had been forced to lie on the ground spread-eagle and been subjected to invasive searches, after which the police found nothing. And, important, he had taken meticulous notes of all this—every stop, every date, every badge number. "I was getting more and more excited," Alexander told me, "because I thought this was our plaintiff."

30   However, at the end of his presentation, the man shared one final fact: he had a felony record, having been busted for a drug offense years earlier

and convicted as an adult. Alexander stopped him there. "I explained to him that I couldn't take his case," she told me. "It wouldn't be fair to him or to us. With his felony record he'd have no credibility on the witness stand; he'd be cross-examined about his past."

Alexander tried to explain to the young man that it wouldn't work out, but he pushed back in protest. He said that the conviction was for a minor offense, and that he'd just taken a plea deal to avoid more jail time. He said his past should have no bearing on the repeated abuse he had experienced.

But Alexander didn't budge, and eventually the young man had enough. Fighting back tears, he yelled at her, "You're no better than anyone else! The minute I tell you I have a criminal record, you stop listening. I can't get a job. I can't feed my family. Where am I supposed to sleep? How long am I supposed to pay for my record?"

The man stormed out in a huff, leaving Alexander stunned. At that point, something clicked with her, something that pulled together all of her prior experience in civil rights law and history. Alexander realized that, not unlike the peonage system in the early 20th century, the "war on drugs" had created what she calls a "permanent under-caste" of men convicted of drug offenses. Men who, even after their release from incarceration for relatively minor crimes, would never again be able to navigate the world on equal footing with the rest of us. Men like the young man she met but could not serve.

The full explanation of this permanent under-caste of black men and the devastation it has wrought is meticulously and powerfully delivered in *The New Jim Crow*—Alexander's book about the war on drugs, which was on the *New York Times* bestseller list for nearly a year and today can be found in the hands of decision makers across the country, from federal court-rooms to the halls of Congress. In the book, she describes the ramp-up of criminal-justice spending in the 1980s as the result of an intentional polit-ical strategy rather than a reasoned law enforcement response. The result has been the mass incarceration of African-Americans, mostly men, with little connection to actual rates of crime.

Alexander shows that there are more African-Americans in the correc-   35
tions system today—in prison or on probation or parole—than there were enslaved in 1850. As of 2004, more black men were denied the right to vote because of a criminal record than in 1870, when the Fifteenth Amend-ment was ratified, giving blacks the right to vote. In the three decades since the war on drugs began, the U.S. prison population has exploded from

300,000 to more than 2 million people, giving our country the highest incarceration rate in the world—higher than Russia, China, and other regimes we consider repressive. A significant majority of black men in some urban areas are labeled felons for life; in and around Chicago, when you include prisoners, that number approaches 80 percent.

But isn't this just a function of more crime in black communities? Aren't we arresting violent super-predators, the type we see on television? Alexander makes clear: in most communities, the answer is no.

"It has nothing to do with crime rates," she told me. "Crime rates have fluctuated over time—we're currently at historic lows—but incarceration rates have consistently soared." People of color are arrested in large numbers for relatively minor offenses—four out of five drug arrests in 2005 were for possession, not sales—and then given sentences that outpace their white counterparts. In fact, in the 1990s, when the war on drugs was at its peak, almost 80 percent of the increase in drug arrests was for possession of marijuana.

The result of all of this is the "under-caste," an apt if cringe-worthy term describing the massive numbers of black men who cannot access housing, who are screened out of employment, and who in many states are denied the right to vote. Facing severely limited options and few opportunities for rehabilitation, millions of these men re-offend, creating more victims in our communities and landing themselves back in jail.

These men are increasingly isolated from the rest of America—including from middle-class African-Americans. As the Rev. Al Sharpton, the nationally known civil rights activist and founder of the National Action Network, told me in an interview, "We're in the best of times and worst of times, at the same time." "It's the best-time times," Sharpton continued, "because we have a black president, black attorney general, black CEOs. But it's the worst of times because millions of African-American men are being locked up and left out like never before."

40   Ben Jealous, the president of the NAACP, agrees. In an interview, Jealous declared to me that "black men are the most incarcerated people on the planet . . . warehoused in prison for nonviolent crimes that two decades ago would have resulted in little to no jail time."

But Jealous is also hopeful. The NAACP is going state by state, attaching practical solutions to Alexander's thesis. And because of strained prison budgets and concern about bloated government, they are finding receptive audiences not just among liberals but among conservatives too. For example, they are presently working with Gov. Nathan Deal of Georgia, a Tea Party Republican, to, in Jealous's words, "make their prison system dramatically smaller." "Our allies on the right are beginning to think about criminal-justice reform," Jealous says. "They are finally getting beyond 'tough on crime' slogans, and actually focusing on what works."

In fact, bipartisan efforts on criminal-justice reform are growing. On the Democratic side, Attorney General Eric Holder has confronted the issue head on, spearheading an initiative to tackle youth violence and create new reentry programs for returning offenders, while working with Congress to reduce racial disparities in sentencing. He's been joined on the right by Republican Congressman Frank Wolf, who has taken a particular interest in "smart on crime" approaches, driven by his relationship with Prison Fellowship, an evangelical Christian organization that believes in giving second chances to people who've been incarcerated.

Meanwhile, from the halls of Congress to statehouses across the country, people are reading Michelle Alexander's book. On a recent afternoon, I drove to the office of U.S. Congressman Bobby Rush, sitting for an hour with this stalwart of the Congressional Black Caucus whose experience on the issue of black men in America spans from a stint in the Black Panther party to Christian pulpits to losing his own son to gun violence. Rush recently had a spat with a fellow Illinoisan, Republican Sen. Mark Kirk, who made headlines recommending that Chicago spend $30 million more to lock up young gang members. "I sent him a copy of *The New Jim Crow*," Rush told me. "He promised me that he would read it."

If Michelle Alexander is worried about black men's criminal records, John Hope Bryant is concerned with their wallets. "I believe that 99 percent of black leaders are digging in the wrong hole," Bryant told me. "If you're poor, your health care's going to suck, your housing is going to suck, your infrastructure is going to suck if you're poor, everything sucks."

Bryant speaks like Martin Luther King on an auctioneer's stand—a frenetic ball of energy and ideas, seamlessly mixing civil rights maxims with financial advice at 100 miles an hour. He started his first business in Compton, California, at the age of 10, when the corner store in his neighborhood stopped selling the type of candy kids wanted. He opened up his own store in his mother's living room, and in three months was so successful that, in his words, "I put the corner store out of business." 45

Since then, Bryant has been convinced that the way out for black men is through a burgeoning bank account, not a social service program.

"The whole world pivots on economic issues. If you don't solve that, you can't solve anything else," Bryant says. "But if you do solve that, you have a chance at solving everything else."

Bryant has put his money—and substantial energy—where his mouth is. He runs the largest network of financial literacy centers in the country—HOPE Financial Dignity Centers—which help low-income Americans access credit for small businesses, manage their budgets, open bank accounts, and purchase homes.

Like Michelle Alexander and others, Bryant is concerned with the mass incarceration of young black men but from a slightly different angle. "There's a very good chance that we're actually locking up the only potential we've got to revitalize inner-city neighborhoods in America," Bryant told me. "Drug dealers, gang organizers—they're all natural entrepreneurs. They get up early, they work late, they hustle—but they have misplaced values and terrible role models."

Bryant created the HOPE Business in a Box program to help troubled youth start, fund, and operate small businesses. He also thinks that black businessmen should help young black boys ditch the "rappers and ball players" that they currently hold up as role models, and look in a different direction for examples of success. "These young men are the best chance we have to create jobs and GDP in our neighborhoods," Bryant says, "if we can just get them back on the right track."

50   Bryant's effort is just one of a growing number of innovative private and public programs that are making real inroads on this issue. Many of these initiatives are taking place under the umbrella of George Soros's Open Society Foundations, which has created a Campaign for Black Male Achievement and a Leadership and Sustainability Institute to knit together previously disparate programs for black men and boys, and help the field outlast funding from any one source. The effort is led by Shawn Dove, a burly man who speaks with a thick New York accent that has hints of all five boroughs at once. In fact, he's lived in all of them, but he cut his teeth mostly at 80th Street and Amsterdam Avenue.

It was on that corner that Dove sold loose joints as a teenager, teetering between a strict Jamaican household, where his single mother ruled with an iron fist, and the warm glow of New York evenings and the allure that hustling brings.

One day some friends invited Shawn to a basketball game on the Upper West Side, and he met a guy named John Simon, who ran a youth program called DOME (Developing Opportunities for Meaningful Education). Simon told Shawn that he had the potential for greatness if he would only focus. "I took him up on his offer," Shawn told me.

From there it was a fast track to Wesleyan University, a stint in the garment industry, and a career as a shining star among nonprofit executives in New York. But several years ago, Shawn received a call that would change his life.

It was from the Open Society Institute—now Open Society Foundations. They were looking for someone to start a project on low-income black men, and wondered if Shawn would be interested in the job. Shawn said yes, and six years later he has helped create an entire field of "black male achievement," an ecosystem of organizations, programs, and leaders with one straightforward if daunting goal: give low-income African-American men and boys an opportunity to succeed, a pathway to the American dream.

Under this umbrella is a Black Male Achievement Fellows Program,   55 which supports social entrepreneurs in urban communities, in partnership with the Echoing Green Foundation. Then there is "BMe," a collection of thousands of video testimonials that allow black men to tell their story in their own voices. Dove's institute has also partnered with Mayor Michael Bloomberg in New York on the Young Men's Initiative, a citywide effort to redirect black and Latino boys bound for prison to another path. Linda Gibbs, the deputy mayor of health and human services of New York, told me that the Young Men's Initiative is about building a "continuum of services," including job training, mentoring, and male-friendly health care to give troubled young men the best chance to succeed. In less than two years of running the program, Gibbs says they've seen a "dramatic reduction in the number of young men who are serving time," as well as a reduction in re-arrests. (The program has sparked a similar effort in other cities called Cities United—in which Mayor Mitch Landrieu of New Orleans, Mayor Michael Nutter of Philadelphia, Casey Family Programs, and the National League of Cities are leading participants.)

Dove has also convened other major funders—including William Bell of Casey and Robert Ross at the California Endowment—into a new Black Male Achievement Funders coalition, each with a different approach to a previously intractable problem. Ross, the California Endowment's president and a pediatrician from the South Bronx who took a three-month sabbatical to study the issue of young black men in America, focuses on behavioral health and education. The California Endowment is funding programs to close the achievement gap in third-grade reading scores and develop alternative approaches to suspension when dealing with troubled boys. "Overly harsh discipline and suspension marginalizes, stigmatizes, and criminalizes these boys," Ross told me. "When an African-American male in eighth grade has defiant behavior in the classroom, it's like seeing a burn on their body; we need to treat their behavior as evidence of a problem to be solved rather than a kid to lock up."

There's powerful work happening outside of Dove's network as well. For example, Michael Curtin, CEO of D.C. Central Kitchen, believes the food industry can help to empower black men and women. Since 1989, the kitchen has served over 25 million meals to low-income people in the D.C. area—but don't call it a food bank. Instead, Curtin, a former restaurateur, runs a rigorous culinary job-training program, using the process of meal preparation to help formerly homeless, addicted, and incarcerated men and women learn culinary skills and then find employment in the hospitality industry.

I visited D.C. Central Kitchen recently and saw lines of men and women who were previously on the streets chopping vegetables, barking orders, and managing a full-scale industrial operation. Curtin told me at the time, "When I look back on my personal experience, I recognized that I was incredibly fortunate—I had a phenomenal family, I grew up in safe communities, and went to good schools. I made reckless decisions, but always had someone there to put me back on track. Many of the men and women who come to us grew up in very different circumstances—when they messed up, they didn't have someone to help get them back on track. What we're trying to do at D.C. Central Kitchen is provide people with that opportunity."

The fight for black men is being waged through policy and programs, as the work of Shawn Dove and Michelle Alexander shows. But there's also a concurrent fight going on for their culture and soul—and in that battle, Ta-Nehisi Coates is at the forefront.

60   Coates, a senior editor at *The Atlantic*, is a reluctant spokesman. He has shut down his Twitter account more than once. After penning several landmark columns for the *New York Times*, he declined the Times' offer of a permanent weekly slot. And he does not write solely, or even primarily, about race. His recent topics of interest range from the conflict in Syria to Kurt Vonnegut. He speaks fluent French, and analyzes the hit show *Mad Men* with gusto.

But try as he might, Coates cannot escape the mantle of leading cultural envoy. He writes in a way that's inherently viral, moving fast from black hands to white and then around the world. What Henry Louis Gates says about race painstakingly, like an intricate symphony, and Cornel West declares elliptically, like a Pentecostal preacher or alto saxophonist, Coates offers straight up, with just a splash of hip-hop as a chaser.

Consider his *New York Times* essay "The Good, Racist People," which summed up in nine paragraphs what black men have been trying to get off their chests for the last 30 years. Through personal stories, he cast racism in America as "invisible violence," perpetrated by well-meaning folks all around. Or his landmark piece for *The Atlantic*, "Fear of a Black President," about what he calls the "false promise and double standard of integration" in the era of President Obama.

Coates is at the fulcrum of a resurgent cultural conversation about black men, one that is advancing in a number of sectors. There is the painter Kehinde Wiley, who mixes classical techniques with contemporary subjects to create stunning portraits of blacks in America. There are rappers like Lupe Fiasco and Kendrick Lamar, who are using their lyrics to put new spins on old truths. In sports, Miami Heat great Dwyane Wade has teamed up with a cast of unlikely characters—including Grammy Award–winning artist Lecrae and conservative funder Foster Friess—to launch the "This Is Fatherhood" challenge, which encourages young people around the country, and particularly black men, to tell stories of what fatherhood means to them. In film, the talent agent Tamara Houston has launched a new organization, ICON MANN, to create a space for Hollywood's leading black male actors to learn from one another and project their values to the world.

But Coates is in many ways this movement's biographer. In an interview, he told me that the goal of his writing is not to "fix" race relations in America. "I have folks who write me and want me to help out with their racist uncle; I don't want any part of that," he said with light-hearted sarcasm. But when pushed, he admitted that he does see himself as "an agent in pursuit of the truth of this country, of which I'm a citizen, in which I was raised, which I love." "I want to understand it," he continued. "I want to explore it, and make that exploration as honest as I can."

I asked Coates about the best way to help black men who are struggling, 65 and he didn't point to a particular program. Instead, he said, "If there's one thing that's missing in our country, it's an acknowledgment of the broad humanity of black folks. Racism—and anti-black racism in particular—is the belief that there's something wrong with black people and I mean something in our bones." He continued, "In our own community, we've internalized this. We wonder if we lack moral courage."

"I want the country to understand that there's nothing wrong with us," Coates says, with urgency in his voice. "Things have happened in this country, but there's nothing wrong with us. My job is to help close the gap between what they see in us and who we actually are."

"Who we actually are." It took Joe Jones about two decades to figure that out. That's how long he was strung out—after his dad pulled off in the Thunderbird, his mom went away to work, and he made a series of bad decisions on Edmonson Avenue; after jail made him more of a criminal and a junkie, not less. By 1986, Joe was spending $800 to $900 a day on a mixture of heroin and crack.

There were some bright moments—the birth of his son, a job at the Social Security Administration. But in one way or another, they all were deflated, pricked by the same needle that he regularly thrust into his arm.

Finally, facing a five-year prison sentence for drug possession, Joe argued and cajoled his way into an in-patient treatment program instead. He told me: "There was a six-month wait for the program, but I knew I needed to get in now. The only way you could get in was if you were crazy, so I acted as crazy as I could."

70   It worked. And from the moment he got serious treatment, things kept working for Joe. I asked him how it all came together, and he told me it was pretty simple: people listened to him, got to know him, and they liked him.

There was the staff at the treatment center who grew to know Joe Jones as not just an addict but a man, "counselors and therapists who could help me understand why I did the things that I did."

There was the dean at Baltimore City Community College, who admitted Joe despite his criminal record. He and Joe became so close that Joe ended up counseling the dean when the dean's son was struggling with his own drug addiction. Joe graduated from the college with an accounting degree, at the top of his class. There was also the young woman Joe met in the financial aid office at this community college—she liked him so much that she later became his wife.

This phenomenon of knowing, and liking, was repeated over and over in my interviews with experts on troubled youth. As Geoffrey Canada, CEO of the Harlem Children's Zone—our country's go-to model for turning around tough neighborhoods—told me, "First you have to know them, and then you have to like them, enough to respect what they're going through but not accept responses that may be inappropriate."

Canada continued, "You really do have to like them. Boys, when they're threatened and angry, they act out in ways that make them difficult to deal with. They can become threatening, sullen, disrespectful. They learn to be frightening as a defense mechanism in the environments they have to navigate."

"When you don't like them," he said, "those are reasons to get rid of them—to put them out of programs, put them out of schools, to call the police to deal with them, lock them up. But when they're kids that you actually know, and actually like, they will listen to you, and you will listen to them. And that's where change starts."

A few people got to know Joe Jones, and then like him. And his life changed. Joe entered a series of nonprofit jobs, from HIV counseling to health care, and eventually began working for the Baltimore Health Department. He persuaded the city of Baltimore to start a fatherhood program, along with programs on maternal and child health. These efforts were so successful that the mayor of Baltimore at the time, Kurt Schmoke, helped Joe spin them off into a larger, independent organization, which became the Center for Urban Families, the organization that Joe runs today.

At CFUF, Joe uses evidenced-based models to help the same types of men and women he grew up around. Funded in part by Shawn Dove's campaign, Joe's center has a successful job-training program, including partnerships with major Baltimore employers. They have a fatherhood program that gives dads practical skills to reconnect with their kids and pay back child support. Joe also wrote state legislation called "Couples Advancing Together"; it's based on a simple but powerful idea that low-income men and women who are romantically involved should develop life plans and financial goals together. Social programs focusing on job training and financial literacy have traditionally served these couples separately, instead of acknowledging that their goals and life plans are inherently intertwined. Joe's couples-services concept has the potential to dramatically change how these programs work; it passed the Maryland legislature in April and was signed into law by Gov. Martin O'Malley in May.

And a few weeks ago, something special happened. The man who perhaps most radically symbolizes both the hope of black men in America and the challenges from which they spring stopped by to see Joe Jones.

President Obama, himself a product of a single-parent household, visited the Center for Urban Families to say hello to Joe and the men he serves. Obama met with employers, people being trained for jobs, and dads getting back on track. His remarks were private, candid, and—based on accounts from those in attendance—had quite an impact on a bunch of guys from West Baltimore who were struggling to make it by.

Later that same weekend, Obama traveled to Morehouse College in Atlanta to deliver a speech to the black male graduates there. He was to talk about fatherhood and responsibility, and what African-American men must do to compete in the world. But in one brief, unscripted moment at Morehouse, the two dichotomized worlds of black men—Joe's new one and his old one; the soaring heights of the presidency and the depths of the streets—briefly and powerfully collided.

80   I had been a small part of the planning process for the speech. Obama's relationship with his father—years of absence and brief flickers of presence—is one of the defining aspects of his life. While I grew up with a strong and supportive stepfather, my own biological father had a beautiful, tragic, and deeply complicated story—a black man who received a Ph.D. from Cornell University, and ended his life in a federal penitentiary in North Carolina. Out of this common set of experiences, I worked for years with the president on his fatherhood initiative, an effort to help absent fathers around the country get back on the right track.

I had the text in front of me as Obama was delivering the speech. So it came as a surprise when, as the president neared his close, something pulled him away from the prepared remarks. He was supposed to be moving to a final story about one of the graduates, but instead started talking about men who had been left behind. I have to imagine he was picturing men like those he saw at the Center for Urban Families, men like those he had known his whole life. Men like Joe.

"Whatever success I have achieved," the president said, "whatever positions of leadership I have held have depended less on Ivy League degrees or SAT scores or GPAs, and have instead been due to that sense of connection and empathy—the special obligation I felt, as a black man like you, to help those who need it most, people who didn't have the opportunities that I had."

He continued, "Because there but for the grace of God go I. I might have been in their shoes. I might have been in prison"—a jarring thing to hear from the president of the United States. "I might have been unemployed. I might not have been able to support a family. And that motivates me."

Obama's voice faded off into a trail of emotion and applause, and he returned to the text. But the point was made.

We have walked a winding road with black men in this country, with 85
no small amount of pain and tears along the way. But all Americans
have walked that road together. Our connection to each other is, as James
Baldwin once said of the relationship between blacks and whites, "far
deeper and more passionate than any of us like to think." And it's that
connection, that empathy, that "there but for the grace of God go I" mentality, that must motivate our society's efforts on behalf of low-income
black men. Because our history, our present circumstance, and our humanity demand it. Because there are boys walking the streets of this country
with the brightest of futures—the next Shawn Dove, the next Joe Jones,
the next Barack Obama—if only they were given a shot.

Analyze

1. DuBois summarizes Joe Jones's life: "It was a jumble of inputs—bad
   parenting and bad policy, misguided culture and tragic history—
   resulting in one clear output: a woefully lost kid." Does this combination of scientific language ("inputs" and "outputs") and heartfelt
   compassion ("woefully lost kid") work? What does it reveal about the
   challenges of talking about the policies and people of poverty?
2. Why does DuBois claim that understanding the history of black
   men in the U.S. is critical for understanding what he calls the current
   "crisis"? For example, what is "peonage," and what does it teach us
   about the current situation of black men?
3. What factors contribute to DuBois's ethos (character and credibility)
   in this essay? Identify specific places in the text where we learn about
   him personally—his status, history, connections, attitudes, etc. How does
   that information lead us to trust and/or see bias in his argument?

Explore

1. In discussing the post-Civil Rights era struggles of some black men,
   DuBois claims that the reasons for this don't fit neatly into the standard litany of causes: "The reasons are as complicated as the difficult
   history, and simple debates about government spending versus personal responsibility are woefully insufficient." Has the public debate

about poverty become oversimplified? If so, what damage is done? Who benefits from oversimplification?

2. Choose one of the people or programs DuBois mentions but does not explore in depth. Write a researched profile similar to the ones on Alexander or Bryant's HOPE Financial Dignity Center. Write as if DuBois will include this as an additional case study in his essay. Model your writing style after DuBois—sentence length and arrangement, language level, tone, etc.

3. DuBois tells us that "the fight for black men is being waged through policy and programs." Research a policy, program, or person not mentioned here whose work and vision might help address DuBois's concerns. This might not be specifically or exclusively for black men but would likely help address the underlying problems that DuBois addresses. Or, think like a social entrepreneur, as Bryant does, and propose an antipoverty program or policy (local, national, or global). Imagine how DuBois would write your profile in the future.

NPR
"'Life, Death and Politics': Treating Chicago's Uninsured"

Reaching audiences through radio, podcasts, and its website, *NPR* hosts a variety of programs that cover news stories and cultural commentaries on issues of national conversation. In this piece, *NPR* reports on and provides a sample of the work of Dr. David Ansell, a Chicago-based physician who writes about tackling disparities in access to healthcare. The book excerpt that follows, from his memoir *County: Life, Death and Politics at Chicago's Public Hospital*, explores this unequal access to healthcare.

What is the public's responsibility to ensure equal access to healthcare for people who are poor?

The first time Dr. David Ansell went into the men's room at Cook County Hospital in Chicago, he immediately ran out. "It was so bad, I couldn't use it," he says. "I ran across the street and had to use the bathroom there. It was quite an introduction to my first day at County."

Ansell is now the vice president for clinical affairs and chief medical officer at Rush University Medical Center. But he began his medical career in 1978 at County, Chicago's public hospital, where he worked as an attending physician for almost two decades. His social history of the hospital, *County: Life, Death and Politics at Chicago's Public Hospital*, details his own time on the wards—and examines health care in America from the perspective of the uninsured.

Working at County, Ansell says, made him realize just how much the current payment system drives health care inequalities. "There's a misunderstanding that if you just go to the [emergency room], that's health care," he says. "It's not.... And I don't think the public or politicians really understand that. I think the last health reform attempt which is being bandied about—we don't know what's going to happen—is likely to fall short with regards to equity."

Doctors within Borders

Cook County Hospital, where Ansell worked, was a public hospital, a place that treated people with nowhere else to go. Physicians and residents who worked at County, meanwhile, were entering an environment with underfunding, mismanagement, high patient demand, safety concerns and antiquated equipment.

"I went into medicine because I wanted to help people, and when I went to medical school, I found it very disillusioning," Ansell says. "County was a place that many of us went because we believed that disease had social etiologies—the idea that disease just emanated from the individual and wasn't somehow constrained or influenced by societal factors. Going to a place like Cook County Hospital was a place where we could live those beliefs out."

Health care at County was very different from care at private or university hospitals. When Ansell first started treating patients, County had no air conditioning, poor sanitation and limited patient privacy. "The beds were lined up one after another, separated by curtains, but there was really no privacy," he says. "Patients would roll in and they'd be lined up around the walls of this one room, and the middle was lined with stretchers and wheelchairs. You were forced to take histories and examine patients under these conditions."

5   In 2002, a new hospital called the John H. Stroger Jr. Hospital opened in Chicago, replacing Cook County. The facility provides more dignified conditions for patients. But the new facility, Ansell says, cannot compensate for social inequalities and limited access to preventive health care.

"Just yesterday I had a conversation with a physician [who] says there's a many-months wait to see the eye doctor," he says. "There are 4,000 patients waiting to get a colonoscopy. This is not a screening colonoscopy—they've got blood in their stool. . . . The new hospital and the doctors and the nurses and the clinics are spectacular, [but] if you look at the whole system and you look at the outcomes we're getting . . . people are going blind waiting to see the eye doctor, in a country where it doesn't have to be."

Health Inequalities

On the South Side of Chicago, the life expectancy of an African-American male is eight years lower than that of a Caucasian man, Ansell explains.

"When you look at the reasons for it, at least half of this is [because of] heart disease and cancer and things that could be treated," he says. "One of the problems with our current system is segregating people by insurance status, which ends up limiting the options of care—especially when you get down to the specialty care that people need."

During his 17 years at Cook County, few if any of Ansell's patients could get their hips replaced—or other medically necessary but not trauma-related treatments.

10   "The only fair way to do this is where people have a card that gets them in, where that card is accepted widely and broadly by everyone, and [giving people] choice," he says. "So you could go anywhere you want, you get the care you want, and choose your own doctors—and that would be some sort of universal plan—Medicare for all, single-payer. We need a system that really gives patients—poor or rich—adequate care."

August, 1978. Dog days in Chicago. The windows overlooking Ogden Avenue were open in a futile attempt to induce a breeze. A kamikaze fly buzzed my head. The air was thick as syrup. My shirt was Saran Wrap plastered to my body. A distant rumble from trucks and cars that barreled past the clinic on Ogden waltzed its way up the four floors to the cubicle where I sat. The room was no larger than a closet. A chair and an examination table wedged in. No sink. A partition, about seven feet high, separated my stall from the next one. A polyester curtain provided a flimsy barrier between the exam room and peeping eyes from the hall outside. A pile of dog-eared manila folders and blank yellow-lined progress notes that passed for patient charts were stacked on the desk in front of me.

During the three years of residency, each internal medicine resident was assigned a half-day every week in the clinic. Interns were thrown in every August, just handed a schedule and told to show up. After a month on the County wards you were deemed ready to tackle outpatient medicine. I was led to my cubicle by a hard-nosed clinic nurse. Part clinician and part traffic cop, these nurses ran the clinics. The waiting area resembled Union Station, with back-to-back, church-pew-like benches, lined end-to-end down the center of the hallway. Stuffed with patients. Their eyes followed me as I passed by.

Technically, we were supervised by an attending physician. Mine was a well-known schmoozer. From my cubicle I could look down the hall to the office where he was ensconced like a night watchman, the door ajar, his legs on the desk and a phone receiver wedged between his shoulder and his ear. A sweet arrangement. We ignored him. He ignored us. Voices carried from cubicle to cubicle. No privacy. I learned outpatient medicine by eavesdropping on the conversations that other young doctors in the stalls around me had with their patients.

In the midst of the politics, the chaos, the poor physical condition of County Hospital, the hard urban rudeness of the clerks and other staff, my clinic cubicle would become a place of refuge for me. I was home. It was my calling to be a primary care doctor. There I discovered my patients and how their lives and illnesses were intertwined. It is where I learned to be a doctor over the next three years. Mostly taught by my patients. When I told people that I worked at Cook County Hospital, their imaginations took off. They conjured up images of the emergency room; urban violence; the Saturday night "knife and gun club"; grit and despair; track-marked heroin addicts who shivered and vomited in withdrawal; toothless Skid Row winos who slept off weekend benders. Urban trauma, alcoholism and heroin punctuated the story of Cook County Hospital, but there was much more to the place.

Fantus Clinic was a Soviet-style yellow-brick and cement ambulatory 15 office building appended to the west side of the main hospital by a corridor. Grey city pigeons lined up side by side on the concrete ledges outside the Fantus casement windows that faced Harrison Street as if mimicking the long lines of people inside the building. Across the street was a hamburger joint and Login's Medical Bookstore, where generations of doctors and students bought stethoscopes and medical textbooks. George, a grizzled, homeless schizophrenic, dressed Eskimo-like in layers of clothes and winter coats (even in summer), staked his claim to the Fantus Harrison Street entrance sometime in the late 1970s. All day he stood outside. At night he slept in the hospital. A de-facto doorman, he muttered and gesticulated at his internal tormentors. There was always a gaggle of assorted city people congregated near him puffing cigarettes under clouds of blue smoke. The Harrison Street bus rumbled to a stop in front of the Fantus entrance in twenty-minute cycles and let out load after load of passengers, a tide of humanity who surged past George into the Fantus lobby.

The lobby was clogged with patients. Standing. Limping. Shuffling. Sitting. On crutches. Rolling in wooden wheelchairs. Old. Young. Frail. Pregnant. In every nook and corner, they sprawled on benches. Jammed the elevators. They came to County to get outpatient care denied or unavailable elsewhere. Four-hundred-thousand each year. This was the County that did not make the evening news or the TV shows. Regular people who just needed to see a doctor and had nowhere else to go. They waited hours, endured rude clerks and inexperienced doctors like me. Lines ringed the clinic. They snaked down the hallways and around the corners. Lines for registration, for appointments, and even longer lines for the pharmacy. The patients armed themselves with bags filled with food. They were here for the long haul. Everyone knew you had to wait at County.

Most clinics had no set appointment times. The morning patients were told to come at 8:00 a.m. and the afternoon patients at 1:00 p.m. Once they showed up, it was first come first served. The oral surgery clinic had a perverse policy. They would treat only fifty patients daily. No appointments. Fantus' doors opened at 7:00 a.m. Patients with toothaches, loose teeth, oral tumors and mouth abscesses lined up in painful silence during the dark hours of the early morning. When the doors to Fantus were opened, it was like the starting gate at Arlington race track. They're off! The crowd scrambled through the open Fantus gates. Patients, some in wheelchairs, others with canes and crutches, raced to get to the Oral Surgery clinic to win one of the fifty prized slots that guaranteed a dentist would see them. This system had persisted through the years despite its inhumanity. Those who were too slow, too feeble, or too late to get one of those numbers would often leave, resigned to suffer and try again another day.

Why did County patients tolerate these waits and abusive conditions? Our patients declared that they came because County had "the best doctors." This was not true. There is no way we were the best. We were young, uninitiated, and worse, unsupervised. But many of our patients had been turned away from other institutions or had family or friends with the same experience. Maybe it was cognitive dissonance. Were their tributes to our medical prowess born of our lifesaving deeds or had they been conjured out of the cold fact that we were among the only doctors in the city who would see them without judgment? That it was worth the wait because County doctors were the best? Or maybe it was the only way they could justify to themselves the humiliation and abuse they endured. I felt unprepared to live up to my patients' expectations of me.

My first patient experience in clinic was inauspicious. There was no chart. Just a blank piece of yellow-lined paper. I called the patient into my cubicle and he sat in the chair, arms crossed, face gripped in an angry frown. A skinny, thin-haired middle-aged white guy, with bugged eyes. "I just need my phenobarbital, nothing more," he said. Epilepsy medication. He had been waiting for hours. The outpatients at Fantus had to change doctors every three years as a new batch of residents matriculated and the graduating ones departed. The luck of the draw. He scowled at me as if I was the short straw.

Maybe we would not have had the altercation had the chart been there. 20 But it was missing. More often than not the patient charts never appeared. Maybe if the medication he was demanding had not been phenobarbital, a barbiturate and a controlled substance, I would not have challenged him. But with no chart, and no playbook, I was flustered. I felt the tension escalate in the tiny space as the blood rose to my face. He just wanted his script and nothing more. This was my first outpatient experience. I had never written a prescription before and this guy wanted me to take him at his word. For a barbiturate. "Now wait one minute, mister. Not so fast," I thought. I questioned him to be sure that he truly had the disease he claimed. "How do I know you have epilepsy?" I asked.

Purple splotches appeared on his neck and cheeks and rose to his ears with the challenge. His pupils narrowed. I had done it now. He stood up, now fully red-faced, fists clenched and yelled. His voice rebounded across the clinic. "Why would I make up epilepsy?" he screamed. "Give me my phenobarbital." I let loose in return. I might be young and inexperienced but I was not a pushover. I was nose to nose with my first patient—not what I had imagined when I opted for a career in primary care.

My mind raced as I considered my options. Phenobarbital was a controlled substance. What if he was a drug user? I gazed at the pile of charts in front of me. It was hot. The air was muggy. I had patients waiting for me in the hospital when I was done with clinic. Why would anyone fake epilepsy? He had a point. I had no frame of reference. I could not afford to get bogged down. I took a deep breath. "What the fuck?" I mused. I took his word, wrote out a prescription for three months of a medication I had only read about in a pharmacology book. He grabbed the script out of my hand, as soon as I wrote it, eyebrows furrowed.

I was at a crossroads. Ready or not, here I was, "Presenting Dr. Ansell." A "real" doctor. And while I felt like a poseur, a fraud, I decided that despite my insecurity and inexperience, I needed to act as if I knew what the hell I was doing.

One month into my internship, on the West Side of Chicago, in a steamy corner of the fourth floor of Fantus clinic, at the County Hospital. An epiphany. I suppressed a wave of panic and shoved my doubts aside. Oh. I got it. I was a "real" doctor now. The patients expected no less.

25   Somehow, that experience freed me up to dive in to outpatient medicine. My patients' lives were a window into a slice of American life I had never known—sharecroppers, wooden shacks on dusty backroads, backbreaking cotton picking for pennies a pound. Towns whose names littered civil rights history—Philadelphia, McComb, Indianola, Yahoo City, Little Rock, Montgomery, Birmingham. Life under Jim Crow. "Yes, suh. No, suh." The humiliation of survival in places where being black meant no chance for justice. The Illinois Central ride to Chicago. The promise of jobs. The disappointment of segregation and the urban violence that greeted them.

I learned about the lives of my patients in Chicago every week in that clinic. Hyper-segregated neighborhoods. Unsafe streets. Unemployment or backbreaking jobs in factories and foundries. Women followed when they walked around Loop clothing stores. My black male patients had all been stopped by the police for traffic violations—"Driving while black." They taught me the routine. Something I had never experienced myself. Flashing red lights. A floodlight blasts through the back window illuminating the interior of the car. Every black parent taught his or her children how to respond to a police stop. White kids were taught to trust the police. Black kids were taught to be cautious around the police. There was a routine that black men had learned to follow when stopped by the police. Open the window. Put your hands up. Easy does it. On top of the steering wheel where they could be seen as the cop approached the car. Sit still. The police flashlight aimed at the driver's side and then throughout the interior of the car. Look straight ahead. Don't move your hands unless the cop orders you to. No quick moves. Say "Yes, sir and no sir." Do not argue.

This was just part of the reality of black life in Chicago. The hand of institutional racism was invisible to most white people, including my friends, who tended to avoid institutions or neighborhoods that catered to black people out of fear for their own safety or discomfort. My weekly session with my patients in the General Medicine Clinic heightened my sensitivity to the issues of race in America. In 1906, W. E. B. DuBois said, "The problem of the twentieth century is the problem of the color line." I was a middle-class white man from a small city in upstate New York. I had never been in a position to understand the meaning of these words until I was immersed in the lives of my patients that revealed their truth so powerfully and so tragically.

It did not take long for me to peel back the doctor-patient relationship more and discover other difficulties my patients faced. One of my patients was an elderly black woman, stoic and quiet, her hardscrabble life etched into the deep creases that traversed her face in such a way that her skin, had it been cloth, would have taken days to iron out. She sat quietly, in a button-down cotton dress, threadbare and almost colorless from many washings. Under it, her breasts sagged. Her steel wool wiry hair was iron gray and held in place with a bandana. She arrived in my office for a routine visit. Her blood pressure was through the roof. I leafed through the chart and noted it had been controlled in the past. I began to dig to see if I could identify a cause.

"How do you feel?" I probed.
"All right," she mumbled with her Arkansas accent.
"Are you having any chest pain or problems breathing?" 30
"No suh."
I tried another line of questioning before moving on. "Have you had any recent stress in your life?"
Jackpot. Her eyes welled. Her voice remained emotionless.
"My gran-chillin, got kilt. On my fron poich," she said.

35   Two teenage boys. Out of school. On their way to see her. Chased by gang members. They sprinted to her house. Bounded up the porch stairs. Frantic, the gang close behind, guns ablaze. Bullets ricocheted. Knock, knock, knock, they banged on the door. "Mama, mama, mama," they called for their grandma. She heard the shots and the banging, and thought the gang was trying to break in. She cowered in panic on the other side of the door, inches from her grandchildren.

"Ah was a-scared to open it. Ah din know it were them. Ah din know it were them," she repeated.

When she opened the door after the shooting stopped, she discovered the two young boys. Dead. Full of bullets, their blood joined in a pool on the porch. She wailed. "Jesus, Jesus, Jesus." Her blood pressure shot up. And remained high two weeks later.

If I had not asked, she would not have told me. I might have just adjusted her medicine and had her return in three months. I did not learn how to treat this in medical school. There was no medicine for grief, for the inevitability of urban violence. I felt powerless. I mumbled my sympathy and asked her to return in a month to recheck her blood pressure.

I heard similar stories from my other patients. The violent deaths of family members and friends, drugs and imprisonment. Children in gangs. Just about every man had a scar from a knife or bullet wound. Almost every woman had lost a close family member to violence. The names of lost loves and relatives were tattooed onto the arms and in the memories of my patients. Many years later one of my patients lost her high-school-aged son in a drive-by shooting, a block away from home. It happened on a summer night in Chicago when thirty-one children were shot and eight died. He was killed when he pushed a girl out of the way of the bullets. My patient, the mother of the dead boy, climbed into bed with her mother, also my patient, and they held each other and cried together. Her two surviving children struggled at school. She developed diabetes and hypertension and some heart abnormalities. The grandmother's health deteriorated as well. How can these experiences not affect health and accelerate death in our patients? Each story left me, mouth agape, in shock and dismay. My condolences rang hollow.

Many years later, colleagues of mine conducted door-to-door health surveys in Chicago's poorest neighborhoods. More than a third of those surveyed had higher rates of depression, asthma, hypertension and smoking than those in white communities. Racism, poverty and violence took their toll. As an observer to the lives of my patients I could attest to the fact that poverty was as exhausting as it was deadly. I saw the damage it caused in the faces and bodies of my patients. These were painful lessons for me to learn as a twenty-six-year-old. But I could not imagine being anywhere else.

Sometimes, I got too close to my patients. Mary S. had severe rheumatoid arthritis and lung disease. She had spent her life cleaning white people's houses and raising their children. She moved to Chicago from Mississippi in the 1940s to find work. Now in her sixties, she had to quit work because of her advancing lung disease. She dragged a canister of oxygen with her to my office. In between gasps, she told me she wanted to get better and help raise my newborn son. She expressed no bitterness about her illness or about my inability to cure her. During her last hospitalization, she made one request. She lay in the hospital bed, her chest heaving to get air. We held hands.

"Doctor Ansell?" Her eyes sparkled. "Ah want ta see yo chile. Please, can ah see yo chile?" We hatched a plan. On the next Saturday morning, I brought my son to County Hospital for her to see. She came to the sixth floor window of the Medical A building. I stood outside and held my infant son up over my head like a gift offering to the gods. She smiled and waved at us from the sixth floor window, oxygen tubes dangling from her nose. We waved back. I cried when she died a few days later.

I learned a lot from the patients. I was discovering the tools of medicine from them. Many of my patients and I grew up together. They had seen me become a father for the first time, and they consoled me when my father died. I had seen their children grow up, having children themselves. I had helped them through family crises, tragedies, diseases, and deaths. I had no idea in those first weeks and months of General Medicine Clinic how much I would grow from these relationships. I am on a first-name basis with many of my original patients. From them I gained insight into illness and the dignity with which people can face hardship that has helped me through difficult times in my life. I have taken care of three generations of some families, and have seen the destruction that poverty, poor diet, obesity, diabetes, and hypertension can unleash on a family's tree. I learned that sometimes giving hope or an embrace is as therapeutic as a drug. I sometimes measure my life progress by thinking

40

of the people who have had an impact on my growth as a human being. My parents, my wife, my children, my friends and colleagues. I number my patients among them.

Analyze

1. In the introduction to the excerpt, we learn that a new hospital with improved facilities has been built in Cook County. Why does Ansell say that this won't fix the problem?

2. What reason does Ansell give for patients tolerating the long waits and abusive, undignified treatment they often receive? Do you agree with his explanation? Explain.

3. What does Ansell say he learned about race in America through his sessions at the General Medicine Clinic?

Explore

1. Ansell writes: "As an observer to the lives of my patients I could attest to the fact that poverty was as exhausting as it was deadly." What does Ansell's narrative reveal about the connection between poverty and health? Does poverty cause poor health or vice versa? Write a researched essay analyzing the evidence regarding this connection.

2. Ansell's experience leads him to be firm in recommending that the U.S. needs a single-payer healthcare system where everyone gets good care, whether they are rich or poor. Designers of the Affordable Care Act claim that it improves access to healthcare for the poor. Are the poor in your state being well served by the Affordable Care Act? Write a researched letter to one of your state officials explaining your thoughts on this program as it relates to the poor in your state. Use the hhs.gov/healthcare website as one resource.

3. Wavering between despair and hope, Ansell writes: "There was no medicine for grief, for the inevitability of urban violence. I felt powerless." Later, he writes: "I learned that sometimes giving hope or an embrace is as therapeutic as a drug." Despite the challenges, Ansell says that being a primary care doctor is his "calling." Some people work jobs in which they face problems like poverty that seem "inevitable" or overwhelming. Interview one of those people and write a profile exploring what keeps them going. Explain through his/her perspective why such work can be a life's calling.

Joseph Rowntree Foundation
"100 Questions about Poverty: Identifying Research Priorities for Poverty Prevention and Reduction"

Founded in the United Kingdom in 1904 to advance the understanding and improvement of various social problems, the Joseph Rowntree Foundation concentrates its current work on identifying "the root causes of poverty and injustice," supporting "resilient communities where people thrive," and responding "positively to the opportunities and challenges of an aging society." Frustrated with short-term fixes to social ills, its founder lamented in 1904 that "much of the current philanthropic effort is directed to remedying the more superficial manifestations of weakness or evil, while little thought or effort is directed to search out their underlying causes." Consonant with this view that philanthropic work should address root causes, the foundation proposes that the following questions be studied in order to aid efforts to identify and tackle the causes of poverty. See the researched essay in the appendix for an example of how one student addressed a question on this list.

How does your own vocation or field of interest intersect with some of the root causes of poverty indicated in the following list?

These 100 research questions would, if answered, help to reduce or prevent poverty.

The list includes questions across a number of important themes, including attitudes, education, family, employment, heath, wellbeing, inclusion, markets, housing, taxes, inequality and power.

The questions were identified in an exercise run by JRF and the Centre for Science and Policy at the University of Cambridge, involving 45 participants from government, non-governmental organisations, academia and research.

Attitudes Towards Poverty

1. To what extent does stigma contribute to the experience of living in poverty in the UK, and what could be done to address this?
2. How do images of people in poverty influence policy debates in different countries?

3. What are the levels of awareness and understanding of the importance and effects of poverty among public service professionals (for example, psychiatrists, judges, youth workers, civil servants, teachers, doctors)?
4. What blocks are there to challenging institutional discrimination towards people in poverty?
5. To what extent do public and political discourses (in the media, for example) shape public attitudes to people living in poverty, and to what extent is it the other way round?
6. To what extent are attitudes towards people in poverty affected by the language and stereotyping used by politicians of the day, and how does this vary geographically?
7. What values, frames and narratives are associated with greater support for tackling poverty, and why?
8. What can be learned from interventions devised to challenge negative attitudes of other kinds (for example, racism, smoking, homophobia) that could be helpful for the design of interventions aiming to tackle negative attitudes towards people in poverty?
9. What evidence is there about the existence, nature and effectiveness of interventions designed to tackle negative attitudes towards people in poverty (targeting, for example, politicians, other elites, the media and specific groups of the general public)?
10. Do certain experiences (such as schooling or voluntary work) shape people's support for poverty reduction?
11. Do more affluent groups in society feel that they are entitled to the share of income and wealth they currently have, and if so, why?

Education and Family

1. To what extent do families (including extended families) provide the first line of defence against individual poverty, and what are the limits and geographical variations of this support?
2. How can childcare be provided so that it is both affordable for parents and of high quality, with a proven positive long-term impact on child outcomes?
3. What evidence is there that youth work can have a positive impact on outcomes for young people in poverty?

4. If services for looked-after children were developed from scratch, so that their specific focus was on eliminating poverty, how would they be different, and what can be learned from other countries?

5. How, why and where have poverty rates among minority ethnic groups changed?

6. What are the most effective interventions for reducing the social gap in educational outcomes?

7. What works to radically improve the quality of underperforming schools in deprived areas?

8. What are the most effective methods of increasing involvement and support for the education of children among their parents or guardians?

9. What works in reducing the negative impact of growing up in poverty on a child's life chances?

10. Why is there a weaker link between family disadvantage and child outcomes for some children, families and communities (for example, among some minority ethnic groups)?

11. What are the key mechanisms through which poverty is translated into poorer life chances for children?

Employment

1. What explains variation in wages as a share of GDP internationally?

2. What can countries do to combat low pay without causing unemployment in sectors that cannot move abroad?

3. Why are wages still low for traditionally 'women's' work?

4. What are the most effective and viable mechanisms for shifting responsibility from state to employer for reducing poverty?

5. How effective is the Living Wage at reducing poverty?

6. How could targeting and incentivising payment of the Living Wage make it more effective at reducing household poverty?

7. Is there evidence that different models of business or ownership are more inclusive to disadvantaged groups?

8. How can people be helped to progress out of low-paid employment into better-paid jobs (considering the roles of governments, employers and employees)?

9. How can policy incentivise the creation of high-quality jobs for people at risk of poverty?

10. What is an effective skills-based employment system for poverty reduction?
11. How can a coherent and effective system of back-to-work interventions for those furthest from the labour market be created?
12. What are the longer-term changing dimensions of employment, and what impact will these have on UK poverty?
13. What does effective worker representation look like for reducing poverty?
14. Compared with unemployment, what are the longer-term effects of underemployment and short-term, low-paid employment on later wages, employment and poverty?
15. Does setting up as self-employed or in a small business help to reduce poverty?
16. Is there evidence from other countries of mainstream initiatives that have effectively reduced the number of young people (aged 18–25) not in employment or training, and that have successfully reduced poverty in this group?

Health, Well-Being and Inclusion

1. What is the nature and extent of poverty among those who do not or cannot access the safety net when they need it?
2. What are the health risks associated with poor-quality work (low paid, insecure, poorly regulated etc.) for individuals or households in poverty?
3. What are the causal connections and intersections between poverty and wider social problems (such as homelessness, substance misuse, mental and physical ill health)?
4. What initiatives or assets can help people manage the experience of remaining in poverty?
5. What is an acceptable standard of living for people who are disabled/sick in a way that makes paid employment impossible?
6. What are the factors (local, global and other) that affect the ability of people in poverty to have a healthy diet?
7. How is poverty related to being a victim or perpetrator of crime or violence, and how can such risks be mitigated?
8. What are the causal links between poverty and low subjective well-being (including isolation and loneliness)?

9. What are the positive and negative impacts of digital technologies on poverty?
10. What are the implications of changing demography for people in poverty?

Markets, Service and the Cost of Living

1. What transport measures and interventions have the greatest negative/ positive impact on poverty?
2. What is the impact of up-front charging in public services on people in poverty?
3. What interventions have been shown to improve the extent to which people living in poverty benefit from services, and why?
4. In which services could there be benefits from universalism in tackling poverty, and what are the trade-offs?
5. Does universalism build solidarity and make it easier to justify public expenditure on anti-poverty measures?
6. How can essential goods and services provided by the private and regulated sectors become affordable, accessible and inclusive to people in poverty?
7. How do environmental and social regulations or obligations affect prices for those in poverty?
8. How can consumer markets be made to work better for people in poverty?
9. How can better contracting within the delivery of publicly funded services lead to improved outcomes for people in poverty?
10. What are the most effective ways to improve the quality, affordability and choice of food on sale in disadvantaged areas?

Place and Housing

1. What is the effect of housing-related welfare changes on people and places in poverty?
2. What can be done to ensure that enough homes are provided with sufficient security of tenure and at rent levels that will address the needs of those in poverty?
3. How can local authorities and other stakeholders integrate anti-poverty work into their approaches to housing, regeneration and economic development?

4. Are there examples of localities in the UK where poverty has significantly reduced/been reversed in the last 20 years, what caused this and was it sustained?
5. What evidence is there of successful community development practice in addressing poverty in the UK?
6. What are the possible solutions to poverty in parts of the country that have been in decline for a long time (often places that were formerly industrialised that have not recovered)?
7. What are the most effective classes of intervention able to be implemented by devolved administrations?
8. How can access to opportunities be improved in isolated or disconnected areas that can reduce persistent poverty?

Tax, Benefits and Inequality

1. What would be the impacts on poverty of different models of more contributory benefit schemes?
2. How can the effect on poverty of issues of diversity, such as ethnicity, disability, age, gender, sexual orientation or religion, be better understood and addressed?
3. What relevance does inequality in the top half of the income distribution have for the reduction of poverty?
4. The claim is often made that high personal and business taxation leads to disinvestment—for example, people and businesses leaving the UK for lower tax regimes. Taking into account international experience and evidence, how robust is this claim?
5. Would different policy conclusions be reached about reducing poverty if there were a focus on individuals and lifetimes rather than households and snapshots?
6. What could be the relative contribution of income, consumption and asset taxation to a successful anti-poverty strategy?
7. What is the relative importance of security of resources to people living in poverty, and what contribution could the tax/benefit system make?
8. What is the most effective balance between supply-side and demand-side interventions in meeting additional needs and costs (for example, in the provision of childcare)?
9. If the primary objective of Universal Credit were to tackle poverty, what changes would need to be made?

10. How can the social security system become more focused on achieving beneficial long-term outcomes for individuals?
11. What would be the impact on different individuals or households of being paid benefits in a restrictive way (for example, direct payment or benefit cards)?
12. What might social mobility look like if relative poverty were eradicated without addressing inequality in the top half of the redistribution?

Policy, Power and Agency

1. What forms of institutional structures, processes and reforms enable people living in poverty to hold state and non-state actors to account?
2. Where are there effective examples of the redistribution of power within (labour or consumer) markets, and why are they effective?
3. What are the barriers to political participation (including, but not restricted to, voting) for people in poverty, and how are they best overcome?
4. What are the (political) barriers to implementing anti-poverty policies based on existing (and extensive) evidence?
5. To what extent do different ideologies within the governing institutions of the UK, Northern Ireland, Scotland and Wales shape poverty-reduction initiatives?
6. How can decision-makers and decision-making processes be made more responsive to the needs of people experiencing poverty?
7. In what ways can people experiencing poverty develop, deliver and evaluate policy and practice?
8. What is the quality of service received by people in poverty from professionals (such as teachers or GPs) and what are the effects of this?
9. Which poverty campaigns have been most successful at reducing poverty, and what can be learned from them?
10. What is the relative scope and capacity of different levels of government to affect poverty?

The Bigger Picture

1. What are the most cost-effective interventions to prevent poverty over the life course?

2. What differentiates the effects of poverty on men and women in terms of the impact on both their own quality of life and that of their families?
3. Considering how much money has been spent on poverty alleviation, why has it not had more of an effect?
4. What are the costs of poverty to the individual, society and the economy, and who benefits most from reducing those costs?
5. Who benefits from poverty, and how?
6. What evidence is there that economic growth reduces poverty overall, and under what circumstances?
7. What are the current structural economic drivers of poverty?
8. What cost-effective measures would ensure that those who escape poverty stay out of poverty?
9. What are the dynamics of how people experience poverty through their life-course—for example, moving in and out of poverty, versus brief spells, versus living in poverty for a long time—and why?
10. Who is at risk of poverty in the UK, and why?
11. What are the implications of deep and/or widespread poverty for democracy?
12. What is the role of organisations outside central governments in tackling poverty, and how do they do it?

Analyze

1. Select one question from three different categories and discuss how you would begin to answer those questions. What type of research would you do—interviews, focus groups, surveys, rhetorical analysis, statistical analysis? How would you know if you had answered the question well?
2. Select one category that interests you, and read all the questions carefully. If you could recruit any two people in the world to help you answer those questions, who would you choose and why? What knowledge and skills would they contribute?
3. Do these questions help us get to the causes of poverty or do they make assumptions about those causes? Point to places in the text that lead you to that conclusion.

Explore

1. What is the value of identifying *questions* about poverty? Should the people who brainstormed these questions have spent their time trying to *answer* just one of them instead of thinking of 100? Explain.

2. Do the questions asked here require input from people in poverty to be answered well? What value or challenges would including those voices present?

3. Write a research report in which you address one of these questions in the U.S. context.

Forging Connections

1. The readings in this chapter explore arguments about the root causes of persistent poverty. Haskins and Sawhill write that Americans are divided on whether they think poverty is generally caused by "personal effort" or "outside circumstances," but they argue that most people see some truth in perspectives on both ends of this spectrum. Choose three readings from this chapter and cite places in the text that suggest where the author appears to fall on this spectrum. Next, locate common ground among those different authors. What statement or action could they all get behind? Explain.

2. Burd-Sharps and Lewis identify four domains of structural inequality that can cause poverty or limit prosperity: health, environment, education, and wealth. Drawing from readings in this chapter, write an essay that recommends one of these four domains as the best starting point for a new national campaign to reduce poverty. For example, if you think education is the key, then your proposal might recommend an increase in interest-free government loans for higher education and a tightening of regulations on for-profit colleges.

Looking Further

1. Readings in this chapter (e.g., Alexander, DuBois, Haskins and Sawhill, Wright) and throughout this book (e.g., Bauer and Ramírez, DNLee, Ehrenreich, Iceland, Kaufmann, Marks, Martin, McMillan Cottom, Mehta, Poo, Shriver, Serwer, Solnit, Sullivan-Hackley, Webb)

argue that discrimination based on race, gender, sexuality, criminal history, and other differentiating features remains a cause of poverty, or at least a contributing factor. Others doubt the scale of this problem. Conduct library research—and interviews with relevant stakeholders, if possible—to better understand the connection between discrimination, opportunity, and prosperity in one specific demographic group. Write a research report in which you inform readers of the history and future prospects of reducing discrimination in that area. Note potential threats to progress, as well as promising policies and programs that seem likely to increase opportunity and prosperity for this group.

2. Readings in this chapter (e.g., Ansell, Sessions) and throughout this book (e.g., Garrity; Karlan and Appel; *The Economist*, "Penury Portrait"; *The Economist*, "The Rich Are Different"; Offenheiser; Rector and Sheffield; Solnit) suggest that a lack of compassion causes poverty; or, stated in the positive, they argue that compassion is a solution for poverty, or at least a precondition for change. They say that we must care deeply about the dignity and humanity of every human being for people to flourish. In their book *Compassion*, Henri Nouwen et al. write: "Compassion requires us to be weak with the weak, vulnerable with the vulnerable, and powerless with the powerless. Compassion means full immersion in the condition of being human" (4). Is it possible for institutions, such as governments or nonprofits, to be compassionate in this way? What would that look like? Discuss examples that show compassion at the level of institutions—or give examples of institutions whose actions, even in the name of good intentions, dehumanize or diminish people.

3

Consequences: Who Is Poor?

A girl tries to reach a feeding station during a famine in Sudan as a vulture watches. Kevin Carter won the 1994 Pulitzer Prize for this stark representation of the crisis in Africa. Is telling the story of poverty—through images and words—activism or neutral observation?

INTRODUCTION

As we discussed in chapter 2, it is often hard to distinguish a cause from a consequence in the dynamic cycle of poverty. For example, poverty can prohibit people from buying health insurance, which can lead them to avoid preventative care, which can lead to delayed discovery of a disease such as diabetes, which then requires expensive treatment. That expensive treatment can lead to other cutbacks, perhaps forgoing additional education that would lead to higher wages. Or, possibly seeking a loan from a payday lender whose fees could reach 400% APR, helping in the short term but causing more harm in the long term as the family falls deeper into debt. And so on. A decision to avoid expensive licensed childcare by having children stay with an acquaintance could provide a short-term solution, but if children aren't properly supervised, they have fewer safeguards against physical or sexual abuse. Thus, decisions made in the financial domain often have consequences in social and psychological domains. These unintended consequences happen at the level of institutions, as well as at the level of individuals. Governments that look for a quick fix to poverty or that try only to protect their own interests often find that they have accomplished neither, such as with the farm subsidies described in this chapter. Perhaps what is most important to consider about the consequences of poverty is that they can take many shapes—from poor health outcomes, to less education, to social isolation and exclusion, to more poverty.

In this chapter, Gabriel Thompson investigates the unseen world of people living in "extreme poverty" in the U.S., where people often rely on informal safety nets. Mary Bauer and Mónica Ramírez's essay also explores a hidden world, that of migrant farmworkers who live on the margins, often with no recourse from abusive employers. Mind the Meal

Gap provides a visual reminder of food insecurity in the U.S., a consequence of poverty. Monica Potts profiles yet another hidden type of poverty, the working poor in rural Appalachia, and the unintended consequences of seeking higher education. In his essay, Senator Bernie Sanders of Vermont claims that federal budget cuts will lead to additional deaths of poor Americans. Creative writer Sonja Livingston offers an intimate portrait of the subtle but significant consequences of not having the means to fit in, a cruel hardship for children in poverty. Laura Sullivan-Hackley narrates a case of class-based discrimination that forges her resolve to erase her accent and thereby her public identification with her home. In a chapter by novelist Sherman Alexie, the young narrator tells a painful story of not having the resources to save his best friend, an experience underscoring the pain of poverty. Crystal Gammon explains research exploring the connection between poverty, pollutants, and race in East St. Louis, a public health crisis emerging worldwide. Maria Shriver examines research outlining the distinct vulnerability of women in poverty and exhorts readers, particularly women, to unite against the policies that threaten their success. Greg J. Duncan and Katherine Magnuson present research showing that one of the areas where we get a significant long-term return on antipoverty investment is in increasing the income of poor families with children under five years old. Roger R. Blunt and Paul D. Monroe argue that American poverty hurts the quality of military recruiting, but perhaps even more destructive, they argue, the existence of poverty in the U.S. suggests to other world powers that the American way of life might not be ideal. Maura O'Connor shows how the good intention of helping American farmers through government subsidies has had the unintended consequence of generating artificially low prices in foreign markets such as Haiti, where poor farmers who can't compete get poorer.

Gabriel Thompson
"Could You Survive on $2 a Day?"

Gabriel Thompson is an author and independent journalist whose work centers on social issues such as immigration and workers' rights. The author of three books, his writing has also been published in *The Nation*, the *New York Times*, *Colorlines*, and *Huffington Post*. In this piece, published in *Mother Jones*, Thompson recounts how Americans experience hardship living on incomes far below the poverty line.

How can people who work full-time still experience "deep poverty"?

Two years ago, Harvard professor Kathryn Edin was in Baltimore interviewing public housing residents about how they got by. As a sociologist who had spent a quarter century studying poverty, she was no stranger to the trappings of life on the edge: families doubling or tripling up in apartments, relying on handouts from friends and relatives, selling blood plasma for cash. But as her fieldwork progressed, Edin began to notice a disturbing pattern. "Nobody was working and nobody was getting welfare," she says. Her research subjects were always pretty strapped, but "this was different. These people had nothing coming in."

Edin shared her observations with H. Luke Shaefer, a colleague from the University of Michigan. While the income numbers weren't literally nothing, they were pretty darn close. Families were subsisting on just a few thousand bucks a year. "We pretty much assumed that incomes this low are really, really rare," Shaefer told me. "It hadn't occurred to us to even look."

Curious, they began pulling together detailed household Census data for the past 15 years. There was reason for pessimism. Welfare reform had placed strict time limits on general assistance and America's ongoing economic woes were demonstrating just how far the jobless could fall in the absence of a strong safety net. The researchers were already aware of a rise in "deep poverty," a term used to describe households living at less than half of the federal poverty threshold, or $11,000 a year for a family of four. Since 2000, the number of people in that category has grown to more than 20 million—a whopping 60 percent increase. And the rate has grown from 4.5 percent of the population to 6.6 percent in 2011, the highest in recent memory save 2010, which was just a tad worse (6.7 percent).

But Edin and Shaefer wanted to see just how deep that poverty went. In doing so, they relied on a World Bank marker used to study the poor in developing nations: This designation, which they dubbed "extreme" poverty, makes deep poverty look like a cakewalk. It means scraping by on less than $2 per person per day, or $2,920 per year for a family of four.

In a report published earlier this year by the University of Michigan's National Poverty Center, Edin and Shaefer estimated that nearly 1 in 5 low-income American households has been living in extreme poverty; since 1996, the number of households in that category had increased by about 130 percent. Among the truly destitute were 2.8 million children. Even if you counted food stamps as cash, half of those kids were still being raised in homes whose weekly take wasn't enough to cover a trip to Applebee's. (Figure 3.1 reflects their data.)

> "'[E]xtreme' poverty, makes deep poverty look like a cakewalk."

In the researchers' eyes, it was a bombshell. But the media barely noticed. "Nobody's talking about it," Edin gripes. Even during a presidential campaign focusing on the economy, only a few local and regional news

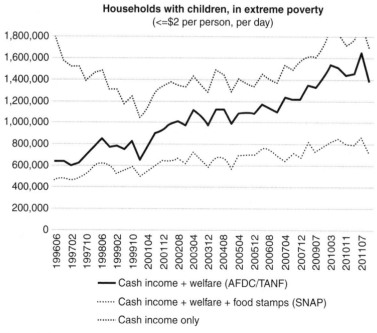

Households with children, in extreme poverty
(<=$2 per person, per day)

Legend:
— Cash income + welfare (AFDC/TANF)
······ Cash income + welfare + food stamps (SNAP)
······ Cash income only

Figure 3.1

outlets took note of their report on the plight of America's poorest families. Mitt Romney told CNN that he wasn't concerned about the "very poor," who, after all, could rely on the nation's "very ample safety net." Even President Obama was reticent to champion any constituent worse off than the middle class. As journalist Paul Tough noted in the *New York Times Magazine* this past August, the politician who cut his teeth as an organizer in inner-city Chicago hasn't made a single speech devoted to poverty as president of the United States. (Paul Ryan has.)

If you want to explore the dire new landscape of American poverty, there's perhaps no better place to visit than Fresno, a sprawling, smoggy city in California's fertile Central Valley. Heading south on Highway 99, I pass acres of grapevines and newly constructed subdivisions before reaching the city limit, where a sign welcomes me to California's Frontier City. Ahead, no doubt, is a city, but all I see is brown haze. It's as if a giant dirt clod had been dropped from space. The frontier looks bleak.

In 2005, after Hurricane Katrina briefly focused the nation's attention on the plight of the poor, the Brookings Institution published a study looking at concentrated poverty. Only one city fared worse than New Orleans: You guessed it, Fresno. Earlier this year, the US Census identified Fresno County as the nation's second-poorest large metropolitan area. Its population has nearly doubled over the past three decades, which means more competition for minimum-wage farm and service-sector jobs, and a quarter of the county's residents fall below the federal poverty threshold. With fewer than 20 percent of adults 25 and up holding bachelors degrees, there's little prospect of better-paying industries flocking here.

For those living on the margins here, daily life can be a long string of emergencies. "There's this whole roiling of folks," says Edie Jessup, a long-time local anti-poverty activist. "They are homeless, move in someplace else, lose their jobs and are evicted, maybe end up in motels."

10   If I want to see how bad things are, Jessup advises, I should check out the area southwest of downtown. She gives me directions, and after crossing some train tracks near a pristine minor-league baseball stadium, I find myself in a virtual shantytown. Amid boarded up warehouses and vacant lots, the streets begin to narrow. They are filled with structures made of pallets, plywood, and upended shopping carts. A truck pulls up filled with bottles of water, and a long line of thirsty people forms.

Amid the makeshift shelters, one section of pavement has been cleaned up, fenced off, and filled with more than 60 Tuff Sheds—prefab tool sheds brought in to provide emergency housing for Fresno's growing street population. "It's not ideal," concedes Kathryn Weakland of the Poverello House, the nonprofit that oversees the encampment and doles out 1,200 hot meals a day. "But like one of the homeless told me, it beats sleeping in a cardboard box."

The collection of sheds even has a name: "Village of Hope."

In the wee hours of the following morning, I pay a visit to Josefa, a 37-year-old single mother from Mexico who lives in a low-slung apartment complex just north of downtown. She's awake and ready by 3 a.m. when the first family knocks on her door. A Latino couple hands off two children and a sleeping baby and then disappears into the dark, heading for fields outside of town. Over the next half hour, two more farmworker families do the same. The small living room is soon filled with kids in various states of somnolence. Some nestle together on couches; others spread out on blankets on the floor. Josefa heads down the hallway to her bedroom, cradling the baby girl and walking quietly to avoid waking her 10-year-old daughter in the next room.

Four hours later, she has accomplished the morning's major chores: Five of the six kids are awake, fed, and dressed. The only holdout is a feisty toddler who is waging a mighty fuss over the prospect of wearing a t-shirt. Josefa gives the edges of the boy's shirt a sharp downward tug and smiles, winning a small but important battle. After pulling her curly black hair into a ponytail she looks at her watch. "Let's go!" she calls, waving her hands toward the door. "We're going to be late."

The group heads down a dirt alleyway, led by a tiny girl wearing a pink Dora the Explorer backpack that looks big enough to double as a pup tent. The school is three blocks away. Along the way, we pass modest but tidy single-family homes, a few shoddy apartment complexes, and two boarded-up buildings. On the surface, there's little to distinguish this neighborhood—known as Lowell—from other hardscrabble sections of Fresno. But Lowell is, in fact, the poorest tract in the city and among the poorest stretches of real estate in America. More than half of its residents, including nearly two-thirds of its children, live in poverty. One in four families earns less than $10,000 a year. 15

In a county where unemployment now hovers around 14 percent, Josefa is lucky to have work. Even better, she loves her job, and 10 minutes in her company is enough to realize she's got a gift with children. "They run up on the street and hug me," she says, beaming. "What could be better?"

What she lacks is money. Her farmworker clients are barely scraping by, so she only charges them $10 a day per child. At the moment it's late September, the heart of the grape season, so she's got a full house. But at times when there's less demand for farm work, or the weather is wet, she gets by largely on her monthly $200 allotment of food stamps. "I don't even have enough to pay for a childcare license," Josefa says. (Because of this, I've agreed to change her name for this story.)

Josefa estimates that her childcare business brings in $7,000 a year. She visits local churches for donated food and clothes, and has taken in relatives to help cover her $600 rent. Until earlier this year, Josefa and her daughter shared their small apartment with her niece's family. It was hardly ideal—some days, there were 12 people sardined in there. "Of course I need more money," Josefa tells me, pushing a stroller and holding the toddler's hand as we arrive back at her place. "But how can I charge more when no one has any more to give?"

Her niece, Guillermina Ramirez, is sitting in the apartment complex's small courtyard and overhears Josefa's last comment. "The key is to learn English," she announces. Guillermina, like Josefa, is undocumented, but she's married to a US citizen and says she will be a legal resident soon. She recently enrolled in English classes and anticipates securing "a really good job" once she's done. "That's what you need to get ahead."

20   Gary Villa and Jim Harper speak English and both are American citizens—as a member of the Northern Cheyenne Nation, Harper's lineage goes way back—but neither would say he's getting ahead. I run into the two men outside a temp agency three miles from Josefa's apartment. They've been waiting around since well before sunrise in hopes of finding something.

Villa, a stocky 23-year-old with a shaved head and goatee, tells me that he was pulling in a decent paycheck installing phone boxes for an AT&T subcontractor before he got laid off in 2008. He was evicted from his apartment and now lives with his mother—"It's kind of embarrassing," he mutters—while his girlfriend and two kids moved in with a relative. "You can't pay $800 in rent making $8 an hour."

Villa peers inside the job office, trying to discern any movement.

"At least we have family to fall back on," says Harper, 33, who keeps his long brown hair tucked beneath a red-and-blue Fresno State cap. After being let go from his job delivering radiators, he tried starting a handyman business called Jim's Everything Service. It didn't work out, so now he begins each day by calling seven temp agencies. But Fresno was slammed hard by the housing bust, and it remains a tough place for unemployed blue-collar workers. Harper, who is staying with his stepfather, says he's lucky to pull in more than $200 a month. His monthly food stamp allotment tacks on another $200, for an annual income of $4,800.

By now the sun is well above the horizon and it's shaping up to be yet another day without a paycheck. "The working class isn't the working class if there's no work, right?" says Harper, who is wearing paint-stained Dickies and a faded t-shirt. "We're getting pretty desperate out here."

"I like to joke that I'll take any job short of being a male whore," he adds.   25

True enough, when the temp office clerk announces that there's a job available, Harper leaps at it even though the gig starts at 2 a.m. and he knows he'll have to arrive at the work site in the early evening, thanks to Fresno's limited bus service. He shrugs off the six hours he'll waste "twiddling his thumbs." What matters, Harper says, is to keep knocking on doors and making the calls, because "you never know when you might get your foot in the door."

Fleeing Fresno's hostile job market might seem like the logical solution, but it's never that simple. As frequently happens with the very poor—especially in light of the restrictions put in place with welfare reform—the informal safety nets that help keep people afloat also tend to keep them rooted in place. Losing his delivery job left Harper homeless. For a few months he lived out of his car or in a room in Fresno's "motel row," notorious for drugs and prostitution. But since moving into his stepfather's house, he's been able to use food stamps in lieu of rent. Leaving town would mean running the risk of being homeless again. And given Harper's income, there's no room for error.

Neither is there a clear path out of deep poverty for Josefa. She puts in twelve-hour days six days a week, so there's not much room to increase her workload. By allowing six other families to work, she plays a small but key role in making Fresno an agriculture powerhouse, but her cut is miniscule. "That's why it's so important for my daughter to study," she says.

The last time I speak to Harper, he tells me he's landed a stint working overnight at a series of grocery stores that are overhauling their freezer compartments. "It looks like it will be a 10-day job," he says, excited. In Fresno, that counts as a big success. I ask where he hopes to find himself in five years. He pauses and takes a deep breath. "Best case scenario, as sad as it sounds, is to be no worse off than I am right now," he says. "That's about all I can hope for."

Analyze

1. Use the text to define "deep poverty" and "extreme poverty."
2. What "bombshell" findings do researchers Edin and Shaefer discover?
3. What does Thompson write is one consequence of people relying on "informal safety nets" to stay afloat?

Explore

1. Why are people using "informal safety nets" as opposed to "formal" ones? What programs constitute the "formal" safety net in the U.S.? Use government sites to explore these programs. Use a timeline-producing tool such as dipity.com or tiki-toki.com to create a multi-media production showing when these programs were started.
2. This article includes two types of evidence: research data and original narratives based on personal interviews. Thompson quotes Edin as saying that the media barely noticed their shocking research. The workers profiled in this article—Josefa, Villa, and Harper—might feel that their shocking stories are equally overlooked. What does it take to get the public's attention and concern about poverty? Are we more likely to listen to research, personal testimonies, or articles like this one that combine both?
3. This article concludes with one of the day workers, Harper, stating that his greatest hope for his well-being in five years is that he's "no worse off." What tone does this set at the conclusion? Is it effective? Is it consistent with the rest of the article? How would you conduct research to find out if that attitude is representative of Americans at different levels of society? What sources could you use to find reliable data on public attitudes? Finally, how does his attitude compare to your attitude about life five years from now? Speculate about why your attitudes are the same or different.

Mary Bauer and Mónica Ramírez
"Injustice on Our Plates: Immigrant Women in the U.S. Food Industry"

The Southern Poverty Law Center describes itself as "dedicated to fighting hate and bigotry and to seeking justice for the most vulnerable." To ensure that civil rights extend to all, the center offers legal services and support, an innovative program to support the teaching of tolerance, and researched reports on hate, immigration, LGBT rights, and other public issues. The following is one such report, and it describes how undocumented workers, on whose labor America depends, are not afforded the basic workers' and human rights that protect documented workers and American citizens. The report's authors, Mary Bauer and Mónica Ramírez, are both lawyers with the Southern Poverty Law Center. Bauer has devoted her career to legally representing farmworkers and other low-wage immigrant workers in various civil rights lawsuits. Ramírez, the daughter and granddaughter of migrant workers in the U.S., has similarly devoted her career to advocating for women farmworkers and migrant workers, fighting to prevent sexual violence and gender discrimination.

How should Americans respond to what the report calls the "shameful exploitation" of undocumented workers?

Executive Summary

> The migrants have no lobby. Only an enlightened, aroused and perhaps angered public opinion can do anything about the migrants. The people you have seen have the strength to harvest your fruit and vegetables. They do not have the strength to influence legislation.
> —Edward R. Murrow

They're the backbone of our food supply.

Their hands sliced the chicken breast we had for lunch. Their sweat brought the fresh tomato to our plates. Their backs bent to pick the lettuce in our salads.

They are America's undocumented workers. Every single day, virtually all of us rely on their labor. At least six in 10 of our country's farmworkers are undocumented immigrants—probably many more. On farms across America, they help produce billions of dollars worth of grapes, tomatoes, strawberries, melons, beans and other grocery store staples.

Despite their contribution to our economy, these immigrants live at the margins of U.S. society—subsisting on poverty wages, enduring humiliation and exploitation in the workplace, and living in constant fear that their families will be shattered if they are detected.

5   Because of their status, they remain in the shadows, their voices silent. They are unable to speak out about the indignities they suffer and the crimes committed against them. As one 59-year-old Mexican woman says: "No one sees the people in the field. We're ignored."

This report is based on extensive interviews conducted with 150 immigrant women from Mexico, Guatemala and other Latin-American countries. They live and work in Florida, California, North Carolina, New York, Iowa, Arkansas and other states. All have worked in the fields or in the factories that produce our food. They are among the 4 million undocumented women living in the U.S.

They are the linchpin of the immigrant family. And they are surely the most vulnerable of all workers in America—seen by their employers as easily exploitable and, at the end of the day, disposable.

Their stories are remarkably similar. Virtually all say they came to the United States to escape devastating poverty and to try, like waves of immigrants before them, to lay a foundation for their children's future. They tell harrowing stories of survival in the desert they crossed to get here. They tell of being cheated out of hard-earned wages by unscrupulous employers. They tell of working in dangerous conditions without adequate safety precautions. And they tell of enduring near-constant sexual harassment in the fields and factories.

The laws that protect these workers are grossly inadequate. More importantly, the workers' ability to enforce what protections they have is generally nonexistent.

10   When the debate over immigration policy once again reaches Congress—the only venue where it can be resolved—it's important to understand the motivation that drives these women across our borders, their role in our economy and our communities, and the exploitation they face.

They are economic refugees—pushed from their home countries by abject poverty, hunger and desperation. They're pulled north by the alluring images in their heads of a bountiful country overflowing with opportunity—a meritocracy where one need only work hard to have enough food to eat and to provide decent clothes and shelter. They don't come here expecting a handout.

Some find their American dream is little more than a mirage. Others, finding a modicum of success, are able to put their children on an upward path and help sustain their relatives back home. Many come to the U.S. for what they believe will be a temporary stay but find their plans to return home complicated by community ties, their desire to give their children the opportunity the U.S. offers and tighter border controls.

These women live at the bottom of a world where titans of finance send capital across borders at the speed of light and transnational corporations move factories—and jobs—around the globe like a chess match to take advantage of the lowest labor costs. It's a world where trade and foreign policies established in Washington and other faraway places can mean a job or no job to people who have no say in the matter. Though the world's economy has never before been so interwoven, it's still a world where the workers who run the factories and whose labor helps enrich those at the top are supposed to stay within the lines.

America is now at war with the immigrant hands that feed us. Communities and states across the country are enacting a patchwork of highly restrictive laws that will only drive undocumented immigrants further underground and make them even more exploitable by the businesses that employ them and the criminals who prey on them. Immigrant women face the additional danger of sexual assault and rape, crimes they often are afraid to report to police because it could lead to deportation.

Not only is this war costing taxpayers many billions, it is eroding wage and workplace protections for U.S. workers as well, especially for low-skilled workers, as businesses find they can exploit immigrant labor with virtual impunity. 15

U.S. immigration policy has not kept pace with these challenges. Border security has been greatly enhanced. But the reality is that about 11 million people are now living and working in the U.S. without documentation. Millions of them are raising U.S.-born children. Deporting all of these immigrants, according to one recent study, would leave a $2.6 trillion hole in the U.S. economy over the next decade. That does not include the billions of dollars that would be required to enforce such a policy. And it does not take into account the massive human rights violations that would inevitably occur.

Fifty years ago this Thanksgiving, CBS broadcast *Harvest of Shame*, an Edward R. Murrow documentary that chronicled the plight of migrant farmworkers. Murrow closed the program with this commentary: "The migrants have no lobby. Only an enlightened, aroused and perhaps angered public opinion can do anything about the migrants. The people you have seen have the strength to harvest your fruit and vegetables. They do not have the strength to influence legislation."

Not much has changed.

Congress must address this crisis in a comprehensive way—a way that recognizes the contributions of these immigrants to our country and our fundamental values of fairness and dignity. Our recommendations for doing so appear at the conclusion of this report.

Analyze

1. How many farmworkers in the U.S. are undocumented? What does it mean to be an "economic refugee"?
2. If these workers are treated so unfairly, why don't they speak up or do something about it?
3. What is the significance of noting that the workers' stories are "remarkably similar"?

Explore

1. What is the purpose of this research? What audiences are the authors trying to reach? What attitudes are they trying to change?
2. The authors make a bold claim: "America is now at war with the immigrant hands that feed us." What evidence do the authors provide to support this? Do your own research and write your own argument either supporting or challenging this claim with evidence.
3. Watch the CBS broadcast *Harvest of Shame* and read the full report of "Injustice on Our Plates: Immigrant Women in the U.S. Food Industry," both available online. Research conditions of migrant farmworkers in the 1960s and compare them to conditions today. What has changed, and how did it change? What type of change should still happen in Congress or elsewhere?

Feeding America
"Map the Meal Gap"

Feeding America is a nonprofit organization devoted to relieving hunger in the U.S. by coordinating and supporting a nationwide network of member food banks. In particular, Feeding America helps communities respond to their own unique food insecurity problems by collecting and organizing local data beyond just poverty statistics since many in poverty are not food insecure and many who do go hungry are not necessarily living in poverty. In the following infographic, Feeding America illustrates the general distribution of the population who is food insecure throughout the U.S. The interactive map on Feeding America's website offers more specific information for each area in the U.S.

How can those not living in poverty have less food to eat than those who are living in poverty?

Feeding America first published the Map the Meal Gap project in early 2011, with the generous support of the Howard G. Buffett Foundation and the Nielsen Company, to learn more about the face of hunger at the local level. In August, 2011, with the support of the ConAgra Foods Foundation, child food insecurity data was added to the project. The map shown on the next page reflects 2009–2012 data[1], and will be updated [online] every year with new data.

Nationwide[1] food insecurity rate

15.9 percent. Food insecure people: 48,966,000.

Income bands within food insecurity population

57 percent below SNAP threshold of 130 percent.

17 percent between 130 to 185 percent poverty.

27 percent above nutrition pgm threshold of 185 percent poverty.

Additional money required to meet food needs in 2012: $23,497,478,000.

Average cost of a meal: $2.74.

[1]USDA

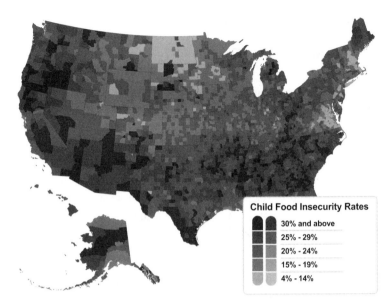

Figure 3.2

What Is Food Insecurity and What Does It Look Like in America?

Food insecurity refers to USDA's measure of lack of access, at times, to enough food for an active, healthy life for all household members and limited or uncertain availability of nutritionally adequate foods.

Food insecure households are not necessarily food insecure all the time. Food insecurity may reflect a household's need to make trade-offs between important basic needs, such as housing or medical bills, and purchasing nutritionally adequate foods.

5   Select your state and county from our interactive map [online] and start learning more about your neighbors struggling with hunger and the food banks that serve them.

Read more about the findings of Map the Meal Gap in our Executive Summary, see food insecurity by Congressional District or learn how we got this data.

Feeding America undertook the Map the Meal Gap project, with the generous support of the Howard G. Buffett Foundation and the Nielsen Company, to learn more about food insecurity at the local community level.

What Do the Income Bands Mean?

Program eligibility is determined by income. The income bands shown reflect percentages of the federally established poverty line[2], which varies based on household size. These percentages are used to set eligibility thresholds for nutrition programs.

How is food insecurity related to poverty? Although related, food insecurity and poverty are not the same. We know that 27 percent of food insecure households live above 185 percent of the poverty level (Coleman-Jensen et al., 2013). Note below, however, that 185 percent of the poverty level is only $43,568 for a family of four. For families with medical expenses or who are located in areas with a high cost-of-living, it's easy to see how quickly resources can get drained. We also know from Hunger in America 2010 that 25 percent of Feeding America network clients were found to be food insecure. This may be because they are able to access emergency food resources or participate in federal nutrition programs at times when their own resources are scarce.

What does it mean to live in poverty? Poverty rates are provided as supplemental information to the food insecurity rates. Poverty rates are determined by the number of members in a household and their annual income.

Household #	100%	130%	185%
🧍	$11,170	$14,521	$20,665
🧍🧍🧍	$19,090	$24,817	$35,317
🧍🧍🧍🧍	$23,050	$29,965	$42,643

Figure 3.3
Source: Federal Register, Vol. 78, No. 17, January 24, 2013, pp. 5182–5183.

These rates do not vary from state to state (except in AK and HI), despite significant differences in cost-of-living.

What Is the Safety Net for People Who Are Food Insecure?

Availability of government support for households varies based (in part) on the household income as it relates to the poverty level. The thresholds shown in Figure 3.4 apply to the national average; it is important to know that individual states can and have increased their Supplemental Nutritional

[2]Due to rounding, totals range from 99–101%.

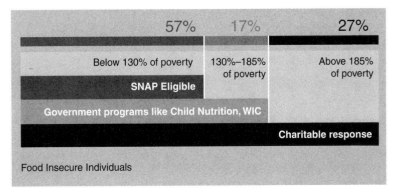

Figure 3.4

Assistance Program (SNAP, formerly the food stamp program) thresholds up to 200 percent of the poverty level. This increases the number of people who are eligible for SNAP, the cornerstone of the federal nutrition safety net.

How Do You Calculate the Dollars Needed and the Meal Costs?

Using actual food sales data, the Nielsen Company created a county-level multiplier to reflect the local cost of food. To develop the average cost of a meal, we use this multiplier to weight the national average amount spent on a meal by the food secure—$2.74.

We also use the county-level multiplier to weight the national average of additional money a food insecure person reports needing per week in order to meet his/her food needs—$15.82. To calculate the total additional money required to meet food needs in 2012, we multiply the weekly amount by the number of food insecure people in the selected geography, then by 52 weeks, and finally by 60 percent (7/12)—the average portion of the year in which a food insecure person experiences food insecurity.

Analyze

1. What is the food insecurity rate in the U.S.?
2. Visit the interactive version of this map online to answer these questions (http://feedingamerica.org/hunger-in-america/hunger-studies/map-the-meal-gap.aspx): How does your state and county's food insecurity rate compare to the national average? Find the counties in your state with the highest and lowest levels of food insecurity. Why

do you think these counties have that status? What are the trends for child food insecurity in your state from 2009 to the present?

Explore

1. This map visualizes the numbers behind food insecurity. The Feeding America website and other sources, such as the documentary *A Place at the Table*, also tell the personal stories of people experiencing food insecurity. Locate one of these stories and do a rhetorical analysis of the story and how it is presented in that context. If you review more than one story, note common or differing themes and frames.

2. Write your own story about food security in your home or in a home you have observed. Have you or persons in your study ever struggled to eat well due to financial constraints? If not, tell the story of food security, which is also important to understand. In your observation, what is the connection between food and health, happiness, and dignity within a family?

Monica Potts
"Pressing on the Upward Way"

Monica Potts is a senior writer for *The American Prospect*, a print and online magazine that explains, "We're liberal, progressive, lefty—call it what you want, we're proud of it." Commentating broadly on the issue of poverty, her writing has also appeared in newspapers such as the *New York Times*, *Connecticut Post*, and *Stamford Advocate*. In the following award-winning story, which served as the centerpiece for *American Prospect's* special issue on poverty, Potts chronicles the efforts of impoverished Americans whose hard work and piecemeal progress are often not enough for them to overcome poverty.

If someone doesn't go to college right after high school, what are the risks and rewards of enrolling later in life?

By her second semester of college, in the spring of 2008, Sue Christian was about as tired as she'd ever been in her 40 years. It wasn't that her studies kept her working hard; she was used to long hours. It wasn't that she was missing her salary; she was already good at fretting over bills. It wasn't that the daily trip from her home in Booneville, Kentucky, was more than an hour long, a drive that, when rains washed out a one-lane bridge, took her over the nauseating Hatton Holler Mountain. It was more that, listening to lecture after lecture in crowded classrooms with people half her age, Sue felt her brain was stretched as far as it would go. "I thought, 'I'm so dumb, I'm not good at college,'" she says. "Professors seemed to be more focused toward that age group fresh out of high school. So, if you're past that, it's like, 'Catch up or get out.'"

Going to college was an accident of timing. The previous spring, SourceCorp, the data-entry company where Sue worked, had closed, which had come as a shock. The company had received a five-year contract from the federal government, but a year and a half into it, the company shut down its Booneville office. "It's like these data-entry companies either work you to death or lay you off," Sue told her husband, J.C. Since the age of 15, Sue had used her only marketable skill—typing fast—to get minimum-wage jobs at data-entry companies. They were the only ones around. While her two children, Kody and Ciara, were in elementary school, she often worked the second shift to earn night pay. For most of their adult lives, the Christians have made less than $22,113 a year, the poverty line for a family of four. This makes them like a lot of families in Owsley County, where 40 percent of the population lives in poverty and 30 percent lives just above it. More families rely on food stamps than make the national median household income of $49,445.

Sue describes herself as introverted, but she is so ready to tell you about her shyness that she proves herself wrong. She is private and slow to start a conversation but also slow to stop it. She's quick to a giggly laugh, a happy look that makes her dark eyes disappear. At five feet four inches, she's shorter than her kids, and they tease her for her short arms, which tend to dart up while she talks. Her hair is black as coal next to her pale skin—she straightens it every morning into a neat bob—and it's lined with an increasing number of silver strands.

She might have worked at data entry forever had SourceCorp not laid her off. "I used to do the only thing I thought I could earn money from," she says, "but I was kind of content." Not content in a happy way but content in that she wasn't looking for any other type of work. "It's sometimes easier to stay where you're at, instead of trying to get to someplace else."

For as long as people could remember, the biggest employer in Owsley County has been the school system, and people lucky enough to get hired hold on for life. Beginning teachers start out at $28,000, which makes those jobs some of the most sought after. Senior teachers can earn as much as $55,000, which makes them rich by Owsley County standards. Losing her data-entry job got Sue to thinking about teaching. She had always enjoyed teaching Sunday school and liked working with kids. So when a friend told her about a social-services agency that could help her pay for college, she decided to apply to Eastern Kentucky University, an hour away in Richmond. She decided to major in middle-school education. What she had not taken into account, though, was that she had always been the family's steadiest—and usually biggest—wage earner. Without her money coming in, and with Kody heading to college and Ciara entering high school, the Christians were about to enter four of their toughest years.

Now Sue was stuck in science and math courses, next to students fresh out of high school, talking about meta-this and osmosis-that. She was used to setting to a task and working in a fury until it was done, but maybe going to college was a bad idea, maybe she had reached the limits of her mental ability. If a data-entry company had been hiring on, she would have taken the job. When she'd go home, she'd tell J.C., "I don't think I can do college."

Sue felt like whenever someone from Owsley County went out into the world, the world went out of its way to poke them in the eye. One professor, who spoke at an orientation seminar, encouraged the freshman class to rub out their accents. "It's all right to be from Eastern Kentucky," he told them, "but you don't need to sound like you're from here." Eastern Kentucky University was supposedly in the same region as Owsley County, but as far as Sue was concerned, that hour's drive into the rolling hills of the Bluegrass was on the other side of the country. The limestone runoff from the Appalachians enriched the Bluegrass, making it ideal for tobacco, horses, and bourbon. Even the soil, it seemed, took what it wanted from the mountains and made itself rich.

Then, in her second semester, Sue took a class called "Educational Foundations" from a professor named Roger Cleveland. He had taught in some big city, Louisville or Cincinnati—Sue could never remember—in a school for teenagers who lived in gang-ridden neighborhoods. Part of his job was to go to the kids and say, "Don't look so close at the situation you're in now. Look at where you want to be," and that resonated with Sue. He asked Sue once, "Christian, do you feel like, because you're from Eastern Kentucky, people try to put you in a box?" She said, "Well, yeah, I do." It was weird, but it was this man from the city who seemed to understand her and her people, and that was a way to win Sue over.

Cleveland gave all his students a test that identified their learning styles. For Sue the test was a revelation. It said that she absorbed material better by doing projects with her hands than by listening to lectures or reading textbooks. The learning-styles test became a talisman for Sue to ward against the danger of feeling dumb. She changed the way she studied. By the time she got her degree, in May 2011, she'd won an award for being on the dean's list. She graduated along with about 300 other middle-school education students, who would compete with one another for jobs in Eastern Kentucky. Sue hadn't found a job by graduation, but that didn't matter. "Have you ever impressed your own self with what you're capable of doing?" she says. "That's how I felt when I got my degree."

10   While most of Appalachia is poor, Southeast Kentucky, where the mountains start turning into hills, is the worst off. There was never enough coal for deep mining that would at least provide well-paying jobs. The ground, mostly black slate, is too rocky for farming, though some families grew tobacco on a few flat bottomland pastures until the government bought them out in the 1990s. Five of the poorest counties in the United States—Owsley, Clay, Lee, Knox, and Wolfe—touch here, huddled along a swath of wilderness, the Daniel Boone National Forest, that divides them from the rest of the state. Owsley County does the rest of these small, poor counties the favor of being a little bit smaller and a little bit poorer. Less than 200 square miles, slightly bigger than the city of New Orleans, it's shaped like a bowl with hills on the edges and the low, slow south fork of the Kentucky River cutting through. It has the distinction of being the poorest county in the United States with a majority-white population.

Kentucky began calling Owsley County a "pauper county" as far back as the 1890s, because it took more state tax revenue than it contributed. Since the federal government began tracking poverty rates in 1959, Owsley has ranked as one of the nation's poorest counties. By the 1960s, when much of the United States had moved into prosperity, Southern

Appalachia's shoeless children, living in mountain shacks without electricity or plumbing, seemed like relics—trapped in a sticky poverty that modernity had yet to solve. The people of Owsley County translated all the attention as criticism. They weren't descendents of pioneers. They were a problem.

Sue's was the first generation to live in Owsley County after Lyndon B. Johnson declared his War on Poverty, and this part of Kentucky was Omaha Beach. Do-gooders, ministers, and bureaucrats came and never stopped coming. Grants poured in. Programs were created. The Appalachian Regional Commission. AmeriCorps VISTA. The Community Action Program. The Christian Appalachian Project. The Children's Dental Health Initiative. Endow Kentucky. Head Start got kids into school and free lunches fed them. All these initiatives solved the problem of basic survival, but they didn't solve the problem of an increasingly depopulated region: not enough consumers to support business, old trail roads that kept big trucks out and kept the cost of goods high, companies that only opened their doors because they could pay the populace, hungry for jobs, less than they would have to pay people elsewhere. Because the government programs were the most visible, well-functioning industry in town, many locals set on them with a special brand of ire. They were helping a lot of people—more than anyone wanted to acknowledge—but they also seemed like an attack on a way of life. Sue felt the same way. "I think we've been helped so much," she says, "we're getting helped to death." Government benefits, from welfare to Social Security to the Earned Income Tax Credit, account for 53 percent of all the county's income.

For many years, the way to be successful in Owsley County was to leave—the students who could make it to college stayed away. The population, which in 2010 was 4,755, started to fall seven decades ago. There were few opportunities to keep young people in Owsley County, and the first thing that federal anti-poverty programs did was connect the poor here to opportunities elsewhere. What was good for individuals drained the community as a whole. About 40 miles in any direction there's a bigger town with a Walmart and enough jobs for Owsley County's young to go make their living.

When Sue was born in Owsley County, in 1967, most families lived like hers—up a holler, piecing together work through manual labor and growing most of the food they needed to eat. Her parents, Ruby and Puddin Thomas, had lost their first child to pneumonia before having Sue and her brother. Puddin earned money on his own, going into the logwoods with a small dozer. This sense of self-reliance bred confidence—you'll never go hungry if you grow your own food. When Sue was in first grade, Puddin broke his arm in seven places. That winter a local church brought over food and Christmas presents. Puddin's working life ended when he was 53 after part of a tree fell on his head, a near-fatal injury that kept him in recovery for more than two months, and even then he checked out of a rehabilitation center early. The injury aggravated his body, especially his arm. "If I knew it wouldn't kill me and I wouldn't go to hell," he'd grouse, "I'd cut my own arm off." He's been drawing disability and, later, Social Security ever since.

15   When Sue was 15, in 1983, she fell for a 25-year-old from the next county north, Lee County, and got married. Maybe the attentions of an older man were too tempting for a bashful teenager to resist, maybe it was because Puddin disapproved, but Sue set at that marriage in a stubborn way. She moved with her husband to a house with no indoor plumbing. He was unemployed. Although she remained in high school, she got her first data-entry job, working nights; most of her paycheck went to the electricity bill. Her husband, without a word to Sue, joined the Navy. When he was transferred to Jacksonville, Florida, she decided to finish school there, but she was used to a rural high school where kids lined up, orderly, for lunch; this new world was too aggressive, and she dropped out. Far from home, in a marriage she stuck to for spite, Sue was conquered and miserable.

Four years after getting married, Sue and her husband divorced. Soon after, Sue met J.C. when she applied for a job at his mom and stepfather's window-installation business in Jacksonville. Tall and slim, J.C.—which stands for James Christian—was six years older than Sue. He had tawny skin and tattoos up and down both arms, but he kept his black hair close-cropped and he dressed neatly for the job. When Sue saw him, she thought: "Clean-cut." J.C. had a girlfriend he fought with all the time, and one day Sue asked, "How serious are you and that girl?" and J.C. said, "Why? Do you want to go out?" In Christian family lore, this means Sue had made the first move. Five months after her divorce, Sue and J.C. married.

In 1988, they moved to a trailer outside Winston-Salem, North Carolina, where Kody was born, and later to West Virginia, to a trailer outside Charleston. When Kody was two, J.C. asked Sue why they didn't just move to Owsley County and be near her parents. J.C. could see life there, quiet, up a holler. Sue's answer was quick: "There are no jobs." J.C. lined up a job with an electrician, and they spent their last $600 getting to town.

Booneville's downtown is only one square, where three state highways meet and wrap around a courthouse. A plaque marks a spot where Daniel Boone might have camped; the town was christened on so slight an honor as passing through. Two cafes, two churches, and five empty storefronts surround the courthouse. Just off the square, there's a Dollar General, a Family Dollar, a Shopwise market, and three gas stations that serve biscuits and gravy. There are three pharmacies, one doctor, one dentist, and a pain-treatment clinic. There's the Owsley County Action Team office, an unofficial, ancillary government and social-services agency paid for by donations and government grants. Down the road sits the husk of a building with brown aluminum siding, covered with graffiti, which was a movie theater when Sue was growing up. By the theater, a Baptist mission operates a food bank out of an old motel, which also provides lodging to volunteers who come to build houses in the summer. In 2005, the drive-in movie theater just south of town closed, leaving the cinder-block projection wall standing by the road that leads toward an empty industrial park built to lure businesses that never came.

By the time Sue and J.C. moved to Booneville, his job had fallen through. The electrician who promised J.C. work said he didn't have enough calls to justify his hire. After that, J.C. held a series of jobs—bagging groceries, clerking at a hardware store, working at a factory one county over—and either quit in a huff or got fired from each. J.C. doesn't talk much about his dad, except to say that he was a mean drunk. J.C. owns that he's inherited a watered-down version of that anger. When he drank or had to take medication because he was injured, he got worse. After five years in Owsley County, he decided to become a handyman. He figured his best boss was his own self—if he got mad, he couldn't storm off and quit. It took years, though, for J.C. to get hired regularly around town. Like a lot of small places, Owsley County is suspicious of outsiders. "J.C.," folks later explained to him, "we didn't know you." That first year in Booneville, J.C. brought in $11,000, and for a six-month stretch, the family relied on food stamps. The next year, when Sue started working as a data-entry keyer, their income grew to $17,000.

In July 1993, Sue became pregnant with Ciara. The visits to Sue's doctor 20
took them past one of her favorite spots, a little rock that jutted over the highway west of town like the bow of a ship. It was quiet and removed. Sue would think that if she could just put her family up there, they would be safe. The land, no more than a quarter-acre, belonged to her cousins, who

said Sue and J.C. could have it for $4,200. They had hopped from one rent house to another in Owsley County. "I wanted to settle and be still," she says. She also wanted her children to know where home was. The couple borrowed $3,800 from the bank, and J.C. paid off the rest by helping Sue's cousins in their tobacco fields. Sue and J.C. bought their first trailer, run-down and tiny as a cracker box, for $1,000. Puddin lent them the money, a debt that J.C. settled by working on his father-in-law's farm. They gave their kids the bedrooms, one at either end. J.C. and Sue slept in the living room, pushing two blue couches they had together at night and pulling them apart again in the day. "That was pretty rough," Sue says.

Most people will tell you that two kinds of folks live in Owsley County—those who draw and those who work. There are families who receive aid and families who don't, and, because the county has only one grocery store left, everyone knows who they are. There are families who send their children to school neat and clean and fed, and those who don't. It's easy to think appearances don't matter, but country poverty has its own wardrobe, and, sometimes, seeming less poor is about clever costume design.

When nearly everyone in the county is poor, the distinction between have and have-not becomes meaningless. There are have-very-little's, but even they wouldn't always call themselves poor. Neither would the Christians. As far as Sue was concerned, "poor" was the word for giving up. It took drive to make a living in Owsley County—you had to create your own work on your own steam—and Sue had seen plenty of people run out of it before they got anywhere. "They're good kids," people will say about Kody and Ciara. "Their parents both work." Sue and J.C. performed a service for their children that was less tangible than getting the bills paid. They made sure no one in town looked down their noses at them.

Beginning in 2002, things began to improve. Sue had started inputting for SourceCorp a couple of years earlier. At first, it was from home and catch-as-catch-can. There were nights when she underestimated the amount of time it would take her to finish, and she would work until morning to meet deadlines. SourceCorp then hired Sue full time, which meant going into their office and steady pay. J.C. had managed to turn his handyman and electrician services into something that could rightly be called a business. For five years, from 2002 to 2007, they managed to finally make enough money to cover the bills and have a little extra left over for drive-in movies with the kids on Saturdays. They financed a new doublewide, which had a master bedroom and a decent-size kitchen. They set it on their little hill, and J.C. built a porch on the front. Those years they made a touch more than $30,000. That's how much the Christians needed to be comfortable.

Then in 2007, SourceCorp closed, and the Christians were down to J.C.'s bumpy income. The only other decent-paying job Sue was qualified for was to be an aide at the nursing home outside of town. "I'm very squeamish," she says, "and I thought, 'I can't do that.'" Sue decided to go to college. She'd been a bad student in middle and high school, but when Kody and Ciara had started in Owsley County schools, she'd chaperoned trips and parties and eventually become president of the Parent-Teacher-Student Organization. When she thought about where she could work, the school, with its well-paying jobs, seemed like the best bet. She was already there so often. College was just a necessity, something she could work like a job at SourceCorp, steeled with faith that, this time, she'd be a better student.

Still, it was a huge gamble. Sue didn't drive in the snow, so some days, 25 J.C. would have to take her to Richmond and sit, all day, waiting for her to get out of class. She and J.C. knew college would add to their expenses. Even with help from various programs, she would have to pay for some of her gas, lunch, and books. But what they hadn't taken into account was how much they would miss Sue's income. Sue didn't allow herself the title of breadwinner—that would have been too hard on J.C.—but in truth she was. Even in their best years, J.C. had off months—long winters when no one called him for home repairs—and Sue's paycheck had kept them going. Sue had also provided health insurance for the family through her jobs. Her work had pushed them above the poverty line and, now that her work was gone, they had dropped below it again. Like many of America's poor, the Christians had a few tantalizingly good years that set a standard of living they struggle to maintain during the bad ones. What they hadn't known, of course, when they made the decision for Sue to go to college was that the global economy was about to collapse and J.C.'s work was about to dry up.

On top of everything, Kody had quit Asbury College, a religious school near Lexington, after his freshman year and was back home. He had enrolled at the same time Sue started at Eastern Kentucky. Kody had told everyone that he was desperately ready to leave Booneville, but the extent of his rebellion was refusing to come home on weekends. He wanted to become a preacher and was planning to get a degree in theology. Then, during a cross-country meet, he blew out a knee and lost his scholarship.

When school ended, he left with a girl he was sure God wanted him to marry. The relationship turned bad after two months, and he returned home. When Kody came back, what Sue saw was her 19-year-old son looking gaunt and baggy-eyed, fresh from a place where no one had cared for him.

For a time, Kody worked with J.C. to save money and maybe go back to college. When the pastor at his Methodist church asked if Kody would be the music leader, though, he decided that God was calling him to stay in Owsley County. He spent all the money he saved on music equipment and a van. Sue was happy to have him home. "College wasn't for Kody," she'd say. He would find his way, she was sure. Still, he was having as much trouble holding a job as J.C. once had. J.C.'s mom likes to say Kody was J.C. made over, with a bit of his temper but without his dark skin. Kody had never quite fit in Owsley County—he was quiet and artistic and liked to spend his free time in church and practice the guitar. "He always was kind of nerdy," Sue says. He straightened his dark hair every morning and wore it spiked or swooped down over his eyes. His favorite shoes were a pair of Converse with a Batman design. In college, he'd made friends with other musicians, and when he was back in Booneville he started to play in Christian rock bands and sell comic fan art online.

Ciara entered high school the year Kody came back home. She was learning to drive and wanting money for gas and clothes. She was beginning to realize her parents couldn't always give money because they didn't have it to give. Ciara's friends were all high-achieving, academic-team, straight-A students, and Ciara started to shine in 4-H contests and on the occasional morning newscast she helped produce for one of her classes. Ciara liked being a star. Bubbly and outgoing, she decided a career as a news anchor would keep her at the center of attention, and she wanted to study broadcasting in college. Ciara was the opposite of what Sue had been as a teenager. Sue teased Ciara and called her their little diva, but she was also protective. Sue knew how the pretty girl in school could be the focus of the wrong kind of attention. Plus, Sue knew that looks faded. She didn't want Ciara to go into the cutthroat world of broadcast, where she would have to lose her accent and live far from her family. Still, Sue saw that Ciara's way of helping the family was to promise that she would win every scholarship she could, finish college, and have a successful career. What Kody heard when Ciara said this was "I'm not going to be like Kody."

Sue had always been what she called a dweller, someone who fretted over things. When her mind got hold of a worry, she couldn't let it go. But she says her real worries didn't start until she became a mother. She met J.C. when she was only 20, and they both liked to party. She would spend a lot of time with people who did things they shouldn't have. She'd ridden in cars with people who liked to drink or get high. Being pregnant, being responsible for someone else, made Sue deeply regret her youth. It hung over her like a penance.

She had been dragged as a child to a Pentecostal church on the few 30 occasions Ruby had decided Puddin needed some religion, but she had never been deeply religious. Then, when Kody was two, Sue watched the *700 Club* on TV and heard a born-again Christian testify that being saved had lifted all his burdens, and Sue thought, "I would like that, too." She knelt on the crooked linoleum floor Kody had learned to toddle on and recited the sinner's prayer. Sue's religion was personal, guided by her own interpretation of her relationship with God. She didn't understand denominations—she felt like people were always trying to put God in a box—and for many years she and the kids attended a small nondenominational church far out in the county. It was Kody who inspired them to go to the United Methodist Church in town. The pastor was his track coach, and the church had a popular youth-group service on Wednesday nights that he wanted to join.

Becoming a Christian didn't relieve Sue's problems like she thought it would. She was prone to panic attacks, frozen by overwhelming dread. During the attacks, she told Kody, she felt like she was alone in the world, screaming, without anyone to hear her. Other times, it was like she was pressed into a dark, tight space, held down by a heavy weight. The attacks usually hit when she was by herself, and she'd call J.C., who would stop what he was doing and talk to her until she was calm again.

The attacks became less frequent as she got older, but not because her problems left her. Turning them over still kept her up at night, and most of the time her problems were her bills. Sue liked to say that she didn't want fancy things. Her family had what they needed, and that's all she cared about. While Sue had gotten saved after Kody's birth, J.C. had gotten a Suzuki GS750 motorcycle. Sue always saw it as a childish luxury, a money suck. Sue wanted J.C. to care about paying the bills as much as she did. She'd yell at him to grow up, but J.C. knew what it meant to grow up—it meant to lose your sense of humor, and he wasn't interested. He liked to joke that he didn't need to be born again because he was born a Christian the first time.

Kody remembers his parents fighting over money throughout his childhood. He was close to both of them, but even as a kid he felt that J.C. was the parent he had fun with, and Sue was the parent he spoke about serious things with. Sue was in charge of the bills, the food, and, increasingly, everything else—discipline, getting to places on time, going to church. Kody would pray that his father would get saved. Like Sue, he was zealous. If J.C. became a Christian, Kody thought, he would take more responsibility. Then his parents would talk to each other the way Christian couples should and stop fighting over bills.

By the winter of 2010–2011, Sue's last year in college, the Christians' financial worries began to seep into every conversation. J.C.'s work usually slowed down in the cold months anyway, but this winter was even worse. The weather and the economy were keeping families down to the most necessary repairs. J.C.'s biggest jobs had always been hooking new mobile homes up to electricity. He could make as much as $600 a hookup. But almost no one was buying a new mobile home—that's how the housing crisis came to Owsley County.

35   Like most of the families they knew, the Christians had become masters at rotating their payments. They could skip a few months of paying on time before their water or electricity would be shut off, but Sue didn't like to be late on bills that people in town could know about. It was better to miss the unnecessary amenities they'd gotten used to in the good years—like their satellite TV. J.C. had to drop his favorite channel, which showed Westerns nonstop. Sue teased him that Westerns were all he liked to watch or read. "How many home-on-the-range things can you read about?" she asked. "They do the same thing every day."

Other things were harder to get rid of. All four family members had gotten cell phones, and it cost them more to cancel their plans than it did to keep paying them for the rest of the contract. J.C. played a game on Xbox called *Black Ops* and had signed up for an online gaming service that withdrew from their bank account automatically. It often overdrew their account, costing them fees. Their water bill went up. The electric company started adding a surcharge, and it cost nearly $400 a month to heat their trailer in the winter. Sue was driving a rickety Chevy Lumina to school every day, and she knew it wouldn't last long. The grants from the program that helped her pay for school had fallen short, and she'd had to spend more for textbooks. Most years, Sue tried to take care of property taxes by December because she'd get a $100 discount. The Christians had missed that date, and it looked to Sue like they might be late for the final deadline in April, which would mean they'd have to pay even more money. The real penalty, as far as Sue was concerned, was that their names would be listed in the paper. They got the payment in just before it was due.

School was always a means to an end for Sue, but when her last semester started, it started to feel like a luxury. J.C. was working too little and playing *Black Ops* too much. She talked about quitting and going back to data entry. It was J.C. who didn't want her to. J.C. was the one who went on about how employers always mistreated their workers, but even Sue had to admit that sitting and typing for 12 hours had started to cause her aches and pains. She told J.C. she'd stick it out.

When Owsley County's leaders, official and unofficial, talk about what Owsley County needs, they identify different problems all with the same urgency. For the schools superintendent, Tim Bobrowski, it's essential that the high school prepare students for college, which is difficult to do when you can't recruit physics or chemistry teachers. Molly Turner, who runs the Owsley County Action Team, wants a new highway that will make it easier for folks to live in the county but work outside it. Molly's brother, former county executive Cale Turner, argues that the county needs housing—real, solid houses, ones with foundations. Tim's brother, Nelson, who runs the bank, thinks the town should have more entertainment, like the golf course he helped build, to lure college graduates. (Others in town said that Nelson just likes to golf.) Jamie Brunk, the Methodist minister, believes the town needs a drug-recovery program to halt the rampant use of prescription painkillers. All of them want more young people to stay or, to be more precise, they want more young people to go to college and then come home. They like to say Owsley County needs more energy, and it needs a critical mass of young people to create it.

With that in mind, they ought to have thrown Kody a parade when he decided to stay and take over a business in Booneville. Late in the winter of 2011, the couple who owned a T-shirt printing business in town came to Kody and J.C. and offered to sell it. Kody had worked for them briefly as a graphic artist. They had tried to sell before, but they always wanted too much money. Now they were willing to go down to $30,000, and that seemed like something Kody could do. Kody wanted a job for J.C. where he could be less physical. He'd already seen how his grandfather suffered from a lifetime of hard labor. Looking at his dad's arthritic hands, which J.C. plunged into hot wax every night to ease the pain, Kody thought he could help by going into business with J.C. When they went into the only bank in Booneville to see about a loan, the officer asked, "Where's Sue at?" Even when they tried to run things, Kody and J.C. couldn't escape the notion that Sue was in charge.

40   Kody renamed the business Robots in Disguise (he's a *Transformers* fan). He made sure the store could be found on Google Maps and opened Facebook and Twitter accounts. But problems cropped up right away. Another couple had opened a T-shirt-printing business on the square. Booneville was going to have a hard enough time supporting one T-shirt-printing store, but two?

Sue didn't have a job after she graduated that spring and also began working at the shop. Kody needed the free labor, but Sue was good at driving him crazy. Sue says that she doesn't ask anyone to work harder than she worked, and Kody says that's the problem. Sue needs for everything to be perfect. Kody wanted her to understand that, sometimes, you did the best you could do in the time you had. For Kody, that meant occasionally cutting corners in ways that he didn't think people would notice. When Kody had worked for the previous owners, the Owsley County Action Team ordered signs for their drug-and-alcohol-free party after prom. Some signs came in red and white instead of the ordered maroon and white—the high school's colors. The party organizers said Kody's response was "I thought you might want a little bit of variety." It would have been better, they said, if he had just admitted that he ran out of maroon paint.

The biggest problem was that charging people money vexed Kody. He often arrived at a price that factored in the cost of the goods but not much else. When J.C. had to drive an hour to Richmond to pick up a blanket for a last-minute order, Kody didn't take into account the price of gas. More disconcerting, Kody often didn't charge for the time he spent designing the logos and getting them ready for screen-printing. His time, he says, is invaluable. When he thinks about pricing, he's guided by one thing: Would he pay that much? "I don't see it as I need to make one huge lump sum in a sitting," he says. "I see it as if I charge them this amount, they'll eventually come back and order more." Kody didn't always understand that a business is supposed to make a profit. Its first year, the shop covered all its expenses, but Kody himself only made $600 and J.C. $877. With three working adults, the family's income for 2011 was a combined $21,000, right on the poverty line.

In November, six months after she graduated, Sue finally landed a job. She had looked at every middle school within an hour's drive of her home but had found nothing. She had resigned herself to working at Kody's shop until the beginning of the next school year when she heard that Berea College was running a federal initiative called Promise Neighborhoods. With adjacent Jackson and Clay counties, Owsley was one of the few rural areas to receive a grant. Based on the Harlem Children's Zone, the program hired counselors to work with children from cradle to high school and prepare them for college. Sue was hired to help middle school students. Armed with the learning-styles test, she would provide one-on-one counseling to struggling students.

Restless and on a whim, Kody announced that he wanted to drive to New York to watch the Macy's Thanksgiving Day Parade. Almost at the last moment, Sue, J.C., and Ciara, in a celebratory mood, decided to go with him. The Christians didn't tell anyone, because they didn't want the town to know that their house would be empty for a few days. They found a cheap hotel in New Jersey and drove the 12 hours in a straight shot.

They hadn't known it would cost $12 in tolls just to get into New York   45
City or $40 for parking. They couldn't really see the parade from their crowded spot along Broadway, except Ciara, who perched on top of a postal box. She held a two-year-old from South Carolina in her lap. They were cold and miserable. They got lost and turned around in traffic and yelled at by a lady police officer they asked for help. The next day, they went to see the Empire State Building, but it cost $23 to go to the top, so they passed. They decided to go to the Statue of Liberty but were, again, put off by the cost. Sue skipped lunch—she said she wasn't hungry—and the rest followed her lead and skipped lunch, too. Kody said that they wouldn't have wanted to be shocked by the check anyway. During the few days they spent in New York, they often didn't eat until 11 at night, when they got back to the New Jersey hotel and picked up food from a nearby Subway. Their first advice to others when they got back to Booneville was "Don't go—stay home and watch it on TV."

By the winter, the Christians had settled into a routine. Sue and Ciara went to school around 7:30 in the morning, J.C. and Kody went to the shop, and they all gathered there late in the afternoon. Sue ran the embroidery machine. After a while, customers started bringing her dresses to hem, broken zippers to fix, and other things to sew. It wasn't really what the shop was supposed to do, but Sue would still do it—she brought her sewing machine into the shop's office and was often perched there, at night, tired. When J.C. and the kids got hungry, they still turned to Sue to ask about dinner. There was a time when she would have rushed home to make chicken and dumplings or beans. She used to never let her kids eat hot dogs or pizza. But Sue was letting go of some of those things she used to have so much control over.

There were other things to worry about, anyway. Sue thought Kody and J.C. spent too much time sitting at the shop, hoping new customers came in. She had gotten into the habit of drawing charts to show J.C. and Kody their progress. She knew the test would be not whether the shop's revenues could cover its expenses but whether the business was growing year over year. Their loan lasted for ten, but if the shop wasn't doing well after two years, they might need to think of a different way to cover that loan than working, as a whole family, on a shop that couldn't make money.

It also bothered Sue that Ciara was so dead set on majoring in broadcasting. Broadcasting would take Ciara far away. Ciara was as ready to leave as Kody had been. By early 2012, she'd settled on Morehead State University, but Sue didn't like Morehead—it was liberal and the kind of place where Ciara would forget who she was—so she worked on Ciara to change her mind. As Ciara moved toward graduation, she decided to go to the University of the Cumberlands, a Christian school near the Tennessee border. She also decided that she'd become a 4-H agent. Ciara had always loved 4-H. Sue liked that, as long as it was what she really wanted to do, because it meant Ciara might work close to home after college.

Sue wasn't so sure about this new job, either. Many days, she had to spend more time doing paperwork to show she was working than actually doing the work with the kids. Worse, Berea officials were butting heads with local school administrators. Sue's work overlapped, her supervisors were starting to see, with an older grant program called Gear Up, which also aimed to get students ready for college. After a few months on the job, everyone started to argue over Sue's head about what her job should be, and they decided that for the following school year, Sue would be in charge of parent outreach for every student in the school system, from Head Start to high school. It was a daunting prospect. Sue had been listening ever since Kody and Ciara were born to how teachers talk, and she knew they talked their own language—a language that it took Sue four years of college to decipher. "No wonder parents are scared of y'all," she thought. "They probably think you'll make them feel dumb if they come. Chances are, you probably will. Not that you mean to." That was the bridge Sue was going to have to build, and she wasn't sure she could do it.

This was also the first salary job Sue had, and it made her nervous. She   50
was used to her pay being tied to results. With this job she never knew, on
any given day, whether she was doing enough work to merit her salary,
which for 2012 would be $30,000. It was enough, more than enough, Sue
knew, to pay the bills. But it wasn't enough to calm her worries. Berea had
assured everybody that the grant would last five years. Sue, though, had
heard that before.

Analyze

1. What is one significant negative consequence for Sue going back to
   school? What is one significant positive consequence?
2. Why was Owsley County called a "pauper county"?
3. Potts writes: "For many years, the way to be successful in Owsley
   County was to _____." How does that attitude compare with the
   message your hometown sends to its young residents?

Explore

1. Commenting on the history of federal and private aid delivered to the
   Appalachia region over decades, Sue says: "I think we've been helped so
   much, we're getting helped to death." What does she mean? Where else
   in the U.S. or internationally might someone claim there is too much
   aid? What are the consequences of that attention? Conduct research
   on the influx of media attention to the Appalachia region during the
   1960s. Watch Elizabeth Barrett's documentary *Stranger with a
   Camera*, in which she asks, "Can filmmakers portray poverty without
   shaming the people we portray?" Write a researched essay responding
   to that question.
2. Potts writes: "When nearly everyone in the county is poor, the distinction between have and have-not becomes meaningless." Indeed, research suggests that societies that have less inequality—less distance
   between those who have and those who don't—tend to be more stable.
   Does this support Potts's claim? Explain.
3. Describe the writing style of this article. Why does Potts write the
   article this way? What is the value or lesson in getting to know Sue, her
   family, and their struggles?

Bernie Sanders
"Poverty in America: A Death Sentence"

Bernie Sanders is a U.S. senator representing Vermont as a nonpartisan Independent. During Sanders's public service, he has devoted himself to the issue of income inequality, aiming to reverse the trends of the decreasing middle class and the widening income gap. He wrote the following essay in 2011 for Spotlight on Poverty, an organization founded to facilitate a nonpartisan forum for conversations about poverty.

What do Senator Sanders's fellow senators—Democrats and Republicans— have to gain in supporting policies that help people in poverty?

The crisis of poverty in America is one of the great moral and economic issues facing our country. It is very rarely talked about in the mainstream media. It gets even less attention in Congress. Why should people care? Many poor people don't vote. They certainly don't make large campaign contributions, and they don't have powerful lobbyists representing their interests.

That's why I held a hearing on September 13th, the same day the Census Bureau's new poverty estimates were released. These numbers make clear why we all should care.

There are 46 million Americans—about one in six—living below the poverty line. That's the largest number on record, according to the new report released last week by the Census Bureau. Additionally, about 49.9 million Americans lacked health insurance. That number has soared by 13.3 million since 2000.

According to the Organization for Economic Cooperation and Development, the United States has both the highest overall poverty rate and the highest childhood poverty rate of any major industrialized country on earth.

5   When we talk about poverty in America, we tend to have in mind human suffering—people who are unable to meet basic needs including securing appropriate housing, food, transportation, and medical care.

Yet, I want to focus on an enormously important point. Poverty in America today leads not only to anxiety, unhappiness, discomfort, and a lack of material goods—it also leads to death. Poverty in America today is a death sentence for tens of thousands of our people, which is why the high childhood poverty rate in our country is such an outrage.

It is important to keep a few key facts in mind.

- At a time when we are seeing major medical breakthroughs in cancer and other terrible diseases for the people who can afford those treatments, the reality is that life expectancy for low-income women has declined over the past 20 years in 313 counties in our country. In other words, in some areas of America, women are now dying at a younger age than in the past.
- In America today, people in the highest income group level, the top 20 percent, live, on average, at least 6.5 years longer than those in the lowest income group.
- In America today, adult men and women who have graduated from college can expect to live at least five years longer than people who have not finished high school.
- In America today tens of thousands of our fellow citizens die unnecessarily because they cannot get the medical care they need. According to a 2009 report in Reuters, nearly 45,000 people die in the United States each year—one every 12 minutes—in large part because they lack health insurance and cannot get good care.
- According to the Office of Minority Health at HHS, the infant mortality rate for African American infants was twice that of white infants.

I recite these facts because I believe that as bad as the current situation is with regard to poverty, it will likely get worse in the immediate future. As a result of the greed, recklessness, and illegal behavior of Wall Street we are now in the midst of the worst economic downturn since the 1930s. Millions of workers have lost their jobs and have slipped out of the middle class and into poverty. Poverty is increasing.

Despite the reality that our deficit problem has been caused by the recession and declining revenue, two unpaid for wars, and tax breaks for the wealthy, there are some in Congress who wish to decimate the existing safety net, which provides a modicum of security for the elderly, the sick, children, and lower income people. Despite an increase in poverty, some of these people would like to cut or end Social Security, Medicare, Medicaid, food stamps, home heating assistance, nutrition programs, and help for the disabled and the homeless.

10   To the degree that they are successful, there is no question in my mind that many more thousands of men, women, and children will die unnecessarily.

From a moral perspective, it is not acceptable that we allow so much unnecessary suffering and preventable death to continue. From an economic perspective and as we try to fight our way out of this terrible recession, it makes no sense that we push to the fringe so many people who could be of such great help to us.

Analyze

1. What two poverty-related distinctions does the U.S. have among other major industrialized countries at the time of this essay?
2. What is the significance of the title of this essay?
3. What reason does Sanders give for why he shares these facts?

Explore

1. Research one of the five "key facts" Sanders lists and write a more substantive summary of this situation. What are the causes of this situation? Who are the stakeholders? Who is researching this further or working to improve the situation?
2. Sanders takes a jab at Wall Street, claiming that the economic downturn driving more people into poverty is a direct consequence of the "greed, recklessness, and illegal behavior" of Wall Street workers. How does this affect his ethos (character and credibility)? Will he gain or lose readers by making that point here? Is it a successful rhetorical move?
3. Sanders then attacks "those who wish to decimate the existing safety net" through budget cuts at a time when poverty is increasing. He claims that the consequence of such cuts is the unnecessary death of people who are poor. Examine the tone and rhetoric of Sanders's claims. Is this an effective strategy? Who is Sanders's intended audience, and how might that influence his tone? If you were someone who proposed budget cuts to the programs Sanders names, how would you respond?

Sonja Livingston
"Shame"

Sonja Livingston is a professor at the University of Memphis, teaching in the M.F.A. degree program and specializing in writing memoirs and women's non-fiction. The following excerpt is from her award-winning memoir *Ghostbread*, in which she details the physical, emotional, and mental hardships of growing up in poverty in the 1970s.

For what, if anything, should people living in poverty feel ashamed?

The thing is; it has a dent in it.

A scar runs across the face of the metal box. It's chipped and rusted in spots, pushes inward, and presses together whatever unfortunate food item has been placed inside.

There's nothing pretty about my lunchbox, nothing to see but the huge old head of Kwai Chang Caine, the crime-fighting monk from TV. If you look at it, that's all you'll see—Caine's bald head, cracked by the dent, looking like the shell of an overcooked egg.

The dent was there long before I ever got hold of it. It was a hand-me-down from my oldest brother, Bob, who is as quiet and strange as the box. And don't think I don't try covering Kung-Fu's rocky head with a carefully placed hand or two. I try. And try. But the head is hungry and wide and way too big for covering. Big, buttery, and unsmiling, Kung-Fu's head is the first thing people notice about me on the bus to Albion Primary School or at the Brownies. Having the head of Mohammed Ali or Evel Knievel hover on my box—even the entire Walton Family—would be far less painful.

I never tell my mother how much I hate it. I don't want to be seen as weak.   5
I prefer to look greedy, and so beg regularly for a Josie and the Pussycats Box. And when begging doesn't work, I bang my head against Kwai Chang's on the school bus; the first time on accident, but after that, for the easy laughs it earns me, and the chance of damaging it beyond repair. And finally, when knocking heads with Kwai Chang Caine fails to ruin the box, I simply leave it at home and hold off eating till after school.

On those autumn nights when flocks of Brownies gather in fidgety groups in the school gymnasium and open their sewing boxes in search of thread and needle to fashion dolls from empty Palmolive bottles, I look genuinely surprised that my own box had gone missing and ask my cousin Dori for a needle and some thread.

"Where's your sewing kit?" my mother asks when the troop leader reports that I'd forgotten it again and had to borrow from Dori, whose box is everything a sewing kit should be—clear plastic with powder-yellow handles, stuffed to capacity with yarn and thread and a rainbow of fabric scraps.

I shrug, keep to myself the fact that mine is not even a real sewing kit; that I'd prefer to pull needle and thread from a plain brown bag than carry around sewing supplies in Kung-Fu's big old head. I say nothing, and keep as a secondary source of shame the fact that I care about such things.

I decide to be rid of the subject once and for all by convincing my mother that I hate Brownies. And I must be a good liar because my mother somehow believes my aversion to singing and sewing and dipping peeled apples into brown sugar and cinnamon, pushing them onto the ends of broken branches, then turning them over an open fire. I hate the songs, the snacks, and the parades, I say while praying she doesn't look into my eyes.

10   "Just let me quit," I say.

And just like that, she does.

Analyze

1. In this text, what is the narrator supposed to use the Kung-Fu lunchbox for? What does this repurposing suggest to readers about her family's financial status?
2. How does the narrator try to get rid of the lunchbox?
3. Why doesn't the narrator come prepared for Brownies?

Explore

1. The narrator writes: "I never tell my mother how much I hate it. I don't want to be seen as weak. I prefer to look greedy, and so I beg regularly for a Josie and the Pussycats Box." Why does the narrator choose to project greed over weakness to her mother? What is the nature of that weakness? Explain.
2. When her mother asks why she didn't have her sewing kit at Brownies, the narrator shrugs and doesn't say what she's thinking, that hers "is not even a real sewing kit." Instead, she says nothing, "and keeps as a

secondary source of shame the fact that [she] care[s] about such things." If this is a secondary shame, what is the primary shame?

3. In this story, the lunchbox becomes a symbol for something larger, a visible sign of difference. What are the ultimate consequences (negative and positive) of the narrator's refusal to brand herself with the lunchbox?

Laura Sullivan-Hackley
"Speech Pathology: The Deflowering of an Accent"

Laura Sullivan-Hackley is a graphic designer who graduated with a degree in journalism from Western Kentucky University. She published the following prose in *Kalliope*, a literary magazine featuring poetry, nonfiction, fiction, and artwork. This piece also appears in the book *Reclaiming Class: Women, Poverty, and the Promise of Higher Education*, edited by Vivyan C. Adair and Sandra L. Dalhberg, a collection of essays written by women who sought higher education as an opportunity to overcome poverty. In her writing, Sullivan-Hackley conveys the pressure to erase unique and sometimes shaming marks of poverty, such as accents.

Has someone's criticism ever prompted you to want to mask unique characteristics that define a certain part of you?

Each schoolday was a raveling Pavlovian chain. First a flicker of naked bulb shocking us out of bed. Then Bus 64's engine grinding uphill, belching sour diesel exhaust in our path like a taunt, daring us in this chase. Once aboard, we watched the neighborhood's grey Etch-a-Sketch landscape scroll past our windows until it disappeared into fog behind us. We dreaded the air brake sighing that sigh of a tired old man, our cue to wade through Marlboro clouds toward the clatter and nag of homeroom bell.

When Bus 64 screeched and coughed to a stop in front of school one Tuesday, the driver refused to let us off. We sat, watching all other buses unload, spilling classmates into a new schoolday. At 8:01, a long sedan parked over our shadowed silhouettes in the bus lane. The county school superintendent thrust himself out of that black Lincoln, then boarded our bus two steps at a time. Grim like somebody had just died or egged his house, he appeared to be masturbating with his necktie, gripping and tugging and rearranging with one fist.

"Hogtrash." He flung the word out over us all like a Frisbee rimmed with mud for extra spin, then waited for it to settle.

"Every last one of you. Hogtrash. Never amount to nothing."

5   We would have searched each other's faces for clues, but our gazes drove forward, hard swizzlestick skewers this man might impale himself on. Bus 64 seemed to shrink, its brown vinyl closing around us like cupped hands of beggars until we were no longer passengers parked outside our destination; we were stepchildren bumming a ride.

The superintendent gave his tie one more fierce yank before spinning on his heels, knocking the door open with his fist. He tripped on the last step down, but his gaffe came too late to elicit even the slightest snag of an upper lip.

The slow stream of us snaked from Bus 64 to the linoleum school foyer. Stepping down to asphalt, my jaw clamped shut. By the ring of first-period bell, I had slated my own lesson plan: to master a new language, no matter how bitter or foreign its flavor on my tongue.

My words became bullets, severe and staccato. Rappelling the cliffs where *g*s and hard *o*s had always dropped off the ends of things, I fought past the *in*s and *uh*s my lips liked to rest upon. I stiffened against the easy lean of *ain't*, the lively rhythm of twang. I bit down on all the lacy fringe of my mother's words, the slurred segues between my father's syllables, that peppery patois of the neighborhood.

The prize I knew when I heard it pronounced, years and miles from Bus 64's shuttling: "You don't sound like you come from anywhere."

Analyze

1. Who is the unexpected visitor to Bus 64? What is his purpose?
2. What does the visitor call the students? What is the significance of that particular insult?
3. What self-directed "lesson plan" does the narrator write for herself after this incident?

Explore

1. Bus 64 becomes a character in this narrative. How does it symbolize its passengers before and after the incident?

2. The narrator describes her effort to erase her accent, deliberately fighting against the speech patterns she inherited from her mother and father. Why has the accent become a source of shame? Research this phenomenon, common to both rural and urban residents, of erasing an accent to conceal a heritage deemed socially undesirable. Write an academic essay or narrative on this issue using descriptive writing.

3. In the conclusion, the narrator claims that she has won the prize because she no longer has an accent that tells others where she comes from. Is she genuinely satisfied, or is there some regret in that accomplishment? What does it mean not to seem to come from anywhere? Think of economic disparities in your home region. Are the affluent areas and low-income areas clearly marked? What are the signs of that difference—verbal accents or physical amenities like parks, gates, and structures that inscribe those boundaries? Can people tell who is from "the wrong side of the tracks"? Census data show that some of the richest counties in the U.S. are next to the poorest. This is common around the world. Use a tool such as the Measure of America map (measureofamerica.org/map) to research your home region, or a region that interests you, to analyze local economic patterns. Now research causes for these sharp differences. What policies or practices (local, national, or global) contribute to this phenomenon of starkly unequal neighbors?

Sherman Alexie
"Why Chicken Means So Much to Me"

Sherman Alexie was raised on the Spokane Indian Reservation, and much of his writing, poetry, and filmmaking reflects his experience growing up as a Native American. The following excerpt is from his novel *The Absolutely True Diary of a Part-Time Indian*, which is based on events in Alexie's life. In it, the

narrator confronts the many consequences of growing up as a poor Native
American struggling with health problems and bullying.

---

*Why do the poor need others to "pay attention to their dreams in order to
have the chance to be something else"?*

Okay, so now you know that I'm a cartoonist. And I think I'm pretty
good at it, too. But no matter how good I am, my cartoons will never
take the place of food or money. I wish I could draw a peanut butter and
jelly sandwich, or a fist full of twenty dollar bills, and perform some magic
trick and make it real. But I can't do that. Nobody can do that, not even the
hungriest magician in the world.

I wish I were magical, but I am really just a poor-ass reservation kid living
with his poor-ass family on the poor-ass Spokane Indian Reservation.

Do you know the worst thing about being poor? Oh, maybe you've done
the math in your head and you figure:

Poverty = empty refrigerator + empty stomach

And sure, sometimes, my family misses a meal, and sleep is the only thing
we have for dinner, but I know that, sooner or later, my parents will come
bursting through the door with a bucket of Kentucky Fried Chicken.

Original Recipe.

5   And hey, in a weird way, being hungry makes food taste better. There is
nothing better than a chicken leg when you haven't eaten for (approximately) eighteen-and-a-half hours. And believe me, a good piece of chicken
can make anybody believe in the existence of God.

So hunger is not the worst thing about being poor.

And now I'm sure you're asking, "Okay, okay, Mr. Hunger Artist,
Mr. Mouth-Full-of-Words, Mr. Woe-Is-Me, Mr. Secret Recipe, what is
the worst thing about being poor?"

So, okay, I'll tell you the worst thing.

Last week, my best friend Oscar got really sick.

10   At first, I thought he just had heat exhaustion or something. I mean,
it was a crazy-hot July day (102 degrees with 90 percent humidity), and
plenty of people were falling over from heat exhaustion, so why not a little
dog wearing a fur coat?

I tried to give him some water, but he didn't want any of that.

He was lying on his bed with red, watery, snotty eyes. He whimpered in pain. When I touched him, he yelped like crazy.

It was like his nerves were poking out three inches from his skin.

I figured he'd be okay with some rest, but then he started vomiting, and diarrhea blasted out of him, and he had these seizures where his little legs just kicked and kicked and kicked.

And sure, Oscar was only an adopted stray mutt, but he was the only   15
living thing that I could depend on. He was more dependable than my parents, grandmother, aunts, uncles, cousins, and big sister. He taught me more than any teachers ever did.

Honestly, Oscar was a better person than any human I had ever known.

"Mom," I said. "We have to take Oscar to the vet."
"He'll be all right," she said.

But she was *lying.* Her eyes always got darker in the middle when she lied. She was a Spokane Indian and a bad liar, which didn't make any sense. We Indians really should be better liars, considering how often we've been lied to.

"He's really sick, Mom," I said. "He's going to die if we don't take him to   20
the doctor."

She looked hard at me. And her eyes weren't dark anymore, so I knew that she was going to tell me the truth. And trust me, there are times when the *last thing* you want to hear is the truth.

"Junior, sweetheart," Mom said. "I'm sorry, but we don't have any money for Oscar."
"I'll pay you back," I said. "I promise."
"Honey, it'll cost hundreds of dollars, maybe a thousand."
"I'll pay back the doctor. I'll get a job."   25

Mom smiled all sad and hugged me hard.

Jeez, how stupid was I? What kind of job can a reservation Indian boy get? I was too young to deal blackjack at the casino, there were only about fifteen green grass lawns on the reservation (and none of their owners outsourced the mowing jobs), and the only paper route was owned by a tribal elder named Wally. And he had to deliver only fifty papers, so his job was more like a hobby.

There was nothing I could do to save Oscar.

Nothing.

30   Nothing.

Nothing.

So I lay down on the floor beside him and patted his head and whispered his name *for hours.*

Then Dad came home from *wherever* and had one of those long talks with Mom, and they decided something *without me.*

And then Dad pulled down his rifle and bullets from the closet.

35   "Junior," he said. "Carry Oscar outside."

"No!" I screamed.

"He's suffering," Dad said. "We have to help him."

"You can't do it!" I shouted.

I wanted to punch my dad in the face. I wanted to punch him in the nose and make him bleed. I wanted to punch him in the eye and make him blind. I wanted to kick him in the balls and make him pass out.

40   I was hot mad. Volcano mad. Tsunami mad.

Dad just looked down at me with the saddest look in his eyes. He was crying. He looked *weak.*

I wanted to hate him for his weakness.

I wanted to hate Dad and Mom for our poverty.

I wanted to blame them for my sick dog and for all the other sickness in the world.

45   But I can't blame my parents for our poverty because my mother and father are the twin suns around which I orbit and my world would EXPLODE without them.

And it's not like my mother and father were born into wealth. It's not like they gambled away their family fortunes. My parents came from poor people who came from poor people who came from poor people, all the way back to the very first poor people.

Adam and Eve covered their privates with fig leaves; the first Indians covered their privates *with their tiny hands.*

Seriously, I know my mother and father had their dreams when they were kids. They dreamed about being something other than poor, but they never got the chance to be anything because nobody paid attention to their dreams.

Given the chance, my mother would have gone to college.

50   She still reads books like crazy. She buys them by the pound. And she remembers everything she reads. She can recite whole pages by memory.

Figure 3.5

She's a human tape recorder. Really, my mom can read the newspaper in fifteen minutes and tell me baseball scores, the location of every war, the latest guy to win the Lottery, and the high temperature in Des Moines, Iowa.

Given the chance, my father would have been a musician.

When he gets drunk, he sings old country songs. And blues, too. And he sounds good. Like a pro. Like he should be on the radio. He plays the guitar and the piano a little bit. And he has this old saxophone from high school that he keeps all clean and shiny, like he's going to join a band at any moment.

But we reservation Indians don't get to realize our dreams. We don't get those chances. Or choices. We're just poor. That's all we are.

It sucks to be poor, and it sucks to feel that you somehow *deserve* to be poor. You start believing that you're poor because you're stupid and ugly. And then you start believing that you're stupid and ugly because you're Indian. And because you're Indian you start believing you're destined to be poor. It's an ugly circle and *there's nothing you can do about it.*

55   Poverty doesn't give you strength or teach you lessons about perseverance. No, poverty only teaches you how to be poor.

So, poor and small and weak, I picked up Oscar. He licked my face because he loved and trusted me. And I carried him out to the lawn, and I laid him down beneath our green apple tree.

"I love you, Oscar." I said.

He looked at me and I swear to you that he understood what was happening. He knew what Dad was going to do. But Oscar wasn't scared. He was relieved.

But not me.

60   I ran away from there as fast as I could.

I wanted to run faster than the speed of sound, but nobody, no matter how much pain they're in, can run that fast. So I heard the boom of my father's rifle when he shot my best friend.

A bullet only costs about two cents, and anybody can afford that.

Analyze

1. The narrator offers to get a job and pay back his parents for the vet bill. Why won't that solution work?

2. Why does the narrator say he can't blame his parents for their poverty?

3. What does the narrator say his mother would do "if given the chance"? What would his father do "if given the chance"? What does that phrase mean here?

Explore

1. This story shows the excruciating sense of powerlessness when the poor can do "Nothing. Nothing. Nothing." Write an example similar to this story about a time when financial resources fell too short to provide an emotional or spiritual safety net for you or someone you know. Or write an example in which having financial resources provided someone with the ability to protect or expand vital capabilities, such as visiting a loved one at a critical time, going on a vacation or retreat to reenergize, or getting counseling.

2. The narrator names many emotional consequences of poverty: "It sucks to be poor, and it sucks to feel that you somehow *deserve* to be poor. You start believing that you're poor because you're stupid and ugly. And then you start believing that you're stupid and ugly because you're Indian. And because you're Indian you start believing that you're destined to be poor. It's an ugly circle and *there's nothing you can do about it.*" Analyze this passage drawing from the readings in this chapter and book that help you think about such issues as discrimination, shame, and the importance of emotional well-being.

3. The narrator writes: "Poverty doesn't give you strength or teach you lessons about perseverance. No, poverty only teaches you how to be poor." This seems to rebut arguments made outside the text that sometimes romanticize poverty, suggesting that suffering ennobles the poor. Analyze this passage in your own words, drawing from narratives of people in poverty (e.g., Sue in the Potts article) who reveal their own wavering sense of self-worth as they navigate life in poverty.

Crystal Gammon
"Pollution, Poverty, and People of Color: Asthma and the Inner City"

Crystal Gammon holds a master's degree in journalism from New York University with an emphasis on science, health, and environmental reporting. She serves as the web editor of *Yale Environment 360,* an online magazine that reports and offers analysis on global environmental issues. In this article, published in the *Environmental Health News* special series on pollution, poverty, and people of color, Gammon asserts that high poverty rates, coupled with environmental pollution, contribute to high asthma rates.

How does living in poverty compound the problem of living in an unhealthy environment?

E east St. Louis—On a clear spring day, the four-year-olds laughed as they ran out on the playground at the start of morning recess. Within minutes, one boy stopped, a terrified look on his face. Brenda Crisp and her staff immediately realized what was happening: Asthma attack.

"He escalated from zero symptoms to a severe attack in no time at all," said Crisp, director of the Uni-Pres Kindercottage daycare center. "It came out of the clear blue."

An ambulance rushed the boy to the hospital, where it took him two days to recover. Two years later, he still suffers unexpected asthma attacks and must take his nebulizer, a device that delivers a dose of corticosteroids and oxygen, wherever he goes.

This wasn't the first—or the last—near-deadly attack Crisp and her staff have witnessed at the daycare center. When it comes to asthma, the children of their community are at high risk.

5   Nearly all are African American and living in poverty. Incinerators, metal producers, power plants, chemical manufacturers and other industries ring the city. Exhaust from cars and trucks on nearby highways blankets the area, as well.

This socioeconomic profile and long history of environmental hazards have left East St. Louis with what experts suspect is one of the highest asthma rates in the nation.

Seven million American children—nearly one out of every ten—have asthma, and the rate has been climbing for the past few decades, reaching epidemic proportions. For black children, it's even worse—one out of every six—and the reported rate has risen 50 percent between 2001 and 2010, according to data from the Centers for Disease Control and Prevention.

"We are seeing higher asthma numbers in emergency departments, and we're realizing it's on the rise," said Anna Hardy, a public health nurse at the East Side Health District in East St. Louis.

What is it about this city—and other poor, African American cities across the nation—that leaves children with a disproportionate burden of respiratory disease? Is it the factories? The traffic exhaust? The substandard housing? For two decades, medical experts have struggled to unravel the mysterious connections between inner-city life and asthma, and while they have reached no conclusions yet, they suspect they know the answer: All of the above.

Crippling Poverty

Located across the Mississippi River from St. Louis, Mo., East St. Louis   10
is on the wrong side of the tracks, so to speak.

Of its 27,000 residents, 15 percent are unemployed, almost 44 percent are below the poverty line and the median family income is around $22,000, according to census reports. Its violent crime and murder rates are consistently among the nation's highest. Eighty-two percent of East St. Louis children depend on food stamps, 28 percent of births are to teen mothers and 22 percent of mothers receive no or inadequate prenatal care, according to the nonprofit group Vision for Children at Risk.

Housing in the city ranges from, at best, small homes that often house multiple families to crowded, low-income apartment complexes. Some people live in burned-out buildings and tents.

There are few grocery stores, so residents buy most of their food at convenience marts. A quart of milk costs around $6 and a bottle of children's Tylenol is $15 at one such store, according to nurses at a local clinic run by Community Nursing Services of Southern Illinois University-Edwardsville.

Raw sewage backs up into homes, businesses and schools whenever the volume overwhelms the city's decaying 150-year-old pipes. Garbage collection, which halted completely from 1987 to 1992, now is only available to households that pay out-of-pocket for the service. Most trash is burned in back yards, adding to the polluted air, or dumped in vacant lots.

A survey by the Southern Illinois University nursing group counted   15
2,200 dumped tires and 27 registered strip clubs within a 10-block radius of the clinic. In fact, for all appearances, strip clubs are the city's dominant industry.

That wasn't always the case. At the turn of the 20th century, East St. Louis was a booming industrial center with abundant employment opportunities. A Monsanto chemical plant, an aluminum refinery and the St. Louis National Stockyards Company, among others, set up shop there.

But most industrial facilities had split off from East St. Louis by the early 1900s, forming their own company towns to avoid the city's regulations and taxes. The Monsanto chemical plant, now Solutia, is in one of those towns, in the village of Sauget, on East St. Louis' southern edge. Sauget also is home to many other chemical plants, a hazardous waste incinerator, a copper smelter and a wastewater treatment plant. The Aluminum Ore Company established the town of Alorton, also along East St. Louis' southern border, and the St. Louis National Stockyards Company, now defunct, incorporated National City in 1907.

Plummeting city revenue combined with job losses, a corrupt city government and increasing racial tensions. Most upper- and middle-class white residents moved out of East St. Louis by the 1960s. The poor, largely African American population that remained was left with a city that couldn't afford to take care of itself.

The city receives no revenue from the neighboring companies. But unlike the tax dollars, the pollutants don't stop at city limits.

Whichever Way the Wind Blows

20 "East St. Louis gets the pollution, but none of the funds," said Kathy Andria, president of the American Bottom Conservancy and conservation chair of the Kaskaskia group of the Illinois Sierra Club. "Whichever way the wind blows, the city gets industrial emissions."

To the city's north, U.S. Steel-Granite City Works is a major source of carbon monoxide—more than 13,000 tons—as well as 3,500 tons of particulates in 2010. Its coke facility emitted another 1,900 tons of sulfur dioxide and 500 tons of particulates. The Dynegy Midwest Generation plant, a coal-burning power plant, had nearly 10,000 tons of sulfur dioxide emissions in 2010. The ConocoPhillips Wood River refinery also released nearly 5,000 tons of sulfur dioxide, 4,000 tons of nitrogen oxides and 2,000 tons of volatile organic matter, according to data from the U.S. Environmental Protection Agency. To the east, CenterPoint Energy, a natural gas compression facility, contributed 54 tons of nitrogen oxides. South of East St. Louis, the industrial plants in Sauget release hundreds of tons of volatile organic matter, sulfur dioxide and nitrogen oxides each year.

Seven of those facilities each emit at least 10 annual tons of hazardous air pollutants, including the carcinogens benzene and formaldehyde. Dozens of additional polluters are scattered throughout the metro area, too.

Traffic is also a significant pollution source for East St. Louis residents, as the city sits at the intersection of three interstate highways and U.S. Highway 40. Westbound traffic is often funneled into a single lane across the Mississippi River, which means traffic is constantly jammed and engines idle on the highways throughout the day. Also, because it's a low-income area, local traffic consists of older and more polluting cars and buses.

The region's levels of ozone and particulate matter, two pollutants caused by both automobiles and industry, exceed national air quality standards.

"We think ozone and particulate matter in this region usually come   25 50/50 from mobile sources, such as cars and trucks, and from stationary facilities," said Jim Ross, air pollution control division manager at the Illinois Environmental Protection Agency.

Particulate matter accumulates in the respiratory system and can lodge deep within lungs, triggering asthma attacks and other respiratory and cardiovascular problems. Ozone, volatile organic matter and sulfur and nitrogen oxides can irritate airways and also trigger asthma attacks.

"Particulates, ozone, oxides of nitrogen and sulfur—they all have strong biological mechanisms for making asthma worse," said Dr. Rob McConnell, an asthma researcher at the University of Southern California.

Air pollution has decreased over the past few decades, but residents still may be dealing with the lasting effects on their health.

"Twenty, 30 years ago, you would step outside and see clouds of smoke, and the air would smell like stale smoke all the time," Crisp said. "It's gotten better, but I think those companies were killing our children."

A Complex Disease

Experts have been unable to figure out why rates of asthma—a chronic   30 disease in which airways are inflamed and constricted—have risen so dramatically over the past few decades.

Doctors have long recognized that allergens, such as dust, mold and pet dander, and air pollutants can trigger asthma attacks. Much less clear, however, is what causes people to develop the disease in the first place.

"There's an emerging consensus that air pollution also causes new onset asthma, but that's not accepted by everybody," McConnell said.

Traffic pollution may be the biggest culprit. Over the last two decades dozens of studies have associated increases in asthma rates with pollution near roadways.

"We've known for a long time that PM2.5 [fine particulate matter] exposure is a trigger; now there's emerging evidence that exposure can be associated with development of asthma, too," said Dr. Rachel Miller, an asthma researcher at Columbia University Medical Center.

35   In Southern California communities, exposure to air pollution and traffic emissions stunts children's lung growth, according to USC research. Traffic pollution near a child's home and school also was related to the child's risk of developing asthma, and regular freeway commutes of just a few minutes increased a child's asthma risk. Children in families and communities with low socioeconomic status had a higher risk of developing the disease.

In Dominican and African American families from poor areas of New York City, living in a neighborhood with dense traffic and industrial facilities increased a child's risk of developing asthma, according to Miller and other Columbia University researchers. These children had higher levels of an immune marker associated with asthma the closer they lived to a highway.

Also, in a poor area near Lima, Peru, researchers found that living near a major road doubled both asthma and allergy risks. People near the roadway were exposed to significantly higher levels of black carbon, a component of diesel vehicle exhaust.

"We know that traffic-related pollution can be very allergenic. It could . . . make an individual more susceptible to developing an allergic sensitization to a specific allergen," said Dr. William Checkley, a Johns Hopkins pulmonologist who led the Peru study.

Nevertheless, some experts believe outdoor air quality plays only a minor role in asthma disparities. Instead, they focus on cockroaches, mold and other problems related to poverty or substandard housing.

40   For those living below the poverty line, 12 percent of U.S. children have the disease, compared with eight percent with family incomes more than twice the poverty level.

"Asthma rates and lead poisoning rates often track pretty closely," said Dr. William Kincaid, chairman of the St. Louis Regional Asthma

Consortium and a professor at Saint Louis University. "Everyone breathes the same outdoor air. But if you're in an older home, you're more likely to have lead paint, and you're also more likely to have mold, mildew, a leaky roof and all those other issues that predispose you to asthma."

Miller said that labeling pollutants as "indoor" versus "outdoor" oversimplifies the issue.

"Most of the outdoor pollutants people encounter readily penetrate indoors," she said. "In particular, black carbon, the soot that can come from diesel engines, penetrates from outdoors to indoors, and from indoors to outdoors."

In addition, scientists suspect that the stress of living in low-income areas with high rates of crime and other stressors may make children more vulnerable to the effects of pollutants, perhaps by altering their hormones and immune systems.

There also is evidence that some pollutants and allergens may interact 45 synergistically to cause asthma or trigger an attack. For example, diesel exposure and allergen exposure can each trigger allergic reactions. However, people exposed to both diesel exhaust and another allergen simultaneously often have a reaction that is more severe than the sum of their diesel-only and allergen-only reactions, McConnell said.

"I think the evidence for outdoor, near-roadway pollution is as strong as the evidence that indoor allergens cause asthma—maybe stronger—but I don't see it as one or the other," McConnell said.

"Asthma is a complex disease, and there are probably multiple causes," he said.

A Triple Whammy for East St. Louis

East St. Louis is prime territory for both indoor and outdoor pollution, as well as poverty.

"Their housing stock generally is older and not so well-maintained," which exposes residents to a variety of indoor air pollutants, said Amy Funk, an air quality specialist with the Metro East Citizens Air Project at the University of Illinois. "The housing stock also sits directly on a major interstate, so obviously you're going to have an impact from mobile pollution sources, too."

St. Louis ranks seventh on the Asthma and Allergy Foundation of 50 America's list of asthma capitals. About 14 percent of children have asthma in the St. Louis metro area, compared with 9.4 percent nationwide, according to the St. Louis Regional Asthma Consortium.

Data on East St. Louis itself is nearly impossible to track down, but its asthma rate is likely higher. Ninety-eight percent of the city is black, and black children have double the asthma rate of whites.

One person who's not waiting for more asthma data is Crisp of Kindercottage. Five generations of her family have lived in East St. Louis, and nine family members—including Crisp herself—have suffered from asthma.

After caring for dozens of asthmatic children over the last 42 years, including her own son and daughter, Crisp knows how to make immediate differences in their lives. Kindercottage partners with local physicians and pharmacy representatives so children have access to check-ups and asthma medications.

Crisp also teaches children to remind their parents not to smoke around them, and to ask drivers to avoid revving car engines in their driveways.

55   "We start asthma education early so children can take charge of their own care," Crisp said. "It's about empowering kids to know they can control their asthma."

Analyze

1. Gammon frames the article with a series of research questions to be addressed through a case study of East St. Louis. As a reader, do you find this helpful? Explain why you would or would not use this strategy in your own writing.

2. What percentage of children living below the poverty line have asthma? How does that compare with families living at twice the poverty level? How does that compare to figures in East St. Louis?

3. What is the "triple whammy" in East St. Louis? What is the grim significance of this trifecta?

Explore

1. Why does Gammon spend so much time explaining the history and geography of the city? How does understanding the physical and industrial history of East St. Louis help us understand its human history?

2. Gammon writes that while the pollutants flow into East St. Louis, the tax dollars for those companies do not because the companies

intentionally locate outside city limits. What could a poor resident of East St. Louis do about this situation? Research similar situations in which high-poverty communities have encountered serious environmental health concerns and did something about it. What are the particular challenges of creating changes in low-income communities?

3. After reading this article, are you convinced that poor health, such as asthma, might be a consequence of poverty? What does race have to do with these cascading consequences? Research another health issue closely associated with poverty in the U.S. or abroad. What is the connection between poverty and poor health in that context? From your research, are you able to draw any broader conclusions about the connection between poverty and poor health?

Maria Shriver
"The Female Face of Poverty"

Maria Shriver is a network news anchor and writer whose journalistic work centers on societal trends that are significant to women. That focus continues through the new Shriver Report, a nonprofit media initiative. As the former first lady of California, Shriver changed the nature of her position, transforming the role into one with a responsibility for social change. In her position, she pioneered social programs for women, the working poor, military families, and the intellectually and developmentally disabled. In the following essay published in *The Atlantic*, she argues that women in poverty experience unique hardships, and while the government must work to alleviate these, the American public is responsible too.

Why might poor women be more disadvantaged than poor men?

Let me state the obvious: I have never lived on the brink. I've never been in foreclosure, never applied for food stamps, never had to choose between feeding my children or paying the rent, and never feared I'd lose my paycheck when I had to take time off to care for a sick child or parent.

I'm not thrown into crisis mode if I have to pay a parking ticket, or if the rent goes up. If my car breaks down, my life doesn't descend into chaos.

But the fact is, one in three people in the United States do live with this kind of stress, struggle, and anxiety every day. More than 100 million Americans either live near the brink of poverty or churn in and out of it, and nearly 70 percent of these Americans are women and children.

Fifty years ago, President Lyndon Johnson envisioned the Great Society and called for a War on Poverty, naming my father, Sargent Shriver, the architect of that endeavor. The program worked: Over the next decade, the poverty rate fell by 43 percent.

In those days, the phrase "poverty in America" came with images of poor children in Appalachian shacks and inner-city alleys. Fifty years later, the lines separating the middle class from the working poor and the working poor from those in absolute poverty have blurred. The new iconic image of the economically insecure American is a working mother dashing around getting ready in the morning, brushing her kid's hair with one hand and doling out medication to her own aging mother with the other.

5   For the millions of American women who live this way, the dream of "having it all" has morphed into "just hanging on." Everywhere they look, every magazine cover and talk show and website tells them women are supposed to be feeling more "empowered" than ever, but they don't feel empowered. They feel exhausted.

Many of these women feel they are just a single incident—one broken bone, one broken-down car, one missed paycheck—away from the brink. And they're not crazy to feel that way:

- Women are nearly two-thirds of minimum-wage workers in the country.
- More than 70 percent of low-wage workers get no paid sick days at all.
- Forty percent of all households with children under the age of 18 include mothers who are either the sole or primary source of income.
- The median earnings of full-time female workers are still just 77 percent of the median earnings of their male counterparts.

For this year's *Shriver Report, A Woman's Nation Pushes Back from the Brink*, we polled more than 3,000 adults to determine how Americans feel about the economy, gender, marriage, education, and the future.

Here are some highlights from the poll respondents who are low-income women:

- Seventy-five percent of them wish they had put a higher priority on their education and career, compared to 58 percent of the general population
- Seventy-three percent wish they had made better financial choices (as did 65 percent of all those we polled)
- They were less likely to be married (37 percent, compared to 49 percent of all the men and women we polled) . . .
- And more likely than men to regret marrying when they did (52 percent, compared to 33 percent of low-income men)
- Nearly a third of those with children wished they had delayed having kids or had fewer of them

Overwhelmingly they favor changes that will help balance work and family responsibilities. Eighty-seven percent of low-income women—and 96 percent of single moms—identify paid sick leave as something that would be very useful to their lives.

What's more, the opinion of the general public is on their side: 73 percent of Americans said that in order to raise the incomes of working women and families, the government should ensure that women get equal pay for equal work. And 78 percent said the government should expand access to high-quality, affordable childcare for working families.

The typical American family isn't what it used to be. Only a fifth of   10 our families have a male breadwinner and a female homemaker. The solutions we need today are also different. We don't need a new New Deal, because the New Deal was an all-government solution, and that's not enough anymore. And my father's War on Poverty isn't enough anymore either.

Our government programs, business practices, educational system, and media messages don't take into account a fundamental truth: This nation cannot have sustained economic prosperity and well-being until women's central role is recognized and women's economic health is used as a measure to shape policy.

In other words, leave out the women, and you don't have a full and robust economy. Lead with the women, and you do. It's that simple, and Americans know it.

Women have enormous power. Politicians knock themselves out wooing us because we're the majority of voters in this country. Every corporate marketer and advertiser is after us because we make as much as 70 percent of this country's consumer decisions and more than 80 percent of the healthcare decisions.

With this power, we women can exert real pressure on our government to change course on many of the issues we care about and deliver on what women need now. Isn't it strange, for instance, that the United States is the only industrialized nation without mandatory paid maternity leave?

And how about those of us who aren't in jeopardy? Do we pay the women we hire a living wage—not because it's the law, but because it's fair? Do we give them flexibility when they need to take time for caregiving? If we run businesses, do we educate our workers about public policies and programs that can help them?

But the truth is that for so long, America's women have been divided: women who are mothers versus women who are not, women who work at home versus women who work outside the home, those who are married versus those who aren't, pro-life women versus pro-choice, white women versus women of color, Democrat versus Republican, gay versus straight, and young versus old. It feels like the last issue where women came together was fighting for the right to vote.

It's time to come together again. By pushing back and putting into practice the solutions we're proposing in *The Shriver Report*, we can re-ignite the American Dream—for ourselves, for our daughters and sons, for our mothers and fathers, for our nation. We have the power—not just to launch a new War on Poverty, but a new campaign for equity, for visibility, for fairness, for worth, for care.

Analyze

1. Shriver's first sentence anticipates the objections that will arise from her writing an article about poverty when she has never experienced it firsthand. She acknowledges that fact and swiftly shifts to focus on those who have. Is this an effective rhetorical strategy? Does it get your attention? Does it both acknowledge and downplay her celebrity status? Does it help you focus on the real issues?

2. Describe the iconic picture of poverty in the 1960s compared to the picture of poverty Shriver sees today.
3. Who is Shriver's intended audience? What cues in the text suggest that?

Explore

1. Shriver's survey data suggest that in some key areas, the attitudes of low-income women align well with the attitudes of the general public in ways to improve their circumstances. What are those key areas? Research one and write a report explaining the status and likelihood of changes in this area.
2. In closing, Shriver catalogs the many ways that women have been divided. What does this article tell readers she is bringing them together for? What is the consequence of having so many women in poverty? Is this exhortation effective? Do a rhetorical analysis of this essay to explain specifically where it succeeds and where it falls short.
3. Shriver mentions her father twice: once to name him as the architect of the War on Poverty, and once to say that his war isn't enough anymore. Research Sargent Shriver and the War on Poverty to understand more fully this point of reference. To what extent does Shriver's father connection boost her ethos (character and credibility), and to what extent does this family connection complicate her message? If you were her consultant, how would you counsel Shriver to navigate this salient connection?

Greg J. Duncan and Katherine Magnuson "The Long Reach of Early Childhood Poverty"

Greg J. Duncan is a professor of education at the University of California–Irvine, specializing in researching the influences of families, peers, neighborhoods, and public policies on life chances of children and adolescents.

Katherine Magnuson is a professor of social work at the University of Wisconsin–Madison, examining, among other research interests, how maternal education impacts childhood development. In the following, Duncan and Magnuson study and write about the effects of economic disparities on childhood development, exploring the impacts of policies and programs designed to compensate for these disparities.

How would your childhood have been affected if you had grown up under significantly different economic circumstances?

U sing a poverty line of about $22,000 for a family of four, the Census Bureau counted more than 15 million U.S. children living in poor families in 2009. Poor children begin school well behind their more affluent age mates and, if anything, lose ground during the school years. On average, poor kindergarten children have lower levels of reading and math skills and are rated by their teachers as less well behaved than their more affluent peers (see Figure 3.6). Children from poor families also go on to complete less schooling, work less, and earn less than others.

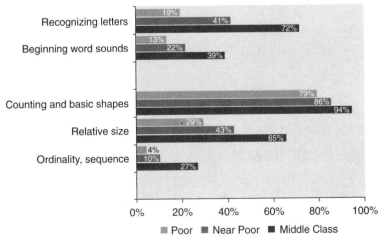

Figure 3.6   Rates of kindergarten proficiencies for poor, near poor, and middle-class children.

Source: Authors' calculations from the Early Childhood Longitudinal Survey—Kindergarten Cohort.

Social scientists have been investigating links between family poverty and subsequent child outcomes for decades. Yet, careful thought about the timing of economic hardship across childhood and adolescence is almost universally neglected. Emerging research in neuroscience and developmental psychology suggests that poverty early in a child's life may be particularly harmful because the astonishingly rapid development of young children's brains leaves them sensitive (and vulnerable) to environmental conditions.

After a brief review of possible mechanisms and the highest quality evidence linking poverty to negative childhood outcomes, we highlight emerging research linking poverty occurring as early as the prenatal year to adult outcomes as far as the fourth decade of life. Based on this evidence, we discuss how policy might better focus on deep and persistent poverty occurring very early in the childhoods of the poor.

American Poverty and Its Consequences for Children

If we were to draw the poverty line at 50 percent of median disposable income (about $29,000 for a family of three in today's dollars), as is common in much cross-national research on poverty, nearly one-quarter of U.S. children would be classified as poor (Figure 3.7). Comparing across countries,

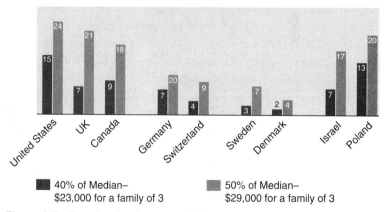

Figure 3.7 Poverty rates for young children.

Source: Gornick, J. and Jantti, M. (forthcoming). "Child poverty in upper-income countries: Lessons from the Luxembourg Income Study." In S. B. Kamerman, S. Phipps, and A. Ben-Arieh (Eds.), From Child Welfare to Child Well-Being: An International Perspective on Knowledge in the Service of Making Policy. A Special Volume in Honor of Alfred J. Kahn. Springer Publishing Company.

the U.S. fares badly, though not too much worse than countries like the UK, Canada, and Poland. More striking are the cross-country differences when the poverty threshold is set at a more spartan 40 percent of median disposable income (about $23,000). In this instance, the 15 percent U.S. childhood poverty rate is more than half again as high as any country other than Poland. Clearly, deep poverty is considerably more pervasive for children in the U.S. than among children in most Western industrialized countries.

5   What are the consequences of growing up in a poor household? Economists, sociologists, developmental psychologists, and neuroscientists emphasize different pathways by which poverty may influence children's development. Economic models of child development focus on what money can buy. They view families with greater economic resources as being better able to purchase or produce important "inputs" into their young children's development (e.g., nutritious meals; enriched home learning environments and child care settings outside the home; and safe and stimulating neighborhood environments), and higher-quality schools and post-secondary education for older children. The cost of the inputs and family income constraints are therefore the key considerations for understanding poverty's effects on children.

Psychologists and sociologists point to the quality of family relationships to explain poverty's detrimental effects on children. These theoretical models point out that higher incomes may improve parents' psychological well-being and their ability to engage in positive family processes, in particular high-quality parental interactions with children. A long line of research has found that low-income parents are more likely than others to use an authoritarian and punitive parenting style and less likely to provide their children with stimulating learning experiences in the home. Poverty and economic insecurity take a toll on a parents' mental health, which may be an important cause of low-income parents' non-supportive parenting. Depression and other forms of psychological distress can profoundly affect parents' interactions with their children. But as we argue below, it is not just the fact that these relationships exist that matters, but *when*.

Why Early Poverty May Matter Most

It is not solely poverty that matters for children's outcomes, but also the *timing* of child poverty. For some outcomes later in life, particularly those related to achievement skills and cognitive development, poverty *early* in a child's life may be especially harmful. Emerging evidence from both human and animal studies highlights the critical importance of early childhood in brain development and for establishing the neural functions and structures that shape future cognitive, social, emotional, and health outcomes. There is also clear evidence emerging from neuroscience that demonstrates strong correlations between socioeconomic status and various aspects of brain function in young children. For clear and compelling evidence on these points, look no further than the pieces in this very issue of *Pathways*.

Intensive programs aimed at providing early care and educational experiences for high-risk infants and toddlers also support the idea that children's early years are a fruitful time for intervention. The best known of these are the Abecedarian program, which provided a full-day, center-based, educational program for children who were at high risk for school failure, starting in early infancy and continuing until school entry, and the Perry Preschool program, which provided one or two years of intensive center-based education for preschoolers. Both of these programs have been shown to generate impressive long-term improvements in subsequent education and employment. Perry also produced large reductions in adult crime.

A Causal Story?

Regardless of the timing of low income, isolating its causal impact on children's well-being is difficult. Poverty is associated with other experiences of disadvantage (such as poor schools or being raised by a single parent), making it difficult to know for certain whether it is poverty per se that really matters or other related experiences. The best method for identifying the extent to which income really matters would be an experiment that compares families who receive some additional money to similar parents who do not receive such money. The only large-scale randomized interventions to alter family income directly were the Negative Income Tax Experiments, which were conducted between 1968 and 1982 with the primary goal of identifying the influence of a guaranteed income on parents' labor force participation. Researchers found that elementary school children whose families enjoyed a 50 percent boost in family income from the program exhibited higher levels of early academic achievement and school attendance than children who did not. No test score differences were found for adolescents, although youth who received the income boost did have higher rates of high school completion and educational attainment. This suggests that higher income may indeed cause higher achievement, although even in this case it is impossible to distinguish the effects of income from the possible benefits to children from the reductions in parental work effort that accompanied the income increases.

10   According to newer experimental welfare reform evaluations in the 1990s, though, providing income support to working poor parents through wage supplements does improve children's achievement. One study analyzed data from seven random-assignment welfare and antipoverty policies. All of these policies increased parental employment, while only some increased family income. These analyses indicated improved academic achievement for preschool and elementary school children by programs that boosted both income and parental employment, but not by programs that only increased employment.

These experimental findings suggest that income plays a causal role in boosting younger children's achievement, although here it should be kept in mind that the beneficial welfare-to-work programs increased both income and parental employment. However, combining these results with those from the 1970s experiments, we note that both kinds of programs increased income but produced opposing impacts on work hours. This suggests that the income boost may have been the most active ingredient in promoting children's achievement.

Non-experimental studies that take care to ensure they are comparing families who differ in terms of income, but who are otherwise similar, can also provide strong evidence. One such study took advantage of an increase in the maximum Earned Income Tax Credit for working poor families with more than two children by more than $2,000 between the years of 1993 and 1997. This generous increase in tax benefits enabled researchers to compare the school achievement of children in otherwise similar—and even the same—working families before and after the increase in the tax credit. And indeed, improvements in low-income children's achievement in middle childhood coincided with the policy change. A second, Canadian study found similar results when researchers took advantage of variation across Canadian provinces in the generosity of Canada's National Child Benefit program to estimate income impacts on child achievement. Thus, the weight of the evidence suggests that increases in income for poor families are causally related to improvements in children's outcomes.

The Long Reach

None of this past income literature has been able to examine family income early in a child's life in relation to that child's adult attainments. This limitation comes largely from the lack of data on both early childhood income and later adult outcomes. Recent research by Duncan and his colleagues, however, has now made this link using recently-released data from the Panel Study of Income Dynamics, which has followed a nationally representative sample of U.S. families and their children since 1968. The study is based on children born between 1968 and 1975, for whom adult outcomes were collected between ages 30 and 37.

Measures of income were available in every year of a child's life from the prenatal period through age 15. This enabled Duncan and his colleagues to measure poverty across several distinct periods of childhood, distinguishing income early in life (prenatal through age 5) from income in middle childhood and adolescence. The simple associations between income early in life and adult outcomes are striking (Table 3.1). Compared with children whose families had incomes of at least twice the poverty line during their early childhood, poor children completed two fewer years of schooling, earned less than half as much money, worked 451 fewer hours per year, received $826 per year more in food stamps, and are nearly three times as likely to report poor overall health. Poor males are more than twice as likely to be arrested. For females, poverty is associated with a more than five-fold increase in the likelihood of bearing a child out of wedlock prior to age 21.

None of these simple comparisons, however, considered the various factors that go along with growing up in poverty that also might explain poorer adult outcomes (e.g., single parenthood or lack of motivation). To account for this, we also adjusted for an extensive set of background control variables, all of which were measured either before or near the time of birth. This effort to separate income from other related disadvantages and characteristics of poor children produces smaller correlations than in the absence of these statistical controls. This suggests that a substantial portion of the simple correlation between childhood income and most adult outcomes can be accounted for by the disadvantageous conditions associated with birth into a low-income household.

But what about the timing of poverty? To better understand whether poverty in early childhood is particularly important, Duncan and colleagues replaced the average childhood income measure with three stage-specific

Table 3.1 **Adult outcomes by poverty status between the prenatal year and age five**

	Income below the official U.S. poverty line	Income between one and two times the poverty line	Income more than twice the poverty line
	Mean or %	*Mean or %*	*Mean or %*
Completed schooling	11.8 yrs	12.7 yrs	14.0 yrs
Earnings ($10,000)	$17.9	$26.8	$39.7
Annual work hours	1,512	1,839	1,963
Food stamps	$896	$337	$70
Poor health	13%	13%	5%
Arrested (men only)	26%	21%	13%
Nonmarital birth (women only)	50%	28%	9%

Note: Earnings and food stamp values are in 2005 dollars.

measures of income. As before, adjustments are made for the effects of the extensive array of background conditions.

In the case of adult earnings and work hours, early childhood income appears to matter much more than later income. For some measures, like work hours, there appears to even be a negligible role for income beyond age 5. Early income also appears to matter for completed schooling, but in this case adolescent family income seems to matter even more. In contrast, the strong association between overall childhood income and health and non-marital birth seems to be largely attributable to income during adolescence, rather than earlier in childhood.

More detailed analyses show that for families with average early childhood incomes below $25,000, a $3,000 annual boost to family income is associated with a 17 percent increase in adult earnings (Figure 3.8). Results for work hours are broadly similar to those for earnings. In this case, a $3,000 annual increase in the prenatal-to-age-5 income of low-income families is associated with 135 additional work hours per year after age 25. In contrast, increments to early-childhood income for higher-income

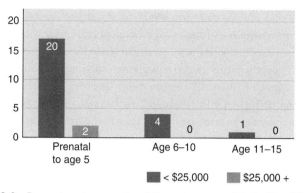

Figure 3.8 Percentage increase in adult earnings associated with a $3,000 annual increase in childhood income.

children were not significantly associated with higher adult earnings or work hours. The implication is clear: If we are hoping that giving parents extra income will bolster their children's chances for success, early childhood is the time to do it.

Refashioning Income Supports

Early childhood is a particularly sensitive period in which economic deprivation may compromise children's life achievement and employment opportunities. Research continues to confirm a remarkable sensitivity (and growing number) of developing brain structures and functions that are related to growing up in an impoverished home.

We also have convincing evidence linking early poverty with both child achievement and adult employment. The achievement studies employ unusually rigorous methods for estimating causal relationships between income early in life and achievement test scores as children age. The effect sizes estimated in these studies are broadly similar. An annual income increase of $3,000 sustained for several years appears to boost children's achievement by roughly one-fifth of a standard deviation. In the early grades, children's achievement increases by nearly one standard deviation per year, so 20 percent of a standard deviation amounts to about two months' advantage in school.

Very recent research has linked poverty early in childhood to adult earnings and work hours. Although non-experimental, the study's key finding—that income early in childhood appears to matter much more than income later in childhood for a range of employment outcomes—is strikingly consistent with the achievement studies.

Taken together, this research suggests that greater policy attention should be given to remediating situations involving deep and persistent poverty occurring early in childhood. In the case of welfare policies, we should take care to ensure that sanctions and other regulations do not deny benefits to families with very young children. Not only do young children appear to be most vulnerable to the consequences of deep poverty, but mothers with very young children are also least able to support themselves through employment in the labor market.

A more generous, and perhaps smarter, approach would be enacting income transfer policies that provide more income to families with young children. In the case of work support programs like the Earned Income Tax Credit, this might mean extending more generous credits to families with young children. In the case of child tax credits, this could mean making the credit refundable and also providing larger credits to families with young children.

Interestingly, several European countries gear time-limited benefits to the age of children. In Germany, a modest parental allowance is available to a mother working fewer than 20 hours per week until her child is 18 months old. France guarantees a modest minimum income to most of its citizens, including families with children of all ages. Supplementing this basic support is the Allocation de Parent Isolé (API) program for single parents with children under age 3. In effect, the API program acknowledges a special need for income support during this period, especially if a parent wishes to care for very young children and forgo income from employment. The state-funded child care system in France that begins at age 3 alleviates the problems associated with a parent's transition into the labor force.

25   In emphasizing the potential importance of policies to boost income in early childhood, we do not mean to imply that focusing on this area is the only policy path worth pursuing. Obviously investments later in life, including those that provide direct services to children and families, may also be well-advised. Economic logic requires a comparison of the costs and benefits of the various programs that seek to promote the development of disadvantaged children throughout the life course. In this context, expenditures on income-transfer and service-delivery programs should be placed side by side and judged by their costs and benefits, with the utmost goal of making our social investments as profitable as possible.

Analyze

1. How does the poverty rate for children in the U.S. compare to that of other Western industrialized countries?
2. Why is it hard to isolate poverty as a factor in research? What factors is it so closely associated with that researchers sometimes have trouble determining causal effects?
3. Duncan and Magnuson argue that research clearly shows that if we want to give low-income parents extra money to help their children succeed, the best time to do so is when?

Explore

1. What do Duncan and Magnuson say are the policy implications of research surrounding childhood poverty? What might some of those policies look like?
2. Because evidence is mounting that intervention in early childhood produces long-term significant gains, do the authors recommend stopping interventions with adults? What are some of the reasons they give for why it's important to have research that shows which interventions are most effective?
3. Research one of the other sources mentioned briefly in this article to understand more fully how this research adds to existing knowledge. For example, research the Abecedarian program or the Perry Preschool program. How was this research used to direct policies or programs for low-income children?

Roger R. Blunt and Paul D. Monroe Jr.
"We Have a Wealth Gap, and Military Is Poorer for It"

Roger R. Blunt is a retired general and a Distinguished Service Medal recipient who now serves to advance development work in Africa through U.S. economic investments. Paul D. Monroe Jr. is a retired two-star general, having served in the U.S. Army and the California Army National Guard for over 46 years. In this piece, Blunt and Monroe add another problem to the list of poverty's ill effects, explaining that the U.S.'s ability to recruit new service members and pay for military resources is hampered by America's poverty.

How might your own life be affected by the reduced capacity of the military to function due to poverty?

In recent weeks, members of Congress and Pentagon officials have been talking a great deal about how our military will be weakened by the economic uncertainty created by the sequester's across-the-board cuts. We agree that our leaders must quickly resolve these issues or our military preparedness will suffer greatly. But the conversation must not stop there. We must also face one of the greatest threats to our economic strength over the long term—the growing number of working poor in America—because our military strength and standing in the world is dependent on our nation's economic health.

As President Barack Obama's 2010 National Security Strategy reminded us, "Our prosperity serves as a wellspring for our power." Any threat to our economic strength is a threat to our military and our standing in the world. Attempting to maintain a robust national military without addressing domestic poverty is like building a house on sinking sand; no matter how solid the house is, it will fall without a strong foundation to support it.

Currently 1 in 3 Americans lives below or near the poverty line. Today there are 26 million Americans who make so little that even full-time work does not provide enough income to lift their families out of poverty. Economist Emmanuel Saez recently reported that the wealth generated by our postrecession economy has gone almost entirely to the wealthiest Americans. The problem is not that the wealthy are making money but that many workers are falling behind. Without a sufficiently broad economic base, we will not be able to fund our military, and crises will only worsen as we scramble to respond to threats from around the world.

High rates of poverty directly affect our ability to recruit the best and brightest to defend our country. Three-quarters of our young adults are ineligible for military service because they cannot meet the military's basic physical, educational or behavioral requirements. Think about that: Three out of 4 Americans who should be able to serve cannot because of obesity, lack of a high school education, or significant criminal history.

Poverty is a central factor in each of these problems. Children in low-income families are twice as likely to be obese as those in middle and upper income brackets; they are also seven times more likely to drop out of high school, and they are at much higher risk for falling into cycles of escalating crime. As a result, fewer young adults are eligible for military recruitment, which hampers our ability to maintain a top-notch, all-volunteer army and compromises our mission readiness.

The U.S. is the greatest nation on earth, but our freedoms and our economic, military and political power have always been rooted in the belief that if you work hard, you can get ahead and provide a better life for your children. When one of the best indications a person is poor in America is that they are working multiple jobs, it is clear that the American dream is in jeopardy. There are clearly moral and economic problems when millions of Americans are desperate for work and unable to meet their families' basic needs. This also opens the door for other rapidly growing economic powers to tilt the balance of global power in their favor.

This is more than an issue of dollars and cents; it is about the example we set. A free-market system that does not provide opportunities for all of us to succeed undermines one of our most convincing arguments against totalitarian regimes and state-run economies that often oppose our interests abroad. The idea that is America is one of our greatest military assets. It is also an incalculable benefit to every military mission we undertake. America stands for more than just a specific place bounded by geography; it stands for the idea that all its people should have the opportunity to reach their God-given potential. Throughout the world, even in countries that are our enemies, millions aspire to the American dream because our example shows it is possible. That is a force that often dwarfs our guns, tanks and warships.

But every time a child in Appalachian coal country goes to bed hungry, we lose some of our moral strength. Each time a single mother has to take on a third or a fourth job just to make ends meet, we squander our credibility. After the recession, with so many hardworking American households falling back into poverty as the richest among us capture even more of America's wealth, our global example is becoming undermined.

As our members of Congress evaluate budget priorities to strengthen our military, they should also look inward at the health and vitality of our economic structures. They must contend with this reality: If we are to continue as the world's sole superpower, we must focus on investments at home that will benefit all Americans.

Analyze

1. "Attempting to maintain a robust national military without addressing domestic poverty is like building a house on sinking sand; no matter how solid the house is, it will fall without a strong foundation to support it." What is the name of the rhetorical device used in this sentence? Is the device effective?
2. How many Americans does the article say work full-time but still can't lift their families out of poverty?
3. Blunt and Monroe state explicitly that the problem is *not* what?

Explore

1. Blunt and Monroe write: "Three out of 4 Americans who should be able to serve [in the military] cannot because of obesity, lack of high school education, or significant criminal history." Poverty, they claim, is a factor in each of these problems. What therefore happens to the American military as a consequence of high poverty rates?
2. Blunt and Monroe argue: "When one of the best indications a person is poor in America is that they are working multiple jobs, it is clear that the American dream is in jeopardy. There are clearly moral and economic problems when millions of Americans are desperate for work and unable to meet their families' basic needs. This also opens the door for other rapidly growing economic powers to tilt the balance of global power in their favor." What is the effect of offering both moral and economic reasons for addressing poverty? Is this strategy successful? Who is their target audience? Explain.
3. Blunt and Monroe claim that the idea of the American dream is more powerful than "guns, tanks and warships," so if others see our free-market system failing, Americans suffering, and the dream crumbling, then there are global consequences. Are you convinced by this argument? Write a professional letter to the authors in which you respond fully to their argument—agreeing, disagreeing, or extending it with well-researched support.

Maura O'Connor
"Subsidizing Starvation"

Maura O'Connor is a journalist who writes on criminal justice issues and news for *New York World*. She also writes on international subjects regarding foreign aid and humanitarian issues, reporting from Afghanistan, Africa, Haiti, and Sri Lanka. The following article was published in *Foreign Policy*, in partnership with *The Investigative Fund* at Nation Institute, which describes itself as supporting "important investigative stories with the potential for social impact, particularly on issues that may be bypassed by the mainstream media." In it, O'Connor considers how ongoing American taxpayer-funded farm subsidies hurt local economies abroad.

How should American leaders weigh national economic interests against consequences that might increase poverty abroad?

In the wake of Haiti's devastating 7.0-magnitude earthquake exactly three years ago, former U.S. President Bill Clinton issued an unusual and now infamous apology. Calling his subsidies to American rice farmers in the 1990s a mistake because it undercut rice production in Haiti, Clinton said he had struck a "devil's bargain" that ultimately resulted in greater poverty and food insecurity in Haiti.

"It may have been good for some of my farmers in Arkansas, but it has not worked," he said. "I have to live every day with the consequences of the lost capacity to produce a rice crop in Haiti to feed those people, because of what I did."

Despite Clinton's dramatic confession and his role as the United Nations' special envoy for Haiti, little has changed in the last three years for the Caribbean country's farmers. If anything, they appear worse off. Before Hurricane Sandy hit the eastern seaboard, its rain and flooding caused $234 million in agricultural losses in Haiti. For a brief moment, coverage of the disaster in the American media shone a light on the miserable conditions that the country's farmers are faced with—a lack of infrastructure, capital, and markets that could help their families and the country prosper.

Meanwhile, for the last year a piece of U.S. legislation that could have arguably changed the playing field for Haiti's farmers has been stalled in

Washington, D.C. A new $500 billion, five-year farm bill that might have cut subsidies to American rice farmers was never passed. And in the final hours of 2012, politicians extended the old one for another nine months.

5   The move effectively kicked the can down the road for changes to America's decades-old agricultural policies—changes that could represent the first challenge to the "devil's bargain" Haiti and Arkansas have been a part of for so long.

Rice is a big deal in Arkansas—the state produces half of the United States' total rice crop—and Stuttgart, a small community nestled in thousands of acres of rice fields south of Little Rock, is no exception. For a long time, it was considered an offense in Stuttgart to buy any beer but Budweiser. Even if you could find a Coors, drinking it was viewed as self-defeating, seeing as Anheuser-Busch was a significant purchaser of the region's rice.

The world's two largest rice mills are located in the center of Stuttgart and process 40 percent of the country's rice crop, shipping the product to domestic and foreign markets on trains and river barges. These mills, rising out of the farmland like glacial erratics, are cooperatives owned by over 9,000 farmers in the region.

In Stuttgart, the farm bill has been a tremendous source of anxiety over the last year. For rice farmer Dow Brantley, the consequences are huge. Cuts to subsidy programs would take away his safety net and the risk of growing rice would become prohibitive, forcing him to turn his fields to corn or soybeans. "There's a lot of fear in the countryside," he said.

Brantley's family has been farming in Arkansas for 100 years, starting out as sharecroppers on a small plot. Today they own a 9,000-acre farm in Stuttgart. Rice is Brantley's highest-grossing crop, and a third of the farm's acreage is dedicated to paddy that he harvests and delivers to Riceland Foods, Stuttgart's largest mill.

10   Brantley's farm is a marvel of modern farming technology. Thirteen satellite-guided tractors level his fields to pancake flatness, extensive irrigation pipes stream water from aquifers deep in the ground, and crop-dusting planes drop fertilizer and pesticides throughout the growing season. It takes just three employees to monitor 3,000 acres of rice once the crop is planted.

Thanks to modern farms such as Brantley's, and the efficiency and scale of rice production in Arkansas, the United States has been a major player in the global rice trade since the 1970s. The country may only produce around

2 percent of global output, but it is consistently among the top five exporters in the world. Arkansas rice is eaten around the world—from Japan to Mexico to Turkey—and roughly half of the rice grown in the state is sold in foreign markets. "People don't realize how much that plays into what we do here, this itty-bitty community in Arkansas," Brantley explained.

One early morning in June, I drove with Brantley around his farm as he checked the water levels in the verdant rice fields. He pointed out the irrigation pumps his dad invested in years ago and talked about his deep love for agriculture. But his mind was in Washington, D.C., where the Senate was debating the farm bill. The legislation was being touted by many politicians on both sides of the aisle as a fiscally responsible measure that would yield $23 billion in savings for American taxpayers, but those savings were created in part by cutting a subsidy program known as "direct payments"—one that rice farmers in Arkansas have heavily relied on for years.

According to the Environmental Working Group, Arkansas farmers received more than $2 billion in direct payments from the federal government between 1995 and 2011, half of which was for rice production. Riceland Foods and Producers Rice Mill, the first- and second-largest recipients of federal subsidies in the state, received over $868 million in subsidies during the same period. The new proposal in the Senate's farm bill was a crop insurance program designed to protect farmers in the event of shortfalls in yield. But rice is an irrigated crop and not dependent on rain, meaning yields are consistent; rice farmers would stop getting direct payments and the crop insurance program would likely never pay out for them.

Just hours after Brantley toured his farm with me, the Senate passed the bill by a vote of 64 to 35. The House of Representatives' version, which includes a "price loss coverage" system to support growers in the event of falling rice prices, never made it to a vote.

"If you take away these direct payments and the domestic market does 15 not make up the difference, odds are farmers are going to grow more soybeans and corn," explained Keith Glover, the president and CEO of Producers Rice Mill. "What remaining rice is grown will obviously be at a higher price, and we're going to be less competitive in the world market. Over the long haul, if we're less competitive that means less exports."

While this prospect is a bleak one for the domestic rice industry, others view it as a long-overdue change. For years, organizations from Oxfam to the Cato Institute have harshly criticized American rice subsidies for enabling the United States to dump its product in developing countries at depressed prices, making it difficult for small-scale farmers to export their own rice or compete in their local markets. As these critics see it, taxpayer dollars have inflated America's competitiveness in global markets while destroying agriculture sectors in countries from Ghana to Indonesia.

Perhaps the most devastating example of this trade distortion, critics say, is Haiti. Since 1995, when it dropped its import tariffs on rice from 50 to 3 percent as part of a structural adjustment program run by the International Monetary Fund (IMF) and World Bank, Haiti has steadily increased its imports of rice from the north. Today it is the fifth-largest importer of American rice in the world despite having a population of just 10 million. Much of Haiti's rice comes from Arkansas; each year, Riceland Foods and Producers Rice Mill send millions of tons of rice down the Mississippi river on barges to New Orleans, where the rice is loaded onto container ships, taken to port in Haiti, and packaged as popular brands such as Tchaco or Mega Rice. Haiti today imports over 80 percent of its rice from the United States, making it a critical market for farmers in Arkansas.

Development experts argue that while U.S. exports may feed people cheaply in the short run, they have exacerbated poverty and food insecurity over time, and subsidies are largely to blame. "The support that U.S. rice producers receive is a big factor in why they are a big player in the global rice market and the leading source of imported rice in Haiti," said Marc Cohen, a senior researcher on humanitarian policy and climate change at Oxfam America. "If governments that preached trade liberalization in Geneva would practice it—and that includes reducing domestic support measures that affect trade—if everything was on a level playing field, that would be very helpful to Haiti."

"You have a country which is 70 percent farmers and you're importing 60 to 70 percent of your food," added Regine Barjon, the marketing director of the Miami-based Haitian-American Chamber of Commerce, in reference to Haiti. The country may have 700,000 hectares of underutilized arable land, according to Barjon's estimate, but it nevertheless maintains chronic trade deficits and has levels of food security that are only slightly better than those of Somalia and the Democratic Republic of Congo.

20   Still, changes to U.S. farm subsidy policy could arguably destabilize Haiti's food security if American agricultural products can't be replaced by equally cheap imports or the country's farmers cannot increase their own production. One ton of Haitian rice is around $300 more expensive than

American rice on the Haitian market, according to Haitian importers. If imports drop and prices rise, not only will there not be enough local product to feed the population, but it will likely be difficult for average Haitian citizens, 75 percent of whom live on less than $2 a day, to afford the household staple. Keith Glover of Producers Rice Mill likened American rice in Haiti to a Wal-Mart in a small southern town. "It hurts some people there and it helps other people have more purchasing power," he said. "We are able to ship rice at a better price that gives the average family in Haiti more purchasing power." But in 2011, the World Food Program reported Haitians' purchasing power fell by 10 percent because of rising food prices and widespread unemployment, raising questions about whether the Wal-Mart model is what Haitians need to ensure the country's food security.

Others don't see food security as the goal, they want food sovereignty— Haitians feeding Haitians, like they used to. "When I was growing up, Haiti exported rice, sugar, coffee, beans, a lot of things," said Josette Perard, who runs an organization in Port-au-Prince called the Lambi Fund that funnels money for development to farmer collectives in the countryside. Like a lot of Haitians, the 72-year-old Perard is keenly aware of the history that has contributed to the dismal state of agriculture today—a reality that she says has its roots in Haiti's declaration of independence from France in 1804, when foreign nations refused to trade with a country run by former slaves. "The United States, the British, the French, the Spanish, and the Portuguese had slaves in their colonies," Perard explained. "They were afraid that Haiti would export its revolution."

Shut out of global markets, Haiti's farmers managed to survive, feeding the population and producing trade surpluses into the 20th century. Throughout the 1970s, Haiti imported a mere 19 percent of its food. The regimes of François Duvalier and his son Jean-Claude ("Baby Doc") Duvalier had abysmal human rights records, but they largely protected farmers from foreign competition by instituting virtual bans on foreign food with tariffs that neared 100 percent. The country was self-sufficient when it came to rice production in part because Haitians only ate rice two or three times a week as part of a diverse diet that included corn and sorghum. According to Perard and many others from an older generation, the country was better off nutritionally as well.

In the 1980s, Baby Doc initiated a period of economic liberalization as part of an effort to establish a thriving manufacturing- and export-based economy that would create jobs for a large and cheap labor force. For a time, this vision seemed manifest. According to Ernest Preeg, the U.S. Ambassador to Haiti from 1981 to 1983, the country had around 200 domestic and foreign manufacturing companies and was producing everything from baseballs to clothing to tomato sauce. "Haiti was just as far along as anyone else," said Preeg. "People came to Port-au-Prince to get jobs because it was a burgeoning export economy." Preeg wrote an article in 1984 in which he echoed the view of many others that Haiti could be the "Taiwan of the Caribbean."

A series of international trade embargos in the early 1990s—prompted by a military coup against President Jean-Bertrand Aristide—not only destroyed the country's business sector, but also depressed agriculture by cutting off imports of raw materials like fertilizer. When the embargo was finally lifted in 1994, the IMF and World Bank stepped into the void and promoted structural adjustment programs aimed at setting the country's economy back on track. Among their conditions was lowering tariffs on food imports—a policy Haitian farmers now call *plan lanmo*, or the "death plan" in Creole. Soon after, President Clinton signed the Federal Agricultural Improvement and Reform Act of 1996, which shifted farm policy to direct payments for farmers. It was this legislation that Clinton dramatically apologized for in 2010.

25   Open markets, virtually no access to banks and credit, and a lack of private and public sector investment made it impossible for Haitian farmers to thrive. Today, most farmers have an income level of just $400 per year and they view the policies that brought them to this state as not just bad economics for Haitians, but also as an ongoing assault by foreigners on their cultural independence. "It was a campaign against Haitian culture," said Ferry Pierre-Charles, an agronomist with the Lambi Fund. "We have a lot of big white people here, but they are coming to take care of their own interests; they don't really care about local production."

Symeus Doval is one of 130,000 rice farmers in Haiti's rural Artibonite Valley in the north, and she remembers when she first started to see American rice in the market. "It was almost for free," she recalled while we sat on wooden stools in the crowded Croix Des Bossales market in Port-au-Prince. "Like a gift." Demand for the affordable new rice increased as poverty levels rose and Haitians grew dependent on the grain.

Today, Doval, who has been farming for five decades, grows her rice crop in much the same way that her parents did before her. She plants the one

hectare of paddy field she owns by hand, relying on rain and small irrigation canals to flood the crop. After the harvest, she dries the rice on cement
slabs in the sun before processing it with a small mechanical mill. Then
she brings her product to Croix Des Bossales, where it sometimes sells for
twice as much as the American rice hawked in nearby stalls. "This rice is
good for you," explained Doval. "People want to buy it but they don't have
the money." To compete with American rice, she needs the resources to
improve her crop and grow more of it. "We don't have money or credit so we
can buy more equipment and seed," she said.

Doval isn't alone. In the Artibonite town of Petite-Rivière, members of
a farming collective called AIM explained that between their 600 farmers,
they lack a single tractor and the ability to sell their rice when markets
are favorable. "We don't have financing," said Gilbert Meulus, a farmer and
one of the leaders of AIM. "If we had that we could do better and not sell
[our rice] to pay for school or the hospital."

International development organizations have begun to recognize the
importance of agriculture in Haiti after decades of prioritizing other
sectors and delivering food aid that some say only further depressed local
markets. In recent months, the Inter-American Development Bank ap-
proved both a $27 million land tenure security project and a $15 million
agricultural reform project. USAID made "food and economic security"
one of its four "pillars" of development in Haiti following the country's
2010 earthquake, and the World Food Program is beginning to procure
some of its food aid from local sources (4 percent of Haiti's rice imports
come in the form of food aid).

But the key partner in implementing these programs is the Haitian   30
government, which has a history of neglecting its peasant base and relying
on foreign countries for over half of its anemic budget. "Changes in U.S.
farm policy will only promote agriculture development and food security
if the government of Haiti adopts polices that put agriculture higher on
the agenda," argued Regine Barjon of the Haitian-American Chamber of
Commerce. "The [government] said they want to reduce Haiti's reliance on
food imports by 25 percent over the next four years. In order to do that,
they need money."

In June, one month after he assumed his role as Haiti's minister of
agriculture, natural resources, and rural development, Thomas Jacques met
me at his ministry's temporary offices. The original ministry building—
a stunning French colonial-looking behemoth—was damaged in the

earthquake and stands empty, rubble still pouring through its front doors as though it were frozen in January 2010. Jacques explained that he had spent six years in the ministry focusing on the question of rice, and one of his first acts as minister in the coming months would be to create a rice commission made up of agronomists, government officials, and businessmen that would focus on increasing domestic production. Not only would the commission create technology "packages" for farmers, he added, but it would also consider raising import tariffs to protect the local market. "The main function is to make sure that the price of the product is accessible and people can afford it," Jacques said. "It's a balance of production and importation. It has to be a fair balance." He admitted that the ministry's paltry budget is a "big problem" standing in the way of his goal.

Most significantly, Jacques said that Haiti's rice importers would be part of the commission. The business is dominated by a handful of figures, some of whom have longstanding business relationships with mills in Arkansas. According to a 2010 USAID report, a mere six importers control 70 percent of the import market and often exhibit rent-seeking behavior—seeking profits without creating new wealth—that can further exacerbate food insecurity in the country. It is arguably these importers that have the greatest interest in Haiti's dependence on imports, but they are also uniquely capable of making significant investments in local agriculture if they could be convinced that doing so would be profitable. Although a price-control commission for food commodities was created in September, there have been no reports of a rice production commission beginning its work.

One of Haiti's major rice importers is SAJ Holdings, which Steeve Khawly's father started in the early 1990s. At one time, the company represented about 10 percent of the rice import market in the country, according to Khawly, who now runs the business. Khawly said he believes importers cannot invest in Haitian agriculture without government leadership to offset the considerable risks. "Only the government can invest in irrigation and the rehabilitation of the land," he noted. "And if all those conditions were met, the importers can then say, 'I want to be part of the process. I'm going to invest in the industry myself since I already have the distribution.'"

Ten years ago, Khawly bought a rice mill in Guyana, disassembled it, and shipped it to Haiti. "When I realized there were 40,000 hectares of land in Haiti and not one single rice mill, I said there must be rice to process," he explained. But even with a monopoly on Haiti's only mill, he could not process and sell enough rice on the local market to make the endeavor profitable. He was forced to disassemble the mill and ship it back to Guyana. In spite of this failure, Khawly still marvels at the possibilities. "If we were to do the same tonnage that the U.S. does per hectare, that would mean 160,000 tons of rice per season. Every six months, we could do it."

Some experts believe investment will have to come from abroad, possibly in the form of large U.S. companies who invest in entire value chains, from farms to processing plants. But the barriers to entry in Haiti are formidable, particularly with a government bureaucracy that is sometimes its own worst enemy. Four years ago, Carl Brothers, the vice president of marketing for Riceland Foods in Stuttgart, began to think of ways that the company could invest in Haiti's agriculture sector. "It's an important market to us, we value our relationship with the Haitian people," Brothers explained. "We met with the last two Haitian presidents and talked to them about how we could help."

Brothers said he believes rice is simply too expensive to grow in Haiti but felt that investments in corn or other fruits and vegetables could give Haitian farmers a competitive advantage. Despite Riceland's efforts, however, the company was unable to make progress. "Everyone gets fervored up and we call and call and call and can't get anyone to call back," Brothers recalled.

A congressional effort to scale back U.S. farm subsidies as part of a new farm bill could give Haiti a rare window of opportunity to begin growing its own food. But if the country does not move fast enough, it may simply shift its dependence from the United States to other countries. Last year, in what may be a glimpse of things to come, Brazil moved over a million tons of rice onto the world market—including thousands of tons of rice into Haiti.

The stakes could not be higher for Haiti as it attempts to rebound from the 2010 earthquake, as well as decades of stagnant economic growth and political instability. Food sovereignty, a quaint and impractical idea to some, is fraught with symbolism in Haiti—a country where foreign NGOs are often more visible than the national government and U.N. peacekeeping forces are in their ninth year patrolling the streets. "We are losing our identity," said Josette Perard, the nonprofit chief in Port-au-Prince. "When your belly is in the hand of the foreigner, you lose your respect. And people want to regain their self-respect."

Analyze

1. In 2010, what policy decision did former President Bill Clinton famously apologize for? Why did he call it a "devil's bargain"?
2. What is a "subsidy"? What is "food security"? What is "food sovereignty"?
3. Why do Haitian farmers now call the International Monetary Fund (IMF) and World Bank's 1994 requirement that they lower tariffs on food imports (thus encouraging the free influx of foreign goods) the "death plan"?

Explore

1. On one level, this story is about unintended consequences. While trying to help one group succeed, another group is harmed. Explain in your own words how subsidizing rice farmers in Arkansas hurt rice farmers in Haiti. Then explain how cutting spending in the Farm Bill by reducing subsidies could hurt Arkansas farmers.
2. O'Connor writes: "Development experts argue that while U.S. exports may feed people cheaply in the short run, they have exacerbated poverty and food insecurity over time, and subsidies are largely to blame." Why do subsidies, which often provide inexpensive food to hungry markets, sometimes cause poverty and food insecurity? What happens to local producers when these goods arrive? Research other examples that help explain this dynamic.
3. Explain what Josette Perard, the nonprofit chief in Port-au-Prince, means when she says: "We are losing our identity. When your belly is in the hand of the foreigner, you lose your respect. And people want to regain their self-respect." Is losing self-respect an unfortunate but necessary consequence of foreign aid? Do the poor who receive aid have a right to self-respect? Why does O'Connor end her article with this quote? Write an essay exploring the relationship between receiving aid and receiving respect.

Forging Connections

1. Many readings in this chapter explore the consequences for children living in poverty. Drawing from at least two readings in this chapter and additional outside sources (e.g., the Annie E. Casey Foundation),

write a researched argument in which you explain the unique challenges of children in poverty and recommend programs or policies that
can improve their well-being.

2. Advocates for the poor want people to understand the physical and
emotional consequences of poverty, but it can be challenging to present the suffering of others without exploiting them. Sometimes advocates are criticized for making those appeals with too much pathos
(emotion or sentimentality), using the "sob story" rather than constructing compelling arguments based on logos (logic and reason).
Journalists and researchers are ethically obligated to tell stories that
are representative and reliable, yet they retain the power of editing
data and quotes that shape how readers receive information. Personal
narratives and memoirs allow people to tell their own stories on their
own terms, yet vulnerable persons don't often have the time, inclina-
tion, or access to write about their suffering. This chapter includes a
variety of storytelling styles that express the consequences of poverty.
Write an essay analyzing the success of the appeals used in this chapter.
Are the poor ever exploited in such storytelling?

Looking Further

1. An honored value of American culture is that we are dreamers who
are always looking to improve our circumstances. Some of the readings
in this chapter (e.g., Alexie, Bauer and Ramírez, Livingston, Potts,
Sullivan-Hackley, Thompson) and in this book (e.g., Adair, Haskins
and Sawhill, McMillan Cottom, Wright) explore the negative consequences of dreaming or aspiring for more. Write an essay on what it
means to buy into the American Dream. Is buying into it ever too costly?

2. Shame and low self-esteem often punctuate the personal narratives of
people who experience poverty, yet we also see a pattern of resolve and
determination to change those material circumstances, to pursue the
American dream. Sometimes that has dire consequences, as we see in
the plight of migrant farmworkers (Bauer and Ramírez). Compare
readings in this chapter (e.g., Bauer and Ramírez, Blunt and Monroe,
Livingston, Potts, Sullivan-Hackley, Thompson) and throughout the
book (e.g., Adair, DNLee, DuBois, Kenny, Marks, McMillan Cottom,
Poo, Rector and Sheffield, Wright) that explore the sometimes toxic
tension between aspiration and material limits. Why do people choose

to buy an education (Wright) or material goods (McMillan Cottom, Rector and Sheffield) that exceed their means? David Shipler, author of *The Working Poor: Invisible in America*, writes: "[The poor] are caught between America's hedonism and its dictum that the poor are supposed to sacrifice, suffer, and certainly not purchase any fun for themselves" (27). Research the psychological effects of poverty and inequality. How do people adapt, cope, and motivate themselves to see beyond hard times?

4

Privilege: Who Isn't Poor?

This illustration by William Balfour Ker (c. 1906) visualizes class struggle in the 18th century. Depicted are people we might call the privileged elite and the working poor. How would you visualize privilege and poverty today?

INTRODUCTION

Does privilege exist? Haven't we *mandated* equality for all, and don't we *believe* in equal opportunity? Do some people really get a break based on their race, gender, ability, ethnicity, sexuality, etc.? If so, how does that privilege manifest itself and what should we do about it? Most of this book looks at people in poverty, defining poverty as a dynamic state—something reinforced by environmental, legal, and social forces. Some say that people have a lot of help getting poor. Likewise, some say that people have a lot of help getting rich, and wealth reinforces wealth. While we all face risk, wealth can help people buy a bigger safety net to make sure that when those crises inevitably come—disease, divorce, unemployment, natural disasters, etc.—they are only temporary setbacks, not catastrophes. The readings in this chapter explore the extent to which factors such as legal and social discrimination actively reinforce the status quo—further privileging the rich and impoverishing the poor.

Although we have made progress, the readings in this chapter suggest that being white, male, and rich remains a powerful status in the U.S. For example, Equal Pay Day marks the number of extra days into the next calendar year that a woman has to work to earn the same pay as a man doing the same job. When we break those figures down by race, we find that white women fare better than other women. When we look at incarceration, we see that white men are incarcerated at lower rates and for less time than other men who have committed the same crime. Researchers have carefully calculated these discrepancies, but other race- and gender-based losses are less easy to quantify—the loss of a job for not sending the right cultural cues through clothing or language, for example. These readings suggest that when the gatekeepers of social norms and social mobility continue to be dominated by white men (note the gender and racial composition of the U.S. Congress, for example), those values get codified—intentionally or unintentionally—at the expense of others. Furthermore, these readings explore the sense of "entitlement to help," or "cultural colonization," that can also come with that privilege. They examine cases in which privileged individuals or institutions impose their vision of a better world onto poor, vulnerable populations without honoring the vision and skills poor people can contribute.

The readings in this chapter are framed by Courtney Martin's call not only to identify all our privileges—racial, gender, financial, physical ability, mental ability, etc.—but to act on that knowledge. Yet Teju Cole warns us that the desire for privileged people to act, to "make a difference," doesn't mean they have the insight to do so; harm rather than help is too often the consequence of good intentions. In his blog post, Gene Marks, a self-proclaimed "middle aged white guy," posits himself as a "poor black kid," imagining how he would take advantage of the technological and educational opportunities he claims are available to everyone. DNLee rebuts Marks's argument, imagining herself as a wealthy white suburbanite who doesn't quite get why aspiration alone isn't sufficient to overcome the structural barriers that keep some poor kids from high achievement. Responding to those who don't understand why some poor people buy luxury items, Tressie McMillan Cottom explains that spending on material items can be a shrewd investment to win over the "gatekeepers" who daily reinforce class boundaries and thwart social mobility. Senator James Webb argues that current diversity programs simply favor anyone who is not white and should be abolished. Adam Serwer rebuts Webb, emphasizing the "gaping hole" in his argument that fails to acknowledge the decades in which government programs were designed to help whites. *The Economist* reports on paradoxical new research showing that the poor are more charitable than the rich. Anthony Zurcher examines the story of a Texas teen who killed four people while driving drunk and then went to rehab instead of jail because his parents could afford it and because the judge thought his pampered upbringing made it difficult for him to comprehend consequences, what some have dubbed the "affluenza" defense.

Courtney Martin
"Moving Past Acknowledging Privilege"

Courtney Martin is a prolific writer and speaker, engaging audiences with cultural critiques on activism, feminism, and social justice. She founded the

Secret Society for Creative Philanthropy and other organizations devoted to social justice work, and she won the Elie Wiesel Prize in ethics in 2002. In the following essay, Martin encourages her readers not only to acknowledge their privilege but also to act, in collaboration with others, to correct unequal access to resources.

In what aspects of your life do you feel privileged and able to act to change the systems that lend you that privilege?

Last week, we experienced a funny study in our public dialogue on race. On Monday, a video of Chris Rock—in which he discussed how backward it is to say the nation had made "progress" in racial relations because, in fact, white people had "become less crazy"—went viral. By Thursday, Donald Trump was bragging about his solid relationship with "the Blacks."

Perhaps this week Chris Rock will have to release a statement rescinding his previous vote of confidence in "the Whites" and while he's at it, apologize to disability rights activists who have long been fighting for people to stop using words like "crazy."

It seems like we, as a nation, are still either inflamed in name-calling (sexist! racist! Communist!), or noticeably silent on more substantive issues like unearned privilege, guilt, and tokenism. Twenty-three years after Peggy McIntosh first wrote her signature article, "White Privilege: Unpacking the Invisible Knapsack," we're still unpacking, and not particularly skillfully.

All those years ago, McIntosh wrote, "As a white person, I realized I had been taught about racism as something which puts others at a disadvantage, but had been taught not to see one of its corollary aspects, white privilege which puts me at an advantage." In other words, part of the work of any person with white privilege—and relatedly, heterosexual privilege, class privilege, etc.—is to get real about the ways in which life is just plain easier for some of us because of ongoing institutional and cultural discrimination.

> "[L]ife is just plain easier for some of us."

5   But part of why McIntosh's article is still being taught so widely, I fear, is because we haven't made much progress in this discussion in the last

couple of decades. Today, white kids from Williamsburg to Berkeley are still trying to grasp the vast implications of being born white, wealthy, able-bodied, etc. This will always be a critical practice, but we have to also push beyond this stage. After we see through the fog of privilege, what do we do with that new vision?

Unfortunately, too many people whom I encounter—particularly on college campuses—get sort of stuck in a muck of guilt. They become invested in testifying to their own lack of ignorance in public spaces (read: "I'm one of the good ones") but then don't constructively reimagine what those spaces might look like in a more just world, and enact the necessary changes. As I traveled from Seattle to Richmond speaking on panels for Women's History Month, I heard many a well-intentioned student stand up at a Q&A session, requesting more inclusion without offering systemic analysis, real stories, or actionable recommendations. The impulse to do some of the intellectual and emotional labor of calling out unchecked privilege, as a person benefiting from some version of it, is a valuable one, but it can't end there.

As educators Dena Simmons and Chrissy Etienne wrote in a presentation they prepared for schoolteachers: "To acknowledge one's privilege is not a moral condemnation. Rather, it is a call to action that requires collective work in order to evenly distribute access to power and to resources so that human agency can be reclaimed and claimed by all. Our intention is not to inspire guilt but to inspire action."

We have to stop treating privilege like a common cold, when it's more like a multifaceted virus. "Privilege" doesn't just mean white, or male, or rich. It is a facet of most everybody's identity and experience, one that is both deeply personal and incredibly political. My friend Chris Gandin Le brought much-needed humor to the topic, writing on my Facebook page: "I feel like an Alanis Morissette song when I think about privilege: 'I'm straight but I'm a refugee/I'm a minority but I'm educationally privileged/ I'm married, but interracially, baby!'"

This humor serves a purpose, though. It's time to tackle different questions.

What would it look like to actually redistribute economic resources? 10 Resource Generation, a New York-nonprofit is organizing wealth inheritors to consider and act on that very question. What would it look like to form genuinely diverse coalitions on critical social issues like environmentalism?

The environmental-justice movement—which draws on leaders from the South Bronx to rural West Virginia—has something to teach us all about that kind of collaboration. What would it look like to focus on critical mass? The National Council for Research on Women has studied this transformative effect in the financial sector.

Talking about privilege is one step better than the Donald Trump version of diversity that we sadly call dialogue in this culture. But it's not enough. The question is not just about what unearned privileges we have been walking around with but also about what it would take to change the systems that gave us these privileges in the first place. We must move beyond acknowledgment and guilt, panels and conferences, and start living, working, organizing, consuming, and loving differently.

Analyze

1. This article explores the claim that racism is often discussed as something that puts someone else at a disadvantage, but what, according to Martin, is it that we haven't always explored?

2. What point is Martin trying to make when she quotes her friend saying that acknowledging privilege is like living an Alanis Morissette song? Is this strategy effective?

3. When she talks to college students, Martin says they often call for more inclusion, but they often fail to offer what?

Explore

1. Martin argues that we are still "either inflamed in name-calling (Sexist! Racist! Communist!), or noticeably silent on more substantive issues like unearned privilege, guilt, and tokenism." Do you agree with that observation? Use examples to support your response.

2. Martin references a seminal article by Peggy McIntosh, "White Privilege: Unpacking the Invisible Knapsack," that leads readers through the process of identifying and naming their own privileges (we *all* have something, she suggests)—gender, racial, ability, religious, economic, etc. Write a personal narrative or create a visual (PowerPoint, Prezi, collage, comic, etc.) in which you identify your own privileges. In what way might those privileges make life "just plain easier" for you compared to those who don't have those privileges? Read McIntosh's essay (available online) to help you work through this "unpacking."

3. After identifying our privileges, though, Martin says we must get past the "muck of guilt" and take action. What action does Martin propose? What action is necessary or even possible after acknowledging those privileges? Is privilege reversible? Or is action necessary at all?

Teju Cole
"The White Savior Industrial Complex"

Raised in Nigeria and currently residing in Brooklyn, Teju Cole is a writer, art historian, and photographer. He is the author of two books, including *Open Road*, which earned numerous awards. He also contributes writing to the *New York Times*, *The New Yorker*, *The Atlantic*, and several other magazines. In the following article, originally published in *The Atlantic*, Cole critiques the sentimental reasons that inspire some people to help others.

How does your own privilege motivate you to help others?

A week and a half ago, I watched the Kony 2012 video. Afterward, I wrote a brief seven-part response, which I posted in sequence on my Twitter account:

1- From Sachs to Kristof to Invisible Children to TED, the fastest growth industry in the US is the White Savior Industrial Complex.

12:33 PM - 8 Mar 2012

1,105 RETWEETS **331** FAVORITES

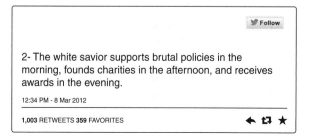

2- The white savior supports brutal policies in the morning, founds charities in the afternoon, and receives awards in the evening.

12:34 PM - 8 Mar 2012

1,003 RETWEETS **359** FAVORITES

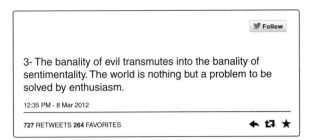

3- The banality of evil transmutes into the banality of sentimentality. The world is nothing but a problem to be solved by enthusiasm.

12:35 PM - 8 Mar 2012

727 RETWEETS 264 FAVORITES

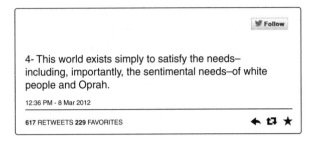

4- This world exists simply to satisfy the needs–including, importantly, the sentimental needs–of white people and Oprah.

12:36 PM - 8 Mar 2012

617 RETWEETS 229 FAVORITES

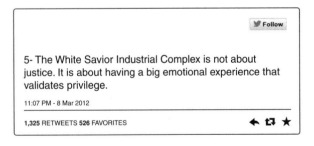

5- The White Savior Industrial Complex is not about justice. It is about having a big emotional experience that validates privilege.

11:07 PM - 8 Mar 2012

1,325 RETWEETS 526 FAVORITES

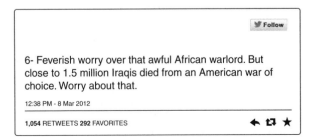

6- Feverish worry over that awful African warlord. But close to 1.5 million Iraqis died from an American war of choice. Worry about that.

12:38 PM - 8 Mar 2012

1,054 RETWEETS 292 FAVORITES

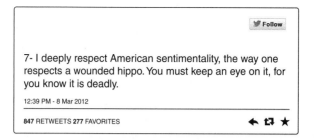

These tweets were retweeted, forwarded, and widely shared by readers. They migrated beyond Twitter to blogs, Tumblr, Facebook, and other sites; I'm told they generated fierce arguments. As the days went by, the tweets were reproduced in their entirety on the websites of the *Atlantic* and the *New York Times*, and they showed up on German, Spanish, and Portuguese sites. A friend e-mailed to tell me that the fourth tweet, which cheekily name-checks Oprah, was mentioned on Fox television.

These sentences of mine, written without much premeditation, had touched a nerve. I heard back from many people who were grateful to have read them. I heard back from many others who were disappointed or furious. Many people, too many to count, called me a racist. One person likened me to the Mau Mau. The *Atlantic* writer who'd reproduced them, while agreeing with my broader points, described the language in which they were expressed as "resentment."

This weekend, I listened to a radio interview given by the Pulitzer Prize-winning journalist Nicholas Kristof. Kristof is best known for his regular column in the *New York Times* in which he often gives accounts of his activism or that of other Westerners. When I saw the Kony 2012 video, I found it tonally similar to Kristof's approach, and that was why I mentioned him in the first of my seven tweets.

Those tweets, though unpremeditated, were intentional in their irony and seriousness. I did not write them to score cheap points, much less to hurt anyone's feelings. I believed that a certain kind of language is too infrequently seen in our public discourse. I am a novelist. I traffic in subtleties, and my goal in writing a novel is to leave the reader not knowing what to think. A good novel shouldn't have a point.

But there's a place in the political sphere for direct speech and, in the past few years in the U.S., there has been a chilling effect on a certain kind of direct speech pertaining to rights. The president is wary of being seen as   5 the "angry black man." People of color, women, and gays—who now have greater access to the centers of influence than ever before—are under pressure to be well-behaved when talking about their struggles. There is an expectation that we can talk about sins but no one must be identified as a sinner: newspapers love to describe words or deeds as "racially charged" even in those cases when it would be more honest to say "racist"; we agree that there is rampant misogyny, but misogynists are nowhere to be found; homophobia is a problem but no one is homophobic. One cumulative effect of this policed language is that when someone dares to point out something as obvious as white privilege, it is seen as unduly provocative. Marginalized voices in America have fewer and fewer avenues to speak plainly about what they suffer; the effect of this enforced civility is that those voices are falsified or blocked entirely from the discourse.

It's only in the context of this neutered language that my rather tame tweets can be seen as extreme. The interviewer on the radio show I listened to asked Kristof if he had heard of me. "Of course," he said. She asked him what he made of my criticisms. His answer was considered and genial, but what he said worried me more than an angry outburst would have:

> There has been a real discomfort and backlash among middle-class educated Africans, Ugandans in particular in this case, but people more broadly, about having Africa as they see it defined by a warlord who does particularly brutal things, and about the perception that Americans are going to ride in on a white horse and resolve it. To me though, it seems even more uncomfortable to think that we as white Americans should not intervene in a humanitarian disaster because the victims are of a different skin color.

Here are some of the "middle-class educated Africans" Kristof, whether he is familiar with all of them and their work or not, chose to take issue with: Ugandan journalist Rosebell Kagumire, who covered the Lord's Resistance Army in 2005 and made an eloquent video response to Kony 2012; Ugandan scholar Mahmood Mamdani, one of the world's leading specialists on Uganda and the author of a thorough riposte to the political wrong-headedness of Invisible Children; and Ethiopian-American novelist Dinaw Mengestu, who sought out Joseph Kony, met his lieutenants, and recently wrote a brilliant essay about how Kony 2012 gets the issues wrong. They have a different take on what Kristof calls a "humanitarian disaster," and this may be because they see the larger disasters behind it: militarization of poorer countries, short-sighted agricultural policies, resource extraction, the propping up of corrupt governments, and the astonishing complexity of long-running violent conflicts over a wide and varied terrain.

I want to tread carefully here: I do not accuse Kristof of racism nor do I believe he is in any way racist. I have no doubt that he has a good heart. Listening to him on the radio, I began to think we could iron the whole thing out over a couple of beers. But that, precisely, is what worries me. That is what made me compare American sentimentality to a "wounded hippo." His good heart does not always allow him to think constellationally. He does not connect the dots or see the patterns of power behind the isolated "disasters." All he sees are hungry mouths, and he, in his own advocacy-by-journalism way, is putting food in those mouths as fast as he can. All he sees is need, and he sees no need to reason out the need for the need.

But I disagree with the approach taken by Invisible Children in particular, and by the White Savior Industrial Complex in general, because there is much more to doing good work than "making a difference." There is the principle of first do no harm. There is the idea that those who are being helped ought to be consulted over the matters that concern them.

I write all this from multiple positions. I write as an African, a black   10
man living in America. I am every day subject to the many microaggressions of American racism. I also write this as an American, enjoying the many privileges that the American passport affords and that residence in this country makes possible. I involve myself in this critique of privilege: my own privileges of class, gender, and sexuality are insufficiently examined. My cell phone was likely manufactured by poorly treated workers in a Chinese factory. The coltan in the phone can probably be traced to the conflict-riven Congo. I don't fool myself that I am not implicated in these transnational networks of oppressive practices.

And I also write all this as a novelist and story-writer: I am sensitive to the power of narratives. When Jason Russell, narrator of the Kony 2012 video, showed his cheerful blonde toddler a photo of Joseph Kony as the embodiment of evil (a glowering dark man), and of his friend Jacob as the representative of helplessness (a sweet-faced African), I wondered how Russell's little boy would develop a nuanced sense of the lives of others, particularly others of a different race from his own. How would that little boy come to understand that others have autonomy; that their right to life is not exclusive of a right to self-respect? In a different context, John Berger once wrote, "A singer may be innocent; never the song."

One song we hear too often is the one in which Africa serves as a backdrop for white fantasies of conquest and heroism. From the colonial project to *Out of Africa* to *The Constant Gardener* and Kony 2012, Africa has provided a space onto which white egos can conveniently be projected. It is a liberated space in which the usual rules do not apply: a nobody from America or Europe can go to Africa and become a godlike savior or, at the very least, have his or her emotional needs satisfied. Many have done it under the banner of "making a difference." To state this obvious and well-attested truth does not make me a racist or a Mau Mau. It does give me away as an "educated middle-class African," and I plead guilty as charged. (It is also worth noting that there are other educated middle-class Africans who see this matter differently from me. That is what people, educated and otherwise, do: they assess information and sometimes disagree with each other.)

In any case, Kristof and I are in profound agreement about one thing: there is much happening in many parts of the African continent that is not as it ought to be. I have been fortunate in life, but that doesn't mean I haven't seen or experienced African poverty first-hand. I grew up in a land of military coups and economically devastating, IMF-imposed "structural adjustment" programs. The genuine hurt of Africa is no fiction.

And we also agree on something else: that there is an internal ethical urge that demands that each of us serve justice as much as he or she can. But beyond the immediate attention that he rightly pays hungry mouths, child soldiers, or raped civilians, there are more complex and more widespread problems. There are serious problems of governance, of infrastructure, of democracy, and of law and order. These problems are neither simple in themselves nor are they reducible to slogans. Such problems are both intricate and intensely local.

15   How, for example, could a well-meaning American "help" a place like Uganda today? It begins, I believe, with some humility with regards to the people in those places. It begins with some respect for the agency of the people of Uganda in their own lives. A great deal of work had been done, and continues to be done, by Ugandans to improve their own country, and ignorant comments (I've seen many) about how "we have to save them because they can't save themselves" can't change that fact.

Let me draw into this discussion an example from an African country I know very well. Earlier this year, hundreds of thousands of Nigerians took to their country's streets to protest the government's decision to remove a subsidy on petrol. This subsidy was widely seen as one of the few blessings of the country's otherwise catastrophic oil wealth. But what made these protests so heartening is that they were about more than the subsidy removal. Nigeria has one of the most corrupt governments in the world and protesters clearly demanded that something be done about this. The protests went on for days, at considerable personal risk to the protesters. Several young people were shot dead, and the movement was eventually doused when union leaders capitulated and the army deployed on the streets. The movement did not "succeed" in conventional terms. But something important had changed in the political consciousness of the Nigerian populace. For me and for a number of people I know, the protests gave us an opportunity to be proud of Nigeria, many of us for the first time in our lives.

This is not the sort of story that is easy to summarize in an article, much less make a viral video about. After all, there is no simple demand to be made and—since corruption is endemic—no single villain to topple. There is certainly no "bridge character," Kristof's euphemism for white saviors in Third World narratives who make the story more palatable to American viewers. And yet, the story of Nigeria's protest movement is one of the most important from sub-Saharan Africa so far this year. Men and women, of all classes and ages, stood up for what they felt was right; they marched peacefully; they defended each other, and gave each other food and drink; Christians stood guard while Muslims prayed and vice-versa; and they spoke without fear to their leaders about the kind of country they wanted to see. All of it happened with no cool American 20-something heroes in sight.

Joseph Kony is no longer in Uganda and he is no longer the threat he was, but he is a convenient villain for those who need a convenient villain. What Africa needs more pressingly than Kony's indictment is more equitable civil society, more robust democracy, and a fairer system of justice. This is the scaffolding from which infrastructure, security, healthcare, and education can be built. How do we encourage voices like those of the Nigerian masses who marched this January, or those who are engaged in the struggle to develop Ugandan democracy?

If Americans want to care about Africa, maybe they should consider evaluating American foreign policy, which they already play a direct role in through elections, before they impose themselves on Africa itself. The fact of the matter is that Nigeria is one of the top five oil suppliers to the U.S., and American policy is interested first and foremost in the flow of that oil.

The American government did not see fit to support the Nigeria protests. (Though the State Department issued a supportive statement—"our view on that is that the Nigerian people have the right to peaceful protest, we want to see them protest peacefully, and we're also urging the Nigerian security services to respect the right of popular protest and conduct themselves professionally in dealing with the strikes"—it reeked of boilerplate rhetoric and, unsurprisingly, nothing tangible came of it.) This was as expected; under the banner of "American interests," the oil comes first. Under that same banner, the livelihood of corn farmers in Mexico has been destroyed by NAFTA. Haitian rice farmers have suffered appalling losses due to Haiti being flooded with subsidized American rice. A nightmare has been playing out in Honduras in the past three years: an American-backed coup and American militarization of that country have contributed to a conflict in which hundreds of activists and journalists have already been murdered. The Egyptian military, which is now suppressing the country's once-hopeful movement for democracy and killing dozens of activists in the process, subsists on $1.3 billion in annual U.S. aid. This is a litany that will be familiar to some. To others, it will be news. But, familiar or not, it has a bearing on our notions of innocence and our right to "help."

20   Let us begin our activism right here: with the money-driven villainy at the heart of American foreign policy. To do this would be to give up the illusion that the sentimental need to "make a difference" trumps all other considerations. What innocent heroes don't always understand is that they play a useful role for people who have much more cynical motives. The White Savior Industrial Complex is a valve for releasing the unbearable pressures that build in a system built on pillage. We can participate in the economic destruction of Haiti over long years, but when the earthquake strikes it feels good to send $10 each to the rescue fund. I have no opposition, in principle, to such donations (I frequently make them myself), but we must do such things only with awareness of what else is involved. If we are going to interfere in the lives of others, a little due diligence is a minimum requirement.

Success for Kony 2012 would mean increased militarization of the anti-democratic Yoweri Museveni government, which has been in power in Uganda since 1986 and has played a major role in the world's deadliest ongoing conflict, the war in the Congo. But those whom privilege allows to deny constellational thinking would enjoy ignoring this fact. There are other troubling connections, not least of them being that Museveni appears to be a U.S. proxy in its shadowy battles against militants in Sudan and, especially, in Somalia. Who sanctions these conflicts? Under whose authority and oversight are they conducted? Who is being killed and why?

All of this takes us rather far afield from fresh-faced young Americans using the power of YouTube, Facebook, and pure enthusiasm to change the world. A singer may be innocent; never the song.

Analyze

1. What does Cole say were generally the two types of responses to his tweets about the White Savior Industrial Complex?
2. Cole says he writes from multiple positions. Identify them.
3. Although he critiques Kristof, Cole says they also agree in several ways. Identify those points of agreement.

Explore

1. Cole considers the following phrase so instrumental to his argument that he repeats it twice, the second time as the essay's final sentence: "A singer may be innocent; never the song." What does this mean? Why is this central to Cole?
2. In his critique of the White Savior Industrial Complex—defined by an unencumbered, uninformed urge to help—Cole writes that "there is much more in doing good work than 'making a difference.' There is the principle of first do no harm. There is the idea that those who are being helped ought to be consulted over the matters that concern them." Explain what this means. Consider examples in which an effort to help might have done harm. How might that unintended harm have been prevented?
3. Where do you see yourself and your peers in relation to the "fresh-faced young Americans using the power of YouTube, Facebook, and pure enthusiasm to change the world" Cole describes? Does he get that picture right? Is "poverty porn"—a term describing typically white, privileged people displaying pictures of themselves as heroes to typically non-white children or vulnerable adults—a common visual frame among your peers or online? How should "fresh-faced" young Americans respond to this critique? Is apathy the answer? Write a researched response to Cole.

Gene Marks
"If I Were a Poor Black Kid"

A business consultant with his own firm, Gene Marks also regularly writes for the *New York Times*, the *Huffington Post*, Inc.com, and *Philadelphia Magazine*. He also contributes unpaid writing to *Forbes*, a magazine focused on business news and financial information. The following piece, originally published on Forbes.com, contains Marks's opinions on how poor children should seek opportunities to overcome their common adversities.

Do poor children have the same access to resources as their affluent counterparts, even if they need to work harder to find them?

President Obama gave an excellent speech last week in Kansas about inequality in America.

"This is the defining issue of our time." He said. "This is a make-or-break moment for the middle class, and for all those who are fighting to get into the middle class. Because what's at stake is whether this will be a country where working people can earn enough to raise a family, build a modest savings, own a home, secure their retirement."

He's right. The spread between rich and poor has gotten wider over the decades. And the opportunities for the 99% have become harder to realize.

The president's speech got me thinking. My kids are no smarter than similar kids their age from the inner city. My kids have it much easier than their counterparts from West Philadelphia. The world is not fair to those kids mainly because they had the misfortune of being born two miles away into a more difficult part of the world and with a skin color that makes realizing the opportunities that the president spoke about that much harder. This is a fact. In 2011.

5   I am not a poor black kid. I am a middle aged white guy who comes from a middle class white background. So life was easier for me. But that doesn't mean that the prospects are impossible for those kids from the inner city. It doesn't mean that there are no opportunities for them. Or that the 1% control the world and the rest of us have to fight over the scraps left behind. I don't believe that. I believe that everyone in this country has a chance to succeed. Still. In 2011. Even a poor black kid in West Philadelphia.

It takes brains. It takes hard work. It takes a little luck. And a little help from others. It takes the ability and the know-how to use the resources that are available. Like technology. As a person who sells and has worked with technology all my life I also know this.

If I was a poor black kid I would first and most importantly work to make sure I got the best grades possible. I would make it my #1 priority to be able to read sufficiently. I wouldn't care if I was a student at the worst public middle school in the worst inner city. Even the worst have their best. And the very best students, even at the worst schools, have more opportunities. Getting good grades is the key to having more options. With good grades you can choose different, better paths. If you do poorly in school, particularly in a lousy school, you're severely limiting the limited opportunities you have.

And I would use the technology available to me as a student. I know a few school teachers and they tell me that many inner city parents usually have or can afford cheap computers and Internet service nowadays. That because (and sadly) it's oftentimes a necessary thing to keep their kids safe at home than on the streets. And libraries and schools have computers available too. Computers can be purchased cheaply at outlets like TigerDirect and Dell's Outlet. Professional organizations like accountants and architects often offer used computers from their members, sometimes at no cost at all.

If I was a poor black kid I'd use the free technology available to help me study. I'd become expert at Google Scholar. I'd visit study sites like SparkNotes and CliffsNotes to help me understand books. I'd watch relevant teachings on Academic Earth, TED and the Khan Academy. (I say relevant because some of these lectures may not be related to my work or too advanced for my age. But there are plenty of videos on these sites that are suitable to my studies and would help me stand out.) I would also, when possible, get my books for free at Project Gutenberg and learn how to do research at the CIA World Factbook and Wikipedia to help me with my studies.

I would use homework tools like Backpack, and Diigo to help me store 10 and share my work with other classmates. I would use Skype to study with other students who also want to do well in my school. I would take advantage of study websites like Evernote, Study Rails, Flashcard Machine, Quizlet, and free online calculators.

Is this easy? No it's not. It's hard. It takes a special kind of kid to succeed. And to succeed even with these tools is much harder for a black kid from West Philadelphia than a white kid from the suburbs. But it's not impossible. The tools are there. The technology is there. And the opportunities there.

In Philadelphia, there are nationally recognized magnet schools like Central, Girls High and Masterman. These schools are free. But they are hard to get into. You need good grades and good test scores. And there are also other good magnet and charter schools in the city. You also need good grades to get into those. In a school system that is so broken these are bright spots. Getting into one of these schools opens up a world of opportunities. More than 90% of the kids that go to Central go on to college. I would use the Internet to research each one of these schools so I could find out how I could be admitted. I would find out the names of the admissions people and go to meet with them. If I was a poor black kid I would make it my goal to get into one of these schools.

Or even a private school. Most private schools I know are filled to the brim with the 1%. That's because these schools are exclusive and expensive, costing anywhere between $20 and $50k per year. But there's a secret about them. Most have scholarship programs. Most have boards of trustees that want to give opportunities to kids that can't afford the tuition. Many would provide funding for not only tuition but also for transportation or even boarding. Trust me, they want to show diversity. They want to show smiling, smart kids of many different colors and races on their fundraising brochures. If I was a poor black kid I'd be using technology to research these schools on the Internet, too, and making them know that I exist and that I get good grades and want to go to their school.

And once admitted to one of these schools the first person I'd introduce myself to would be the school's guidance counselor. This is the person who will one day help me go to a college. This is the person who knows everything there is to know about financial aid, grants, minority programs and the like. This is the person who may also know of job programs and co-op learning opportunities that I could participate in. This is the person who could help me get summer employment at a law firm or a business owned by the 1% where I could meet people and show off my stuff.

15   If I was a poor black kid I would get technical. I would learn software. I would learn how to write code. I would seek out courses in my high school that teach these skills or figure out where to learn more online. I would study on my own. I would make sure my writing and communication skills stay polished.

Because a poor black kid who gets good grades, has a part-time job and becomes proficient with a technical skill will go to college. There is financial aid available. There are programs available. And no matter what he or she majors in that person will have opportunities. They will find jobs in a country of business owners like me who are starved for smart, skilled people. They will succeed.

President Obama was right in his speech last week. The division between rich and poor is a national problem. But the biggest challenge we face isn't inequality. It's ignorance. So many kids from West Philadelphia don't even know these opportunities exist for them. Many come from single-parent families whose mom or dad (or in many cases their grand mom) is working two jobs to survive and are just (understandably) too plain tired to do anything else in the few short hours they're home. Many have teachers who are overburdened and too stressed to find the time to help every kid that needs it. Many of these kids don't have the brains to figure this out themselves—like my kids. Except that my kids are just lucky enough to have parents and a well-funded school system around to push them in the right direction.

Technology can help these kids. But only if the kids want to be helped. Yes, there is much inequality. But the opportunity is still there in this country for those that are smart enough to go for it.

Analyze

1. Name at least three things Marks says he would do to supplement his education if he were a "poor black kid."
2. Who is Marks writing to? Point to evidence from the text to support your response.
3. Marks agrees with President Obama's claim that "the division between the rich and the poor is a national problem." But, Marks says, the biggest challenge we face isn't inequality, it is what? Explain.

Explore

1. To what extent is the conceit of Marks's blog post useful for imagining what he would do if he had been born into different circumstances? Is it empathetic? Insulting? Illuminating? Explain.
2. While some critics of this article, such as DNLee (in this chapter), critique Marks for his argument, others, such as fellow *Forbes* journalist

Kashmir Hill, claim that some people write inflammatory posts on hot topics like race just to "bait" people into viewing and responding. This drives up site visit counts that benefit the writer—personally, professionally, and/or financially. If Marks is strategically seeking shock value, does that change how you would respond to him? If you disagree with his argument, should you ignore it or respond publicly as others have? In general, should we engage differently with people who seem intent on "stirring the pot" or "trolling" the Internet?

3. Compose a researched response to Marks's post in which you support or challenge his recommendations.

DNLee
"If I Were a Wealthy White Suburbanite"

A biologist by trade, Danielle N. Lee studies animal behavior and behavioral ecology. She uses popular culture and social media to teach science to general audiences, especially those who are underserved. Lee writes the Urban Scientist blog for *Scientific American*, on which this post was originally published. In this post, Lee rebuts an argument by Gene Marks published in *Forbes* titled "If I Were a Poor Black Kid" (in this chapter). Here, Lee offers alternative explanations for the prevailing poverty that concerns Marks, noting reasons why Marks's solutions might not work.

If you wanted to break into the next socioeconomic class, how would you prepare yourself to do that?

Small business expert and contributor to Forbes recently wrote an interesting and compelling article, "If I [Were] a Poor Black Kid." Piggybacking on the inspiring and truth-telling recent speech of President Obama about the nation's economy, Gene Marks, offers his own high-five to the president plus his own recommendations for how people can gain access to the middle-class. Which got me thinking, what would I do to change the realities of the socio-economic equation of this nation?

If I were a wealthy white suburbanite . . . then I would host holiday coat drives for the inner-city children. I would rally others to contribute money to give away free gadgets and gizmos for them. I would sponsor bus rides and offer them free admission to the science museums. I would come and speak to them at their community events and tell them how much more reading and writing and arithmetic they ought to be doing. I would completely insult them, their families, and their communities by not acknowledging how much work is already being done by their parents, their teachers, their neighbors, community organizations, or their churches like the African Methodist Episcopal Church, or civic organizations like the National Urban League or the NAACP or by chapters of National Panhellenic Council, that share these very same messages plus physical, fiscal, and spiritual support and have done so for many, many years.

The nerve of him (and so many others) who think they can tell other people not only what's wrong with them, but also rattle off solutions as if it were as easy as casting seeds unto ground and like magic, new crops will sprout! Instantly. Effortlessly. Easy.

You don't know? Other than the fact, this, *THIS* guy is presenting his thesis to poor black kids about gaining access to the middle-class in which he and his children are so well-rooted, then pull up a chair. Let me count the ways. . . .

1. The author assumes that his nirvana is brand new, as if the fact that poor black inner city kids (or any poor kid, for that matter), have never, ever, never been told to make education a priority or that education is the key to having more options. Yeah, I guess Carter G. Woodson was just talking into a vacuum or heck, their parents, pastors, teachers, and grannies never said it. Thank you so much Mark Genes, for spelling that out! Whew, that great path to opportunity is crystal clear, now.

    It takes brains. It takes hard work. It takes a little luck. And a little help from others. It takes the ability and the know-how to use the resources that are available. Like technology.

2. The assumption that he thinks he really is addressing poor black kids, writing under the tent of FORBES Magazine . . . *Yeah, everybody in the 'hood reads that.*

3. The presumption that being born to a poor or working class family and being black automatically means your values for achievement, success, ambition are low. Those kids in West Phillies come from communities and have families that want as much as families from his nice neighborhood.

4. He only addresses children in his trope. Why is he only talking to kids, as if they have no parents or other adults in their lives who want the exact same thing for them?!

5   My mouth fell open as I read line after line of his recommendations, imparting his values on them and I have seen it in real life, too. Individuals and organizations inserting themselves into the lives of needy children, and completely ignoring or even dismissing the parental guardians in their lives.

> *Many of these kids don't have the brains to figure this out themselves—like my kids. Except that my kids are just lucky enough to have parents and a well-funded school system around to push them in the right direction.*

Privilege: All Day, Everyday

Gene Marks has a massive dose of privilege syndrome—of the white and middle-class variety.

> *My kids have it much easier than their counterparts from West Philadelphia. The world is not fair to those kids mainly because they had the misfortune of being born two miles away into a more difficult part of the world and with a skin color that makes realizing the opportunities that the president spoke about that much harder.*

Uh, Mark, your kids have it easier than those West Philly kids because *YOU* are their father . . . the same man who writes about Tech and Business for *Forbes* (the magazine about money and wealth), who is a certified public accountant, and former senior manager at KPMG, and now the owner your own accounting, auditing, and consulting business. *Mediocre, my ass!*

Gene Marks' privilege allows him to make self-deprecating comments about himself and still be taken seriously as a professional accountant. Yeah, that trick doesn't work for the poor kids born 2 miles away with darker skin tones. Heck, that trick doesn't work for grown black women with PhDs. I'm smart, I know it and have to reassert that fact often. And the misfortune isn't the GPS coordinates of where those children were born, it's about the wealth state they were born into and which neighborhood they occupy which is influenced by the economic resources available to their parents.

Gene Marks (and I have met way too many like him, worked with them, too, sadly) has got a really bad case of White (and/or Middle-class) Savior Complex. I think of all of the ways to insult someone, the savior offensive is perhaps the worst and most divisive. Thanks to a variety of experiences and opportunities of being the sole colored person in the room, I am very sensitive of the Savior-to-all-most-unlike-me.

The sense of privilege that he, a multi-generation white middle class guy has to share his awesome wisdom with all of those 'poor black socially-orphaned children out there in the West Phillies of the world' is astounding. *White Daddy has spoken and said you, too, my chillins, can inherit the world, just work, real, real hard for it and maybe you can get a little nibble at the pie in the sky.*

Much like the malevolent step-mother in Cinderella who promises to let Cinderella go to the ball, if she does ALL of her chores and doesn't get into trouble, telling someone working hard is all that it takes is only part of the story. Cinderella sadly learned that after busting her hump all day, Step-Mother and her daughters of privilege nix all of her dreams of a fair shot. They throw in last minute obstacles and other excuses of why she still hasn't earned the right to go to the party. Plus, what will she wear and how will she get there? 10

That's what it's like growing up as a poor black or brown kid in most cities and other economically distressed places in this nation. In other words, there's more to getting a foot-hold in middle class than simply knowing how to use Google Scholar. There are a number of complex and tangle-ly mazes to maneuver when one is climbing up the socioeconomic ladder. Working hard is important; but let's not be naïve. Gene Marks gives no real mention of the hard road ahead it will be for this kids like—access to a full range of technology, transportation to these those fancy-pants magnet schools. And what about supplies, equipment, oh and perquisite education just not offered at those lousy public schools. You see, no matter how hard a kid tries, when the smartest student from a poor-functioning school district walks into my freshman biology class, I can tell. And from day one, she or he is playing catch-up with the kids who attended those private or suburban school districts.

Are his recommendations for working hard, making good grades, and trying to get into better schools bad? No, not all. It's just that those recommendations are being made and followed everyday by poor black kids all over this nation. If he (and others like him) want to make a real difference in the lives of these communities, then I recommend working with folks and organizations already in place and leveraging that privilege to get more resources to those poorer parts of town.

Analyze

1. Why does DNLee imagine herself as a "wealthy white suburbanite"?
2. DNLee expresses frustration that, like Marks, many people list problems and then "rattle off a list of solutions" as if what?
3. In your own words, what are DNLee's four key critiques of Marks's essay?

Explore

1. How does DNLee define "privilege syndrome"? Give examples from Marks's writing that lead her to diagnose him as suffering from this. She also paints him as suffering from the "White (and/or Middle-class) Savior Complex." Is this the same thing? Explain.
2. What adjectives would you use to describe the tone of DNLee's response to Marks? Does the tone change at any point? Identify places in the text that lead you to that assessment. Is the tone effective? Explain.
3. DNLee uses the analogy of Cinderella and her evil stepmother and stepsisters to explore the challenges of the "poor black kid" Marks exhorts. Is this an effective analogy? In what ways does it work? In what ways does it fail?

Tressie McMillan Cottom
"Why Do Poor People 'Waste' Money on Luxury Goods?"

Lecturing and publishing widely on the subjects of inequality, education, race, and gender, Tressie McMillan Cottom is a sociologist and regular columnist for *Slate*. Her work appears in academic journals and in mainstream publications including *The Atlantic, NPR, The Chronicle of Higher Education*, and many more. McMillan Cottom served as a fellow at the Center for Poverty Research at the University of California-Davis when she wrote this essay, originally published on *Talking Points Memo*, an online political news organization. In this essay, McMillan Cottom explains how investing in outward displays of wealth and education, such as professional clothing, can help low-income people get past the social gatekeepers who award mobility.

Have you ever desired—or purchased—something well beyond your budget in order to feel like you belong?

We hates us some poor people. First, they insist on being poor when it is so easy to not be poor. They do things like buy expensive designer belts and $2500 luxury handbags.

To be fair, this isn't about Errol Louis [McMillan Cottom is responding to Errol Louis's tweet: "I totally get that it's horrible and illegal to profile people. But still #SMFH over a not-filthy-rich person spending $2,500 on a handbag."]. His is a belief held by many people, including lots of black people, poor people, formerly poor people, etc. It is, I suspect, an honest expression of incredulity. If you are poor, why do you spend money on useless status symbols like handbags and belts and clothes and shoes and televisions and cars?

One thing I've learned is that one person's illogical belief is another person's survival skill. And nothing is more logical than trying to survive.

My family is a classic black American migration family. We have rural Southern roots, moved north and almost all have returned. I grew up watching my great-grandmother, and later my grandmother and mother, use our minimal resources to help other people make ends meet. We were those good poors, the kind who live mostly within our means. We had a little luck when a male relative got extra military pay when they came home a paraplegic or used the VA to buy a Jim Walter house. If you were really blessed when a relative died with a paid up insurance policy you might be gifted a lump sum to buy the land that Jim Walters used as collateral to secure your home lease. That's how generational wealth happens where I'm from: lose a leg, a part of your spine, die right and maybe you can lease-to-own a modular home.

5   We had a little of that kind of rural black wealth so we were often in a position to help folks less fortunate. But perhaps the greatest resource we had was a bit more education. We were big readers and we encouraged the girl children, especially, to go to some kind of college. Consequently, my grandmother and mother had a particular set of social resources that helped us navigate mostly white bureaucracies to our benefit. We could, as my grandfather would say, talk like white folks. We loaned that privilege out to folks a lot.

I remember my mother taking a next door neighbor down to the social service agency. The elderly woman had been denied benefits to care for the granddaughter she was raising. The woman had been denied in the genteel bureaucratic way—lots of waiting, forms, and deadlines she could not quite navigate. I watched my mother put on her best Diana Ross "Mahogany" outfit: a camel colored cape with matching slacks and knee high boots. I was miffed, as only an only child could be, about sharing my mother's time with the neighbor girl. I must have said something about why we had to do this. Vivian fixed me with a stare as she was slipping on her pearl earrings and told me that people who can do, must do. It took half a day but something about my mother's performance of respectable black person—her Queen's English, her Mahogany outfit, her straight bob and pearl earrings—got done what the elderly lady next door had not been able to get done in over a year. I learned, watching my mother, that there was a price we had to pay to signal to gatekeepers that we were worthy of engaging. It meant dressing well and speaking well. It might not work. It likely wouldn't work but on the off chance that it would, you had to try. It was unfair but, as Vivian also always said, "life isn't fair little girl."

I internalized that lesson and I think it has worked out for me, if unevenly. A woman at Belk's once refused to show me the Dooney and Burke purse I was interested in buying. Vivian once made a salesgirl cry after she ignored us in an empty store. I have walked away from many hotly desired purchases, like the impractical off-white winter coat I desperately wanted, after some bigot at the counter insulted me and my mother. But, I have half a PhD and I support myself aping the white male privileged life of the mind. It's a mixed bag. Of course, the trick is you can never know the counterfactual of your life. There is no evidence of access denied. Who knows what I was not granted for not enacting the right status behaviors or symbols at the right time for an agreeable authority? Respectability rewards are a crap-shoot but we do what we can within the limits of the constraints imposed by a complex set of structural and social interactions designed to limit access to status, wealth, and power.

I do not know how much my mother spent on her camel colored cape or knee-high boots but I know that whatever she paid it returned in hard-to-measure dividends. How do you put a price on the double-take of a clerk at the welfare office who decides you might not be like those other trifling women in the waiting room and provides an extra bit of information about completing a form that you would not have known to ask about? What is the retail value of a school principal who defers a bit more to your child because your mother's presentation of self signals that she might unleash the bureaucratic savvy of middle class parents to advocate for her child? I don't know the price of these critical engagements with organizations and gatekeepers relative to our poverty when I was growing up. But, I am living proof of its investment yield.

Why do poor people make stupid, illogical decisions to buy status symbols? For the same reason all but only the most wealthy buy status symbols, I suppose. We want to belong. And, not just for the psychic rewards, but belonging to one group at the right time can mean the difference between unemployment and employment, a good job as opposed to a bad job, housing or a shelter, and so on. Someone mentioned on Twitter that poor people can be presentable with affordable options from Kmart. But the issue is not about being presentable. Presentable is the bare minimum of social civility. It means being clean, not smelling, wearing shirts and shoes for service and the like. Presentable as a sufficient condition for gainful, dignified work or successful social interactions is a privilege. It's the aging white hippie who can cut the ponytail of his youthful rebellion and walk into senior management while aging black panthers can never completely outrun the effects of stigmatization against which they were courting a revolution. Presentable is relative and, like life, it ain't fair.

In contrast, "acceptable" is about gaining access to a limited set of rewards granted upon group membership. I cannot know exactly how often my presentation of acceptable has helped me but I have enough feedback to know it is not inconsequential. One manager at the apartment complex where I worked while in college told me, repeatedly, that she knew I was "Okay" because my little Nissan was clean. That I had worn a Jones New York suit to the interview really sealed the deal. She could call the suit by name because she asked me about the label in the interview. Another hiring manager at my first professional job looked me up and down in the waiting room, cataloging my outfit, and later told me that she had decided I was too classy to be on the call center floor. I was hired as a trainer instead. The difference meant no shift work, greater prestige, better pay and a baseline salary for all my future employment.

I have about a half dozen other stories like this. What is remarkable is not that this happened. There is empirical evidence that women and people of color are judged by appearances differently and more harshly than are white men. What is remarkable is that these gatekeepers *told me the story*. They wanted me to know how I had properly signaled that I was not a typical black or a typical woman, two identities that in combination are almost always conflated with being poor.

I sat in on an interview for a new administrative assistant once. My regional vice president was doing the hiring. A long line of mostly black and brown women applied because we were a cosmetology school. Trade schools at the margins of skilled labor in a gendered field are necessarily classed and raced. I found one candidate particularly charming. She was trying to get out of a salon because 10 hours on her feet cutting hair would average out to an hourly rate below minimum wage. A desk job with 40 set hours and medical benefits represented mobility for her. When she left my VP turned to me and said, "did you see that tank top she had on under her blouse?! OMG, you wear a silk *shell*, not a tank top!" Both of the women were black.

The VP had constructed her job as senior management. She drove a brand new BMW because she "should treat herself" and liked to tell us that ours was an image business. A girl wearing a cotton tank top as a shell was incompatible with BMW-driving VPs in the image business. Gatekeeping is a complex job of managing boundaries that do not just define others but that also define ourselves. Status symbols—silk shells, designer shoes, luxury handbags—become keys to unlock these gates. If I need a job that will save my lower back and move my baby from Medicaid to an HMO, how much should I spend signaling to people like my former VP that I will not compromise her status by opening the door to me? That candidate maybe could not afford a proper shell. I will never know. But I do know that had she gone hungry for two days to pay for it or missed wages for a trip to the store to buy it, she may have been rewarded a job that could have lifted her above minimum wage. Shells aren't designer handbags, perhaps. But a cosmetology school in a strip mall isn't a job at Bank of America, either.

At the heart of these incredulous statements about the poor decisions poor people make is a belief that we would never be like them. We would know better. We would know to save our money, eschew status symbols, cut coupons, practice puritanical sacrifice to amass a million dollars. There is a regular news story of a lunch lady who, unbeknownst to all who knew her, died rich and leaves it all to a cat or a charity or some such. Books about the modest lives of the rich like to tell us how they drive Buicks instead of BMWs. What we forget, if we ever know, is that what we know now about status and wealth creation and sacrifice are predicated on who we are, i.e., not poor. If you change the conditions of your not-poor status, you change everything you know as a result of being a not-poor. You have no idea what you would do if you were poor until you are poor. And not intermittently poor or formerly not-poor, but born poor, expected to be poor and treated by bureaucracies, gatekeepers and well-meaning respectability authorities as inherently poor. Then, and only then, will you understand the relative value of a ridiculous status symbol to someone who intuits that they cannot afford to not have it.

Analyze

1. What specific incident prompts McMillan Cottom to write this article at this time?
2. What does McMillan Cottom mean when she describes her family as "good poors"?
3. What does the author say was perhaps her family's greatest resource? What "capability" does that lead to that becomes a "privilege" they loan out?

Explore

1. Referring to some of her mother's most expensive items of clothing, which were worn at all important social exchanges, McMillan Cottom writes: "I do not know how much my mother spent on her camel colored cape or knee-high boots but I know that whatever she paid it returned in hard-to-measure dividends." Explain. To what extent is this example relevant to the example that triggered the essay?
2. Write one sentence that explains how McMillan Cottom answers the question posed in her title.
3. What is "gatekeeping" and what does it have to do with poverty and social mobility? Cite observations and research.

James Webb
"Diversity and the Myth of White Privilege"

When this article was published in the *Wall Street Journal*, James Webb was serving in the U.S. Senate as a Democrat from Virginia. He previously served as the secretary of the Navy. He is the author of numerous books that draw on his military and historical interests, and he has written several articles published in the mainstream press that address wealth, race, and class struggles. In the following essay, Webb urges his audience to consider how white Americans are unfairly discriminated against by policies that attempt to correct for discrimination against minority groups.

Is it ever acceptable or desirable to consider race when awarding jobs, college admissions, or loans?

The NAACP believes the tea party is racist. The tea party believes the NAACP is racist. And Pat Buchanan got into trouble recently by pointing out that if Elena Kagan is confirmed to the Supreme Court, there will not be a single Protestant Justice, although Protestants make up half the U.S. population and dominated the court for generations.

Forty years ago, as the United States experienced the civil rights movement, the supposed monolith of White Anglo-Saxon Protestant dominance served as the whipping post for almost every debate about power and status in America. After a full generation of such debate, WASP elites have fallen by the wayside and a plethora of government-enforced diversity policies have marginalized many white workers. The time has come to cease the false arguments and allow every American the benefit of a fair chance at the future.

I have dedicated my political career to bringing fairness to America's economic system and to our work force, regardless of what people look like or where they may worship. Unfortunately, present-day diversity programs work against that notion, having expanded so far beyond their original purpose that they now favor anyone who does not happen to be white.

In an odd historical twist that all Americans see but few can understand, many programs allow recently arrived immigrants to move ahead of similarly situated whites whose families have been in the country for generations. These programs have damaged racial harmony. And the more they have grown, the less they have actually helped African-Americans, the intended beneficiaries of affirmative action as it was originally conceived.

How so?   5

Lyndon Johnson's initial program for affirmative action was based on the 13th Amendment and on the Civil Rights Act of 1866, which authorized the federal government to take actions in order to eliminate "the badges of slavery." Affirmative action was designed to recognize the uniquely difficult journey of African-Americans. This policy was justifiable and understandable, even to those who came from white cultural groups that had also suffered in socio-economic terms from the Civil War and its aftermath.

The injustices endured by black Americans at the hands of their own government have no parallel in our history, not only during the period of slavery but also in the Jim Crow era that followed. But the extrapolation of this logic to all "people of color"—especially since 1965, when new immigration laws dramatically altered the demographic makeup of the U.S.—moved affirmative action away from remediation and toward discrimination, this time against whites. It has also lessened the focus on assisting African-Americans, who despite a veneer of successful people at the very top still experience high rates of poverty, drug abuse, incarceration and family breakup.

Those who came to this country in recent decades from Asia, Latin America and Africa did not suffer discrimination from our government, and in fact have frequently been the beneficiaries of special government programs. The same cannot be said of many hard-working white Americans, including those whose roots in America go back more than 200 years.

Contrary to assumptions in the law, white America is hardly a monolith. And the journey of white American cultures is so diverse (yes) that one strains to find the logic that could lump them together for the purpose of public policy.

The clearest example of today's misguided policies comes from examin-   10
ing the history of the American South.

The old South was a three-tiered society, with blacks and hard-put whites both dominated by white elites who manipulated racial tensions in order to retain power. At the height of slavery, in 1860, less than 5% of whites in the South owned slaves. The eminent black historian John Hope Franklin wrote that "fully three-fourths of the white people in the South had neither slaves nor an immediate economic interest in the maintenance of slavery."

The Civil War devastated the South, in human and economic terms. And from post-Civil War Reconstruction to the beginning of World War II, the region was a ravaged place, affecting black and white alike.

In 1938, President Franklin Roosevelt created a national commission to study what he termed "the long and ironic history of the despoiling of this truly American section." At that time, most industries in the South were owned by companies outside the region. Of the South's 1.8 million share-croppers, 1.2 million were white (a mirror of the population, which was 71% white). The illiteracy rate was five times that of the North-Central states and more than twice that of New England and the Middle Atlantic (despite the waves of European immigrants then flowing to those regions). The total endowments of all the colleges and universities in the South were less than the endowments of Harvard and Yale alone. The average school-child in the South had $25 a year spent on his or her education, compared to $141 for children in New York.

Generations of such deficiencies do not disappear overnight, and they affect the momentum of a culture. In 1974, a National Opinion Research Center (NORC) study of white ethnic groups showed that white Baptists nationwide averaged only 10.7 years of education, a level almost identical to blacks' average of 10.6 years, and well below that of most other white groups. A recent NORC Social Survey of white adults born after World War II showed that in the years 1980–2000, only 18.4% of white Baptists and 21.8% of Irish Protestants—the principal ethnic group that settled the South—had obtained college degrees, compared to a national average of 30.1%, a Jewish average of 73.3%, and an average among those of Chinese and Indian descent of 61.9%.

15   Policy makers ignored such disparities within America's white cultures when, in advancing minority diversity programs, they treated whites as a fungible monolith. Also lost on these policy makers were the differences in economic and educational attainment among nonwhite cultures. Thus nonwhite groups received special consideration in a wide variety of areas including business startups, academic admissions, job promotions and lucrative government contracts.

Where should we go from here? Beyond our continuing obligation to assist those African-Americans still in need, government-directed diversity programs should end.

Nondiscrimination laws should be applied equally among all citizens, including those who happen to be white. The need for inclusiveness in our society is undeniable and irreversible, both in our markets and in our communities. Our government should be in the business of enabling opportunity for all, not in picking winners. It can do so by ensuring that artificial distinctions such as race do not determine outcomes.

Memo to my fellow politicians: Drop the Procrustean policies and allow harmony to invade the public mindset. Fairness will happen, and bitterness will fade away.

Analyze

1. Webb argues that diversity programs have evolved such that they now favor anyone who is not what?
2. What does Webb say about President Lyndon Johnson's initial affirmative action program?
3. Webb says that government programs treat "whites as a fungible monolith." What does this mean?

Explore

1. Webb argues that changes in the law since 1965 have "moved affirmative action away from remediation and toward discrimination." What does he mean? Who is being discriminated against now? What factual evidence does Webb provide to support that claim? Why does Webb state that the government is now in the business of "picking winners"?
2. What call to action does Webb close with? Will his recommendations solve the problem he identifies? Why or why not?
3. Write a research brief that you could give to someone who wants to enter the debate on affirmative action. Research all sides of the issue and present them neutrally in a literature review. Note landmark moments in this issue—important legal rulings, key speeches, etc. Your brief should identify the key leaders within the major stakeholder groups. In your conclusion, identify common ground among the stakeholders. State a modest call to action that would fall within that common ground.

Adam Serwer
"Webb and 'White Privilege'"

A reporter for *MSNBC* who covers civil rights and social justice issues, Adam Serwer has written for *Mother Jones*, the *Washington Post*, the *New York Daily News*, and *The American Prospect*. This essay was originally published in *The American Prospect*. In it, Serwer challenges Webb's claims in the previous reading, arguing that white privilege is pervasive in the U.S.

> Do you agree that the social advancement of minorities does not have to come at the expense of white Americans?

There are a number of things about Senator Jim Webb's op-ed "[Diversity and] The Myth of White Privilege" to dislike, starting with the fact that one of the awesome things about the existence of white privilege is that you can be part of a body like the U.S. Senate, which has a total number of zero elected black members, and write something titled "[Diversity and] The Myth of White Privilege" without anyone batting an eyelash. That said, Webb's op-ed is considerably more nuanced than the title, acknowledging that "The injustices endured by black Americans at the hands of their own government have no parallel in our history," although he makes the same mistake as Ross Douthat in repeating the conservative frame of zero-sum competition between whites and people of color.

For some reason, Webb sees the existence of poor whites as proof white privilege doesn't exist, when it's largely a non sequitur. The existence of Southie or Appalachia does not change the fact that a white man with a prison record has an easier time than a black person without one. But what I find really remarkable is this:

> The old South was a three-tiered society, with blacks and hard-put whites both dominated by white elites who manipulated racial tensions in order to retain power. At the height of slavery, in 1860, less than 5% of whites in the South owned slaves. The eminent black historian John Hope Franklin wrote that "fully three-fourths of the white people in the South had neither slaves nor an immediate economic interest in the maintenance of slavery."

Webb cites President Franklin Roosevelt's study of poverty and the region and notes, "Generations of such deficiencies do not disappear overnight, and they affect the momentum of a culture." How true. The gaping hole in Webb's argument, however, is that, as Ira Katznelson has written, the entire force of the American state spent decades helping the white people of the region to the exclusion of African Americans, at the behest of their representatives in the Democratic Party. The Social Security Act's three major provisions were constructed to deliberately exclude blacks, and previous programs with federal money aimed at the relief of poverty also gave discretion to the states for how to spend them precisely so Southern states could make sure they weren't being spent on black people. The National Labor Relations Act was constructed to exclude blacks, the GI Bill gave fewer benefits to black soldiers than to white soldiers, and the Federal Housing Authority's discrimination helped build the modern wealth gap between blacks and whites. These efforts "treated whites as a fungible monolith," to borrow Webb's own language, and in concert with other economic factors, helped speed the integration of white ethnics while maintaining a caste-system based on skin color. As if it isn't also obvious, the price for maintaining a system of apartheid in the South was diminishing the potential economic impact of these programs by excluding a large part of the region's residents.

I'm not uncomfortable with the government using its power to help poor people of any color, or people who are discriminated against. But to write about the poverty of the South without acknowledging the decades of massive government effort geared exclusively toward aiding white people is rather astonishing. More astonishing, perhaps, is that Webb, like all affirmative-action opponents, seems to forget the rather large number of white people helped by affirmative action. Webb notes that Johnson's "initial program for affirmative action" was grounded in the 13th Amendment. Sure. But arguing that Johnson meant for affirmative action simply to address the unique history of discrimination faced by African Americans is incorrect. It was Johnson, after all, who included "creed" and "national origin," along with "race" and "color," and in 1967 expanded his original executive order to include women. It's one thing for Republicans, who oppose government efforts to help the disadvantaged on ideological principle, to focus on race in arguments about affirmative action (or FinReg, or Health Care, etc.) because they think that this is the quickest way to get white people angry. But it's surprising to hear from a Democrat, especially one so clearly concerned with the stark racial injustices of the U.S. prison system.

5   Johnson's decision hints at affirmative action's real purpose, one that has
been muddied by the legal arguments that have been necessary to keep it
alive. The purpose is not merely the "compelling state interest in diversity,"
it is to help correct the societal biases, conscious and unconscious, that continue to curtail opportunity for certain groups of Americans. The fact that
affirmative action, which is a relatively mild form of government action
compared to the Democratic Party's deliberate creation of a modern whites-
only welfare state, arouses so much anger is evidence of how powerful such
biases continue to be.

In general, the argument over affirmative action is broad and non-
specific, and we don't discuss whether we mean college admissions, employment, or allocation of government contracts. I'm comfortable with moving
to a more class-based system of affirmative action in college admissions, and
I think a more aggressive class-based system might actually work better at
creating diversity. But the fact remains that no one knows a white person is
an Irish Protestant or a Baptist when they walk into a job interview. They
do know when someone is black, and they know when someone is a woman,
and we all know that still matters.

Finally, Pat Buchanan did not get into trouble merely for "pointing out
that if Elena Kagan is confirmed to the Supreme Court, there will not be a
single Protestant Justice." That remark was received in the context of
Buchanan being someone whose definition of whiteness excludes white
Jews and whose definition of Americanness excludes anyone who is not
white. He believes any social advancement for people of color or non-
Christians is necessarily to the detriment of white Americans, who are the
people to whom America truly belongs. That perhaps explains why
Buchanan didn't resign from the Reagan administration in protest when
Justice Antonin Scalia was picked because Reagan thought, "We don't have
an Italian American on the court, so we ought to have one." After all, if
there's any lesson from history in all this, it's that certain forms of affirmative action aren't very controversial.

Analyze

1. Describe the tone of Serwer's opening paragraph. What does it suggest
   about Serwer's intended audience and purpose?
2. Serwer says that "Webb sees the existence of poor whites as proof white
   privilege doesn't exist." Serwer labels this argument as a logical fallacy

called a "non sequitur." Define this term. Did he label Webb's argument correctly? Explain.

3. What does Serwer say is the "gaping hole" in Webb's argument?

Explore

1. Research one or more of Serwer's claims about how the U.S. government continued to support white over black Americans even after slavery was abolished. Write a summary that either Webb or Serwer could
use if they continued their discussion on this issue.

2. How does Serwer's account of the purpose of President Johnson's affirmative action policy contradict Webb's account? What is the significance of that different reading? How would you determine if one or
the other reading is more accurate? Describe your process.

3. In the end, Serwer says that he is "comfortable with moving to a more
class-based system of affirmative action" in such areas as college admissions, and he even thinks it might improve diversity. But, in his last
line, he emphasizes what other key problem that affirmative action is
intended to address aside from increasing diversity? Overall, does
Serwer succeed in challenging Webb's argument? Base your assessment not on your own thinking on this issue but on the strength of
Serwer's counterargument. Find at least one more response to Webb's
op-ed (there were many) and determine which is most rhetorically
successful.

The Economist
"The Rich Are Different from You and Me:
Wealth, Poverty and Compassion"

The Economist, in which the following article was published, is a print and
online newspaper that covers journalists' commentaries on international news,
politics, finance, business, science, and technology. The authors remain anonymous, reflecting the writing process as highly collaborative and edited, and
because the newspaper believes that "what is written is more important than

who writes it." The following article explains differences in charitable giving between the rich and the poor.

Why might the poor be more charitable than the rich?

L ife at the bottom is nasty, brutish and short. For this reason, heartless folk might assume that people in the lower social classes will be more self-interested and less inclined to consider the welfare of others than upper-class individuals, who can afford a certain noblesse oblige. A recent study, however, challenges this idea. Experiments by Paul Piff and his colleagues at the University of California, Berkeley, reported this week in the *Journal of Personality and Social Psychology*, suggest precisely the opposite. It is the poor, not the rich, who are inclined to charity.

In their first experiment, Dr. Piff and his team recruited 115 people. To start with, these volunteers were asked to engage in a series of bogus activities, in order to create a misleading impression of the purpose of the research. Eventually, each was told he had been paired with an anonymous partner seated in a different room. Participants were given ten credits and advised that their task was to decide how many of these credits they wanted to keep for themselves and how many (if any) they wished to transfer to their partner. They were also told that the credits they had at the end of the game would be worth real money and that their partners would have no ability to interfere with the outcome.

A week before the game was run, participants were asked their ethnic backgrounds, sex, age, frequency of attendance at religious services and socioeconomic status. During this part of the study, they were presented with a drawing of a ladder with ten rungs on it. Each rung represented people of different levels of education, income and occupational status. They were asked to place an 'X' on the rung they felt corresponded to where they stood relative to others in their own community.

The average number of credits people gave away was 4.1. However, an analysis of the results showed that generosity increased as participants' assessment of their own social status fell. Those who rated themselves at the bottom of the ladder gave away 44% more of their credits than those who put their crosses at the top, even when the effects of age, sex, ethnicity and religiousness had been accounted for.

The Prince and the Pauper

In follow-up experiments, the researchers asked participants to imagine 5
and write about a hypothetical interaction with someone who was extremely wealthy or extremely poor. This sort of storytelling is used routinely by psychologists when they wish to induce a temporary change in someone's point of view.

In this case the change intended was to that of a higher or lower social class than the individual perceived he normally belonged to. The researchers then asked participants to indicate what percentage of a person's income should be spent on charitable donations. They found that both real lower-class participants and those temporarily induced to rank themselves as lower class felt that a greater share of a person's salary should be used to support charity.

Upper-class participants said 2.1% of incomes should be donated. Lower-class individuals felt that 5.6% was the appropriate slice. Upper-class participants who were induced to believe they were lower class suggested 3.1%. And lower-class individuals who had been psychologically promoted thought 3.3% was about right.

A final experiment attempted to test how helpful people of different classes are when actually exposed to a person in need. This time participants were primed with video clips, rather than by storytelling, into more or less compassionate states. The researchers then measured their reaction to another participant (actually a research associate) who turned up late and thus needed help with the experimental procedure.

In this case priming made no difference to the lower classes. They always showed compassion to the latecomer. The upper classes, though, could be influenced. Those shown a compassion-inducing video behaved in a more sympathetic way than those shown emotionally neutral footage. That suggests the rich are capable of compassion, if somebody reminds them, but do not show it spontaneously.

One interpretation of all this might be that selfish people find it easier to 10
become rich. Some of the experiments Dr. Piff conducted, however, sorted people by the income of the family in which the participant grew up. This revealed that whether high status was inherited or earned made no difference so the idea that it is the self-made who are especially selfish does not work. Dr. Piff himself suggests that the increased compassion which seems to exist among the poor increases generosity and helpfulness, and promotes

a level of trust and co-operation that can prove essential for survival during hard times.

Analyze

1. The article says that the rich might be inclined to some "noblesse oblige" given their security and well-being. Define this term. What does it mean in the modern context?
2. What is the main finding of this research, which might counter general expectations on the connection between status and generosity?
3. In the experiment, how did the attitudes about giving to charity among real lower-class participants and those temporarily playing lower-class compare?

Explore

1. Does this research surprise you? Why or why not? Cite examples from your experience and reading that support, challenge, or complicate this conclusion.
2. In the experiment, what was the difference between the real upper- and lower-class individuals in terms of compassion? What does this mean?
3. Is there evidence that inheriting wealth versus creating wealth on your own influences selfishness? Drawing on research from philanthropic studies or related fields, dig deeper into the issues of charity, generosity, and giving. Note how even the rhetoric of giving—the words we use to describe it—defines this dynamic. The article quotes Dr. Piff's theory on the results. Research this issue (watch Dr. Piff's TED talk), then offer your own theory on why it seems that the poor are more generous than the rich.

Anthony Zurcher
"'Affluenza Defence': Rich, Privileged, and Unaccountable"

A prolific political commentator, Anthony Zurcher is an editor of "Echo Chambers," a regular column at *BBCNews* that serves to "unscramble the noise of the global debate, from social media to scholarly journals." In this "Echo Chambers" piece, Zurcher offers a synthesis of arguments responding to a Texas judge's controversial ruling in a fatal drunk driving case committed by a wealthy teenager.

Should wealth determine whether a criminal is punished versus rehabilitated if it can save taxpayer and state resources?

I s there a separate justice system in the US for the rich and powerful? It all depends on whether you believe that Ethan Couch would be in jail right now were it not for his wealthy parents and privileged background.

On 15 June, Ethan, 16, was driving with a blood-alcohol level three times above the legal limit. He lost control of his speeding pick-up truck and killed four pedestrians. On Tuesday, he was sentenced to serve in a high-priced California drug rehabilitation centre paid for by the parents, with no jail time and 10 years of probation.

It's the court case that has made the "affluenza defence" a household word, as Ethan's lawyers successfully argued he had a diminished sense of responsibility due to his wealth, pampered childhood, and absentee parenting. Ever since the sentence came down, the media have been rolling in shock and outrage.

The judge "pretty much did what his parents had always done," writes Mike Hashimoto of the Dallas Morning News, "which is let him skate." It's an example of a two-tiered legal system in the US, he wrote, where the rich are treated better than the poor.

"Blame his parents, who may richly deserve it, but bear in mind that this young man will again be driving the same streets as you and yours one day," he writes. "Watch out for big, speeding red pickups."   5

Other commentators echoed Mr. Hashimoto's disgust. Alexandra Petri of the Washington Post writes that with affluenza, one need not fear consequences.

"I can't possibly be guilty of a crime, officer," you point out, if anything comes up. "I have far too much money." This is sound logic. You dangle a few dollar bills out the window, and suddenly it turns out you weren't speeding at all. Most things, money can buy. And for everything else, there's more money.

CNN featured a lawyer who traced the roots of the "affluenza defence" back to the 1979 "Twinkie defence," in which depression (manifested by eating junk food) was used as a mitigating factor in the defence of Dan White, who had shot and killed San Francisco Mayor George Moscone and Supervisor Harvey Milk.

"The wrong message has been sent in this case about wealth, power and the penalty for killing others while recklessly driving in an intoxicated state," writes Paul Callan. "The law exists to rehabilitate but also to deter unlawful conduct by the rich as well as the poor."

10   Slate's Josh Voorhees agrees: "Given the 'affluenza' defence—along with the fact that the teen's parents will be the ones paying for his stay at a $450,000-a-year, in-patient rehab facility near Newport Beach, Calif.— one doesn't have to squint to see what looks an awful lot like a double-standard predicated on the teen's family wealth."

The editors of the Fort Worth Star-Telegram take a different view, how-ever, writing that media criticisms "fail to take into account all the circum-stances of the case."

The Texas juvenile justice system "is built not on punishment but on taking account of an offender's age, offering a chance at rehabilitation and a productive life," they write. "This case is tragic for all involved. What seemed to make it worse for some was that the teen's parents are wealthy, and he's led a privileged life."

They conclude that the judge in this case, Jean Boyd, decided that justice was best served by sending Ethan to drug abuse treatment and extended probation.

"None among those who say she was wrong have sat in her chair for 26 years," they write. "In this case, she's earned our trust."

15   In Texas, judges campaign for office like other politicians. Ms Boyd, however, has decided not to run for re-election.

UPDATE: An Echo Chambers reader points out another interesting opin-ion piece out of Texas that highlights what a disaster the Texas juvenile justice system is, calling it "a system you'd do anything on earth to keep your own kid out of."

"Because we condemn everybody else's kid to violent prisons, does that mean it's unjust to let any one kid go?" writes Jim Schutze in the Dallas Observer. He argues that the "affluenza defence" is just courtroom blus-ter: "The real defence is: 'This kid's parents can afford a very expensive whiskey school for him, so why toss him onto the human trash heap of a brutal state prison system? Maybe he can be saved by the whiskey doctors. Why not try?'"

It's probably not an answer that will satisfy the families of the victims and those who place retribution over rehabilitation in the justice system. But the system is what it is. He concludes: "Maybe what the rest of us need to do is work to provide a more dignified and decent system of punishment for all kids."

Is the real tragedy of this case the awfulness of the US juvenile justice system and not the privileges of being wealthy?

Analyze

1. What is the "affluenza defense"?
2. Why do people accuse the U.S. of having a "two-tiered legal system"? Is it significant that this case was covered by international news media?
3. What factor seems to change the sentencing in Couch's case?

Explore

1. Some people who defend the judge's sentence point out that the law is meant to *deter* and *rehabilitate*. Couch is afforded a significant opportunity to rehabilitate. Is that a good thing? Is it diminished by the fact that others wouldn't be able to afford the level of counseling, support, and rehabilitation Couch will receive due to his parents' wealth? Explain.
2. Is privilege a burden? Can wealth lead us away from well-being? Consult the readings from *The Economist* and the Brookings Institution in this chapter along with other outside research to inform your argument.
3. Write a letter to Judge Jean Boyd explaining your response to her verdict. Use various types of support to construct a compelling argument: academic research, testimonials, narratives, etc. Close your letter with a call for action.

Forging Connections

1. Several of the readings in this chapter (e.g., Cole, DNLee, McMillan Cottom) critique people with privilege who tell people in poverty what to do. Is that critique justified? What's wrong with trying to help others, trying to "make a difference"? Is it the *message* or the *method*

that seems so objectionable? Explain your answer by writing to one of these authors to express either your support for or your disagreement with his or her essay. Support your claims with readings from this book.

2. We explore the psychological effects of poverty throughout the book, but are there negative psychological effects of privilege? Does research confirm that "affluenza" is a real condition, or are there other types of cognitive, emotional, or physical maladies associated with those who are surrounded by wealth and privilege? What if any connection is there between this and the research showing that the rich are less generous than the poor?

Looking Further

1. Research an area of privilege explored in this book and write a history of how it has evolved over time. Feel free to challenge whether that privilege continues to exist (or ever did). Provide scholarly support for your claims, citing specific examples, laws, and events. Explain what the status of that privilege has to do with poverty. For example, research the "feminization of poverty" or the "racialization of poverty."

2. Discussing both poverty and privilege helps us think about them as dynamic forces that exist in relation to one another, a gap we call inequality. Research shows that higher equality generally leads to greater stability and economic growth within a society. Organizations such as the International Monetary Fund, the World Bank, the Organisation for Economic Co-operation and Development (OECD), and the United Nations all help gather and assess relevant data regarding levels of inequality. We represent the level of income inequality through the Gini coefficient. You needn't be an economist to think about this issue, however. Research the level of inequality in one area (counties, states, countries, regions) and write a report explaining how the level of inequality affects well-being there (Measure of America and the World Bank have helpful research tools online).

photo
gallery

Michael Pharaoh, "The Homeless of L.A."

Michael Pharaoh's photo series "The Homeless of L.A." offers a piercing eye-to-eye encounter with people who are homeless in Los Angeles, California. Pharaoh, a graphic designer based in New Zealand, says he was fascinated by the number of people who were homeless and by their stories of "how they came to live on the streets"; he calls the project "sad yet humbling" (http://www.visualnews.com/2013/09/13/homeless-los-angeles-michael-pharaohs-photographs-capture-spirit/).

Representations of people who are poor help others understand that experience. Yet when those representations are filtered through a writer or artist, such as a photographer, the author's viewpoint can become part of the narrative. Sometimes those representations illuminate suffering; other times they seem to exploit it. Sometimes they illuminate the dignity of the person; other times they seem to evoke so much pathos (emotion and sentimentality) that we seem called only to pity the people portrayed. To show the consequences of poverty, we have to manage issues of tone and ethical representation carefully.

Do a rhetorical analysis of Pharaoh's photos. Use these questions as a guide:

Form: How are the images framed and scaled? What is the relationship between the subject and camera? What might be edited out and why?

Arrangement: How do items in the frame relate to one another in space? What is in the background and foreground? Are we led to read the image in a certain order or sequence?

Color: How does color (natural or artificial) affect the tone and meaning of the images?

Emphasis: Does the image use color, size, pattern, or placement to get our attention and suggest importance?

Content: What is the subject? Is this art and/or argument? Do the photos praise or blame the subject? What does the photographer want the audience to do or think based on these photos? Does this series fit a common narrative frame on this issue, or does it differ?

Michael Pharaoh. "Homeless of LA" appeared in HuffingtonPost.com, 09/23/13

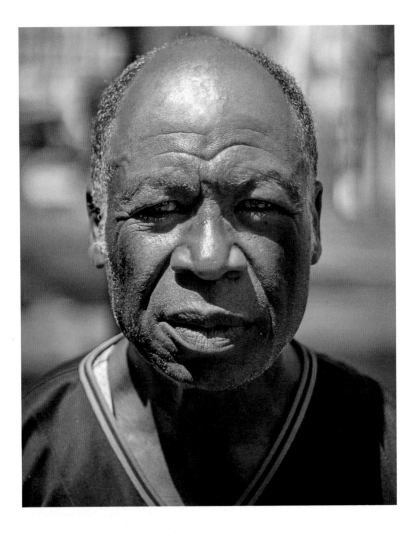

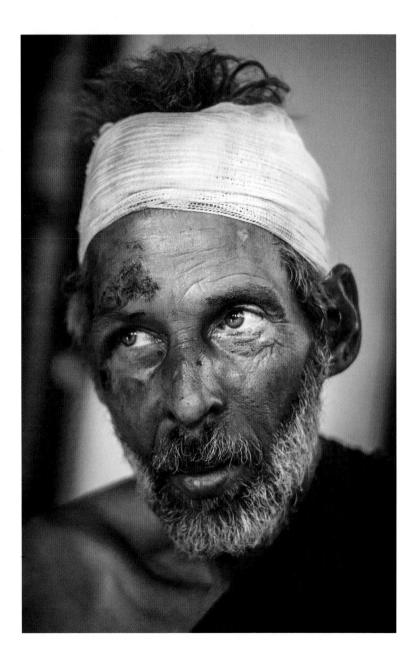

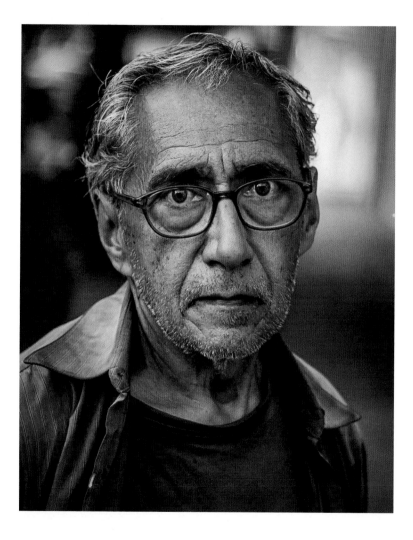

Rhetoric: How Do the Media Represent Poverty?

5

President Lyndon B. Johnson talks with Tom Fletcher and children in Inez, Kentucky (1964). Johnson toured high-poverty areas, including rural Appalachia, to inform the War on Poverty. How does this photo frame the people and the issue it represents?

INTRODUCTION

A truism about poverty reporting in the media states that poverty is either underrepresented or misrepresented. Neither case is heartening. In this chapter we look at the ways poverty is represented—in the media, in our governing bodies, in our policies, in our everyday language. The words and images we use to represent poverty, these readings argue, sometimes *reflect* our attitudes about poverty and sometimes *shape* them. Unfortunately, whether intentional or unintentional, those representations are not always accurate, and misinformation gets magnified in the media spotlight. The image of the "welfare queen" is one of the most dramatic examples of the rhetoric of poverty. Using welfare fraud as a campaign issue, President Ronald Reagan coalesced real stories of welfare fraud into a caricature of the welfare queen—a lazy, sexually promiscuous, African American woman who was bilking honest taxpayers out of hard-earned money. She became the despised face of welfare that helped launch welfare reform by rallying public opinion against a convenient villain. Yet some would say that President Bill Clinton was equally opportunistic in generating photo ops with poor women who succeeded in his welfare to work program. Whether we see ourselves as fighting a "War on Poverty" or succumbing to an "entitlement society," how we talk about poverty and the images we use to represent it often politicize and oversimplify complex issues. The readings in this chapter expose some of the common poverty frames used in the media and challenge us to read against those rhetorical reductions of people and programs.

Simon Kuper frames this chapter by admitting that he and his journalist colleagues often either neglect the poor or misrepresent them, usually by letting non-poor professionals tell the story of those in poverty because it's more convenient and comfortable to do so. Dan Froomkin suggests ways that journalists could drop the typical "sob story" and cover poverty in deep, dynamic ways that not only get at the context of poverty but also draw readers into news outlets that now struggle to attract readers. Emily Brennan's interview with Pulitzer Prize-winning journalist Katherine Boo profiles Boo's thinking that if journalists don't try to represent the stories of the poor and vulnerable, then those stories go "down the memory hole," lost to public consciousness. Rebecca Solnit argues that we "live and die by words and ideas" quite literally when it comes to how we represent the actions of vulnerable people in the aftermath of disasters. Reporter Noel King uses the 50th anniversary of President Lyndon Johnson's announcement of the War on Poverty to explore how American presidents have talked about poverty or strategically avoided it. Nazneen Mehta compares the frame of the American "welfare queen" to the frame of the "third world woman," showing how those frames shape public opinion and policy while misrepresenting the facts and harming vulnerable people. Olson et al. argue that poor women are harmed when their experiences are demonized *and* when they are sanitized, so their article includes the voices of poor women to complicate those polarizing frames. Finally, ads from a United Nations Development Programme campaign to reduce poverty show how an international aid agency represents the poor and represents the public's duty to address global poverty.

Simon Kuper
"Poverty's Poor Show in the Media"

Born in Uganda and raised all over Western Europe and North America, Simon Kuper is a sports writer for *Financial Times*, a British newspaper covering international news with a focus on business and economics. Kuper authored the book *Football Against the Enemy*, and his work, which spans many subjects, has also appeared in *The Observer* and *The Guardian*. In this essay from *Financial Times,* Kuper explains the many reasons journalists often overlook the poor.

If you were asked to interview someone in your community who was poor, how would you go about finding and asking him/her to talk to you?

> "To become news, poor people have to cause disorder."

An actor recently left France after the government tried to raise rich people's taxes. Gérard Depardieu moved to Belgium (to be near friends, excellent meat and Paris's airport, he explained), acquired a Russian passport, and made friends with Vladimir Putin. Meanwhile earlier this month an unemployed father became the fourth Bulgarian to burn himself to death since February in despair at poverty. Guess which victim of the economic crisis got more publicity?

The media have probably always ignored the poor, but we continue to do so even as poverty becomes the most pressing problem in developed countries. One in seven Americans now lives below the official poverty line, ever more jobless people kill themselves, and my colleague Gillian Tett recently wrote of a child in Liverpool chewing the wallpaper as hunger rises in the city. Yet the media still look away. I'm as guilty as anyone. But we can change.

Poverty has never been sexy. In 2008, the Joseph Rowntree Foundation analysed 40 hours of British TV, and found that "the word 'poverty' appeared only twice, both in *Shameless,*" a comedy drama. One reference was to the Live Aid concert; the other to Comic Relief. When poor people did get airtime, it was often as objects of derision on *Jerry Springer*-like shows.

You'd have thought the economic crisis would have made poverty newsy. "If it bleeds, it leads" is a journalistic maxim, and the Cambridge sociologist David Stuckler found sharp increases in suicides in recession-hit European countries after 2008. The crisis arguably caused 1,000 "excess" suicides in England alone.

5   But they weren't news. The global poor—2.5 billion people living on less than $2 a day—are considered even more boring, due to the triple whammy of being non-white, non-Anglophone and poor. To become news, poor people have to cause disorder. Middle-class people raise issues by writing;

poor people do it by rioting. I've read columns by prisoners and by people with terminal cancer, but I've never seen one by someone living on benefits.

The neglect isn't because journalists hate poor people. As the Tea Party likes to point out, most journalists are liberals. However, most are also upper-middle-class folk who never visit the poor areas of their city. We tend to interview people like us. There are rightwing media and leftwing media, but all are controlled by the well-fed. So are social media. On a map measuring global Twitter activity, the Netherlands dwarfs India, South Africa and Nigeria put together. And though journalists may be liberals, our proprietors and advertisers mostly aren't.

It's easier to meet a corporate PR for coffee in a nice hotel lobby near the office than to trek out to a chilly ghetto with poor transport links to find interviewees. Even when you get there, you don't always end up using their quotes. Something that's taboo to mention: poor Europeans (if asked) often express views on immigration that most journalists consider racist.

Poor people's analyses rarely fit neatly into the formats through which the ruling class interprets the world. A colleague told me how in Tunisia recently he'd interviewed a poor man who said he supported the ruling Islamist party. Then the man said he might vote for the secular far left. And then he expressed nostalgia for the departed dictator Zine el Abidine Ben Ali. These were probably valid responses to Tunisia's turmoil, but they didn't sound politically sophisticated, and my colleague was baffled.

I blame myself too. In the Palestinian West Bank this winter I interviewed a poor Bedouin family harassed by the Israeli authorities. I didn't write about them. Casting poor people as victims is boring. Anyway, nobody pressures you to quote them. Journalists get called up by corporate PRs, not by Bedouins.

Despite everything, there is a vigorous media debate about inequality. 10 However, it focuses on the 1 percent at the top. Most people profiled in the media—artists, athletes and many politicians—are millionaires. Depardieu probably received more coverage as an individual than the bottom 2.5 billion combined. That humanised him. Even when attacked, he gets a platform to complain about tax rises; people hurt by benefit cuts are rarely interviewed. It's as if you covered the Great Depression only by speaking to rentiers. In fact, we're exactly the media that an unequal world requires.

We don't have to be. We could take our lead from historians, who generations back dropped their exclusive focus on kings and queens to write "history from below." Fifty years ago E. P. Thompson, in *The Making of the English Working Class*, famously set out to rescue long-dead workers "from the enormous condescension of posterity."

Journalists still condescend, when we bother to notice the poor at all. Rather than presenting them only as victims, we could copy the narratives of triumph over adversity used in working-class women's magazines, suggests Amina Lone, social researcher in Manchester. It worked in *Educating Rita*, a film about a Liverpudlian hairdresser who goes to university. Morals aside: by ignoring the poor we are missing the economic story of the decade.

Analyze

1. "You'd have thought the economic crisis would have made poverty newsy," Kuper writes. What evidence does he provide that it did or did not?
2. What "triple whammy" makes poverty "boring"?
3. Kuper claims that the media neglect people who are poor not because they hate them but why?

Explore

1. Kuper writes: "To become news, poor people have to cause disorder. Middle-class people raise issues by writing; poor people do it by rioting." As support for this claim, Kuper says he's never seen something written by someone on benefits. Have you? How might he be right and/or wrong? Connect with a local social service agency to find someone who has experienced poverty who would like to be interviewed about that experience. Write a narrative or oral history that represents that story. Where could that story be shared?
2. Kuper claims: "[W]e're exactly the media that an unequal world requires." What does this mean? Do you agree or disagree? Explain.
3. Kuper gives both moral and practical reasons why the media's neglect of the poor is a problem. Explain those reasons. Write an essay in which you offer your own assessment of the media's attention to poverty. Cite examples from the media as support.

Dan Froomkin
"It Can't Happen Here: Why Is There Still So Little Coverage of Americans Who Are Struggling with Poverty?"

A senior Washington correspondent for the *Huffington Post*, Dan Froomkin is also a watchdog reporter who scrutinizes journalistic trends on *Nieman Reports*, a site dedicated to increasing accountability in journalism by highlighting questions that the press should ask. In the following article, Froomkin articulates the journalistic pressures that prevent poverty reporting and offers some solutions for restoring quality poverty reporting.

What makes a story about poverty engaging and compelling?

Poverty is hardly a new phenomenon in the hardscrabble highlands of Missouri's Ozarks. But to David Stoeffler, freshly arrived at the helm of the region's main paper, the *Springfield News-Leader*, the fact that two out of five families in the area with children under 18 lived below the poverty line seemed like a huge story. "We certainly had covered these issues," says Stoeffler, who became executive editor in May 2010, "but I would say it was more episodically, and not in any coordinated way."

> **16.1%** Percentage of Americans living in poverty (49.7 million total)[1]
>
> **0.2%** Coverage primarily about poverty in 50 major news outlets 2007–2012[2]

Stoeffler decided the paper needed to do more: "My sense was the community needed a little crusading."

After conversations with community groups and among staffers, the newsroom embarked on a major public service project called "Every Child" examining the range of challenges facing children in the region. There was still a problem, though, the one that plagues all poverty reporting: "What we were trying to do is figure out how could we paint this big broad picture and at the same time not bore everybody to death," Stoeffler says. "The goal was to try to raise awareness and get people to say, 'We need to do something about this.'"

So for five consecutive days last September, Stoeffler published stories across the entire front page of the print edition and the homepage of the paper's website. Each day focused on a specific problem: "No home," "No shoes," "No food," "No car," and "No peace." Many readers were shocked, saying they had no idea so many area families were living in such desperate circumstances. Some reached out to families that had been featured. Members of the community the *News-Leader* had initially brought together as an advisory group formed the Every Child Initiative to push for long-term policy changes. "There seems to be momentum toward wanting to do something sustainable and lasting," Stoeffler says. "We feel like we succeeded in getting the attention of the community."

5   Sadly, the *News-Leader's* success is an anomaly in the news business. Nearly 50 million people—about one in six Americans—live in poverty, defined as income below $23,021 a year for a family of four. And yet most news organizations largely ignore the issue. The Pew Research Center's Project for Excellence in Journalism indexed stories in 52 major mainstream news outlets from 2007 through the first half of 2012 and, according to Mark Jurkowitz, the project's associate director, "in no year did poverty coverage even come close to accounting for as little as one percent of the news hole. It's fair to say that when you look at that particular topic, it's negligible."

Instead, as *Tampa Bay Times* media critic Eric Deggans notes, at most news organizations poverty comes up sporadically. "Poverty becomes a sort of 'very special episode' of journalism that we sort of roll out every so often," he says.

The reasons for the lack of coverage are familiar. Journalists are drawn more to people making things happen than those struggling to pay bills; poverty is not considered a beat; neither advertisers nor readers are likely to demand more coverage, so neither will editors; and poverty stories are almost always enterprise work, requiring extra time and commitment. Yet persistent poverty is in some ways the ultimate accountability story— because, often, poverty happens by design.

"Poverty exists in a wealthy country largely as a result of political choices, not as a result of pure economics," argues Sasha Abramsky, a journalist whose upcoming book is called *The American Way of Poverty*. "The U.S. poverty rate is higher than most other developed nations, and the only way you can square that is there are political choices being made—or not being made—that accept a level of poverty that most wealthy democracies have said is unacceptable. We make these policy choices that perpetuate poverty, and then because poverty is so extreme, it becomes impolite to talk about."

The media could try to force the issue but it doesn't—at least not anymore, according to Philip Bennett, managing editor of PBS's Frontline public affairs series: "There are basic questions about the way the country is today that aren't being addressed by the journalistic institutions that used to address them."

The rise (and fall) of the Occupy movement, along with data about the increasingly skewed distribution of wealth and income in the United States, have led to greater interest in inequality. "There's been lots of really good stuff written about inequality, probably more in the last few years than in the previous 20," says Jason DeParle, who's covered poverty policy for the *New York Times* for 23 years. But much of the debate over inequality has focused on the excesses of the rich rather than the deprivations of the poor.

DeParle also notes that one frequent excuse for ignoring poverty is increasingly anachronistic. "We have tended to congratulate ourselves as a country that 'OK, there's more poverty, but that's because there's also more fluidity in our society,'" he says. But that's just not true anymore. Recent surveys show that Americans now have less economic mobility than Western Europeans. For instance, one study found that 42 percent of Americans raised in the bottom quintile of family income remain stuck there as adults, compared to 30 percent in the historically class-bound United Kingdom. For Bennett, the key unaddressed question is: Has America become a less fair society? "This is a major question of American life," he says. "It's part of our political divide in a really important way. [And yet it] is not receiving the kind of sustained, imaginative, aggressive coverage that it deserves. Shouldn't journalists—and not just one or two—be organizing themselves en masse to ask that question?"

One way to address the question is to confront pernicious myths about poverty. "The reason why people believe that '47 percent nonsense' [Republican presidential candidate Mitt Romney's leaked comment characterizing 47 percent of the population as "dependent upon the government"] that Romney was swinging is because they don't know the working poor," says Deggans, who is also author of "Race-Baiter: How the Media Wields Dangerous Words to Divide a Nation."

Despite stereotypes of "the lazy poor," for example, more than a third of adults in poverty have jobs; they just don't earn enough to support their families. According to the Economic Policy Institute, 28 percent of workers nationally earn less than $11 an hour. Even working full-time year-round, that still leaves a family of four below the poverty line.

10,489 number of presidential campaign stories carried by 8 major print, broadcast news outlets, Jan.–June 2012[1]
17 number of those campaign stories that were substantively about poverty

Modern low-wage workplaces can make for gripping stories. Noting Wal-Mart's promise to hire any recent honorably discharged veteran, Columbia University journalism professor Dale Maharidge suggests reporters follow one of those soldiers around for a few days. Half of Wal-Mart's more than one million U.S. workers make less than $10 an hour. "See how they cope on $8 or $9 an hour," says Maharidge, author of "Someplace Like America: Tales From the New Great Depression." Then consider the Walton family fortune, estimated to be more than $80 billion. "Look at how much money they're making versus how much their workers are making, through this soldier," Maharidge suggests.

15   There are also opportunities for business reporters to broaden questions beyond stock prices and acquisitions. Mimi Corcoran, director of the Special Fund for Poverty Alleviation at the liberal Open Society Foundations, urges journalists to grill CEOs about their companies' compensation plans and the ratio between what their employees make and their own income. "What are you doing to provide livable wages? What's the appropriate balance between return on income versus what you're doing to support your workforce?" Corcoran suggests as model questions.

Gary Rivlin, author of *Broke, USA: From Pawnshops to Poverty, Inc.—How the Working Poor Became Big Business*, points reporters to the businesses (payday lenders, pawnshops and check cashers) that profit from poverty. "Poor people don't just necessarily happen. The poor have a lot of help staying poor," he says. Rivlin and Barbara Ehrenreich, another writer with a long history of covering poverty, recently helped found a nonprofit group, the Economic Hardship Reporting Project, to encourage precisely that kind of coverage.

There's also a wealth of stories in anti-poverty programs. "You always hear, 'We waged a war on poverty and poverty won,'" says Greg Kaufmann, who covers poverty for *The Nation*. But the safety net has caught a lot of people who otherwise would have fallen much further, he points out: "It's like saying the Clean Water Act didn't work because there's still water pollution."

Indeed, one of the most overlooked stories of the decade may be the effects of anti-poverty measures that were part of the 2009 Recovery Act. "They had huge effects; they got virtually no attention," says Michael Grunwald, a *Time* reporter and author of *The New New Deal: The Hidden Story of Change in the Obama Era*. The provisions in the stimulus represent the biggest anti-poverty effort since President Johnson's Great Society in the 1960s.

In addition to expanding anti-poverty programs, the White House and Democrats in Congress made a concerted effort "to really do some innovative—and ultimately, in some areas, remarkably effective—things," Grunwald says. A $1.5 billion homelessness prevention fund allowed local governments to assist at-risk people with things like emergency rent payments, utility bills, and moving expenses. "During the worst economic crisis in 90 years, the homeless population actually decreased," Grunwald notes.

Mark Rank, a social welfare professor at Washington University in St. Louis, argues that poverty reporters also sometimes fall into a trap familiar to political reporters: giving both sides of the issue equal weight.

There's the conservative argument that poverty is largely a function of "people just screwing up, just not having the motivation," Rank says. The other argument, which Rank says is supported by the preponderance of research, is that poverty is the result of structural failings, most commonly, not enough jobs.

The most traditional kind of poverty coverage—the sob story—can actually backfire. A 1990 study by political scientist Shanto Iyengar found that "episodic" television news stories that focused on specific victims of poverty, especially black mothers, actually led white middle class viewers to blame the individuals more than social or government institutions. "In a capitalist society where success is judged in part by how much money you make, there's a strong impulse to want to attach personal choices and deliberate action to whether you are poor," says the *Tampa Bay Times*'s Deggans.

Context is key. Put individual stories in their wider context, look at the social factors at play, and examine possible solutions, says Calvin Sims, a former *New York Times* reporter who now manages the Ford Foundation's portfolio of news media and journalism grants: "Many readers walk away from stories about poverty thinking, 'Well, the poor, they'll always be with us. What can we do?' That's not something that we, as journalists, should leave people with."

News organizations need to "find ways for the work to have resonance in other spaces," according to Sims. That could mean convening follow-up conversations through panel discussions, on video, or through social media, with a particular focus on solutions. He also thinks there's great potential in traditional news organizations for sharing information with others, including the fast-growing ethnic media sector.

25   At the *Springfield News-Leader*, Stoeffler feels a sense of satisfaction. Like other newspapers, his has been retrenching; the newsroom is 20 percent smaller today than it was just three years ago. But Stoeffler argues that going after chronic community problems like poverty is more crucial now than ever. "From a journalistic standpoint, we become less and less relevant if we don't go after some of these bigger issues," he says. "It's the way we can distinguish ourselves from other media."

NOTES

1. Census Bureau Supplemental Poverty Measure.
2. Pew Research Center's Project for Excellence in Journalism.

Analyze

1. What is unusual about the poverty reporting in the *Springfield News-Leader* compared to the general media's poverty coverage?
2. Attention to growing inequality led the media to cover whom instead of the poor?
3. What question does Bennett, quoted in this article, say all journalists should ask?

Explore

1. Name at least two of the potential story areas Froomkin says the media are missing when it comes to covering poverty. Do these topics sound promising? Explain.

2. Why do some people argue that poverty reporters can "fall into a trap familiar to political reporters: giving both sides of the issue equal weight"? What's wrong with that?

3. Froomkin writes: "The most traditional kind of poverty coverage— the sob story—can actually backfire." Do you agree that the "sob story" genre exists in poverty reporting? Identify examples, if you think they exist. Why might this backfire?

Emily Brennan
"Reporting Poverty:
Interview with Katherine Boo"

Emily Brennan is a writer for the *New York Times* Travel section and other publications. In this piece, Brennan interviews Katherine Boo for *Guernica*, an all-volunteer publication focused on art and politics. Boo documents the lives of the poor as an investigative journalist for *The New Yorker* and published the award-winning creative nonfiction book *Behind the Beautiful Forevers* after conducting extensive research and interviews in the slums of Mumbai, India. Boo explains how careful journalism helps readers understand people's unique experiences while struggling through poverty toward upward mobility.

Can a privileged person tell the story of someone who lives in poverty without exploiting that person?

While covering poverty and social welfare for the *Washington Post* in 1993, Katherine Boo was commissioned to write a magazine profile of the new vice president, Al Gore. For most reporters, such an assignment would signal entry into the big leagues. Social issues are regarded as a beat journalists cover until they are deemed important enough to interview politicians, bureaucrats, people of power. "In journalism, if you get to be really hot stuff, that's where you get to go—to the White House!" Boo told *The Guardian* in June. "And that's too bad," she added, "social issues are kind of worthy things that people graduate from."

As soon as she handed in the assignment, Boo returned to the streets, precincts, churches, and shelters where she continued her reporting on low-income communities. She went on to win the Pulitzer Prize for Public Service in 2000 for a *Post* series on government-run group homes for mentally retarded people. The investigation showed how much Boo, far from being uninterested in power, was a great student of it. She understood that the people who wield power often have the most simplistic grasp of its grip on society. She went on to write, for *The New Yorker*, stories on Hurricane Katrina evacuees looking for new homes and Oklahoma City women hoping that marriage-prep classes might help them out of the ghetto.

In her first book, *Behind the Beautiful Forevers*, Boo turns her attention to India and the residents of Annawadi, a Mumbai slum in the shadows of the city's airport and luxury hotels. Of Annawadi's three thousand residents, few have full-time employment. Most sleep in homes of nailed-together scrap metal, plywood, and plastic tarpaulin; some sleep outside. Many children are forced to work instead of attend school. The dwelling's eastern edge borders a vast pool of sewage.

Amid Annawadi's grinding poverty lives Abdul, a teenager who supports his family of eleven by selling scraps of trash. Boo chronicles the struggle of Abdul and other families to get out of poverty by whatever means available: corruption, education, work (NGOs, tellingly, never enter the picture). Their lives illustrate what poverty [can do to] the underclass of a developing country, but Boo never reduces them to case studies. She depicts the residents' relationships, squabbles, opportunities, and misfortunes with eloquence and detail. In its specificity, *Behind the Beautiful Forevers* tells a larger story about India's rapid growth in the global economy, and the people the country is leaving behind. Boo spoke with me over the phone from her mother's house in Virginia.

—Emily Brennan for *Guernica*

5   **Guernica:** After reporting on issues of poverty in the United States for so long, what drew you to write about India?

Katherine Boo: I met my husband, who is from India, in 2001. When I first started going to India, I'd be at these dinner tables where people, claiming a posture of great authority, talked about what was going on in these historically poor communities. They always seemed to fall into two schools of thought: everything had changed with the country's increasing prosperity, or nothing had changed in the lives of low-income people. I wasn't a subscriber to either. In fact, I was familiar with these arguments from my experience of writing about the poor in the United States. Most of the people who do the talking about what it's like for the very poor don't spend much time with them. That circumstance transcends borders.

It was my husband, who had watched my reporting and fact-checking process, the way I use official documents and taped interviews to be quite precise, who first said to me, "Well, this might be something you can do in India." And at first, I thought, "I can't do it. I'm not Indian. If I did write anything, I would just be some stupid white woman writing a stupid thing." But there were people around me who were saying, "If you do it well, then who you are becomes less important." My husband and these others were interested in issues of social equality and fairness in India and thought it would be valuable to know what it was like for low-income people there, know it with a little more depth. There was plenty of reporting going on in India, but specifically what I do—follow people over long periods of time—there wasn't much of that in India. (There are some people in the United States who do it, and do it very well, but there are not a lot of them here, either.) In my kind of work, you don't parachute in after some big, terrible event, which is important and has to be covered, but offers only a glimpse. It's the kind of work in which you ask, what is my understanding of how the world works, and where can I go to see these questions get worked out in individuals' lives? That was really the question for me: whether I had anything to add to what had already been written.

Guernica: What did you decide you could add?

Katherine Boo: Going in, I didn't think so much about what I could add, but what I didn't know: how people get out of poverty. As a reporter, you know the tropes of how stories on poverty work in any country. A reporter will go to an NGO and say, "Tell me about the good work that you're doing and introduce me to the poor people who represent the kind of help you give." It serves to streamline the storytelling, but it gives you a lopsided cosmos in which almost every poor person you read about is involved with a NGO helping him. Our understanding of poverty and how people escape from poverty, in any country, is quite distorted.

10   Mumbai, especially, had so many contradictions. You have this manifest prosperity, but then more than half of its citizens lived in slums. The life expectancy in Mumbai is seven years shorter than the country as a whole. How can that be in one of India's wealthiest cities? So many things didn't make sense to me, and long before I started reporting on the book, I was trying to get answers to those questions for myself. When I did start reporting in 2007, I just followed people in the poor communities at first, looked at whether they prospered while India continued to soar. If I'd add anything, I figured it was the time I'd put in these historically poor communities.

Guernica: How did you balance telling individuals' stories and using those stories to illuminate India's economic inequality?

Katherine Boo: It's a question of foreground and background. The reason I followed Abdul Husain, before he's falsely accused of a crime and the story twists, is that there was this explosion of garbage. All of a sudden people who were gathering trash had more income than they had ever known. When I arrived to Annawadi in 2007, it was about seven months before the Beijing Olympics, and construction in China had pushed up the prices in scrap metal; people doing the recycling had indeed become part of the global economy. There was always this cliché about the abject garbage collector, but most of the people in Annawadi, according to official Indian standards, had risen above the poverty line. These people weren't even poor anymore, according to India, but part of this narrative of global capitalism in India.

When I pick a story, I'm very much aware of the larger issues that it's illuminating. But one of the things that I, as a writer, feel strongly about is that nobody is representative. That's just narrative nonsense. People may be part of a larger story or structure or institution, but they're still people. Making them representative loses sight of that. Which is why a lot of writing about low-income people makes them into saints, perfect in their suffering. But you take Abdul, for instance. He's diffident, he's selfish, he's not very verbal. Even his own family considers him charmless. But when the reader meets him, they sense he's a real person, that he's not a construct. And even Manju—who's good and generous in many ways—she's good and generous as a way of getting back at her mother. The more righteous she can be, the better she can stick it to her mom. So you try to let the reader have a sense of this person and soul, as a recognizable human.

The hope is for the reader to engage with them as individuals and see how these people really do get around social obstacles, when there is a limited distribution of opportunities, when there are institutional problems, be it police corruption or poor public hospitals and schools. I don't think readers will get invested in what potential is being squandered if they don't engage with the people in the story as individuals. When you have a kid who is killed, I want the reader to feel what I felt and what the people of Annawadi felt, and because of that, get involved in the problems of criminal or social justice.

Guernica: In your author's note, you write, "Although I was mindful of the risk of overinterpretation, it felt more distortive to devote my attention to the handful of Annawadians who possessed a verbal dexterity that might have provided more colorful quotes." Does reporting's reliance on interviews too often determine who is featured? What is lost as a result, and how do you try to recover it in your own work?

Katherine Boo: You try everything when you're doing this work. You figure out what works and what doesn't. With questions, you ask them, and sometimes the person's wondering, "What is the right answer? What does she want? What does she think? Let me give her what she's looking for." Listening and observing often work much better [and] reveal much more about the complexity of someone than the answers that they give to questions about themselves. That's certainly true in my life and the life of my friends and family.

Often the people who have the most verbal dexterity have had some amount of education in their lives, and you don't want to limit your reporting to just those people. You take a kid like Sunil, the young scavenger, he's been raising himself, so conducting long interviews and eliciting illustrative anecdotes was out of the question. When I started spending time with him, it became clear that Sunil had an extremely strong aesthetic sense that helped him through life. Moments of natural beauty were very important to him. For example, there were parrots on the other side of the sewage way, and some boys would climb up and capture the parrots and sell them at the market. Sunil felt so strongly that this was wrong. He thought the parrots should be left where they were so that everybody could hear and see them. Another time, he found six purple lotuses blooming on an airport wall and protected them, kept them a secret, so that no one could cut them down and sell them. These aspects of his character emerged over time from observation. I wasn't going to get them through conversation. It's one thing to have somebody talk about what they value in whatever language they have; it's another thing to really see what they value. And with Sunil, after it became clear he had this sense, I could talk to him about it. I still asked questions, and a lot of them—endless questions if you ask some—but what works best for me is when I can observe something and then ask the person about that moment afterward.

Guernica: Does that explain why you report in a place for so long? To collect all of these observations?

Katherine Boo: And to be there when something happens, as it happens, when something gets said, as it's said. There's a moment I describe in the book when Abdul starts talking about what a life is, says something like, "Even a dog has a life. Even if my mother keeps beating me, even if that moment was my entire life, that's a life." It was a moment that came out of nowhere. When I listened to the tape of it, we're talking about so many things—a woman had just tried to kill herself, and all of this stuff was going on in Annawadi—and that comes out of nowhere. Every once in a while, that happens, but it doesn't ever happen in response to a question. Part of the reason that I spend a long time there, day after day, which to others seems tedious and pointless, is so I can be there at those moments when things get articulated, and I can put them on page.

20   **Guernica:** Where did you live when you did your reporting on Annawadi?

Katherine Boo: I ended up staying the most time in an apartment on the same street as Arthur Road Central Jail, some kilometers away from Annawadi.

Guernica: Was it important to you to stay in the vicinity of the community?

Katherine Boo: Quite the contrary. It was important to me, in the course of my reporting in Annawadi, day after day, night after night, to leave and get a sense of the city as a whole. It is a city that until eleven years ago was unknown to me, and is changing all of the time, so I really had to explore it, learn about it. I certainly did a lot reporting around the five-star hotels as well as Annawadi. I did my whole anthropology of five-star bathrooms, each one more lavish than the next. (Laughs.)

Even if I were to stay in Annawadi or something like it, it wouldn't be the same. After Hurricane Katrina, for instance, I did stay in the shelter [when] I did reporting for *The New Yorker*. But me staying in a shelter is not the same as someone who's been evacuated to that shelter. This whole thing of, "I'm walking a mile in their shoes by living this certain way." Well, I'm not living that way. I can turn around and leave. We can do the best we can to get to the core of people's circumstances, but it's ludicrous to think that my being in Annawadi all of that time is walking in their shoes. It's not.

Guernica: At a lecture at American Academy, you recounted that during   25
your reporting on that evacuation shelter for *The New Yorker* a woman told you, "Wait, so you take our stories and put them in a magazine that rich people read, and you get paid and we don't? That's some backward-ass bluffiness, if you ask me." She seemed to sum up the moral dilemma that reporting on poverty raises. Can you speak to some of these ethical questions?

Katherine Boo: She said it better than I did. We take stories and purvey them to people with money. And in the conventions of my profession, which I try to adhere to, we can't pay people for stories. Anyone with a conscience who does this work grapples with that reality, and if they don't, I'd worry. I lie awake at night, and I think, "Am I exploiting them? Am I a vulture?" All of the terrible names anyone could call me, I've called myself worse.

But if writing about people who are not yourself is illegitimate, then the only legitimate work is autobiography; and as a reader and a citizen, I don't want to live in that world. Because if you take a kid like Sunil, who's been denied the possibility of an education that allows him to write his own story, and all of the people who lack the means and access to do so, they go down the memory hole. They're lost. What it comes down to is, the only thing worse than being a poverty reporter is if no one ever wrote about it at all. My work, I hope, helps people understand how much gets lost between the intellection of how to get people out of poverty and how it's actually experienced.

One of the reasons I pore over official documents and reportage is because I'm fascinated by the chasm between the lives that people have and the way they're officially recorded. In Annawadi, when people were killed, they were categorized as sickness deaths because the officials were corrupt, were extorting money from other people, didn't care to investigate the deaths of no-account people, and so on. The tragedy is that the other children in Annawadi knew that these people were murdered, that their lives had no meaning, that they'd be classified and filed away. The corrosive effect of that knowledge is staggering. When you know that anything can happen to you, that there is no possibility of redress because of who you are, because you're an embarrassment in this prosperous city, that's tragic.

Sunil knows people who've been killed and filed away, and he can't bring that to life. But he can tell me and I can get the documents and do the work and bring it to life. And that's a trade-off to make.

Analyze

1. How could studying government-run group homes be a greater opportunity to study power than covering the White House?
2. Boo says that "[m]ost of the people who do the talking about what it's like for the very poor don't spend much time with them. That circumstance transcends borders." What does she mean? Do you agree? Cite examples that support or challenge Boo's claim.
3. Why is Boo initially hesitant to report on India? Why does she decide to do it?

Explore

1. Boo says that when colleagues encouraged her to report on India, her initial thought was that she was an outsider who would be perceived as just "some stupid white woman writing a stupid thing." Others argued that if she did it well, "then who you are becomes less important." How might someone like Teju Cole (chapter 4), who critiques the "white-savior industrial complex" that imposes its desire to help onto others, respond?
2. Boo argues that "nobody is representative. That's just narrative nonsense. People may be part of a larger story or structure or institution, but they're still people. Making them representative loses sight of that." Boo presents her ideas from the point of view of a writer, a journalist who reports through narrative. Do writers have that much control, or do readers impose frames despite the author's intentions?
3. In the interview, Boo agonizes over the fact that her job as a reporter is to "take stories and purvey them to people with money. . . . I lie awake at night, and I think, 'Am I exploiting them? Am I a vulture?' All of the terrible names anyone could call me, I've called myself worse." Do journalists and researchers who work with vulnerable populations like the poor take advantage of them, or is there a "greater good" in purveying those stories? Write a letter to Boo in which you help her think through this ethical dilemma.

Rebecca Solnit
"When the Media Is the Disaster: Covering Haiti"

An independent writer, Rebecca Solnit is an activist and journalist, contributing news and analysis on climate change, Native American land rights, human rights, and anti-war movements. In the following article, Solnit chronicles how the media often exploit poor people when they are most vulnerable, following natural disasters, framing their attempt to survive as criminal activity.

Is it morally acceptable for those living in desperation and deprivation to "loot" goods during disasters?

Soon after almost every disaster the crimes begin: ruthless, selfish, indifferent to human suffering, and generating far more suffering. The perpetrators go unpunished and live to commit further crimes against humanity. They care less for human life than for property. They act without regard for consequences.

I'm talking, of course, about those members of the mass media whose misrepresentation of what goes on in disaster often abets and justifies a second wave of disaster. I'm talking about the treatment of sufferers as criminals, both on the ground and in the news, and the endorsement of a shift of resources from rescue to property patrol. They still have blood on their hands from Hurricane Katrina, and they are staining themselves anew in Haiti.

Within days of the Haitian earthquake, for example, the *Los Angeles Times* ran a series of photographs with captions that kept deploying the word "looting." One was of a man lying face down on the ground with this caption: "A Haitian police officer ties up a suspected looter who was carrying a bag of evaporated milk." The man's sweaty face looks up at the camera, beseeching, anguished.

Another photo was labeled: "Looting continued in Haiti on the third day after the earthquake, although there were more police in downtown Port-au-Prince." It showed a somber crowd wandering amid shattered piles of concrete in a landscape where, visibly, there could be little worth taking anyway.

5   A third image was captioned: "A looter makes off with rolls of fabric from an earthquake-wrecked store." Yet another: "The body of a police officer lies in a Port-au-Prince street. He was accidentally shot by fellow police who mistook him for a looter."

People were then still trapped alive in the rubble. A translator for Australian TV dug out a toddler who'd survived 68 hours without food or water, orphaned but claimed by an uncle who had lost his pregnant wife. Others were hideously wounded and awaiting medical attention that wasn't arriving. Hundreds of thousands, maybe millions, needed, and still need, water, food, shelter, and first aid. The media in disaster bifurcates. Some step out of their usual "objective" roles to respond with kindness and practical aid. Others bring out the arsenal of clichés and pernicious myths and begin to assault the survivors all over again.

The "looter" in the first photo might well have been taking that milk to starving children and babies, but for the news media that wasn't the most urgent problem. The "looter" stooped under the weight of two big bolts of fabric might well have been bringing it to now homeless people trying to shelter from a fierce tropical sun under improvised tents.

The pictures do convey desperation, but they *don't* convey crime. Except perhaps for that shooting of a fellow police officer—his colleagues were so focused on property that they were reckless when it came to human life, and a man died for no good reason in a landscape already saturated with death.

In recent days, there have been scattered accounts of confrontations involving weapons, and these may be a different matter. But the man with the powdered milk? Is he really a criminal? There may be more to know, but with what I've seen I'm not convinced.

What Would You Do?

10   Imagine, reader, that your city is shattered by a disaster. Your home no longer exists, and you spent what cash was in your pockets days ago. Your credit cards are meaningless because there is no longer any power to run credit-card charges. Actually, there are no longer any storekeepers, any banks, any commerce, or much of anything to buy. The economy has ceased to exist.

By day three, you're pretty hungry and the water you grabbed on your way out of your house is gone. The thirst is far worse than the hunger.

You can go for many days without food, but not water. And in the improvised encampment you settle in, there is an old man near you who seems on the edge of death. He no longer responds when you try to reassure him that this ordeal will surely end. Toddlers are now crying constantly, and their mothers infinitely stressed and distressed.

So you go out to see if any relief organization has finally arrived to distribute anything, only to realize that there are a million others like you stranded with nothing, and there isn't likely to be anywhere near enough aid anytime soon. The guy with the corner store has already given away all his goods to the neighbors. That supply's long gone by now. No wonder, when you see the chain pharmacy with the shattered windows or the supermarket, you don't think twice before grabbing a box of PowerBars and a few gallons of water that might keep you alive and help you save a few lives as well.

The old man might not die, the babies might stop their squalling, and the mothers might lose that look on their faces. Other people are calmly wandering in and helping themselves, too. Maybe they're people like you, and that gallon of milk the fellow near you has taken is going to spoil soon anyway. You haven't shoplifted since you were 14, and you have plenty of money to your name. But it doesn't mean anything now.

If you grab that stuff are you a criminal? Should you end up lying in the dirt on your stomach with a cop tying your hands behind your back? Should you end up labeled a looter in the international media? Should you be shot down in the street, since the overreaction in disaster, almost *any* disaster, often includes the imposition of the death penalty without benefit of trial for suspected minor property crimes?

Or are you a rescuer? Is the survival of disaster victims more important than the preservation of everyday property relations? Is that chain pharmacy more vulnerable, more a victim, more in need of help from the National Guard than you are, or those crying kids, or the thousands still trapped in buildings and soon to die? 15

It's pretty obvious what my answers to these questions are, but it isn't obvious to the mass media. And in disaster after disaster, at least since the San Francisco earthquake of 1906, those in power, those with guns and the force of law behind them, are too often more concerned for property than human life. In an emergency, people can, and do, die from those priorities. Or they get gunned down for minor thefts or imagined thefts. The media not only endorses such outcomes, but regularly, repeatedly, helps prepare the way for, and then eggs on, such a reaction.

If Words Could Kill

We need to banish the word "looting" from the English language. It incites madness and obscures realities.

"Loot," the noun and the verb, is a word of Hindi origin meaning the spoils of war or other goods seized roughly. As historian Peter Linebaugh points out, "At one time loot was the soldier's pay." It entered the English language as a good deal of loot from India entered the English economy, both in soldiers' pockets and as imperial seizures.

After years of interviewing survivors of disasters, and reading first-hand accounts and sociological studies from such disasters as the London Blitz and the Mexico City earthquake of 1985, I don't believe in looting. Two things go on in disasters. The great majority of what happens you could call emergency requisitioning. Someone who could be you, someone in the kind of desperate circumstances I outlined above, takes necessary supplies to sustain human life in the absence of any alternative. Not only would I not call that looting, I wouldn't even call that theft.

20   Necessity is a defense for breaking the law in the United States and other countries, though it's usually applied more to, say, confiscating the car keys of a drunk driver than feeding hungry children. Taking things you don't need is theft under any circumstances. It is, says the disaster sociologist Enrico Quarantelli, who has been studying the subject for more than half a century, vanishingly rare in most disasters.

Personal gain is the last thing most people are thinking about in the aftermath of a disaster. In that phase, the survivors are almost invariably more altruistic and less attached to their own property, less concerned with the long-term questions of acquisition, status, wealth, and security, than just about anyone not in such situations imagines possible. (The best accounts from Haiti of how people with next to nothing have patiently tried to share the little they have and support those in even worse shape than them only emphasize this disaster reality.) Crime often drops in the wake of a disaster.

The media are another matter. They tend to arrive obsessed with property (and the headlines that assaults on property can make). Media outlets often call everything looting and thereby incite hostility toward the sufferers as well as a hysterical overreaction on the part of the armed authorities. Or sometimes the journalists on the ground do a good job and the editors back in their safe offices cook up the crazy photo captions and the wrongheaded interpretations and emphases.

They also deploy the word *panic* wrongly. Panic among ordinary people in crisis is profoundly uncommon. The media will call a crowd of people running from certain death a panicking mob, even though running is the only sensible thing to do. In Haiti, they continue to report that food is being withheld from distribution for fear of "stampedes." Do they think Haitians are cattle?

The belief that people in disaster (particularly poor and nonwhite people) are cattle or animals or just crazy and untrustworthy regularly justifies spending far too much energy and far too many resources on control—the American military calls it "security"—rather than relief. A British-accented voiceover on CNN calls people sprinting to where supplies are being dumped from a helicopter a "stampede" and adds that this delivery "risks sparking chaos." The chaos already exists, and you can't blame it on these people desperate for food and water. Or you can, and in doing so help convince your audience that they're unworthy and untrustworthy.

Back to looting: of course you can consider Haiti's dire poverty and   25
failed institutions a long-term disaster that changes the rules of the game. There might be people who are not only interested in taking the things they need to survive in the next few days, but things they've never been entitled to own or things they may need next month. Technically that's theft, but I'm not particularly surprised or distressed by it; the distressing thing is that even before the terrible quake they led lives of deprivation and desperation.

In ordinary times, minor theft is often considered a misdemeanor. No one is harmed. Unchecked, minor thefts could perhaps lead to an environment in which there were more thefts and so forth, and a good argument can be made that, in such a case, the tide needs to be stemmed. But it's not particularly significant in a landscape of terrible suffering and mass death.

A number of radio hosts and other media personnel are still upset that people apparently took TVs after Hurricane Katrina hit New Orleans in August 2005. Since I started thinking about, and talking to people about, disaster aftermaths I've heard a lot about those damned TVs. Now, which matters more to you, televisions or human life? People were dying on rooftops and in overheated attics and freeway overpasses, they were stranded in all kinds of hideous circumstances on the Gulf Coast in 2005 when the mainstream media began to obsess about looting, and the mayor of

New Orleans and the governor of Louisiana made the decision to focus on protecting property, not human life.

A gang of white men on the other side of the river from New Orleans got so worked up about property crimes that they decided to take the law into their own hands and began shooting. They seem to have considered all black men criminals and thieves and shot a number of them. Some apparently died; there were bodies bloating in the September sun far from the region of the floods; one good man trying to evacuate the ruined city barely survived; and the media looked away. It took me months of nagging to even get the story covered. This vigilante gang claimed to be protecting property, though its members never demonstrated that their property was threatened. They boasted of killing black men. And they shared values with the mainstream media and the Louisiana powers that be.

Somehow, when the Bush administration subcontracted emergency services—like providing evacuation buses in Hurricane Katrina—to cronies who profited even while providing incompetent, overpriced, and much delayed service at the moment of greatest urgency, we didn't label that looting.

30   Or when a lot of wealthy Wall Street brokers decide to tinker with a basic human need like housing. . . . Well, you catch my drift.

Woody Guthrie once sang that "some will rob you with a six-gun, and some with a fountain pen." The guys with the six guns (or machetes or sharpened sticks) make for better photographs, and the guys with the fountain pens not only don't end up in jail, they end up in McMansions with four-car garages and, sometimes, in elected—or appointed—office.

Learning to See in Crises

Last Christmas a priest, Father Tim Jones of York, started a ruckus in Britain when he said in a sermon that shoplifting by the desperate from chain stores might be acceptable behavior. Naturally, there was an uproar. Jones told the Associated Press: "The point I'm making is that when we shut down every socially acceptable avenue for people in need, then the only avenue left is the socially unacceptable one."

The response focused almost entirely on why shoplifting is wrong, but the claim was also repeatedly made that it doesn't help. In fact, food helps the hungry, a fact so bald it's bizarre to even have to state it. The means by which it arrives is a separate matter. The focus remained on shoplifting, rather than on why there might be people so desperate in England's green and pleasant land that shoplifting might be their only option, and whether unnecessary human suffering is itself a crime of sorts.

Right now, the point is that people in Haiti need food, and for all the publicity, the international delivery system has, so far, been a visible dud. Under such circumstances, breaking into a U.N. food warehouse—food assumedly meant for the poor of Haiti in a catastrophic moment—might not be "violence," or "looting," or "law-breaking." It might be logic. It might be the most effective way of meeting a desperate need.

Why were so many people in Haiti hungry before the earthquake?   35 Why do we have a planet that produces enough food for all and a distribution system that ensures more than a billion of us don't have a decent share of that bounty? Those are not questions whose answers should be long delayed.

Even more urgently, we need compassion for the sufferers in Haiti and media that tell the truth about them. I'd like to propose alternative captions for those *Los Angeles Times* photographs as models for all future disasters:

Let's start with the picture of the policeman hogtying the figure whose face is so anguished: "Ignoring thousands still trapped in rubble, a policeman accosts a sufferer who took evaporated milk. No adequate food distribution exists for Haiti's starving millions."

And the guy with the bolt of fabric? "As with every disaster, ordinary people show extraordinary powers of improvisation, and fabrics such as these are being used to make sun shelters around Haiti."

For the murdered policeman: "Institutional overzealousness about protecting property leads to a gratuitous murder, as often happens in crises. Meanwhile countless people remain trapped beneath crushed buildings."

And the crowd in the rubble labeled looters? How about: "Resourceful   40 survivors salvage the means of sustaining life from the ruins of their world."

That one might not be totally accurate, but it's likely to be more accurate than the existing label. And what is absolutely accurate, in Haiti right now, and on Earth always, is that human life matters more than property, that the survivors of a catastrophe deserve our compassion and our understanding of their plight, and that we live and die by words and ideas, and it matters desperately that we get them right.

Analyze

1. Solnit claims that in a disaster, the media respond in one of two ways. Name the two responses. Which does she suggest is more appropriate?

2. Define "looting." Explain why Solnit thinks that word should be banished from the English language. Explain the section title "If Words Could Kill."

3. Solnit is frustrated by how the media fixated on people taking TVs in the aftermath of Hurricane Katrina while they neglected to report that so many people were dying unnecessarily. Solnit asks: "Now, which matters more to you, televisions or human life?" Is this a fair question? Does it further or frustrate Solnit's argument? Explain.

Explore

1. In a section of her article titled "What Would You Do?" Solnit puts readers into a disaster situation and asks them to consider how they would respond. Does this rhetorical device help you visualize and identify with the situation? Imagine that you are Solnit's editor. Write to her to either explain why you think it works or offer suggestions for revising this section.

2. Solnit writes that "unnecessary human suffering is itself a crime of sorts." Write an essay in which you agree or disagree with this claim. Construct an argument supporting your position and addressing such issues as who should be prosecuted if we do think such a crime has been committed.

3. Solnit concludes with a forceful series of claims, saying that for Haiti and for the Earth, it is accurate to say "that human life matters more than property, that the survivors of a catastrophe deserve our compassion and our understanding of their plight, and that we live and die by words and ideas, and it matters desperately that we get them right." First, discuss what Solnit means. Next, consider how people might agree with her claims but come to a different conclusion about policies and practices during a catastrophe. Create some of your own first-person scenarios to test your thinking: Role-play as a police officer, as a survivor, as a journalist, as a business owner, as a public health specialist, etc.

Noel King
"American Presidents and the Rhetoric of Poverty"

Noel King is a reporter on wealth and poverty for *Marketplace*, a Los Angeles-based nationally broadcast radio program that focuses on news events related to business and the economy. King graduated from Brown University with a degree in American civilization and has since reported on a variety of national and international topics through media including *BBC World Service*, *NPR*, *CBS Radio*, *Reuters*, and *USA Today*. In the following article, King explores how presidents have historically discussed—or strategically avoided—the issue of poverty.

Should presidents talk about poverty more than they do?

January 8, 2014 marks the fifty-year anniversary of Lyndon B. Johnson's State of the Union address, in which he issued a call to arms against poverty. Sasha Abramsky, author of *The American Way of Poverty: How the Other Half Still Lives*, says it was a remarkable scene.

"You've got to remember," Abramsky said, "this is only six weeks after John F. Kennedy had been assassinated, and the entire country is in a state of shock. And he comes to the podium, and it's a very somber affair. There's none of the bombast, none of the hoopla that you see in a modern State of the Union. And very quietly, but with enormous moral force, he lays out this campaign."

Johnson's stated aim was to win the war against poverty, "in the field, in every private home, in every public office, from the courthouse to the White House." In the five decades since, there has been fierce debate, not only over whether the US has won or lost the war on poverty, but whether the country as a whole is gaining ground or retreating.

Johnson used the word "poverty" nine times in his 1964 address. Most other presidents use the word a maximum of two times during their states of the union, and many don't use it at all, a fact which bothers Abramsky.

"There's almost an invisibilizing of poverty in this country," Abramsky said. "You saw it in 2012, in the presidential election. It's during a period when tens of millions of Americans are struggling massively. They've lost 5 their middle-class footholds and they are falling into what can only realistically be described as lives of poverty. But the language in 2012 was all about the struggling middle class. It wasn't even about the working poor."

And while the middle class is certainly struggling, millions of Americans aren't middle class, they are poor. Because of the stigma attached to poverty, elected officials throughout US history have seen risk in aligning themselves with the poor.

"There's suspicion of poor people that we see in politics today," said Alice O'Connor, a professor of history at UC Santa Barbara, who writes on poverty, social policy and inequality. "The idea being that large numbers of people are simply undeserving of help because they are poor because of some fault of their own."

American attitudes toward "big" government and government relief also shape how politicians talk—or don't talk—about poverty, O'Connor said, pointing to Franklin Delano Roosevelt, architect of the New Deal.

"FDR was very careful to try to distinguish his welfare state from the politics of relief," O'Connor said. "[It] was about protecting people against economic insecurity. It was about putting people back to work. As opposed to providing relief for poor people."

10   While writing *The American Way of Poverty*, Sasha Abramsky crisscrossed the country, speaking to people living below the poverty line. Their erasure from political discourse coexisted with a sense, among many he spoke to, of diminished self-worth.

"When you speak to people [in poverty] it becomes increasingly hard to demonize them," Abramsky said. "They're not all saints but neither are they all sinners. One of the things we've done in this country is we've turned poverty into a sin."

In his 1988 State of the Union address, Ronald Reagan's famous assertion, "some years ago, the federal government declared war on poverty. And poverty won," drew laughter from his audience, suggesting that Johnson's war on poverty had become a punchline. Or perhaps the low rumble of laughter illustrated American discomfort with poverty.

"It works politically to not talk in terms of poverty," said Peter Edelman, author of *So Rich, So Poor: Why it's So Hard to End Poverty in America*. "Poverty connotes welfare. Welfare connotes race to a large extent. These are all things that have a pejorative meaning to millions of people in our country."

And while the country and its elected officials often seem to cleave along partisan lines when discussing solutions to poverty, Edelman says, on the whole, the country agrees on many things.

"If you say, every child ought to have an opportunity, every child ought   15
to be able to go to a good school, everybody ought to be able to have a fair opportunity to succeed in our country, people resonate with that," Edelman said.

President Obama will deliver his next State of the Union address on 28 January, just over fifty years after Johnson declared his war. In 2013, Obama used the word poverty five times, notably while critiquing the minimum wage.

"Even with the tax relief we've put in place, a family with two kids that earns the minimum wage still lives below the poverty line," Obama said at the time. "That's wrong."

Analyze

1. King quotes Sasha Abramsky as claiming that in the U.S., "we've turned poverty into a sin." What does he mean? Do you agree? Give evidence to support your response.

2. King quotes Peter Edelman as saying that there are many things about poverty on which Americans agree. What are those points of agreement? Is his list correct? Add or delete items. Explain your editing.

3. What is the value and what is the limitation of counting the number of times each president uses the word "poverty" in his state of the union address to measure his attention to the issue?

Explore

1. Abramsky describes President Johnson as presenting his plan for the War on Poverty with "enormous moral force." Read the full text and/or listen to Johnson's speech (available online as text and video) and research the details of the War on Poverty. To what extent was this a moral project? To what extent was this a practical project? Many people have disagreed with Johnson's approach to solving poverty in the U.S., and many have disagreed with the sentiment that we should even try. Research those objections and discuss them in the context of

the claim that this war was driven by a "moral" force. What does that suggest about those who opposed it? Explain.

2. King writes that President Ronald Reagan turned Johnson's War on Poverty into a "punchline." Research the circumstances King refers to. What can we really ascribe to a president in terms of success or regression in the fight against poverty? Point to a particular policy or program—or repeal of a policy or program—that shows a president's power to address poverty.

3. Identify a recent significant speech or writing by a world leader that addresses poverty (e.g., State of the Union address, invited talk to a major organization, written statement). Do a rhetorical analysis of that speech analyzing how the person constructs the argument in order to shape or respond to public thinking about poverty. Note word choices, references, assumptions, etc. that support or undermine the strength of the speech.

Nazneen Mehta
"Opposing Images: 'Third World Women' and 'Welfare Queens'"

Nazneen Mehta wrote the following article as a third-year law student at Columbia University. Now serving as counsel for the U.S. Senate Committee on Judiciary, Mehta previously trained low-income women to become early childhood educators through the Connecticut-based nonprofit organization All Our Kin. In this article, Mehta argues that the images people construct of irresponsible "welfare queens" and oppressed "third world women" obscure their realities and negatively impact public policies.

What images of the poor do you see most often today?

Consider two familiar images of poor women: Both women are impoverished, raced, struggling to meet their children's basic needs, and living as marginalized members of their societies. But one woman lives in the

"Third World"—a victim of poverty in a developing country. The other woman lives in America—a "welfare queen" (Hancock 2004). While both images convey poverty and powerlessness, each one implies a different message about the woman's life and her ability to create a better future for herself and her family. These contrasting images and the assumptions they convey have a profound influence on U.S. public policy, creating a sharp contrast between international and domestic policies for assistance to poor women.

International development institutions and U.S. foreign policy makers have internalized the image of the Third World mother as a vulnerable woman who is trapped in a life of poverty because of "underdevelopment." The international and foreign policies created against the backdrop of this image seek to remedy the Third World woman's situation through empowerment; microcredit programs and cooperatives invest in women's economic and social empowerment as the key to increasing the well-being of the overall community and children. By contrast, underlying U.S. welfare policy for poor American women is the idea of the welfare queen—a mother who is seen not as an asset, but instead as a liability to herself, her children, and her community.

Both of these images are deeply problematic. They mask the historical and political processes that led to the poverty and structural inequality shaping these women's lives (Esteva 1992; Roberts 1999). But while the assumptions behind the image of the Third World woman—passivity and deprivation—have led to empowerment programs and policies (UNFPA 2005; U.S. Department of State n.d.), the image of the U.S. welfare queen—characterized as lazy, irresponsible, and uncontrollably fertile—has manifested in disempowering and dispiriting welfare reform laws that dismiss the poor woman's role as a source of strength and leadership to her family and community (Hancock 2004, 8).

Images and Policy: Power and Distortion

These two opposing images are so powerful both because they are literally images, which are flashed on television screens and circulated in print, and because they are fixed in our minds through our associations with labels and descriptions repeatedly cycled through public discourse. The interaction of the media, the public, and policy makers produces the constructed identities ("images") of social groups in public discourse; these images are then part of public debate and projected through social policy (Bickford 1999; Ingram and Schneider 1995).

5   Ange-Marie Hancock illustrates this point in her analysis of the congressional debate surrounding the welfare reform legislation of 1996. She describes the way a congressman read into the congressional record a *U.S. News* magazine report of an unemployed mother on welfare ("Bertha Bridges") as support for his vote to pass the Personal Responsibility and Work Opportunity Reconciliation Act of 1996 (PRWORA). The congressman's use of Bertha's story as representative of the experiences of millions of poor women meant that the journalist's description of Bertha and her "disruptive, severely depressed son" served not only to construct the popular image of a welfare queen, but also to indelibly etch the image into the legal documents of the policy-making process (Hancock 2004, 2).

Lawyers and policy makers may assume that legal policy and popular representations of it are separate, but law is rarely so hermetic. Policy efforts are often beholden to the popular images of law in action (Mégret and Pinto 2003, 468). For example, Frederic Mégret and Frederick Pinto (2003) argue that images in the "war" on global terrorism (photos and footage of detainees, soldiers, and prisons) have shifted legal and policy agendas by turning public attention away from the larger geopolitical issues underlying terrorism and focusing it instead on the few visible aspects of terrorism caught in the frame of a photograph. The images of the welfare queen and the Third World woman have a similar effect on policy agendas, blocking out other considerations and narrowing public attention to the issues we can "see" in the images. The result is policy prescriptions that address only poor women's most visible personal impediments: the welfare queen's failed work ethic and the Third World woman's oppression. What we do not see in these images is the complex web of history, power, and financial control that contributes at least as much as personal choice to the poverty these women experience.

For the Third World woman, the image of a passive victim, trapped and assailed by a poorly governed state, sets up a heroic narrative in which the international community acts as "savior"—the purveyor of financial assistance and protector of rights and economic security (Orford 1999, 696). This image of the Third World woman is set against the backdrop of a global economic hierarchy divided between the politically constructed "First" and "Third" worlds. Enshrining this division, the image of the victimized Third World woman is interwoven with a picture of heroic altruism on the part of the international First World community. This masks the history of the West as colonizers, complicit in causing the poverty and powerlessness of people in the developing world, and as perpetuators of colonial-style economic relations today (Schoepf et al. 2000, 96–101).

Similarly, the image of the welfare queen is the product of a denial of the legacy of slavery and segregation in the United States. These political institutions contributed to the historical denigration of African American motherhood and the economic disenfranchisement that underlies the persisting need for social aid programs (Roberts 1999, 22). By ignoring this history and its effects, the raced image of the welfare queen suggests poverty created by personal moral failing, without reference to social and historical context. Beyond simply ignoring the effects of macro political and economic forces on women's lives, the "welfare queen" image ascribes women agency in the apparent *decision* to live a life of poverty.

Implementing Images through Policy

This dichotomy of images has significant public policy consequences that are visible in the differences between U.S. federal welfare "reform" laws and the poverty alleviation programs promoted by U.S. policy makers and international development institutions.

The congressional and public debates on welfare reform leading up to the passage of the PRWORA were coded in gendered and raced language that targeted poor women's behavior as a root cause of family poverty. Analyzing shifts in the racial images of news coverage of the poor from the 1960s to the 1990s, Martin Gilens found that in the latter part of the period, images of African Americans were used at rates double their actual percentage of America's poor (Gilens 1999, 123). As noted above, the image of the welfare queen was actively invoked in congressional debate on the PRWORA, and the stereotypes underpinning the image seemed to justify the law's harsh restrictive conditions on aid to poor women and their children (Gilens 1999, 92).

The reforms targeted single mothers in poverty by enforcing term limits on their receipt of aid, instituting family caps barring additional aid to mothers who gave birth to children while on welfare, and strictly tying benefits to proof of work, while revoking benefits for mothers who were students (Pierson-Balik 2003). When the PRWORA was reauthorized in 2005, it included more than $100 million a year to implement programs encouraging women receiving welfare to marry (U.S. Department of

Health and Human Services n.d.). The federal law also allowed states to experiment with incentives and restrictions, which led some states to propose voluntary sterilization of poor women in return for more welfare benefits (Pierson-Balik 2003).

These reforms did nothing to cultivate poor women's education level, their autonomy, or their potential as leaders and advocates for their communities. The aim was to get women into work—any work—even if the work was dead-end, low-paying, far from their children, and without benefits (Schleiter and Statham 2002). The marriage initiative suggests one of poor women's problems is their lack of husbands, not opportunities. Thus, the message sent by the PRWORA is one of mistrust and degradation of poor women's life choices—a message made more tolerable to the public by the image of the welfare queen. U.S. foreign policy and international development policy, on the other hand, have sent a completely different message about the impoverished Third World woman. Development policy has been enthusiastic about supporting women's rights and increasing their educational, economic, and political opportunities (Coleman 2004, 82). For example, the World Bank's project to increase single mothers' employment in Tajikistan focused not on finding women any job placement available, but on the creation of microcredit institutions and local women's community centers where poor single mothers could receive the education and skills they need to start their own businesses (World Bank n.d., 8). This was in keeping with the dominant policy trend by international institutions; in 2000, when the United Nations instituted the Millennium Goals on global poverty, the promotion of gender equality and women's empowerment was included as one of the eight goals (United Nations n.d.).

Similarly, U.S. Secretaries of State Condoleezza Rice and Hillary Rodham Clinton have emphasized women's rights and empowerment in developing countries as a key component of U.S. foreign policy efforts to combat global poverty (Brand 2008; Landler 2009). The Obama administration recently created a new post of ambassador for Global Women's Issues to focus U.S. foreign policy efforts on the "political, economic, and social empowerment of women" (U.S. Department of State n.d.). In 2003, Congress specifically invested $10 million to empower Iraqi women by implementing leadership, political advocacy, and media training programs (Coleman 2004, 92). And in 2009, Senator Dick Durbin proposed the Global Resources and Opportunities for Women to Thrive Act (GROWTH Act) to increase funding for programs in developing countries that "ensure that the policies of the United States actively promote development and economic opportunities for women" (GROWTH Act 2009).

At the core of these foreign and international policies is a belief in what Nicholas Kristof and Sheryl WuDunn call the "girl effect," that is, the idea that *if only* women in developing countries had more opportunities, protections, and rights, they could better protect themselves and their children from poverty (Kristof and WuDunn 2009). This suggests optimism that, with the right support, poor women can be transformative actors, changing and improving their own lives as well as those of their children and communities. That message finds no counterpart in U.S. welfare laws; instead, U.S. policy evinces skepticism that U.S. women could be affected by the same kinds of oppressive economic and cultural forces that keep women in poverty in the developing world. This denies the potential of America's poor women to become the strong advocates and leaders of their communities that their sisters in developing countries are believed to be.

Exposing the dichotomy between foreign and domestic policy approaches suggests that U.S. welfare policy has been stunted by the confines of the harmful image of the welfare queen. By enacting welfare policies that seek to punish poor women's behavior, the United States loses out on the positive effects of women's empowerment that are already accepted and highlighted by the United States as sound policy abroad.

15

Analyze

1. Describe in your own words the contrasting images of poor women in the U.S. and poor women in the "third world."
2. What facts does Mehta say these images fail to acknowledge about the structural challenges and history behind these faces?
3. What is the "girl effect"? To whom is it applied?

Explore

1. Mehta argues that the images inspire compassion for the "third world woman" and disgust for the American "welfare queen." What evidence does she give that the images affect public policy? What analogy helps solidify her argument? Identify other cases in which media representations seem to drive public opinion/policy.

2. Locate images of these two types of representations. Do a rhetorical analysis of these images. How is meaning constructed through the way poor women are photographed (or drawn/painted)? How do they invite the type of audience response Mehta describes? Or, find images that challenge the frames Mehta describes. How do these images contradict the frames she defines?

3. Mehta writes: "U.S. policy evinces skepticism that U.S. women could be affected by the same kinds of oppressive economic and cultural forces that keep women in poverty in the developing world." What evidence does Mehta provide to support this claim? Write a researched letter to her in which you explain why you agree or disagree with her thesis.

Miriam Meltzer Olson, Khadijah Muhammad, Laura Rodgers, and Mansura Karim
"Picture This: Images and Realities in Welfare to Work"

Specializing in women's health and women in social work, Miriam Meltzer Olson was a professor of social work at the School of Social Administration at Temple University, where her co-authors in the following piece, Khadijah Muhammad, Laura Rodgers, and Mansura Karim, were students in the social work master's program. In the article, they explain how different portrayals of poor women in the media have left such women increasingly vulnerable.

Have you ever spoken with a woman on welfare, encountered such a voice in readings or viewings, or been on welfare yourself?

Picture this: a full-page newspaper ad, most of it a close-up of a Black woman, probably in her mid-30s. She looks directly at the viewer. Her shoulder-length hair is wavy and makes a soft frame for her handsome face. She seems poised and has a quiet smile. A boy, about 7 years old, leans in close to her. He is wearing a trim polo shirt and looks well groomed. He is also smiling. A mother and son: They are the picture of health.

One might think that the ad is for a breakfast cereal or a computer reading program, but it is part of a state-supported campaign to persuade employers to hire women whose welfare benefits are being severed under the PRWORA. The ad reads as follows:

> How About My Mom.
> Need a Hard Worker?
> Moms Coming Off Welfare are Motivated, Responsible Employees.
> They Have to Be. Hire One Today.

The large picture, the brief message, and the name and telephone number of the sponsoring agency are all there is to this newspaper ad. Similar ads appear on television and billboards, in buses and trains. Brochures, targeted directly to employers, provide specific information about the federal and state benefits that employers receive, highlighting the information that "in the first year alone, a $15,000 hire may cost employers only $4,400 after tax credits and wage subsidies." The brochure also tells potential employers that "no one is more motivated to provide for her family than a mother."

What follows here is not an examination of the efficacy of the ad campaign, which is only one of many devices that are being used across the country to get women from welfare to work. Rather, this article illuminates the image making and image manipulation that are used to define social problems, create social policy, and implement social programs. It examines the ads as a way of understanding the uses made of representations of women on welfare in the media and the rhetoric of public officials. In addition, it offers pictures of poor women based on their own lives and welfare-to-work experiences.

Almost all the women and children in the photographs in the ad campaign are people of color: Blacks, Browns—"ethnics"—with dark hair and dark eyes. The mothers seem to be at least in their early 30s and are usually pictured with one school-aged child, most often a girl. In addition to being nice looking, they all have a modest appearance—they wear little jewelry, their hairstyles and clothing are simple, and there is not a hint of malnutrition or illness.

The Images and Rhetoric

Do these photographs misrepresent women on welfare? Before PRWORA was enacted, the majority of women receiving Aid to Families With Dependent Children (AFDC) were White, although 39% were Black (including some Hispanics); 25% were aged 30 to 34 years (U.S. Bureau of the Census, 1998); and the average number of children per family was 1.9. Although no one collects data on the appearance of people on welfare, there is anecdotal evidence of not just one but many kinds of good looks among them. Despite the well-known associations among low income, poor health, and malnutrition, many women and children on AFDC managed to be in good health and look it. But if the images are not literally false, they nevertheless are manipulated images, carefully constructed (with professional models) to create a particular kind of positive picture of women on welfare.

The good face that the ad campaign seeks to put on "welfare moms" betrays the negative images that have dominated policy debates, public perceptions, and even the self-perceptions of many women on welfare (Axinn & Hirsch 1993; Davis & Hagen 1996; Miranne 1998; Swigonski 1996). The ads reassure the public that women on welfare are nice people, familiar, and unthreatening. They stand in stark contrast to the widespread portrayals of women on welfare as dirty, lazy, dishonest, ignorant, and drugged out.

The ads' tender portraits of the nice, mature women, each with one school-aged child, also create visions of modesty and chastity. They are mirror opposites of the typical representations of women on welfare as sexually promiscuous, producers of one child after another, and/or mindless teenagers with illegitimate babies.

In these images, the demonized welfare mom undergoes a metamorphosis and becomes the good mother—the ultimate emblem of a worthy woman. This transformation is further communicated in the following idealized words of the brochure: "No one is more motivated to provide for her family than a mother."

10   What is the value of this campaign? Some women on welfare and others who are sympathetic to their difficult situations hope that these images will change the public's perception and help the women get jobs. Certainly, if the campaign can disrupt negative stereotypes or reduce the stigma attached to poor women, it could serve a worthwhile purpose. Yet, there is danger in manipulating images to promote social change. That a campaign can be mounted to influence people's perceptions of women on welfare

without providing any information about them, except through pictures and a few words, indicates how susceptible these women are to being cast and recast in any light that serves a political interest.

When President Clinton, a Democrat, under whose administration PRWORA was enacted, presents women to the public who are welfare-to-work "success stories," his image making is a replay of President Reagan's. In the 1976 presidential campaign, Reagan, a Republican, repeatedly told the story of a "Welfare Queen," a woman he described as a high-living, Cadillac-driving, welfare cheat who wove a huge web of deception to defraud the government of hundreds of thousands of dollars. This invented story was based on newspaper coverage of a 47-year-old Chicago woman who had been charged with defrauding the state of $8,000 and was dubbed the Welfare Queen (Zucchino 1999). One political leader singles out some women for applause, and the other does so for derision, but their methods are not different; both have told dramatic stories and distorted or partial truths. Reagan's aim was to discredit social welfare programs, and Clinton sought to undermine the Republicans' attempts to claim welfare reform as their own. Both used women on welfare for their own political gain.

Similarly, Wisconsin governor Tommy Thompson exploited the success story of Michelle Crawford, a mother of five who had been on welfare for 10 years and was now working as a machine operator and supporting her family. Thompson invited Crawford to tell her "inspiring" story before the state legislature and later retold it to conservative supporters at a welfare conference in Washington. Yet, he did not recount Crawford's story of her numerous difficulties. Some, such as panic attacks, are continuations of past distresses. Some are new: barbs from coworkers and relatives who envy her achievements, the arrest of one of her sons twice in 4 months, and the severe strains her work success added to her volatile 2-year marriage. She is still determined to work but recalls a nervous breakdown she had a year earlier that she attributes, in part, to the pressures of Wisconsin Works. Before she got her job, she was required to work for her welfare check. "To me, it was just like slavery," she said, "I couldn't be with my kids." She fears for the pressures and instabilities that remain in her life (DeParle 1999, p. A18).

Like Crawford's experience with Wisconsin Works, the "How About My Mom" campaign is dense with meaning and contradictory messages. For instance, people portrayed in ads generally represent the people to whom the product is being sold. In the "How About My Mom" ad, however, the copy reveals that it is employers, not the mother and son, who are being sold to and that the mother is being sold and the son is delivering the sales pitch. This is not the first time that a child has been placed in such a position; throughout the world, boys in poverty are sent out to sell their mothers' or sisters' sex and, sadly, the same desperation that leads them to do so echoes in this ad.

Along similar lines, there should be no doubt left that moms coming off welfare are motivated, responsible employees, because the ad copy reminds moms and employers that they have to be. Whereas children may sell their mothers only under dire circumstances, threats and coercion are common experiences of all poor mothers.

15   Messages of coercion, blatant and subtle, have long been a part of public support programs for poor people—from the first Mothers' Pensions legislation in 1911, which threatened to deny or withdraw assistance from widows and to remove their children from them if they could not prove that they provided suitable care, to the investigations and midnight raids of women receiving Aid to Dependent Children (ADC; later AFDC) to ensure that the women's conduct was socially and morally correct (Bell 1965). Through searches for men in the homes and for evidence of unreported sources of income, the welfare system inserted itself as the patriarch of the family, demanding obedience and faithfulness in return for its meager support (Glassman 1970). The treatment of mothers on ADC was in sharp contrast to the treatment of widows with children whose husbands had been employed for specified periods; these women received Old Age and Survivors Insurance (OASI) benefits for themselves and their children with no means testing or stigma and with adjustments for increases in the cost of living. Partly because of OASI, the percentage of poor, White widows on welfare declined, and the percentage of poor divorced and single mothers of color increased (Kemp 1995).

These forces converged to draw a line between the worthy—women whose breadwinner husbands died—and the unworthy—divorced and never-married mothers. They also pressed the convergence among poverty, welfare, and race (Mink 1994). Pejorative images of Black women have been created since the time of slavery. Collins (1990) traced the historic development of images, such as breeder, Jezebel, mammy, and welfare mother, that were used to control Black women's reproduction to accommodate the political and economic needs of their time. The present melding of the images of women of color and women on welfare continues the process and supports the punitive character of welfare reform.

The Realities

The following stories tell some truths about the experiences of poor women on welfare, as told to the social work interns who worked with them.

What Khadijah Muhammad Heard

Khadijah conducts a weekly parent support group at a neighborhood church, under the auspices of a private nonprofit agency, with women who have long histories (8–17 years) of drug and/or alcohol abuse, reside in a drug treatment program with their children, and receive TANF. At one meeting, Khadijah asked the women how they felt when they saw or heard the "How About My Mom" ads and what their thoughts were on welfare reform in general.

Toni Smith, aged 34, who is recovering from both drug abuse and 10 years of domestic violence, has three children aged 2, 9, and 11. Toni's response to the question was, "I feel motivated, like I can really get a job. Like I can really do something with my life." Her sentiment was in the minority. Most of the women thought the ad was misleading; they recognized that they would need education and training to get jobs that would allow them to support their families.

Lenora Davis, a 22-year-old mother who did not complete high school   20
and has three children aged 2, 4, and 10, has not had consistent employment and is recovering from 12 years of substance abuse.

> I like the changes in the welfare system; it should change. But I am
> not getting the training and skills I need to get a job and keep it.
> I was told to just get a job; I never had a job before. I don't know
> who thought of these changes, but they should have asked me or
> people like me what I need.

Linda Moore, aged 36 with five children (aged 11 months, 3, 5, 10, and 17 years), stated, "It [the ad] made it seem that you can really get a job, but there are no jobs out there—no job that pays enough for me to really survive." Linda knows about surviving. She lived in several foster homes since the age of 5 after her mother died, and she has been on her own since she was 16.

Betty Brown, aged 30, is the mother of four children aged 6 months and 2, 4, and 5 years. Her infant has severe medical problems, and her 2-year-old is in foster care. Attending to her son's medical problems, visiting her son at the foster care agency, and caring for her other children take up most of her time. Under TANF, she was given a work assignment at the Internal Revenue Service. She recounted the following:

> I went to work for 2 days; on the third day, my baby got sick and had to be admitted to the hospital. I told them [her employer] that I would be out because my baby was in the hospital. Not only did I lose my job, but they cut my food stamps off because they said I did not tell my caseworker what happened. For 2 months, I did not get food stamps. I got money and food from my mother. Thank God for her because I don't know what I would have done.

It took 2 months for Betty's food stamps to get reinstated. While she is residing in the drug treatment program, she is exempt from the work requirement. However, when the allotted time for drug treatment (6 months) expires, Betty will again be required to find a job. She says her hope and prayer is that she can manage the demands of her family responsibilities, maintain sobriety, and adjust to the rules of welfare reform. Khadijah often heard the women say they were disappointed in the new welfare system. Somehow, it did not seem to be meant for them. They thought the ad campaign painted a false picture and gave false hopes.

What Laura Rodgers Heard

Laura works as a case manager and counselor with homeless families and persons with mental health disabilities at a community-based family agency. The two women she asked to share their stories were eager to tell them.

25   Rose Hines, aged 26, is the mother of five children and a survivor of 10 years of domestic violence. As a child and adolescent, she was institutionalized for several years for what she described as anger and fighting behaviors. She is not part of the debate on welfare reform because she is excluded from eligibility for TANF on the basis of her conviction and imprisonment for distributing drugs. Since her release from jail, Rose has been enrolled in an intensively supervised probation program and is considered a model probationer. Rose started her life over without any financial assistance or help from her family. Before her conviction, she had been receiving AFDC off and on. She would work when she could find child care and a job she could get transportation to. She recalled the following:

> I was on welfare . . . and it wasn't enough. I had an electric bill that was $600 [the subsidized housing in which Rose lived was

notorious for high utility bills]. When I went to them at welfare, they said they couldn't pay it and told me with the check I get, $300 and some dollars, I should be able to handle it. But I said to them it's $600, how am I gonna pay for that? So . . . I went up to New York and got some drugs and started selling right away. The money started coming in so fast and so good. I sold drugs there for like 3 years until my house got busted. I just wished it never happened. My kids were so happy, and they're so sad now. I tried to buy my family's love, and they really liked me when I had money, but it still didn't work.

Since Rose was released from jail and was cut off from welfare, she has lived in five different places, sometimes with all her children and sometimes with her children taken in by various people. She has spent much time at a hospital emergency room being treated for the symptoms of her disability rather than receiving ongoing services to remain stable. Today, Rose is working full-time and saving for an apartment while staying with generous friends. She is determined not to get arrested and not to be separated from her children again.

Rose is also a keen observer of others who are struggling to comply with the maze of TANF requirements. She noted, "People out here want to commit crimes because they can't get help for their children. . . . And it's really sad; people are suffering, and . . . the parents can't feed the kids. With them stopping welfare and everything . . . it's really sad."

Sara Vorn, aged 28 and a survivor of domestic violence, lives in a subsidized apartment with her three children. Since the TANF work requirements, she has been in training programs and Workfare and has been employed for a time. She now receives no cash assistance because she has been sanctioned many times. Sara needs a great deal of help with literacy skills, time management, child care, and training to be able to find a stable job at a living wage. She had the following to say about her treatment in the job training program and the welfare department:

> I've been off of welfare now for 3 months, and I've just been trying to take care of my kids. It's like they want me to sit in class again for 3 weeks after all of the training I've been through and the way they talk to you there. . . . It's like they're treating us like kids, and they shouldn't be treating us like that.

Sara witnessed many punitive measures taken in the job-search classes, from making the participants stand in the corner if they are not behaving properly to fining those who are late for class.

30   Sara also gave many examples of inept assessments by unprepared welfare workers. She said,

> And over the past 4 months, there have been people up there in the welfare office . . . telling me I use drugs when I'm not on drugs. I finally talked to this one lady, and she said I'm sorry . . . we know that you are not on drugs.

Sara had never been asked to take a drug test, and it took several months until she was referred to the staff drug-assessment counselor and had her sanction removed.

When her Workfare assignment was to clean streets, Sara was dropped off in a distant part of town and given no instructions about taking breaks or where she might be able to use a bathroom. She also said that she was yelled at in front of an office full of people when she missed work to take care of family necessities.

After Laura invited Sara to attend a weekend meeting of poor people's groups, Sara stated,

> The Poor People's Summit was very nice, and when I saw what was going on, I said we have to bring it down here. . . . I see a lot of people living in the street—older people, people living at the Rescue Mission.

She is now organizing a group in her community. When asked what advice she would give welfare reformers, Sara said, "Number one, they should treat people with respect. . . . I have just been really hurt by the welfare office."

35   Rose and Sara let Laura know that whatever their many struggles, respect was of utmost importance to them. Regardless of what the ads and reformers said, they both felt they had not been respected in their experiences with the welfare system or welfare-to-work program.

What Mansura Karim Heard

Mansura works in a job training program offering case management, life-skills training, and crisis intervention and referrals, as well as job development, job coaching, and job retention services. The clients are mandated to participate in the program and generally enter it unwillingly, scared to exit welfare and afraid to be on their own. They want their lives to be better, but they often do not know where to begin.

Mary Lester, aged 33 and the mother of six children, dropped out of school in the 11th grade when she became pregnant. She seemed especially hopeful at the orientation for training in customer service. Her desire to be free from the welfare system after 14 years drove her to attend daily job-training classes, as well as classes in math, science, and English so she could receive a general equivalency diploma. Mary reported that the training activities, mock job interviews, class discussions, tutoring, field trips to suburban malls for potential jobs, and personal counseling helped her to feel part of the larger world. As she put it,

> I have bills to pay, and it's time for me to get a job. I am tired of going nowhere. Welfare reform is telling me anybody can work. This is my time. [Before] my family came first. [With the youngest now age 6, all the children are in school.] It will be easier now that the older children can help the younger ones. I've been able to volunteer at my children's school and help them. I didn't stay home and do nothing. But I don't want to be told that I have to stay in one job the rest of my life. I don't like the "hire my mom" ads because they make people on welfare feel bad—like all people on welfare are sitting around being told where to go and what to do.

Mary grew up with a mother, grandmother, and uncle who were loving and supportive, even when she "got mixed up with the wrong crowd" as a teenager. She now has a boyfriend who lives with the family and who helps out financially and with child care. Her mother lives nearby and cares for the children in her home while Mary is at school and will continue to do so when Mary is working.

After Mary completed customer service training, she chose to use her housekeeping skills and thought that a job in a major hotel in the city would afford job security, convenient hours, a living wage, and the opportunity for advancement. Mansura helped her get an unpaid internship (the next step in the job training program) at a Marriott hotel, where she would be able to gain skills that would enhance her résumé.

40   Mary and Mansura met with the hotel's human resources director and together designed an 8-week unpaid internship, which consisted of timed room cleanings starting with three rooms and working up to eight. The director assured them that Mary would be ready to enter employment at the end of the training and that jobs were available at the hotel. However, Mary was not hired at the end of training because she did not pass the "flexibility test," although her flexibility level was good enough as long as she was unpaid. On further investigation, Mansura found that Marriott had many contracts with the city to provide entry-level jobs through various training programs and that there was a steady stream of welfare participants for unpaid internships. Mary said of this experience, "I felt used. Everybody needs a chance. I knew they had openings, but they told me they weren't hiring right now. That's why I stopped coming to job club."

Mary then got a housekeeping job at a suburban hotel. Even though she had to commute 45 minutes each way, she thought that the job would work out. Her starting salary would be $7.50 per hour, full-time with health benefits after 6 months, and she would work the 8 to 3 shift.

Did Mary's story have a happy end? Unfortunately, Mary was never able to work full-time because her hours constantly changed with the amount of tourism and travel in the area. Her weekly paychecks were based on anywhere from 19 to 33 hours of work, which made budgeting difficult. Thus, Mary was not able to leave the welfare system and went on the monthly reporting system at the department of welfare that minimally supplemented her low wages.

Mary stayed in the position for 8 months. As she put it, "I was told that the spring would bring more business; then, it was the summer." She wanted to prove to herself that she could hold down a job, that her work had value, and that she was trying to be self-supporting. Her tenacity with this work experience finally allowed her to obtain a job in the city as a dietary aide—a position with guaranteed hours. Mansura saw that Mary found the stigma of welfare that she long felt now followed her in the confusion that surrounded her training and job experiences and that she was hurt by it.

Conclusion

These glimpses of the lives of poor women reveal the vast gap between the reality of their lives and the images and representations of welfare participants in the political rhetoric, the design of PRWORA, and the ad campaigns for welfare-to-work programs. The reality is that women on welfare are a highly diverse population who have widely different reasons for needing assistance, motivations to work, and self-sufficiency and whose health problems and those of their children are even more diverse.

The women in this article represent only themselves, yet their brief 45 stories depict situations that are far more complex than can be captured with slogans and sound bites. Although their experiences are unique, they are also emblematic of the diverse realities of poor women around the country. Mary Lester, despite the stigma, chose to wait until all her children were in school before she sought paid employment. Patty Evans, the mother of three preschool-age children, did not have that choice, nor did she choose her welfare assignment—working with other people's preschool-age children. Betty Brown and Rose Hines also want to be good mothers, but one had to choose between going to her work assignment or staying with her hospitalized baby and jeopardizing her benefits. The other turned from the welfare system to drug dealing to make money and please her children; she failed herself and them and is now ineligible for a welfare-to-work program.

The weight of the women's accumulated experiences demands that social workers look beyond the rhetoric that welfare reform promotes women's self-sufficiency and self-esteem. As with all social policies that blame poor women for their poverty (Abramovitz 1992; Axinn & Hirsch 1993), PRWORA and TANF force welfare participants to work for their welfare stipends, not wages (Workfare); pay fines and other sanctions for their children's absence from school (Learnfare); and be deprived of benefits if they have more children while on welfare (Babyfare) and have limited their lifetime receipt of welfare to 5 years. Such coercive measures do not enhance the women's self-regard. Sara Vorn holds on to her self-respect by working to help others instead of attending demeaning classes and abusive work assignments.

Although many women on welfare, such as Toni Smith and Lenora Davis, are hopeful that welfare-to-work programs will help them fulfill their desire to obtain paid employment, the reality is that they are given little or no education or training, health care, or child care to be able to find living-wage jobs. Eliminating their right to choose between a bare-existence welfare check but staying at home with their children and a minimum-wage job with no flexibility to take care of their children or meet with a concerned teacher is a further assault on their selfhood.

Just as images that demonize poor women and blame them for being poor deny their life experiences, so do images that sanitize their experiences and ignore the realities of the workplace. As Rendell (1999), the mayor of Philadelphia and a critic of welfare reform, succinctly stated, "There simply are not enough jobs, nor is there enough child care, transportation or training" (p. E7). In short, although welfare reform seeks to make the women work-ready, the necessities for creating worker-ready jobs are not in place, and nowhere is the choice for women to work at raising their own children even being considered.

Moreover, there is little basis for expecting that through welfare reform, the women described in this article or most other women on welfare will escape poverty. As the women's stories made clear, what is needed are new social and economic policies to move poor people out of poverty, including establishing a minimum, living wage; providing child care and paid family care leaves; and restoring the safety net for poor people by rescinding the lifetime cap on the receipt of welfare. Social workers can challenge the false images of women on welfare that are propagated in the rhetoric on welfare reform and bring attention to the submerged identities and experiences of real women with real families, real capacities, real problems, and real aspirations, who have the right to be free from coercion and stigma to survive.

Analyze

1. What is PRWORA?
2. What is the purpose of the ad campaign described in this article?
3. Highlight the paragraph in the article that explains the rhetorical situation of the ad (target audience, speakers, message). Draw or digitally create what you think the ads look like. Compare and contrast your image with other students' images.

Explore

1. Although the authors see the good intentions of this ad campaign to disrupt the negative images of women on welfare, they still worry about "how susceptible these women are to being cast and recast in any light that serves a political interest." They claim that both Presidents Reagan and Clinton "used women on welfare for their own political

gain." Is this concern valid? What is at stake for these women? Explain.

2. This article is divided into two sections: "The Images and Rhetoric" and "The Realities." Does the latter correct the former? Explain.

3. The authors conclude: "Just as images that demonize poor women and blame them for being poor deny their life experiences, so do images that sanitize their experiences and ignore the realities of the workplace." If we agree, are we prohibited from making any representations? What methods help us find an authentic middle ground when it comes to representing vulnerable people such as poor women?

United Nations Development Programme Posters
"The UN Has Picked a Group of People to Eliminate World Poverty" and "There Are 8 Things Maria Wants to See Happen by 2015"

Headquartered in New York City, the United Nations Development Programme (UNDP) aims to help connect countries with information, resources, and experience they need in order to help people improve their lives through the United Nations' Millennium Development Goals, eight international development efforts established in 2000. To help achieve these, the UNDP focuses on poverty reduction, HIV/AIDS, democracy, energy and environmental concerns, social development, crisis prevention, and recovery. The following visuals are part of the UNDP's advertising campaign that aims to inform its audience of these goals and recruit their contributions.

What have you done, or could you do, to contribute to the Millennium Development Goal to eradicate extreme poverty and hunger?

THE UNITED NATIONS HAS PICKED A GROUP OF PEOPLE TO ELIMINATE WORLD POVERTY.
YOU'RE ONE OF THEM.

It kills a child every three seconds. It directly affects 1.2 billion people across the globe. 25 million more people every year join its victims. No, it's not war. It's not natural disasters. It's not the result of an economic downturn. This frighteningly powerful phenomenon is extreme poverty. And it entraps one fifth of the world's population, making it

almost impossible for them to utilise their talents, to fulfil their potential.

This waste is no longer justifiable. A United Nations Development Programme analysis has revealed that, for the first time ever, the world possesses the wealth, the technology and the know-how to change this situation.

Millions of people, having been denied the education and the means to have useful, fulfilled lives, can now face a different prospect. One which allows them to be energetic, creative, even prosperous members of the human race.

And exactly how will this happen? Well, what is required is a new commitment. A combination of individual resource, co-operation at all levels of society, a real determination at all levels of government to put this at the top of the agenda. Most importantly, it will involve the mobilisation, perhaps for the first time in this area, of the skills and the drive of the business world.

So, whose name should go against the word: ACTION? The United Nations, in its wisdom, has concluded that you, along with many others like you, are capable of ending extreme poverty over the next ten years.

"Me" we hear you say. "Little old me?" Absolutely. At the United Nations in 2000, world leaders have set eight "Millennium Development Goals", which include halving poverty by 2015. And you are fundamental to their success. Whether as an individual or as a company, a municipality, an association, an institution, or a government.

It may surprise you to know that you, and your organisation, have the skills and the means to help.

But think about it? Business applies energy and acumen to bring television to the remotest parts of the world, make branded food stuffs, soft drinks and sneakers available everywhere, make telephone links that span the entire globe. If we re-apply that energy and acumen, problems of extreme poverty will be resolved forever.

You will have restored the basic values of equity and human dignity to over 1.2 billion people, offering them a healthy, fulfilled existence. A life without humiliating and patronising handouts. Moreover, 1.2 billion people will be earning and spending and creating jobs all over the world in the process. That in turn will make the world a safer place, rid of the insecurity and anger that breeds in poverty.

Together, we will put an end to poverty. To find out how you can help, connect to: www.TeamsToEndPoverty.org. Many of the world's individuals and businessmen and women are already committed to making a difference. UN Secretary General Kofi Annan would like you to be too.

United Nations Development Programme
UNDP, PALAIS DES NATIONS, CH-1211 GENEVA 10, SWITZERLAND
www.undp.org

Everyone will be richer without poverty.

Figure 5.1

THERE ARE 8 THINGS MARIA WANTS TO SEE HAPPEN BY 2015.

BUT SHE NEEDS LEBRON'S HELP.

In September 2000, the world committed to tackle poverty in all its forms. The largest-ever gathering of world leaders at the United Nations adopted goals to be reached by 2015. The eight Millennium Development Goals (MDGs) represent commitments by all countries to halve poverty and hunger, put every child through primary school, protect women's rights, limit the spread of disease and preserve our natural resources.

As a UNDP Goodwill Ambassador, Maria Sharapova has invited NBA star LeBron James to team up against poverty and to help build support for the Millennium Development Goals.

Some progress has been made. 15 years ago one in three people lived on less than a dollar a day. We are now at one in five. But with the 2015 target date fast approaching there's a lot to do.

One billion people still live in extreme poverty. More than one billion people lack access to safe drinking water. 6,000 people die of AIDS each day. 750 million adults cannot read. And those who carry almost zero responsibility for climate change are bearing the brunt of its effects, widening the gap between the haves and the have-nots.

Maria and LeBron are inviting you to team up to learn more about the MDGs and the efforts needed to achieve them.

To learn more about the MDGs and to spread the message, visit www.MDGmonitor.org

United Nations Development Programme
www.undp.org

Figure 5.2

Analyze

1. Why does the first poster claim that wasting human ability is "no longer justifiable"? What has changed such that we can't excuse the existence of poverty anymore?
2. The concluding tag line for the first poster is "Everyone will be richer without poverty." What does this mean? Is it effective? Is it true?
3. What are the eight things Maria wants to see happen by 2015?

Explore

1. What stakeholders does each poster identify as key to making change? How effective is each poster in reaching its target audience?
2. What facts do the posters include? What attitudes or claims do they present? Are the facts or claims more persuasive?
3. The second poster makes an appeal based on the celebrity power of two great athletes, Maria Sharapova and LeBron James. Celebrities are often part of campaigns against poverty (e.g., Bono, Brad Pitt, Susan Sarandon). Clearly, they draw attention, but sometimes they also draw criticism for objectifying the poor in photo shoots or offering only a superficial engagement with the real issues. Imagine you work at the United Nations Development Programme and are charged with designing a campaign to increase awareness of the Millennium Development Goals. Would you include celebrities? What is the rhetorical value or risk of using them in a campaign against poverty? What visuals or slogans would you design?

Forging Connections

1. Boo says she already understood the "tropes of how stories on poverty work in any country" before she started reporting in India. Connect this statement to Mehta's reference to the "welfare queen" and the "third world woman," and to Solnit's critique of the looting trope or frame. Can you liken the use of narrative frames about poverty to other issues that journalists seem to frame predictably as well? Do frames always narrow meaning or do they in any way help to tell stories? Give examples to support your position.

2. Boo says that it is "ludicrous" to think that even her long-term poverty reporting constitutes "walking in their shoes." What does that phrase mean? Give examples that show people claiming to have "walked in the shoes" of others or, like Boo, saying that it isn't possible (see living-onone.org and 40daysinorange.wordpress.com). Write a researched essay explaining your position.

Looking Further

1. Boo says "the only thing worse than being a poverty reporter is if no one ever wrote about it at all." First, what does she mean? Second, find a recent news story that addresses poverty. Do a rhetorical analysis to show how it constructs its argument about poverty and the people who experience it and address it. Does it employ one of the frames discussed in this book (e.g., Mehta, Solnit), or does it use a different frame? Explain. Finally, what seems to motivate that coverage of poverty? Is it the goal of an individual, like Boo, or a group, like the Economic Hardship Reporting Project?

2. In her book *Framing Class: Media Representations of Wealth and Poverty in America*, Diana Elizabeth Kendall argues: "[J]ournalists still employ a sympathetic frame in some articles about the poor and homeless, but most articles and stories about people on the bottom rungs of society either treat them as mere statistics or have a critical edge, portraying the poor as losers, welfare dependents, mentally ill persons, or criminals." List the poverty frames you have seen in this chapter (e.g., Boo, Solnit, Mehta, Olson,), in this book (e.g., Ehrenreich, Rector and Sheffield, Banerjee and Duflo, Yunus), and in your own reading. In what ways is Kendall's claim consistent with or different from your observations? What are the consequences if Kendall's assessment is accurate?

6

Solutions: What Should We Do about Poverty?

A young girl praying before eating a healthy school lunch (c. 1936). President Harry Truman signed the National School Lunch Act in 1946 to feed low-income children and help farmers sell surplus crops. Is subsidizing school lunches and breakfasts effective public policy today?

INTRODUCTION

As we saw in chapter 5, how we talk about poverty—how we frame the issue—determines if and how we respond. If we see poverty as the result of individuals making bad choices, we propose solutions that make individuals accountable. If we see poverty as a result of systemic economic and social inequities, we propose solutions to disrupt or dismantle the structures that drive that system. How we try to address the problem, then, has everything to do with how we define it. If we see poverty as a practical problem, for example, then we might address it with policy adjustments that create jobs with full benefits. If we see poverty as an ethical failing of those with power and privilege, we might empower the poor to lead solutions. But few people fall squarely on one side or the other. As David Shipler, author of *The Working Poor: Invisible in America*, writes: "If problems are interlocking, then so must solutions be" (11). He continues: "We lack the skill to solve some problems and the will to solve others, but one piece of knowledge we now possess: We understand that holistic remedies are vital" (286). The readings in this chapter explore the solutions, mindsets, and methodologies that seek to reduce poverty and promote human flourishing.

The title of this chapter—"Solutions"—is ambitious. Attempts to "solve," "cure," or otherwise "win" the War on Poverty ring hollow in the face of persistent suffering. A more modest and perhaps wise rally cry for those who are moved to action might be: First, do no harm. Too often, good intentions serve the needs of those in the position to help, not those who receive it. In a blistering critique of this mindset, Monsignor Ivan Illich used his 1968 keynote speech at the Conference on InterAmerican Student

Projects in Mexico to scold his American audience for their international service:

> Next to money and guns, the third largest North American export is the U.S. idealist, who turns up in every theater of the world: the teacher, the volunteer, the missionary, the community organizer, the economic developer, and the vacationing do-gooders. Ideally, these people define their role as service. Actually, they frequently wind up alleviating the damage done by money and weapons, or "seducing" the "underdeveloped" to the benefits of the world of affluence and achievement. Perhaps this is the moment to instead bring home to the people of the U.S. the knowledge that the way of life they have chosen simply is not alive enough to be shared.

Ouch! That's a paralyzing blow to compassionate people who want to respond to suffering. Read the full speech (available online) and you will see that Illich in part directs Americans back to their own streets to address the suffering caused by civil rights injustices at that time. The context and climate have certainly changed since Illich spoke these words, but there's still much to learn from his rebuke: "to hell with good intentions!"

The readings in this chapter take us through various methods of engaged problem-solving—scientific research using randomized controlled trials, social entrepreneurism, public policy, and being present to the poor, to name a few. While each method has specific champions, most people acknowledge the necessity of "interlocking" and "holistic" solutions that use many informed approaches. You will likely find that your skills and disposition draw you toward some of these methods and away from others as a career choice and/or as a citizen, but understanding how they all work and how they can all work together is critical to building a theory and foundation for change.

Framing this chapter's exploration of solutions mindsets and methods, Dean S. Karlan and Jacob Appel argue that it takes more than good intentions to solve poverty, but with sound research methods, we can find the most effective means. Peter Buffett doubts that good intentions even exist in some extremely wealthy donors who show little interest in understanding the programs, people, and places they support but who instead use charitable giving as "conscience laundering." Paul Theroux puts this in historical context, showing the recurring damage done by the "telescopic philanthropy" of those who would "fix" Africa from afar. Abhijit Banerjee and Esther Duflo explain how on-the-ground research helps tell a fuller story than the headline-grabbing numbers of such claims as "1 billion hungry" that mislead us about the causes and therefore the solutions to problems. Peter Edelman heralds living-wage benefits-bearing jobs as the key solution to poverty in the U.S., but he warns that those jobs are disappearing. Ai-jen Poo asks readers to support legislation that offers worker rights benefits to domestic care workers. Lori Sanders and Eli Lehrer offer a conservative antipoverty platform that promotes work and family values consistent with Republican politics. In his lecture accepting the Nobel Prize for founding the Grameen Bank to create microcredit for development "from below," Muhammad Yunus assures us that if we truly want a future without poverty, we can create it. Sasha Abramsky reports on a new fundraising method where people who need support appeal directly to potential donors who can give directly to them. Phil Garrity describes two types of service and solutions work—the doing and the non-doing—and argues that the non-doing work of just being present to those in need is a necessary part of healing and solving. David Bornstein et al.'s solutions journalism helps writers avoid "puff press" and "good news" stories to instead write stories that critique solutions based on empirical evidence.

Dean S. Karlan and Jacob Appel
"Introduction: The Monks and the Fish"

As a professor of economics at Yale University, Dean S. Karlan researches, writes, and works on implementing and evaluating micro-financing programs designed to help alleviate poverty in developing countries. Jacob Appel implements and evaluates programs through GOOD/Corps. In their book *More Than Good Intentions: How a New Economics Is Helping to Solve Global Poverty*, from which the following chapter is excerpted, Karlan and Appel explore how to invest money into more effective antipoverty efforts using such research as behavior economics to inform design and implementation of programs.

Should any attempt to address poverty that springs from a "genuinely altruistic impulse" be encouraged?

Morning in the harbor at Marina del Rey in Los Angeles is steely bright, and it smells of brine and of fish, and it is filled with the sound of pelicans. They congregate by the hundreds on the end of the jetty, strutting and chattering and throwing their heads back to slug down great bulging beakfuls of breakfast. Completely absorbed in the guzzling of their food, they seem not to notice the dinghies puttering by.

> "[W]e ought to find out where our money will make the biggest impact, and send it."

Jake was in one of those dinghies with his girlfriend Chelsea and her father, returning from a short ride out on the gentle rolling swell of the Pacific. They passed the gray-brown pelicans on the gray-brown rocks and continued into the marina. Coming down the causeway, they passed the gas pumps, the big prow of the Catalina ferry, and the Buddhist monks.

Yes, the Buddhist monks: those unassuming men and women, some dressed in saffron robes and others in street clothes, standing on the dock around a folding card table on which was erected a little altar with a statue of a sitting Buddha and an oil lamp. On the ground in front of the table was a plastic tub as big as a steamer trunk. From the boat, low in the water, Jake couldn't see what was inside. They were saying prayers over it.

Chelsea's father put the boat into idle and turned in a half-circle to stay even with the monks. They came to the end of their prayer and bowed deeply, and the two closest to the bin took it by the handles and dragged it forward to the edge of the dock. Then they tipped it.

Out came a great torrent of water and minnows, which landed in the   5 causeway with a silvery clatter. The minnows disappeared instantly, darting away in every direction, and the ripples from the splash were drawn down the causeway to the ocean by the outgoing tide. The monks bowed again, deeply, and began to pack up their things.

What Jake had seen, Chelsea told him afterward, was a regular ritual. Those particular Buddhist monks set a tubful of fish free every couple of weeks. It was their small way of setting right something they believed was wrong. They didn't think those fish ought to be killed, so they bought their freedom. They would approach some fishermen, purchase their day's catch, say a prayer, and release the fish into the causeway to return to the ocean.

It was a moving gesture. Jake can attest to that. Whatever can be said against it—that it is merely symbolic, that those minnows might just be caught again later, that it does nothing to change the fact that fishing still goes on every day, that it is at best just a drop in a bucket (or a bucket in the sea)—it doesn't change the facts. The monks believed in something and they acted out of kindness and compassion.

When Jake and I talked about it together, though, there was one question we couldn't get around: The monks had clearly aimed to do a good thing—but could they have done better?

If their goal was to save a day's catch of fish from certain death, why not pay the fishermen ahead of time and just tell them to stay home? That would save the fish the trauma of being caught and dragged out of the water in the first place. It would save the fishermen the effort of waking up at dawn to complete the Sisyphean task of catching fish only to see them thrown back. It would save the gas they used to run the boat. And it would save the bait they used too.

10   The monks clearly had good intentions, but they may not have found the best way to act on them. Granted, some might argue that this is a relatively minor tragedy, that freeing baitfish is not a dire global concern. But the lesson still stands: We need more than good intentions in order to solve problems. Nowhere is this more relevant than in the fight against world poverty—a truly dire and global concern, in the service of which good intentions are usually the first (and all too often the only) resource to be mustered.

A Two-Pronged Attack for Fighting Poverty (and Saving Fish)

It is the best part of us that endeavors to be like the monks, to act out of compassion and do something positive for others. The vast majority of the work being done around the world to fight poverty fits this description, and anything that springs from such a genuinely altruistic impulse should be encouraged.

But there is a lesson in the monks and their tubful of minnows. Sometimes, even when we have all the good intentions in the world, we don't find the most effective or most efficient way to act on them. This is true whether we want to save fish, make microloans, distribute antimalarial bed-nets, or deliver deworming pills. What we really need to know is: How can we act with more than good intentions? How can we find the best solutions?

The only real consensus view on the issue is about the gravity of the problem. Three billion people, about half the world, live on $2.50 per day.

(To be clear, that's $2.50 *adjusted for the cost of living*—so think of it as living on the amount of *actual goods* that you could buy for $2.50 per day in the United States.) In the public dialogue about aid and development—that vast complex of people, organizations, and programs that seeks to alleviate poverty around the world—there are two main competing explanations for why poverty persists on such a massive scale. One camp maintains that we simply haven't spent enough on aid programs and need to massively ramp up our level of engagement. They point out that the world's wealthiest nations dedicate on average less than 1 percent of their money to poverty reduction. In their view, we haven't even given our existing programs a fair chance. The first thing we have to do is give more. A lot more.

The other camp tells a starkly different story: Aid as it exists today doesn't work, and simply throwing money at the problem is futile. They point out that $2.3 trillion *has* been spent by the world's wealthiest nations on poverty reduction over the past fifty years and ask: What have we accomplished with all that money? With poverty and privations still afflicting half the globe, can we really claim to be on the right track? No, they say; we need a fresh start. The aid and development community as it exists today is flabby, uncoordinated, and accountable to nobody in particular. It's bound to fail. They argue that we need to pull away resources from overgrown, cumbersome international organizations like the United Nations, wipe the slate clean, and focus instead on small, agile, homegrown programs.

Each camp claims prominent economists as adherents: Jeffrey Sachs of Columbia University, an adviser to the United Nations, and Bill Easterly of New York University, a former senior official at the World Bank. Sachs and his supporters regale us with picture-perfect transformational stories. Easterly and the other side counter with an equally steady supply of ghastly the-world-is-corrupt-and-everything-fails anecdotes. The result? Disagreement and uncertainty, which leads to stagnation and inertia—in short, a train wreck. And no way forward.

Jake and I propose that there actually *is* a way forward. My hunch is that, at the end of the day, even Sachs and Easterly could agree on the following: Sometimes aid works, and sometimes it does not. That can't be all that controversial a stand!

The critical question, then, is *which* aid works. The debate has been in the sky, but the answers are on the ground. Instead of getting hung up on the extremes, let's zero in on the details. Let's look at a specific challenge or problem that poor people face, try to understand what they're up against, propose a potential solution, and then test to find out whether it works. If that solution works—and if we can demonstrate that it works consistently—then let's scale it up so it can work for more people. If it doesn't work, let's make changes or try something new. We won't eradicate poverty in one fell swoop with this approach (of course, no approach yet has managed to do that), but we can make—and are making—real, measurable, and meaningful progress toward eradicating it. That's the way forward.

To get there, we need a two-pronged attack.

The first prong is to understand the problems in the first place. Some problems are systemic, in the way entire populations interact and exchange information, and in the way they buy, sell, and trade. Increasingly we are recognizing that the problems are also with *us as individuals,* with the way we make decisions. Here we turn to behavioral economics for insight.

20   In the past, economists would have thought about the monks in a pretty wooden, mechanical way. They would have talked about the cost of the fish, the value the monks imputed to their survival, the opportunity cost of the fishermen's time, and the social impact of running the boat on diesel fuel. They would have put you to sleep. More important, at the end of the discussion the monks probably would still be dumping tubs of fish into the Marina del Rey causeway.

This is a narrow view of what makes us tick. Traditional economics gives us economic humans, the archetypes for rational decision-making. Borrowing a term from Richard Thaler and Cass Sunstein (from their book *Nudge*), I call these folks *Econs.* When they need to choose between two alternatives, Econs weigh all the potential costs and benefits, compute an "expected value" for each, and choose the one whose expected value is higher. In addition to keeping a cool head, they are very methodical and reliable calculators. Given accurate information about their options, they always choose the alternative most likely to give them the greatest overall satisfaction.

Behavioral economics expands on narrow definitions of traditional economics in two important ways. The first is simple: Not everything that matters is dollars and cents. In a sense, this is nothing new. For instance, Gary Becker—by many accounts a "traditional" economist—has been using economic analysis to think about marriage, crime, and fertility for years. The second expansion is a bit more radical. Behavioral economics recognizes that, unlike Econs, we do not always arrive at decisions by calculating a cost-benefit analysis (or even act as if we had done so). Sometimes we have different priorities. Other times we are distracted or impulsive. We sometimes slip up on the math. And, more often than we'd like to admit, we are shockingly inconsistent. To mark all of the ways we are different from Econs, Thaler and Sunstein use the powerfully simple term *Humans.* I will do the same.

Behavioral economics incorporates more nuanced behavior, and sometimes inconsistent behavior—like when we continue to sneak an occasional candy bar when we say we want to lose weight, or when we still eat dinners out while we try to pay down our credit card debt. It might suggest that the monks don't care what traditional economics has to say. Maybe they throw the fish back because paying for not-fishing wouldn't serve their purpose. Maybe it's important to them to hear that silvery splash, or to see the minnows dart away like a bursting firecracker. Maybe there is something psychological about the salience of seeing, with one's own eyes, fish jump free. And maybe the monks simply are willing to accept a less efficient solution in exchange for that moment of spiritual connection.

The breakthrough of behavioral economics has been to claim that if we want to understand the monks, then we must know how and why they make the decisions they do. Instead of deducing a way to think from a core set of principles, behavioral economics builds up a model of decision-making from observations of people's actions in the real world. As we will see throughout this book, this way of thinking can help us design better programs to attack poverty.

This does not imply that we should throw out the old models. Behavioral economics is a powerful tool, but the proverb still applies: Just because you have a hammer, doesn't mean everything is a nail. The inspiration for some of the antipoverty programs we'll see comes straight from nuts-and-bolts economics. Combining the old and new approaches gives us the best chance to understand exactly what problems we're up against, and to design and implement the best solutions. 25

This first prong of the attack—understanding the problems we face—is a start, but it's not enough. Imagine you are stranded on a desert island with a rusted-out rowboat. Understanding the problem, even deeply, is like understanding why boats full of holes don't float. That alone will not get you home. You need to find a way to build a better boat.

Hence, the second prong of the attack: rigorous evaluation. Evaluation lets us compare competing solutions—like different boat designs or plugs for the holes—and see which one is most effective. Creative and well-designed evaluations can go even further, and help us understand *why* one works better than another.

Here's how it might work with the monks. I could propose setting up a new market, a market for hiring fishermen to not-fish, which would enable the monks to save fish more efficiently. It might sound good in theory, but then we'd go to the field and test.

Sometimes things that sound good fail. Suppose the monks actually don't care about seeing the splash of the minnows and would be happy to pay fishermen to not-fish; maybe they are simply up against a problem that makes it unfeasible. It could be a trust problem, where the monks fear the fishermen would accept payment for not-fishing and go out fishing anyway. Or maybe it is a monitoring problem, where there just aren't enough monks to tail around all the fishermen on not-fishing days to ensure they keep their word. A rigorous evaluation could point us to the specific problem that keeps the not-fishing market from saving more fish.

30   In the context of development, rigorous evaluation can help resolve the debate about how best to attack global poverty, by going to the field and finding out whether specific projects work. (It turns out that some projects work better—sometimes much, much better—than others.) You might think this goes without saying. You might assume that aid organizations have always routinely conducted careful and rigorous evaluations to see if they're doing the best they can. If so, you would be surprised.

Until recently, we knew astonishingly little about what works and what doesn't in the fight against poverty. We are now beginning to get the hard evidence we've lacked for so long, by measuring the effectiveness of specific development programs, many of which you'll read about in these pages. The next chapter will go into a bit more detail about how we do this.

Microcredit, the provision of small loans to the poor, is a perfect example of an idea that generated tremendous enthusiasm and support long before there was evidence on its impact. The excitement is largely understandable, for the very design of microcredit is appealing. It strikes a lot of chords: Microcredit often targets women, and many believe that the economic empowerment of women redounds to the benefit of the entire family; microcredit often focuses on entrepreneurs, and many believe that such individuals, given access to a modicum of working capital, are capable of dramatically improving their lives through their ingenuity and enterprising spirit; microcredit often involves communities, and many believe that by involving the community rather than just individuals, we are more likely to succeed.

But in some sense the enthusiasm is surprising: It seems to be predicated on a double standard about the useful role of high-interest debt. At the same time that we see millions of dollars pouring into microcredit programs to lend to poor microentrepreneurs at rates ranging from 10 to 120 percent APR (all in the hope of alleviating poverty), we also see millions of people outraged at payday-loans outfits at home, which lend at similar rates to the poor in America.

Without some basic facts about whether these loans actually make people better off, I would not know which side to believe, much less how to reconcile the two positions. But rigorous evaluation can—and does—help. Many were surprised by a study in South Africa, which we will see in chapter 4, that found that access to consumer credit, even at 200 percent APR, made people much better off on average. This does not imply that all credit is good for all people, but it should make us look critically at our strong opinions about what works and what doesn't, about what's good and what's bad. Do we have concrete facts to back them up?

The two-pronged attack we'll see throughout this book is a powerful economic tool. I use it (albeit in a slightly different form) whenever I teach development economics, both to undergraduates and doctoral students. Three questions organize our discussions. First: What is the root cause of the problem? Using both behavioral and traditional economics to answer this question is exactly the first prong of our attack in this book. Then two more questions: Does the "idea" at hand, whether a government policy, NGO intervention, or business, actually solve the problem? And how much better off is the world because of it? Using rigorous evaluations to answer these two questions together is the second prong of our attack.

Jump in Singer's Lake

Even in the absence of hard evidence about specific programs, people find compelling reasons to engage in and support the fight against poverty. One such reason comes from ethics, plain and simple: Suppose you are walking down a street by a lake on your way to a meeting, and if you miss the meeting you will lose two hundred dollars. You see a child drowning in the lake. Do you have an ethical obligation to stop and jump in and save the child, even though it will cost you two hundred dollars?

Most people say yes.

Don't you then also have an ethical obligation to send two hundred dollars right now to one of many organizations delivering aid to the poor, where it can save a child's life? Most people say no—or, at least, they don't cut that check.

The example comes from Peter Singer, a utilitarian philosopher at Princeton University and a hero of mine. I tend to think of it at some very specific moments, like when I am in a store and tempted to buy something that I don't really need. Couldn't that money go toward something better?

40   Singer's basic idea resonates, at least with me, but the logical conclusion of his argument is hard to swallow. The implication of his strict utilitarian reasoning is that we should all give away our money until we are so hard up that we honestly *couldn't* spare two hundred dollars to save a drowning child. Maybe an Econ would feel compelled by the cold force of logic to do so (assuming, of course, he'd had the heart to save the drowning child in the first place). But no Human I know of—not even Singer himself, a tireless advocate for doing more—goes that far.

Because the conclusion to the lake analogy makes us uncomfortable, we grope for holes in the logic. We raise objections. Often people's first response is to point out that when you dive in and pull the child to safety, there is no question that you've made a difference in the world. You can see with your own eyes that you've saved a life. But when you cut a check to an aid organization, the link is much less clear. How can you know your two hundred dollars is really doing good?

Most of this book is an attempt to respond to that objection. I hope that seeing some successes (and failures) up close convinces you that we *can* know we're doing good—if we commit to rigorously testing aid programs and supporting the ones that are proven to work.

The second objection people raise to Singer's lake analogy is about the "identifiable victim"—a vague sense that there's something morally significant about *seeing* the child flailing around in the lake, whereas we can't see the child our two-hundred-dollar check would be saving in, say, Madagascar. Logically, this objection is easy to refute. If someone runs to your house to tell you there is a boy drowning in the lake, you still have to go save him even though you haven't seen him with your own eyes. Wearing a blindfold does not solve ethical conundrums, and we cannot confine our responsibilities to a specific geographic area simply by narrowing our field of vision. A child is a child, wherever he is in the world, even if we cannot see him.

The trouble is that, while this refutation might be logically valid, it isn't viscerally compelling. We cannot simply reason our way into having a feeling of compassion, of responsibility for others. We need to be *moved* to act.

Behavioral Solutions Right Under Our Noses

Aid organizations, which depend for funding on our feelings of compassion, know from experience that appealing only to people's ethical obligations doesn't pay the bills. That's why tactics like the identifiable victim are longstanding staples of fund-raising. Think of Save the Children, which promises a photograph and a handwritten letter from *your* sponsored child in exchange for thirty dollars a month. Rather than approaching donors with facts, figures, and tables—which is what might sway an Econ—aid organizations take full advantage of the fact that we're Humans. They capitalize on our emotions.   45

This is exactly behavioral economics applied to the marketing of charities. Once you get inside the minds of those who give, you can come up with clever strategies to raise more money.

One such fund-raising strategy takes the financial sting out of giving by tacking donations onto other purchases. Recently I was in the checkout line at Whole Foods Market when the cashier asked me if I wanted to donate a dollar to the Whole Planet Foundation. She pointed to a small flyer on the counter. If I wanted to donate, she could scan a bar code on the flyer and add a dollar to my bill.

With a hundred dollars of groceries already rung up, an extra dollar is a tiny hit to take—so tiny you'd hardly notice it. And you get a lot of bang for that buck. Suddenly, you feel good walking out of Whole Foods Market with your bags of groceries. You've done something positive. It's not hard to see why the Whole Planet Foundation has been awash in donations.

Another behavioral approach to fund-raising involves separating the good parts of contributing (i.e., the satisfaction of doing a good deed) from the bad (i.e., the pain of parting with your money). Giving becomes much easier if you can enjoy the satisfaction up front, unencumbered by that irksome feeling that your wallet is thinner, and pay later.

That's exactly what happened in the phenomenally successful "Text to Haiti" campaign in January 2010. In the weeks following the devastating earthquake, people rose up in unprecedented numbers and acted to help those in need. Small individual contributions—the vast majority of them   50 ten dollars or less—piled up at an unbelievable pace. Text donations from the first three days alone totaled more than ten million dollars.

Giving by text message takes a few seconds and is utterly gratifying. You type in "HAITI," press Send, and get an instant response thanking you for your generosity. You hardly have time to think of the phone bill coming at the end of the month. When it does arrive, your ten dollars is easier to part with because it's tacked onto the cost of phone service—a cost you're already prepared to bear.

Unless, that is, you are Cara. The following was pulled from a real Facebook page:

Cara's profile said: "I've texted Haiti to 90999 over 200 times . . . over $2000 dollars [sic] donated to Haiti relief efforts. Join me!"

Comments

Noah: Your parents might not like your cell phone bill this month.

Cara: It's not my money! Hah.

Cara: Wait a second . . . this doesn't get added to the phone bill does it? I thought it was just a free thing. . . .

Aaron: Cara shooot. No every text is $10!!!

Cara: Oh wow, are u sure? This could be very bad for me.

Aaron: Yeah I saw it on the football game they bill it to your cell phone bill.

Chloe: Yeah. Every text is 10 bucks. It said so when the Health and Human Services lady came on and told people about it on the Colbert Report. Uhh, Ask for people to help you pay your phone bill?

Cara: Thanks for letting me know! Haha Haiti must love me!

Kyle: A 2000 dollar phone bill? this is sitting in its own special zone of hilarious.

Aaron: Well . . . you may be screwed but, in this case there's a big upside at least.

Cara: Just counted my texts . . . grand total is 188 texts. $1,880 phone bill . . . this is not hilarious Kyle!!!!!!

55   Never mind, Cara—there are worse ways to make a mistake with $1,880. And this really doesn't happen very often—in the vast majority of cases, people know exactly what they are giving when they give it.

But behavioral marketing approaches can make it so donors may not always know exactly what, or whom, they are giving *to,* and this is more disquieting.

As an example let's look at Kiva.org, a tremendously popular Web site that raises money for microlenders around the world. Ask a user of the site how it works and this is what you're likely to hear: You log on and read through the stories of people who need loans. When you find one you like, you can fund her loan by clicking and sending money through Kiva. When the client repays her loan, you get your money back.

That's what most users would tell you, but most users would be wrong.

Suppose you click to fund a Peruvian client's hundred-dollar loan. Here's what happens behind the scenes: Some weeks before, bank staff went out to the field to take pictures and write up profiles of existing clients. Those profiles are what you see on the Web site. When you click to fund the woman's loan, you make a hundred-dollar no-interest loan to Kiva. Kiva then makes a hundred-dollar no-interest loan to the client's Peruvian microlender. The hundred dollars goes into the microlender's loan portfolio, and is lent out to clients (but not the one you clicked on, who already has her loan) at around 40 to 70 percent APR. If the client you clicked on actually defaults on her loan, you could lose your hundred dollars, but that's rare. Most of the time, either another client repays the loan for her, or the lender pays back the loan itself (in order to keep its "record" on Kiva.org clean, so that it can attract more money). That's how it really works.

In innumerable casual conversations, people have told me that they use 60
Kiva exactly because they love the idea that *their* money goes to *that* particular person whose story they read, whose story moved them. They feel a connection, and that inspires them to give.

I have mixed feelings about this. Raising more money is a good thing, of course. Kiva is out there raising millions (over a hundred million as of November 2009) for microcredit. The problem is that pitching a development program on something other than its impacts puts some distance between the means and the ends. Tactics that work brilliantly to mobilize donations—focusing on the identifiable victim, for instance—don't necessarily work best to design programs that truly help poor people improve their lives.

The very best organizations pursue effectiveness in their fund-raising *and* in their programs with equal tenacity—and they usually end up with very different approaches to each. The point is that they have to recognize and respect that difference. We have to trust them to know that anecdotes are a far cry from real, systematic impact. And then we have to trust that, even as they use anecdotes to court donors, they will demand rigorous evidence to shape their programs.

For an organization to be worthy of that trust is no small feat.

We Can Demand Better

Fortunately, we don't have to rely on development organizations to come around entirely on their own. If we want aid programs to do the most good, we have to recognize that as donors—the ones who pay the bills—we are the people who ultimately have the power to steer the ship. Yes, us. You and me.

65   Large donors—governments, major philanthropic foundations, the World Bank—clearly matter. But small donors matter even more. Individual donors in America contribute over $200 billion to charity every year, three times as much as the sum of all corporations, foundations, and bequests. As we've just seen, aid organizations have spared no effort in developing an acute understanding of what works to raise funds from you and me. You can be sure they'll respond to the incentives we give them.

Jake and I will conclude this book with some practical suggestions for what you, as an individual, can do to help steer the ship. I hope I won't spoil the suspense, though, if I give you one bottom line up-front. Cutting checks is good, but it's not enough—especially when, thanks to behavioral marketing, we can do it with such little effort or deliberation.

Instead, we ought to find out where our money will make the biggest impact, and send it there. Some large donors, like the Bill & Melinda Gates Foundation and the Hewlett Foundation, try to do this as a matter of policy—and, sure enough, organizations respond by showing evidence that their programs work. Naturally, a small donor acting alone can't drive that kind of change. But if enough small donors start to reward aid organizations for providing credible demonstrations of their impacts, you can bet that better programs will ultimately result. And perhaps, if a critical mass of donors does this together, we can slowly but surely contribute to a shift in how we as a society view the act of giving money. This isn't just about making better use of the money raised, but also about helping to convince skeptics, who think aid isn't worth giving, that development can work if done right.

Remember Cara's Facebook page? There's a serious point lurking there. Cara's initial post showed not only that texting to Haiti was easy, but that it was cool—cool enough for her to think it was worth sharing on

Facebook. Whether we like it or not, for most of us there's an element of social display mixed up in our motivations for giving—and aid organizations know this, too, which is why visible signs of donation such as wristbands, stickers, and ribbons are also an effective fund-raising tool.

Anyone acting on good intentions deserves praise, no matter how far from optimal their actions may be. But how much more good could we do in the world if impact-informed giving came to be seen as the coolest kind of all?

Most of the research I'll talk about in this book is evaluation. It gives us concrete evidence, and concrete evidence truly should be the driving force in deciding which development approaches to support. But I don't believe it should be the only consideration. There is room for creativity, for trying new things, and for failure. We need new ideas to push us forward, and as donors we should reward those too.

Jake and I don't claim to have all the answers in this book. As we shall see repeatedly, behavioral economics reveals that, just like everyone else, poor people make mistakes that end up making them poorer, sicker, and less happy. (If they didn't, they could quickly escape poverty by selling self-help classes to the rest of us.) Identifying and correcting these mistakes is a prerequisite for solving global poverty, and we don't have a foolproof way of achieving that any more than we have a foolproof way to make every person in the developed world win all of his or her personal battles.

That said, we in the developed world are beginning to chip away at these insidious and persistent problems for ourselves, one by one. We *have* found specific ways to improve our decisions and make our lives profoundly better. We can and do use new tools—like the Save More Tomorrow program and stickK.com, which we'll see later—to spend smarter, save more, eat better, and lead lives more like the ones we imagine. The leap is in understanding that solutions like these, that have so enriched our own lives, can do the same for the people who need them most.

This book is about finding out which of them really work for the poor, and finding new solutions for the problems that remain.

Analyze

1. Define "Econs" and "Humans" as Karlan and Appel use these terms.
2. What are the two prongs in the two-pronged attack for fighting poverty that Karlan and Appel propose?

3. Karlan and Appel claim that there are two main camps with explanations for why poverty persists on such a massive scale. What are those two camps, and where do Karlan and Appel stand?

Explore

1. Describe Karlan and Appel's attitude toward the monks and their ritual of freeing fish. What do you think of that ritual and their response to it?
2. What key questions drive Karlan and Appel? Are these important? Explain.
3. First, explain how Singer's analogy about saving a drowning child relates to aid. Then, consider Karlan and Appel's response: "We cannot simply reason our way into having a feeling of compassion, of responsibility for others. We need to be *moved* to act." Write a reflection essay in which you recount a time when you were moved to act. *How* were you moved? What got you to donate money, time, or resources? Statistical data? A written narrative? Or was it meeting someone firsthand who was affected by the issue? Would the same approach move others? Explain.

Peter Buffett
"The Charitable-Industrial Complex"

A musician and composer, Peter Buffett is also the co-chair of the Novo Foundation, which seeks to transform "a world of domination and exploitation to one of collaboration and partnership." With his wife Jennifer, he was named in 2009 and 2010 to *Barron's* list of the top 25 most effective philanthropists. In the following op-ed, originally published in the *New York Times*, Buffett critiques the structures that both cause poverty and continue to feed it through misguided charity.

Should donors ask for and/or expect a return on their charitable investments?

I had spent much of my life writing music for commercials, film and television and knew little about the world of philanthropy as practiced by the very wealthy until what I call the big bang happened in 2006. That year, my father, Warren Buffett, made good on his commitment to give nearly all of his accumulated wealth back to society. In addition to making several large donations, he added generously to the three foundations that my parents had created years earlier, one for each of their children to run.

Early on in our philanthropic journey, my wife and I became aware of something I started to call Philanthropic Colonialism. I noticed that a donor had the urge to "save the day" in some fashion. People (including me) who had very little knowledge of a particular place would think that they could solve a local problem. Whether it involved farming methods, education practices, job training or business development, over and over I would hear people discuss transplanting what worked in one setting directly into another with little regard for culture, geography or societal norms.

Often the results of our decisions had unintended consequences; distributing condoms to stop the spread of AIDS in a brothel area ended up creating a higher price for unprotected sex.

But now I think something even more damaging is going on.

Because of who my father is, I've been able to occupy some seats I never 5 expected to sit in. Inside any important philanthropy meeting, you witness heads of state meeting with investment managers and corporate leaders. All are searching for answers with their right hand to problems that others in the room have created with their left. There are plenty of statistics that tell us that inequality is continually rising. At the same time, according to the Urban Institute, the nonprofit sector has been steadily growing. Between 2001 and 2011, the number of nonprofits increased 25 percent. Their growth rate now exceeds that of both the business and government sectors. It's a massive business, with approximately $316 billion given away in 2012 in the United States alone and more than 9.4 million employed.

Philanthropy has become the "it" vehicle to level the playing field and has generated a growing number of gatherings, workshops and affinity groups.

As more lives and communities are destroyed by the system that creates vast amounts of wealth for the few, the more heroic it sounds to "give back." It's what I would call "conscience laundering"—feeling better about accumulating more than any one person could possibly need to live on by sprinkling a little around as an act of charity.

But this just keeps the existing structure of inequality in place. The rich sleep better at night, while others get just enough to keep the pot from boiling over. Nearly every time someone feels better by doing good, on the other side of the world (or street), someone else is further locked into a system that will not allow the true flourishing of his or her nature or the opportunity to live a joyful and fulfilled life.

And with more business-minded folks getting into the act, business principles are trumpeted as an important element to add to the philanthropic sector. I now hear people ask, "what's the R.O.I.?" when it comes to alleviating human suffering, as if return on investment were the only measure of success. Microlending and financial literacy (now I'm going to upset people who are wonderful folks and a few dear friends)—what is this really about? People will certainly learn how to integrate into our system of debt and repayment with interest. People will rise above making $2 a day to enter our world of goods and services so they can buy more. But doesn't all this just feed the beast?

10 I'm really not calling for an end to capitalism; I'm calling for humanism.

Often I hear people say, "if only they had what we have" (clean water, access to health products and free markets, better education, safer living conditions). Yes, these are all important. But no "charitable" (I hate that word) intervention can solve any of these issues. It can only kick the can down the road.

My wife and I know we don't have the answers, but we do know how to listen. As we learn, we will continue to support conditions for systemic change.

It's time for a new operating system. Not a 2.0 or a 3.0, but something built from the ground up. New code.

What we have is a crisis of imagination. Albert Einstein said that you cannot solve a problem with the same mind-set that created it. Foundation dollars should be the best "risk capital" out there.

15 There are people working hard at showing examples of other ways to live in a functioning society that truly creates greater prosperity for all (and I don't mean more people getting to have more stuff).

Money should be spent trying out concepts that shatter current structures and systems that have turned much of the world into one vast market. Is progress really Wi-Fi on every street corner? No. It's when no 13-year-old girl on the planet gets sold for sex. But as long as most folks are patting themselves on the back for charitable acts, we've got a perpetual poverty machine.

It's an old story; we really need a new one.

Analyze

1. What does Buffett mean by the phrase "Philanthropic Colonialism"?
2. What does Buffett suggest is the significance of the recent 25% growth in nonprofits?
3. What does Buffett mean by the phrase "conscience laundering"? Is it a real phenomenon? What evidence supports that perception?

Explore

1. Buffett claims that "[n]early every time someone feels better by doing good, on the other side of the world (or street), someone else is further locked into a system that will not allow the true flourishing of his or her nature or the opportunity to live a joyful and fulfilled life." Assess this claim. What evidence does Buffett offer? Find evidence to support or challenge this claim.
2. Buffett questions those who ask for the R.O.I. of their philanthropic efforts. How might Karlan and Appel respond to this?
3. Buffett claims that charity is the cause of a "perpetual poverty machine." He says the world needs a new operating system, not an improvement on the old. What does he mean? Write a researched letter to Buffett responding to his op-ed.

Paul Theroux
"Africa's Aid Mess"

A travel writer and novelist, Paul Theroux has authored numerous books and published short stories in *The New Yorker*, *Harper's Magazine*, the *New York Times*, *Conde Nast Traveler*, and others. As a Peace Corps volunteer, Theroux taught in a Malawi school in the 1960s, and as a monetary donor to

Africa, he writes about Africans' abilities to aid themselves. In the following article from *Barron's*, Theroux describes why the well-funded efforts of celebrities, agencies, and businesspersons largely fail.

Why does so much philanthropy seem to focus on aiding Africa?

The desire of distant outsiders to fix Africa may be heartfelt, but it is also age-old and even quaint. Curiously repetitive in nature, renewed and revised every decade or so, it is an impulse Charles Dickens described, in a wickedly accurate phrase, as "telescopic philanthropy." That is, a focus from afar to uplift the continent: New York squinting compassionately at Nairobi.

Never have so many people, so many agencies, so many stratagems, so much money been deployed to improve Africa—and yet the majority of the movers are part-timers, merely dropping in, setting up a scheme in the much-mocked "the-safari-that-does-good" manner, then returning to their real lives, as hard-charging businessmen, Hollywood actors, benevolent billionaires, atoning ex-politicians, MacArthur geniuses, or rock stars in funny hats. It's not hard to imagine the future tombstones of the Clintons and Bono and Gates, and many others bitten by the eleemosynary itch, chiseled with the words, Telescopic Philanthropist. The farther away the donors are, the shorter their visits ("Chelsea Clinton took time out of her 10-day humanitarian trip in Africa to meet some of the kids that her AIDS work is benefiting . . ."), and the more passionate their feelings.

Never mind that Africa receives roughly $50 billion in aid annually from foreign governments, and perhaps $13 billion more from private philanthropic institutions, according to Penta's estimate. Never mind that Angola's oil revenues are around $72 billion, and Nigeria's $95 billion; that Africa boasts at least 55 verified and somewhat detached billionaires. I can testify that Africa is much worse off than when I first went there 50 years ago to teach English: poorer, sicker, less educated, and more badly governed. It seems that much of the aid has made things worse.

I am not alone observing this fact. In his new book, *The Great Escape: Health, Wealth, and the Origins of Inequality*, economist Angus Deaton questions the usefulness of all aid, and describes how the greater proportion of the world's poor are found not in Africa but in the booming, yet radically unequal, economies of China and India. Zambian-born economist Dambisa Moyo calls aid a "debilitating drug," arguing that "real per-capita income [in Africa] today is lower than it was in the 1970s, and more than 50% of the population—over 350 million people—live on less than a dollar a day, a figure that has nearly doubled in two decades." The Kenyan economist James Shikwati takes this same line on aid, famously telling the German magazine Der Spiegel, "For God's sake, please stop."

There have, of course, been a few successes. For all his faults, Bill Clinton's strong-arming of pharmaceutical companies to lower the price of one-a-day AIDS medications, to less than a dollar per pill, has delivered real relief to Africa's most vulnerable. But we also need to be honest about such grandiose ambitions: Most fail. (For lessons on what to avoid and what to do in order to execute effective philanthropy in Africa, see the box at end of story.)

The most recent example of a Westerner running amok in Africa appears to be the celebrity-economist Jeffrey Sachs and his $120 million effort to end extreme poverty there. Nina Munk documents in her book *The Idealist* (see *Penta*, Sept. 12) how, among other things, Sachs's Millennium Villages Project poured $2.5 million over three years into a sparsely populated community of nomadic camel herders in Dertu, Kenya, and trumpeted its success.

In actual fact, the charity's paid-for latrines became clogged and overflowing, the dormitories it erected quickly fell into disrepair, and the livestock market it built ignored local nomadic customs and was closed within a few months. An incensed Dertu citizen filed a 15-point written complaint against Sachs's operation, claiming it "created dependence" and that "the project is supposed to be bottom top approached but it is visa [sic] versa."

With such glaring examples of failure, the nature of African assistance is heading in a different direction. Today, there is a new push from wealthy Americans to jump-start self-help capitalism in Africa, rather than feed a bottomless pit of philanthropic aid, and in this group sit the likes of Howard G. Buffett, the philanthropist-farmer investing $100 million in the Great Lakes region of Africa (see *Penta*, Oct. 25); Ron Cordes, the co-chairman of Genworth Financial Wealth Management and a proponent of impact investing; and John Coors, the brewery scion and founder of CoorsTek, hoping to convince like-minded families to invest in a start-up African fund.

But are these efforts really so new? When Coors spoke to me of his One Thousand & One Voices (1K1V) mission—currently a 15-family effort to raise a $300 million Africa fund—he said, "We need to create jobs that people are proud of, and the best mechanism for creating jobs is business." I smiled in recognition. Coors was echoing the sentiments of one of the progenitors of the telescopic breed of Africanophiles, the English baronet Thomas Fowell Buxton (1786–1845)—who was also made wealthy through his brewery and wished to fix Africa with family connections and beer profits.

10   Abolitionist and social reformer Thomas Buxton urged in his book *The African Slave Trade and its Remedy* (1839) that a delegation sail to Africa to conclude treaties with African chiefs and kings, and convince them that, instead of capturing and exporting slaves, they could make a steadier (and more virtuous) profit in manufacture, and the selling of their produce. Through honest commerce, they could buy the guns, beads, cloth, and trinkets they desired. Buxton emphasized the then-novel view that the missionary impulse in Africa was not enough; trade was the key to improving the material side of the continent; business was salvation, at least here on earth.

Buxton's book inspired the Niger Expedition, an early version of the Clinton Global Initiative, which sailed to West Africa in 1841, but it failed, from death, disease, disillusionment and fever; and no treaties or business opportunities resulted. Yet a year earlier, a lecture by Buxton in London energized David Livingstone, who was in the audience. Livingstone set off that same year for Africa, his head filled with Buxtonian dreams of commerce on the Zambezi River, in his eyes a potential thoroughfare of prosperity. It is significant that in 33 years of travel Livingstone outlined many plans for commerce in Africa (white settlement, cotton growing, colonialism), but was a distracted messenger of the Lord's word. He managed to convert only one African to Christianity, according to Tim Jeal's exhaustive biography *Livingstone* (newly republished by Yale University Press), and the man later lapsed from the faith.

Buxton also inspired Charles Dickens, who was in his early thirties as a novelist at the time Buxton was preaching his message of legitimate trade. But this Dickensian inspiration was fictional. All potential telescopic philanthropists ought to read *Bleak House*, in which Dickens satirizes Buxton's effort in the minor but resonant character Mrs. Jellyby. She is a familiar figure and from her passions and predilections she might be one of our own contemporaries, paging through *Barron's*, studying the markets, seeking opportunities in mining and agri-business in Africa. "She was a pretty, very diminutive, plump woman of from forty to fifty, with handsome eyes, though they had a curious habit of seeming to look a long way off. As if . . . they could see nothing nearer than Africa!"

Dickens knew the humiliations of poverty; his improvident father languished for months in Marshalsea Debtors' Prison. He is well-known for his depictions of the London poor in his novels, and he was familiar with benefactors (*Great Expectations* is, among other things, a study in money and patronage). The idea that Mrs. Jellyby—mother of numerous scattered children—ignores her family and spends her time in an effort to fix Africa, Dickens finds a subject ripe for satire. Like Buxton, she ignores the squalor and the culture of paupers in London that pained Dickens and informed his fiction, and as a fundraiser she seeks redemption through her colonists on the Niger River.

It is the most modern of paradoxes. When Mrs. Jellyby says, "We hope by this time next year to have from a hundred and fifty to two hundred healthy families cultivating coffee and educating the natives of Borrioboola-Gha, on the left bank of the Niger," she is echoing not only Buxton, but the mission statement of many modern NGOs and family foundations today. And Mrs. Jellyby's "coffee colonists" will have a further duty: "to teach the natives to turn piano-forte legs and establish an export trade."

I am not criticizing the humane desire to help. My modest point is that, for all the talk of "reinvention," aid to Africa has been discussed in exactly the same terms for 173 years. "Microfinance is the way forward," Ron Cordes, head of the Cordes Foundation, assured me. "We financed an initiative in Uganda. A small fund to provide loans for the village of Buyobo. The work we're doing is influenced by the business I had—business services, banking the unbanked, assisting people in going up the ladder."

That too is Buxtonism, and it's not wrong, it might even work in a small way; it's just nothing new. And as a matter of fact the tiny village of Buyobo is not a benighted clearing in the Impenetrable Forest; it is a short drive from the prosperous Ugandan town of Mbale, with its 17 banks and three universities. I know this to be so. Working in adult education at Uganda's Makerere University, I supervised programs for extra-mural students from Mbale (and Buyobo), and economics was part of the curriculum.

That was 40 years ago—see what I mean by repetition?

My first experience of Africa began at the end of the colonial period, in 1963, in Nyasaland, later Malawi. During the 50 years since, I have listened to the rubious generalities of telescopic philanthropists; I have been one myself—perhaps I still am. I remain in touch with my fellow teachers and some former students; I watch developments in Africa, have written two travel books about traipsing through the continent, *Dark Star Safari: Overland from Cairo to Cape Town* (2003), and *The Last Train to Zona Verde: Overland from Cape Town to Angola* (2013). I give money to help fund an orphanage in Malawi. Out of a population of 15 million people, one million Malawians are orphans, mainly AIDS orphans, the relief of whom is a difficult task for all concerned, but in fact not many Malawians are concerned, another paradox, if not disillusionment, for the aid-givers.

The lamentable fact of so many orphans is something the new investment-minded donors, scornful of check-writing philanthropy, seem to overlook. Unless an orphanage is turned into a Dickensian workhouse, with manual labor as its primary purpose, there is no way for such an institution to turn a profit; and so such places depend on cash handouts, nearly all from telescopic philanthropists, and meanwhile the orphans, like the ones in Malawi Children's Village, try to be self-sufficient by tending vegetable gardens, doing household chores, helping with the upkeep and at the same time studying at local schools.

20   For two years in Malawi, I worked at a secondary school attached to teacher-training Soche Hill College outside the southern highlands town of Limbe. Our mission was to educate younger students, who would then join the college, become teachers and replace the American volunteers. When I returned to my hilltop school and college almost 40 years later, I was dismayed to find that foreign teachers were still the mainstay of the faculty. There remained a dire shortage of Malawi teachers; this is still the case.

This suggests a reason why Africa can't move forward. Training teachers has been a priority of the post-colonial African government of independent Malawi; education was equated with economic salvation. Now, 50 years later, the education system in Malawi is still faltering. Why? Because teaching as a profession in Malawi, and many parts of Africa, is undervalued, if not despised, and poorly paid. Besides, you can always find a foreign teacher willing to do the work: American, British, Japanese, Australian.

"Americans like working in the bush," my African friends used to tell me, and they were probably right. Jiving a little they would add, "We prefer city life." With an almost unlimited supply of foreign teachers sponsored by their own governments, what incentive is there for any African ministry of education to improve conditions? I thought I was part of the solution in Malawi, and the experience changed my life in profound ways—as a man, as a writer, as a traveler; but I see I was part of the problem. The obvious conclusion is that an unlimited supply of foreign teachers funded from the outside makes it possible for Africans to avoid having to spend their lives in a classroom in the bush. What is never commented upon is that the spirit of volunteerism that vitalizes foreign teachers in Africa has not created a similar enthusiasm among enough Africans themselves to take on these tasks.

When I voiced these experiences and apparent contradiction to John Coors, he said he was not deterred. On one of his visits to Kenya, he had an epiphany, he said. Driven to do good and unrelated to the profit motive, he flew a team of dentists and doctors to a village and let it be known that a clinic would be open to treat anyone in the immediate area. In the event, thousands of afflicted people showed up, and over the course of three days many hundreds of people received tooth extractions, root canals, and fillings, and medical needs were met.

The American medical team returned home after three days, "and thousands of people who had been waiting were left untreated," Coors said to me, in tones of genuine concern. He has repeated this story in other interviews, speaking of his "catalyzing moment" and his subsequent move to impact investing. But wait, I said. There is an institution in Kenya called The University of Nairobi School of Dental Sciences. It started as the Department (in the Medical School) of Dental Surgery in 1974 with 18 students, and it has grown, with German government aid, to a university dental school.

The catalyzing moment for me is not that Kenya has no dentists in that village, but the obvious fact that Kenya has been training dentists since 1974, almost 40 years, perhaps thousands of them. And yet there are none in sight—none for those many upcountry with toothaches, witnessed by John Coors. If Kenyan dentists are not willing to travel a few hundred miles into the highlands or the bush to see to the needs of their fellow citizens, why should American dentists travel 10,000 miles to do so? That question also contains the answer: because American telescopic philanthropists provide health care for Kenya and many other African countries, there is little incentive for local doctors to engage in philanthropy.

Uganda, just a short distance up the road, has had a medical school for much longer than Kenya. Makerere University Medical School (as it is known now) has been in existence since 1924—my eldest son was born in Mulago Hospital, the teaching hospital in Kampala, where I lived, as a member of the faculty of Makerere, for four years after leaving Malawi. There are similar medical schools all over Africa, even in Zambia and

Malawi now, places where—another paradox—doctors, dentists, and nurses are in short supply and are eagerly provided by the Gates Foundation and the Clinton Global Initiative, to name just two of the active billion-dollar philanthropies.

My experience with the teachers in Malawi might explain this paradox. With so many outsiders willing to travel upcountry to improve the state of health care, African doctors tend to stay in better-paying jobs in urban areas, or simply leave the country altogether for places where doctors are held in high esteem and amply rewarded. And the well-funded work on AIDS and antiretroviral drug therapy, known as ART, for HIV/AIDS patients, means that many local doctors are lured into these areas. Foreign donors guarantee better salaries and incentives, allowing them to bypass the crucial work of day-to-day doctoring.

Another ominous trend in Africa is the phenomenal pace of urbanization—people flocking to cities, looking for work and finding none, and creating another circle of Hell in the shantytowns of Nairobi, Johannesburg, Cape Town, Dar es Salaam, and Luanda. Three-quarters of the four million people in the shantytowns of Dar es Salaam have no plumbing, according to my local doctor friend. A lack of facilities is no discouragement: African cities are growing so fast it is estimated that by 2030 half of all Africans will live in them.

As a Peace Corps volunteer, I got used to the shocked reaction of newcomers to my district, who believed, faced with mud huts, thatched roofs, and barefoot villagers, that they were seeing destitution. A mud hut and thatched roof is, in fact, renewed every few years; the cement structures and tin roofs built by well-meaning NGOs create maintenance problems. A permanent structure often turns into an unfixable ruin.

30   Underlying all of Africa's problems are the infernalities of bad government. Rhodesia did not become independent Zimbabwe until 1980, when Robert Mugabe assumed power. Thirty-three years later, aged 89, with a young shopaholic second wife, he is still president. Mugabe's policy of violently taking over the white-owned farms has turned Zimbabwe from a well-fed exporter of food to a hungry republic, dependent on handouts from the UN World Food Program and the aid of foreign charities, such as the International Rescue Committee. In October this year, in the country where I help support the orphanage, Malawian President Joyce Banda sacked her entire cabinet for their wholesale thievery of public funds.

I raised the question of government corruption with a number of the new donors, and one surprised me by saying, "It is possible to run successful businesses even in a country where the government is corrupt."

In my experience, a corrupt government, in Africa and elsewhere, always a blighting force, expects a share of profits from successful businesses, just as the Mafia preys on commercial success, in the form of protection rackets. While I lived in Malawi, Indian shopkeepers were routinely shaken down for contributions—both money and merchandise—by hacks from the ruling Malawi Congress Party. In Kenya, as the serving Indian ambassador told me with a sigh, President Jomo Kenyatta demanded the personal gift of Indian-made tractors for his family farm.

These are trifling examples of what is a general tendency; the thefts by one politician in Zambia, as revealed in court in 2007, ran to over $50 million, and as I described in detail in my last book of African travels, oil-rich Angola is rife with corruption. A western diplomat in West Africa told me recently how China has become the new briber and enabler in the continent.

Consider the cautionary tale of Mo Ibrahim. To encourage good governance, Ibrahim, the Sudanese telecom billionaire, established a multimillion-dollar prize "to reward democratically elected African leaders who retire voluntarily at the conclusion of their mandated terms after displaying strong qualities of governance and leadership."

In seven years, it has been awarded only three times, and this year it has again gone unclaimed.

It is provable that the most corrupt and oppressive governments in Africa are the wealthiest—the oil economies of Nigeria and Angola being prime examples of this malaise—while the more transparent governments— Ghana, Cape Verde, Botswana and South Africa—are better for business.

When I began teaching in Malawi, in the first years of an independent government, my students spoke dreamily of wishing to build the nation. No one talked about emigrating. But on my trips through Africa in the past dozen years, all I hear in classrooms, in markets, on buses and trains, is the desire to flee. They emigrate and they shine. That's the universal human drive when corruption has quashed all hope: The most ambitious go where they stand a fighting chance to prosper quietly and safely and raise a family in peace.

My students made me aware that, to see a foreign donor or dignitary hob-nobbing with the hated head of state, is to be severely undermined.

Ugandan president Yoweri Museveni was visited in 1998 by U.S. President Bill Clinton, who described him as "the head of a new breed of African leaders." Then Museveni invaded and tried to overthrow the governments of the Congo and Rwanda, rigged elections, and disdained gays; he no longer seemed like a new breed.

In its naked reality, Africa, the greenest continent, is still the most beautiful, the least developed, the wildest on earth. Vast plains, big animals, hospitable people, who have been enslaved, sidelined, colonized, and converted willy-nilly either to Christianity or Islam. This receptive amphitheater of goodwill and big game inspires megalomania among its foreign visitors who strut upon it—it has always done so, for those who seek the singularity of a little excitement and glory. I sometimes think that if the poorer counties of America's Deep South had rhinos and elephants, instead of raccoons and possums, the philanthropists might direct their attentions to those parts, too.

40   A rich white donor in black Africa is a study in high contrast that puts one in mind of the gallery of role models: Tarzan, Mr. Kurtz, King Leopold, Cecil Rhodes, Livingstone, Mrs. Jellyby, Albert Schweitzer, Hemingway, Henderson the Rain King: the overlords, the opportunists, the exploiters, the visionaries, the hunters, the care-givers, the baptizers, the saviors, all of them preaching the gospel of reform and seeking a kingdom of their own, if not an empire.

Henry David Thoreau, the 19th-century American author, believed that all such outgoing people had something discreditable in their past that through giving they aimed to expiate.

And all are characterized by the rather touching innocence of a billionaire faced with the brutal truth that the relative simplicity of acquiring wealth is nothing compared to the extreme difficulty of giving money away, for the common good.

The real helpers are not the schemers and grandstanders of the eponymous family foundations or charities; they are nameless ill-paid volunteers who spend years in the bush, learning the language and helping in small-scale manageable projects, digging wells, training mid-wives, teaching villagers that unprotected sex spreads HIV; and among these stalwarts are the long-serving teachers who have liberated Africans by simply teaching them English, and are still doing so, even as they make the local governments lazier.

The so-called White Fathers (the Society of Missionaries of Africa) I met in Malawi who ran upcountry clinics used to say, "I guess I'll be buried here."

No one ever says that now, and significantly none of the people I spoke   45
with for this piece ever expressed a wish to spend any serious length of time
in Africa. None speaks an African language. To the detriment of their aims,
they are on better terms with the African politicians than the common
ruck of African people.

Years living simply on the ground in Africa convinced me that there was
more for me to learn from Africans than to teach. I saw there were many
satisfactions in the lives of people who were apparently poor; many deficits
in the lives of the very wealthy. I saw that African families were large and
complex and interdependent; that old age was revered, that Africa's link to
the distant past—to the dawn of the world—was something marvelous and
still intact in many places.

Most of all, I was impressed by the self-sufficiency of ordinary people.
Without much in the way of outside help, the people in the countries I knew
managed to endure, usually through the simplest traditional means, and
finally to prevail. Africa has the schools, the money and the resources to fix
its own problems; it's appalling to think of donors telling them otherwise,
of the whole continent terminally indebted and living on handouts.

AFRICAN PHILANTHROPY DONE RIGHT

Foundation Source is the philanthropic advisor and partner to over 1,100
family foundations. *Penta* asked the organization's chief philanthropic officer, Page Snow, to provide some basic guidelines on how to successfully
execute philanthropic projects in Africa. Her advice:

Beware the panacea. Millions of dollars are wasted on overly ambitious projects claiming to be a "killer app." Projects that employ tried-and-
true interventions, narrower in scope, usually have far greater impact.

Demand responsible management. Ask tough questions if money is
flowing into a charity, but isn't flowing out to charitable causes.

Avoid duplication. Be aware of other efforts already on the ground and
make sure that your program isn't a wasteful repeat but, preferably, lever-
ages off what's there.

Support local, sustainable solutions. Avoid short term fixes by
always seeking input from locals; plan for them to run the project on their
own in the long-run.

(continued)

Beware of poor infrastructure projects. Make sure wells are dug where they're actually needed, that the bridges and roads are integrated into existing plans by government or other NGOs.

Use technology intelligently. Over 90% of households across sub-Saharan Africa don't have access to electricity for their everyday needs, let alone power for laptops. Make sure locals have the skills, resources, and necessary tools to keep tech-dependent elements of your philanthropic project running.

Be prepared to face corruption. Even when a project has been granted governmental approvals, there's no guarantee of official cooperation; corruption and regional conflicts pose considerable challenges.

Be culturally appropriate. Put on your anthropologist's hat. Africans have their own process for dealing with grief and loss; Western-style grief counselors following a natural disaster or war aren't appropriate.

Analyze

1. What is "telescopic philanthropy"? Who coined the phrase?
2. Theroux claims that from what he has witnessed, aid to Africa seems to have done what?
3. Why does Theroux say that history repeats itself when it comes to giving aid to Africa?

Explore

1. Reflecting on his experience teaching in Malawi 50 years ago, Theroux writes: "I thought I was part of the solution in Malawi, and the experience changed my life in profound ways—as a man, as a writer, as a traveler; but I see I was part of the problem." Why does Theroux now see himself as part of the problem? How does Theroux's personal story affect his ethos (character and credibility) in this article? Does it help or hurt his objectives? Write a narrative or poem about a time when you or someone else tried to solve a problem but later found that the action might have made the problem worse.
2. Why does Theroux suggest that some local African professionals—teachers, dentists, doctors, etc.—do not engage in philanthropy?

3. Theroux concludes: "Africa has the schools, the money and the resources to fix its own problems; it's appalling to think of donors telling
   them otherwise, of the whole continent terminally indebted and living
   on handouts." What solution or action is implied in this statement?
   What audience is Theroux trying to reach, and what does he want
   them to do?

Abhijit Banerjee and Esther Duflo
"More Than 1 Billion People Are Hungry in the World"

Abhijit Banerjee and Esther Duflo are both professors of economics at the
Massachusetts Institute of Technology. Together, they founded the Abdul
Latif Jameel Poverty Action Lab, a research network that evaluates programs designed to ameliorate poverty and develop economies. In the following article from *Foreign Policy*, the authors explore whether a scarcity of
food really causes calorie deficiencies among the impoverished.

Have you ever made an irrational choice to treat yourself instead of
buying something you really needed?

For many in the West, poverty is almost synonymous with hunger.
Indeed, the announcement by the United Nations Food and Agriculture Organization in 2009 that more than 1 billion people are suffering from hunger grabbed headlines in a way that any number of
World Bank estimates of how many poor people live on less than a
dollar a day never did.

But is it really true? Are there really more than a billion people going to
bed hungry each night? Our research on this question has taken us to rural
villages and teeming urban slums around the world, collecting data and
speaking with poor people about what they eat and what else they buy,
from Morocco to Kenya, Indonesia to India. We've also tapped into a

wealth of insights from our academic colleagues. What we've found is that the story of hunger, and of poverty more broadly, is far more complex than any one statistic or grand theory; it is a world where those without enough to eat may save up to buy a TV instead, where more money doesn't necessarily translate into more food, and where making rice cheaper can sometimes even lead people to buy less rice.

But unfortunately, this is not always the world as the experts view it. All too many of them still promote sweeping, ideological solutions to problems that defy one-size-fits-all answers, arguing over foreign aid, for example, while the facts on the ground bear little resemblance to the fierce policy battles they wage.

Jeffrey Sachs, an advisor to the United Nations and director of Columbia University's Earth Institute, is one such expert. In books and countless speeches and television appearances, he has argued that poor countries are poor because they are hot, infertile, malaria-infested, and often landlocked; these factors, however, make it hard for them to be productive without an initial large investment to help them deal with such endemic problems. But they cannot pay for the investments precisely because they are poor—they are in what economists call a "poverty trap." Until something is done about these problems, neither free markets nor democracy will do very much for them.

5   But then there are others, equally vocal, who believe that all of Sachs's answers are wrong. William Easterly, who battles Sachs from New York University at the other end of Manhattan, has become one of the most influential aid critics in his books, *The Elusive Quest for Growth* and *The White Man's Burden*. Dambisa Moyo, an economist who worked at Goldman Sachs and the World Bank, has joined her voice to Easterly's with her recent book, *Dead Aid*. Both argue that aid does more bad than good. It prevents people from searching for their own solutions, while corrupting and undermining local institutions and creating a self-perpetuating lobby of aid agencies. The best bet for poor countries, they argue, is to rely on one simple idea: When markets are free and the incentives are right, people can find ways to solve their problems. They do not need handouts from foreigners or their own governments. In this sense, the aid pessimists are actually quite optimistic about the way the world works. According to Easterly, there is no such thing as a poverty trap.

This debate cannot be solved in the abstract. To find out whether there are in fact poverty traps, and, if so, where they are and how to help the poor get out of them, we need to better understand the concrete problems they face. Some aid programs help more than others, but which ones? Finding out required us to step out of the office and look more carefully at the world. In 2003, we founded what became the Abdul Latif Jameel Poverty Action Lab, or J-PAL. A key part of our mission is to research by using randomized control trials—similar to experiments used in medicine to test the effectiveness of a drug—to understand what works and what doesn't in the real-world fight against poverty. In practical terms, that meant we'd have to start understanding how the poor really live their lives.

Take, for example, Pak Solhin, who lives in a small village in West Java, Indonesia. He once explained to us exactly how a poverty trap worked. His parents used to have a bit of land, but they also had 13 children and had to build so many houses for each of them and their families that there was no land left for cultivation. Pak Solhin had been working as a casual agricultural worker, which paid up to 10,000 rupiah per day (about $2) for work in the fields. A recent hike in fertilizer and fuel prices, however, had forced farmers to economize. The local farmers decided not to cut wages, Pak Solhin told us, but to stop hiring workers instead. As a result, in the two months before we met him in 2008, he had not found a single day of agricultural labor. He was too weak for the most physical work, too inexperienced for more skilled labor, and, at 40, too old to be an apprentice. No one would hire him.

Pak Solhin, his wife, and their three children took drastic steps to survive. His wife left for Jakarta, some 80 miles away, where she found a job as a maid. But she did not earn enough to feed the children. The oldest son, a good student, dropped out of school at 12 and started as an apprentice on a construction site. The two younger children were sent to live with their grandparents. Pak Solhin himself survived on the roughly 9 pounds of subsidized rice he got every week from the government and on fish he caught at a nearby lake. His brother fed him once in a while. In the week before we last spoke with him, he had eaten two meals a day for four days, and just one for the other three.

Pak Solhin appeared to be out of options, and he clearly attributed his problem to a lack of food. As he saw it, farmers weren't interested in hiring him because they feared they couldn't pay him enough to avoid starvation; and if he was starving, he would be useless in the field. What he described was the classic nutrition-based poverty trap, as it is known in the academic world. The idea is simple: The human body needs a certain number of calories just to survive. So when someone is very poor, all the food he or she can afford is barely enough to allow for going through the motions of living and earning the meager income used to buy that food. But as people get richer, they can buy more food and that extra food goes into building strength, allowing people to produce much more than they need to eat merely to stay alive. This creates a link between income today and income tomorrow: The very poor earn less than they need to be able to do significant work, but those who have enough to eat can work even more. There's the poverty trap: The poor get poorer, and the rich get richer and eat even better, and get stronger and even richer, and the gap keeps increasing.

10   But though Pak Solhin's explanation of how someone might get trapped in starvation was perfectly logical, there was something vaguely troubling about his narrative. We met him not in war-infested Sudan or in a flooded area of Bangladesh, but in a village in prosperous Java, where, even after the increase in food prices in 2007 and 2008, there was clearly plenty of food available and a basic meal did not cost much. He was still eating enough to survive; why wouldn't someone be willing to offer him the extra bit of nutrition that would make him productive in return for a full day's work? More generally, although a hunger-based poverty trap is certainly a logical possibility, is it really relevant for most poor people today? What's the best way, if any, for the world to help?

The international community has certainly bought into the idea that poverty traps exist—and that they are the reason that millions are starving. The first U.N. Millennium Development Goal, for instance, is to "eradicate extreme poverty and hunger." In many countries, the definition of poverty itself has been connected to food; the thresholds for determining that someone was poor were originally calculated as the budget necessary to buy a certain number of calories, plus some other indispensable purchases, such as housing. A "poor" person has essentially been classified as someone without enough to eat.

So it is no surprise that government efforts to help the poor are largely based on the idea that the poor desperately need food and that quantity is what matters. Food subsidies are ubiquitous in the Middle East: Egypt spent $3.8 billion on food subsidies in the 2008 fiscal year, some 2 percent of its GDP. Indonesia distributes subsidized rice. Many states in India have a similar program. In the state of Orissa, for example, the poor are entitled to 55 pounds of rice a month at about 1 rupee per pound, less than 20 percent of the market price. Currently, the Indian Parliament is debating a Right to

Food Act, which would allow people to sue the government if they are starving. Delivering such food aid is a logistical nightmare. In India it is estimated that more than half of the wheat and one-third of the rice gets "lost" along the way. To support direct food aid in this circumstance, one would have to be quite convinced that what the poor need more than anything is more grain.

But what if the poor are not, in general, eating too little food? What if, instead, they are eating the wrong kinds of food, depriving them of nutrients needed to be successful, healthy adults? What if the poor aren't starving, but choosing to spend their money on other priorities? Development experts and policymakers would have to completely reimagine the way they think about hunger. And governments and aid agencies would need to stop pouring money into failed programs and focus instead on finding new ways to truly improve the lives of the world's poorest.

Consider India, one of the great puzzles in this age of food crises. The standard media story about the country, at least when it comes to food, is about the rapid rise of obesity and diabetes as the urban upper-middle class gets richer. Yet the real story of nutrition in India over the last quarter-century, as Princeton professor Angus Deaton and Jean Drèze, a professor at Allahabad University and a special advisor to the Indian government, have shown, is not that Indians are becoming fatter: It is that they are in fact eating less and less. Despite the country's rapid economic growth, per capita calorie consumption in India has declined; moreover, the consumption of all other nutrients except fat also appears to have gone down among all groups, even the poorest. Today, more than three-quarters of the population live in households whose per capita calorie consumption is less than 2,100 calories in urban areas and 2,400 in rural areas—numbers that are often cited as "minimum requirements" in India for those engaged in manual labor. Richer people still eat more than poorer people. But at all levels of income, the share of the budget devoted to food has declined and people consume fewer calories.

What is going on? The change is not driven by declining incomes; by all 15 accounts, Indians are making more money than ever before. Nor is it because of rising food prices—between the early 1980s and 2005, food prices declined relative to the prices of other things, both in rural and urban India. Although food prices have increased again since 2005, Indians began eating less precisely when the price of food was going down.

So the poor, even those whom the FAO would classify as hungry on the basis of what they eat, do not seem to want to eat much more even when they can. Indeed, they seem to be eating less. What could explain this? Well, to start, let's assume that the poor know what they are doing. After all, they are the ones who eat and work. If they could be tremendously more productive and earn much more by eating more, then they probably would. So could it be that eating more doesn't actually make us particularly more productive, and as a result, there is no nutrition-based poverty trap?

One reason the poverty trap might not exist is that most people have enough to eat. We live in a world today that is theoretically capable of feeding every person on the planet. In 1996, the FAO estimated that world food production was enough to provide at least 2,700 calories per person per day. Starvation still exists, but only as a result of the way food gets shared among us. There is no absolute scarcity. Using price data from the Philippines, we calculated the cost of the cheapest diet sufficient to give 2,400 calories. It would cost only about 21 cents a day, very affordable even for the very poor (the worldwide poverty line is set at roughly a dollar per day). The catch is, it would involve eating only bananas and eggs, something no one would like to do day in, day out. But so long as people are prepared to eat bananas and eggs when they need to, we should find very few people stuck in poverty because they do not get enough to eat. Indian surveys bear this out: The percentage of people who say they do not have enough food has dropped dramatically over time, from 17 percent in 1983 to 2 percent in 2004. So, perhaps people eat less because they are less hungry.

And perhaps they are really less hungry, despite eating fewer calories. It could be that because of improvements in water and sanitation, they are leaking fewer calories in bouts of diarrhea and other ailments. Or maybe they are less hungry because of the decline of heavy physical work. With the availability of drinking water in villages, women do not need to carry heavy loads for long distances; improvements in transportation have reduced the need to travel on foot; in even the poorest villages, flour is now milled using a motorized mill, instead of women grinding it by hand. Using the average calorie requirements calculated by the Indian Council of Medical Research, Deaton and Drèze note that the decline in calorie consumption over the last quarter-century could be entirely explained by a modest decrease in the number of people engaged in heavy physical work.

Beyond India, one hidden assumption in our description of the poverty trap is that the poor eat as much as they can. If there is any chance that by eating a bit more the poor could start doing meaningful work and get out of the poverty trap zone, then they should eat as much as possible. Yet most people living on less than a dollar a day do not seem to act as if they are starving. If they were, surely they would put every available penny into buying more calories. But they do not. In an 18-country data set we assembled on the lives of the poor, food represents 36 to 79 percent of consumption among the rural extremely poor, and 53 to 74 percent among their urban counterparts.

It is not because they spend all the rest on other necessities. In Udaipur, India, for example, we find that the typical poor household could spend up to 30 percent more on food, if it completely cut expenditures on alcohol, tobacco, and festivals. The poor seem to have many choices, and they don't choose to spend as much as they can on food. Equally remarkable is that even the money that people do spend on food is not spent to maximize the intake of calories or micronutrients. Studies have shown that when very poor people get a chance to spend a little bit more on food, they don't put everything into getting more calories. Instead, they buy better-tasting, more expensive calories.

In one study conducted in two regions of China, researchers offered randomly selected poor households a large subsidy on the price of the basic staple (wheat noodles in one region, rice in the other). We usually expect that when the price of something goes down, people buy more of it. The opposite happened. Households that received subsidies for rice or wheat consumed less of those two foods and ate more shrimp and meat, even though their staples now cost less. Overall, the caloric intake of those who received the subsidy did not increase (and may even have decreased), despite the fact that their purchasing power had increased. Nor did the nutritional content improve in any other sense. The likely reason is that because the rice and wheat noodles were cheap but not particularly tasty, feeling richer might actually have made them consume less of those staples. This reasoning suggests that at least among these very poor urban households, getting more calories was not a priority: Getting better-tasting ones was.

All told, many poor people might eat fewer calories than we—or the FAO—think is appropriate. But this does not seem to be because they have no other choice; rather, they are not hungry enough to seize every opportunity to eat more. So perhaps there aren't a billion "hungry" people in the world after all.

None of this is to say that the logic of the hunger-based poverty trap is flawed. The idea that better nutrition would propel someone on the path to prosperity was almost surely very important at some point in history, and it

20

may still be today. Nobel Prize-winning economic historian Robert Fogel calculated that in Europe during the Middle Ages and the Renaissance, food production did not provide enough calories to sustain a full working population. This could explain why there were large numbers of beggars—they were literally incapable of any work. The pressure of just getting enough food to survive seems to have driven some people to take rather extreme steps. There was an epidemic of witch killing in Europe during the Little Ice Age (from the mid-1500s to 1800), when crop failures were common and fish was less abundant. Even today, Tanzania experiences a rash of such killings whenever there is a drought—a convenient way to get rid of an unproductive mouth to feed at times when resources are very tight. Families, it seems, suddenly discover that an older woman living with them (usually a grandmother) is a witch, after which she gets chased away or killed by others in the village.

But the world we live in today is for the most part too rich for the occasional lack of food to be a big part of the story of the persistence of poverty on a large scale. This is of course different during natural or man-made disasters, or in famines that kill and weaken millions. As Nobel laureate Amartya Sen has shown, most recent famines have been caused not because food wasn't available but because of bad governance—institutional failures that led to poor distribution of the available food, or even hoarding and storage in the face of starvation elsewhere. As Sen put it, "No substantial famine has ever occurred in any independent and democratic country with a relatively free press."

25   Should we let it rest there, then? Can we assume that the poor, though they may be eating little, do eat as much as they need to?

That also does not seem plausible. While Indians may prefer to buy things other than food as they get richer, they and their children are certainly not well nourished by any objective standard. Anemia is rampant; body-mass indices are some of the lowest in the world; almost half of children under 5 are much too short for their age, and one-fifth are so skinny that they are considered to be "wasted."

And this is not without consequences. There is a lot of evidence that children suffering from malnutrition generally grow into less successful adults. In Kenya, children who were given deworming pills in school for two years went to school longer and earned, as young adults, 20 percent more than children in comparable schools who received deworming for just one year. Worms contribute to anemia and general malnutrition, essentially because they compete with the child for nutrients. And the negative impact of under-nutrition starts before birth. In Tanzania, to cite just one example, children born to mothers who received sufficient amounts of iodine during pregnancy completed between one-third and one-half of a year more schooling than their siblings who were in utero when their mothers weren't being treated. It is a substantial increase, given that most of these children will complete only four or five years of schooling in total. In fact, the study concludes that if every mother took iodine capsules, there would be a 7.5 percent increase in the total educational attainment of children in Central and Southern Africa. This, in turn, could measurably affect lifetime productivity.

Better nutrition matters for adults, too. In another study, in Indonesia, researchers tested the effects of boosting people's intake of iron, a key nutrient that prevents anemia. They found that iron supplements made men able to work harder and significantly boosted income. A year's supply of iron-fortified fish sauce cost the equivalent of $6, and for a self-employed male, the yearly gain in earnings was nearly $40—an excellent investment.

If the gains are so obvious, why don't the poor eat better? Eating well doesn't have to be prohibitively expensive. Most mothers could surely afford iodized salt, which is now standard in many parts of the world, or one dose of iodine every two years (at 51 cents per dose). Poor households could easily get a lot more calories and other nutrients by spending less on expensive grains (like rice and wheat), sugar, and processed foods, and more on leafy vegetables and coarse grains. But in Kenya, when the NGO that was running the deworming program asked parents in some schools to pay a few cents for deworming their children, almost all refused, thus depriving their children of hundreds of dollars of extra earnings over their lifetime.

Why? And why did anemic Indonesian workers not buy iron-fortified 30 fish sauce on their own? One answer is that they don't believe it will matter—their employers may not realize that they are more productive now. (In fact, in Indonesia, earnings improved only for the self-employed workers.) But this does not explain why all pregnant women in India aren't using only iodine-fortified salt, which is now available in every village. Another possibility is that people may not realize the value of feeding themselves and their children better—not everyone has the right information, even in the United States. Moreover, people tend to be suspicious of outsiders who tell them that they should change their diet. When rice prices went up sharply in 1966 and 1967, the chief minister of West Bengal suggested that eating less rice and more vegetables would be both good for people's health and easier on their budgets. This set off a flurry of outrage, and the chief minister was greeted by protesters bearing garlands of vegetables wherever he went.

It is simply not very easy to learn about the value of many of these nutrients based on personal experience. Iodine might make your children smarter, but the difference is not huge, and in most cases you will not find out either way for many years. Iron, even if it makes people stronger, does not suddenly turn you into a superhero. The $40 extra a year the self-employed man earned may not even have been apparent to him, given the many ups and downs of his weekly income.

So it shouldn't surprise us that the poor choose their foods not mainly for their cheap prices and nutritional value, but for how good they taste. George Orwell, in his masterful description of the life of poor British workers in *The Road to Wigan Pier*, observes:

> The basis of their diet, therefore, is white bread and margarine, corned beef, sugared tea and potatoes—an appalling diet. Would it not be better if they spent more money on wholesome things like oranges and wholemeal bread or if they even, like the writer of the letter to the *New Statesman*, saved on fuel and ate their carrots raw? Yes, it would, but the point is that no ordinary human being is ever going to do such a thing. The ordinary human being would sooner starve than live on brown bread and raw carrots. And the peculiar evil is this, that the less money you have, the less inclined you feel to spend it on wholesome food. A millionaire may enjoy breakfasting off orange juice and Ryvita biscuits; an unemployed man doesn't.... When you are unemployed ... you don't *want* to eat dull wholesome food. You want something a little bit "tasty." There is always some cheaply pleasant thing to tempt you.

The poor often resist the wonderful plans we think up for them because they do not share our faith that those plans work, or work as well as we claim. We shouldn't forget, too, that other things may be more important in their lives than food. Poor people in the developing world spend large amounts on weddings, dowries, and christenings. Part of the reason is probably that they don't want to lose face, when the social custom is to spend a lot on those occasions. In South Africa, poor families often spend so lavishly on funerals that they skimp on food for months afterward.

And don't underestimate the power of factors like boredom. Life can be quite dull in a village. There is no movie theater, no concert hall. And not a lot of work, either. In rural Morocco, Oucha Mbarbk and his two neighbors told us they had worked about 70 days in agriculture and about 30 days in construction that year. Otherwise, they took care of their cattle and waited for jobs to materialize. All three men lived in small houses without water or sanitation. They struggled to find enough money to give their children a good education. But they each had a television, a parabolic antenna, a DVD player, and a cell phone.

This is something that Orwell captured as well, when he described how   35 poor families survived the Depression:

> Instead of raging against their destiny they have made things tolerable by reducing their standards.
>
> But they don't necessarily lower their standards by cutting out luxuries and concentrating on necessities; more often it is the other way around—the more natural way, if you come to think of it. Hence the fact that in a decade of unparalleled depression, the consumption of all cheap luxuries has increased.

These "indulgences" are not the impulsive purchases of people who are not thinking hard about what they are doing. Oucha Mbarbk did not buy his TV on credit—he saved up over many months to scrape enough money together, just as the mother in India starts saving for her young daughter's wedding by buying a small piece of jewelry here and a stainless-steel bucket there.

We often see the world of the poor as a land of missed opportunities and wonder why they don't invest in what would really make their lives better. But the poor may well be more skeptical about supposed opportunities and the possibility of any radical change in their lives. They often behave as if they think that any change that is significant enough to be worth sacrificing for will simply take too long. This could explain why they focus on the here and now, on living their lives as pleasantly as possible and celebrating when occasion demands it.

We asked Oucha Mbarbk what he would do if he had more money. He   40 said he would buy more food. Then we asked him what he would do if he had even more money. He said he would buy better-tasting food. We were starting to feel very bad for him and his family, when we noticed the TV and other high-tech gadgets. Why had he bought all these things if he felt the family did not have enough to eat? He laughed, and said, "Oh, but television is more important than food!"

Analyze

1. What do Banerjee and Duflo mean when they say that the "story" of hunger and poverty is more complex than any one statistic or theory? What are they responding to?
2. Summarize the "poverty trap" debate.
3. What are randomized controlled trials (RCTs)?

Explore

1. Banerjee and Duflo explain: "Studies have shown that when very poor people get a chance to spend a little bit more on food, they don't put everything into getting more calories. Instead, they buy better-tasting, more expensive calories." What does this suggest about food priorities in poor households and about the claim of 1 billion hungry people? Write a descriptive narrative using examples and illustrations describing a time when you made an irrational choice—you indulged in something beyond your budget, made an unhealthy choice, or went against the facts in some way. Explain why you made that irrational choice— or reframe it as a rational choice according to other criteria.
2. Why is it important to get the numbers right in such headline-grabbing claims as 1 billion hungry, and what role do the media play in getting it right or giving misinformation? What narrative frames do they convey about hunger?
3. Why do the authors include the passage from George Orwell in this article even though it is not scientific writing?

Peter Edelman
"The State of Poverty in America"

A professor at Georgetown University Law Center, Peter Edelman served as the assistant secretary of Health and Human Services under President Bill Clinton's administration, resigning when the president supported the Republican welfare reform bill. He often writes for a broader audience about poverty, welfare, juvenile justice, and law. In the following article from

The American Prospect, Edelman identifies the main causes of poverty in the U.S. and offers reasons for why his proposed solutions could alleviate it.

> Aside from the wages themselves, how is the low-wage economy to blame for U.S. poverty?

We have two basic poverty problems in the United States. One is the prevalence of low-wage work. The other concerns those who have almost no work.

The two overlap.

Most people who are poor work as much as they can and go in and out of poverty. Fewer people have little or no work on a continuing basis, but they are in much worse straits and tend to stay poor from one generation to the next.

The numbers in both categories are stunning.

Low-wage work encompasses people with incomes below twice the poverty line—not poor but struggling all the time to make ends meet. They now total 103 million, which means that fully one-third of the population has an income below what would be $36,000 for a family of three.   5

In the bottom tier are 20.5 million people—6.7 percent of the population—who are in deep poverty, with an income less than half the poverty line (below $9,000 for a family of three). Some 6 million people out of those 20.5 million have no income at all other than food stamps.

These dire facts tempt one to believe that there may be some truth to President Ronald Reagan's often-quoted declaration that "we fought a war against poverty and poverty won." But that is not the case. Our public policies have been remarkably successful. Starting with the Social Security Act of 1935, continuing with the burst of activity in the 1960s, and on from there, we have made great progress.

We enacted Medicaid and the Children's Health Insurance Program, and many health indicators for low-income people improved. We enacted food stamps, and the near-starvation conditions we saw in some parts of the country were ameliorated. We enacted the Earned Income Tax Credit and the Child Tax Credit, and the incomes of low-wage workers with children were lifted. We enacted Pell grants, and millions of people could afford college who otherwise couldn't possibly attend. We enacted Supplemental Security Income and thereby raised the income floor for elderly and disabled people whose earnings from work didn't provide enough Social Security. There is much more—housing vouchers, Head Start, child-care assistance, and legal services for the poor, to name a few. The Obama administration and Congress added 16 million people to Medicaid in the Affordable Care Act, appropriated billions to improve the education of low-income children, and spent an impressive amount on the least well-off in the Recovery Act.

All in all, our various public policies kept a remarkable 40 million people from falling into poverty in 2010—about half because of Social Security and half due to the other programs just mentioned. To assert that we fought a war against poverty and poverty won because there is still poverty is like saying that the Clean Air and Clean Water acts failed because there is still pollution.

10   Nonetheless, the level of poverty in the nation changed little between 1970 and 2000 and is much worse now. It was at 11.1 percent in 1973—the lowest level achieved since we began measuring—and after going up sharply during the Reagan and George H. W. Bush years, went back down during the 1990s to 11.3 percent in 2000, as President Bill Clinton left office.

Why didn't it fall further? The economics have been working against us for four decades, exacerbated by trends in family composition. Well-paying industrial jobs disappeared to other countries and to automation. The economy grew, but the fruits of the growth went exclusively to those at the top. Other jobs replaced the ones lost, but most of the new jobs paid much less. The wage of the median-paying job barely grew—by one measure going up only about 7 percent over the 38 years from 1973 to 2011. Half the jobs in the country now pay less than $33,000 a year, and a quarter pay less than the poverty line of $22,000 for a family of four. We have become a low-wage economy to a far greater extent than we realize.

Households with only one wage-earner—typically those headed by single mothers—have found it extremely difficult to support a family. The share of families with children headed by single mothers rose from 12.8 percent in 1970 to 26.2 percent in 2010 (and from 37.1 percent in 1971 to 52.8 percent in 2010 among African Americans). In 2010, 46.9 percent of children under 18 living in households headed by a single mother were poor.

The percentage of people in deep poverty has doubled since 1976. A major reason for this rise is the near death of cash assistance for families with children. Welfare has shrunk from 14 million recipients (too many, in my view) before the Temporary Assistance for Needy Families law (TANF) was enacted in 1996 to 4.2 million today, just 1.5 percent of the population. At last count, Wyoming had 607 people on TANF, or just 2.7 percent of its poor children. Twenty-six states have less than 20 percent of their poor children on TANF. The proportion of poor families with children receiving welfare has shrunk from 68 percent before TANF was enacted to 27 percent today.

What's the agenda going forward? The heart of it is creating jobs that yield a living income. Restoring prosperity, ensuring that the economy functions at or near full employment, is our most powerful anti-poverty weapon. We need more, though—a vital union sector and a higher minimum wage, for two. We also need work supports—health care, child care, and help with the cost of housing and postsecondary education. These are all income equivalents—all policies that will contribute to bringing everyone closer to having a living income.

There's a gigantic problem here, however: We look to be headed to a future of too many low-wage jobs. Wages in China, India, and other emerging economies may be rising, but we can't foresee any substantial increase in the prevailing wage for many millions of American jobs. That means we better start talking about wage supplements that are much bigger than the Earned Income Tax Credit. We need a dose of reality about the future of the American paycheck.

The second big problem is the crisis—and it is a crisis—posed by the 20 million people at the bottom of the economy. We have a huge hole in our safety net. In many states, TANF and food stamps combined don't even get people to half of the poverty line, and a substantial majority of poor families don't receive TANF at all.

Even worse, we have destroyed the safety net for the poorest children in the country. Seven million women and children are among the 20.5 million in deep poverty. One in four children in a household headed by a single mother is in deep poverty. We have to restore the safety net for the poorest of the poor.

Getting serious about investing in our children—from prenatal care and early-childhood assistance on through education at all levels—is also essential if we are to achieve a future without such calamitous levels of poverty. In addition, we must confront the destruction being wrought by the criminal-justice system. These are poverty issues and race issues as well. The schools and the justice system present the civil-rights challenges of this century.

Combining all of the problems in vicious interaction is the question of place—the issues that arise from having too many poor people concentrated in one area, whether in the inner city, Appalachia, the Mississippi Delta, or on Indian reservations. Such places are home to a minority of the poor, but they include a hugely disproportionate share of intergenerational and persistent poverty. Our most serious policy failing over the past four-plus decades has been our neglect of this concentrated poverty. We have held our own in other respects, but we have lost ground here.

20   Finally, we need to be much more forthright about how much all of this has to do with race and gender. It is always important to emphasize that white people make up the largest number of the poor, to counter the stereotype that the face of poverty is one of color. At the same time, though, we must face more squarely that African Americans, Latinos, and Native Americans are all poor at almost three times the rate of whites and ask why that continues to be true. We need as a nation to be more honest about who it is that suffers most from terrible schools and the way we lock people up. Poverty most definitely cuts across racial lines, but it doesn't cut evenly.

There's a lot to do.

Analyze

1. How does Edelman respond to President Ronald Reagan's declaration that "we fought a war against poverty and poverty won"? What analogy does he make to underscore his point? Is that analogy effective?
2. How many Americans does Edelman say were kept out of poverty due to public policy in 2010?
3. Why does Edelman say the poverty rate didn't fall further below 11.3% since 2000 but instead rose? Why does Edelman claim the deep poverty rate has doubled since 1976?

Explore

1. What does Edelman say we need going forward to reduce those poverty rates? Why might that be hard to achieve?
2. What do place, race, and gender have to do with persistent poverty levels, according to Edelman? Research an aspect of this claim and write a report explaining or challenging Edelman's observation.
3. What does Edelman want his audience to do about the issues he outlines? What is his purpose?

Ai-jen Poo
"Building a Caring Economy"

Ai-jen Poo, heralded as one of *TIME*'s "100 Most Influential People in the World" and *Newsweek*'s "150 Fearless Women," directs both the National Domestic Workers Alliance and the Caring Across Generations Campaign. Having helped to spearhead the passage of New York State's historic Domestic Workers Bill of Rights in 2010, Poo has contributed much to improving the lives of the impoverished. In the following essay from the *Huffington Post*, April 22, 2013 (and reprinted by Oxfam), she explains how domestic workers do not earn enough to support their own families, but argues that raising certain labor standards can help to correct this.

What is at stake for all Americans in the passage of worker rights legislation?

Anna, a Filipino live-in nanny in Manhattan, begins her workday at 6 a.m. when the children wake up, and ends around 10 p.m. when she puts the children to bed and finishes cleaning the kitchen. Like many domestic workers, Anna's pay is low; she was promised $1,500 a month but receives only $620, meaning that—on average—she is paid just $1.27 per hour.

There are between 800,000 and two million domestic workers like Anna in the United States—people who work as nannies, housecleaners and caregivers for the elderly. The domestic work industry grew by 10 percent from 2004 to 2010. Domestic workers—who do what is traditionally considered "women's work"—are overwhelmingly female. The Census reports that 95 percent of domestic workers are women. The majority are women of color and immigrants from dozens of nations. Women from Asia and the Pacific Islands, Africa, the Caribbean, Latin America and Eastern Europe fill the ranks of the industry, alongside African American women.

These workers are the backbone of the "care economy," doing the long and hard work of caring for our children, homes and elders. Domestic workers put in long hours, rising early to feed young children or going to bed late at night after helping an elderly person in pain get to sleep. But these women—on whom we count to take care of the most precious people in our lives, our homes, and our families—do not earn enough to take care of their own families. Twenty-three percent of domestic workers earn below the minimum wage; 61 percent of live-in domestic workers earn below minimum wage.

The need for domestic work will only grow. As the baby boom generation reaches retirement age, more and more older Americans will need the support of in-home care providers to live independently. Already, home care is one of the fastest growing occupations in the nation. And with women now the majority of the paid workforce, the need for childcare providers will continue.

5   When this country's foundational worker rights and protections were written in the 1930s, domestic workers—together with farm workers— were excluded, as a concession to Southern legislators who didn't want black workers in their states to have access to these basic rights. Today, 80 years later, domestic workers are still excluded from the right to organize unions, along with other basic workplace protections, blocking them from established pathways for improving their working conditions and quality of life.

And they are not alone. Domestic workers are just one population within the growing ranks of the working poor, workers who are slipping through the cracks of a deteriorating safety net and falling into the growing chasm of economic inequality in this country. Over the last 30 years, the politics of austerity have effectively dismantled the social safety net and weakened the basic floor of social protections that working people fought for and won in the 1930s. A shadow economy—in which working poverty is the norm—has emerged in this country. If we don't stop that shadow economy from growing, it threatens to engulf increasing numbers of working people, including people who were once considered middle class.

We must re-establish a basic floor of protections for working people. Domestic worker organizations in states around the country are working to pass a Domestic Worker Bills of Rights to eliminate exclusions and establish basic labor protections. But winning inclusion in minimum standards for selected groups of workers is not enough; we also need to raise those standards for all workers.

We need to make sure that the working poor have on-ramps to improving their lives: opportunities like workforce training and job development. The Restaurant Opportunities Centers United is organizing to raise the minimum wage for all tipped workers, and many organizations are fighting to pass legislation requiring all businesses to provide paid sick leave and paid family leave to their employees We need an inclusive road to citizenship to ensure that undocumented workers can come out of the shadows, out from under employer threats of deportation. And we need to connect the work to raise standards for workers with efforts to rebuild our social safety net.

Two years ago, the National Domestic Workers Alliance initiated a campaign called Caring Across Generations. This campaign brings together all people who are touched by the care economy: people with disabilities and elders who need quality long-term care, families who need care workers they can entrust with their parents' health and well-being, and workers who need decent jobs and basic economic security. By strengthening labor protections for domestic and care workers, improving wages and creating training opportunities for care workers, we can transform domestic work into quality, dignified jobs. By turning domestic and home-care jobs into quality jobs, we can help ensure quality care and support for every family and individual who needs it. By making care a national public policy priority, we can invest in making it affordable and accessible for everyone who needs it.

More than 100 million Americans—one-third of us—live in or near poverty, struggling every day. We need a lively national conversation about how we can right this wrong.

We must begin to create the kinds of policies that growing numbers of working people need in order to be able to provide for our families. These are the types of policies that will turn the rising tide of inequality and suggest a new vision for our economy that is based on the ethics of equality and care.

Analyze

1. What types of jobs are considered "domestic work"? What types of people usually do these jobs?
2. What two types of workers were excluded from the 1930s worker rights protection laws? Why? Are they still excluded? What does that mean?
3. List the policy changes Poo wants to see for domestic workers and for all who are the fragile working poor.

Explore

1. In what ways does Poo's essay provide a specific example of what Edelman only refers to in his article? Explain.

2. Poo is advocating for policies related to a specific subset of poor Americans. Compare this to more broad-based approaches, such as raising the minimum wage for everyone. What advantages or disadvantages are there in constructing arguments on behalf of such a specific group? How does Poo construct her ethos (character and credibility) to advance her argument?

3. How does Poo say domestic work can be transformed into "quality, dignified jobs"? What stakeholders would support her vision? What stakeholders would not want to see the changes she proposes? Write a letter to any stakeholder on this issue in which you define what "quality, dignified jobs" means to you. Try to persuade those readers to accept your definition based on relevant examples and reasons.

Lori Sanders and Eli Lehrer
"Don't Forget the Poor"

Lori Sanders and Eli Lehrer both work for R Street, a "free market think tank" that supports limited government and environmental stewardship. As R Street's policy analyst, Sanders provides public outreach and education about public policy issues. Lehrer, as R Street's president, oversees the organization's work. In the following article from *The Weekly Standard*, Sanders and Lehrer argue that it behooves conservatives to address antipoverty efforts that are usually spearheaded by ineffective liberal policies.

When applying to college, what sorts of hurdles do you imagine "place a disproportionate burden on those with limited means"?

After five decades of liberal antipoverty programs that have produced only failure and futility, it is more than time for a conservative response to the problem of poverty—one that emphasizes work, family, and economic freedom.

Indeed, if the Republican Party wants to regain the White House and be trusted to run the executive branch's myriad poverty-related programs, it will need an agenda beyond simple budget cuts for poverty programs. Instead, conservatives need a plan to foster a dynamic economy in which far fewer Americans would need to rely on government in the first place.

To produce such a plan requires some knowledge of who the poor are. According to the U.S. Census Bureau, roughly 46 million Americans were living below the poverty line in 2011, about 15 percent of the population. That figure, roughly the same as in 2010, is only 4 points lower than the rate when Lyndon Johnson declared the "War on Poverty" in 1964. After falling to 17.3 percent in 1965 and a low of 11.1 percent in 1973, the poverty rate mostly floated between 11 and 15 percent over the intervening years, briefly crossing the 15 percent threshold in the early 1980s and again in the early 1990s.

But the poverty rate has been on a steady climb these past five years and, by a variety of measures, Americans' chances of escaping poverty have declined consistently since the 1970s. A search for root causes implicates just about every major social trend of the past several decades. To name just a few, technology has increased the returns on education and the penalties for poor skills and work habits; the breakdown of nuclear families has required already-limited resources to be stretched even further to support multiple households; and a growing welfare state has provided many of the wrong incentives. These trends are extraordinarily difficult to reverse.

Conservatives long have made the moral case that the poor, like everyone else, should be held accountable for their choices. And it's true that people who marry, avoid substance abuse, graduate from high school, avoid going to jail, refrain from having children out of wedlock, and hold jobs (even minimum wage ones) for at least a year almost never end up living in poverty. 5

It's also largely true that today's American poor do not face privation to quite the same degree as either earlier generations or the poor elsewhere in the world. In the United States today, poor people rarely miss meals, though they may wonder where the next meal is coming from; they generally don't end up homeless, although they may come close; and they typically can get needed medical care, although it takes a lot of work to do so.

All that said, being poor still involves significant misery, constant insecurity, and material deprivation. Moreover, many of the conditions that trap Americans in poverty are the direct result of government policies, often implemented with good intentions.

The lives of America's poor are ones in which even relatively minor difficulties can quickly spiral out of control, making it almost impossible to plan for the future. A small but telling example: One recent study published in *Pediatrics* detailed how a lack of money to buy diapers can throw a poor family into crisis, causing a mother to skip work to avoid leaving her diaperless child at daycare. Even basic services that most Americans take for granted, like low-cost checking accounts, often are unavailable to those without means, forcing the poor into the expensive and inefficient financial services offered by check-cashing stores and pay-day lenders.

In these and a thousand other ways, the American social system today requires more resources and wherewithal to navigate properly than in the past. In today's market, access to technology is increasingly necessary to find a job, and the number of well-paid jobs available to people with modest education has plummeted.

10   Government regulations exacerbate the problem. A recent report from the libertarian Institute for Justice shows that state licensing laws force workers who aspire to ply an array of moderate-skill trades to spend an average of nine extra months in schools that prepare them for licensing exams, paying hundreds of dollars in fees along the way. Such hurdles place a disproportionate burden on those of limited means.

Meanwhile, government assistance programs often seem better designed to serve the middle class than the poor. Dozens of state and federal college programs offer extra money to help middle-class students attend the college they choose, but the sort of comprehensive support poor students need to even consider attending a four-year university is extraordinarily difficult to come by.

Most of these problems are not new. But with just a few notable exceptions (Jack Kemp; more recently, Rick Santorum), the Republican Party and the conservative movement have been hesitant to offer policies to ameliorate these problems. Why should now be any different?

To start, because writing off some 46 million fellow citizens is simply not viable in a healthy liberal democracy. Democracy requires that everyone have access to opportunity. Concern for the poor, moreover, is a core value for Americans of all political stripes, a fact made abundantly clear in the massive dataset of social-attitude surveys compiled by New York University social psychologist Jonathan Haidt.

And the poor represent a larger part of the conservative coalition than many Republicans realize. Between 28 and 36 percent of people earning less than $15,000 per year give their votes to GOP candidates. That's better than Republicans typically do among African Americans, Jews, or Asians.

But in the end, a conservative poverty agenda ought to be seen as essential to building a democratic society that favors and rewards the industrious and innovative, yet includes the poor. By failing to provide such an agenda, conservatives ignore a prominent national problem—and in doing so abandon the field to the political left.   15

Any conservative antipoverty agenda must begin with work—which presupposes employability: habits of courtesy, responsibility, punctuality, honesty, and so on. Research shows overwhelmingly that work is central to escaping poverty. This is true not only for the obvious reasons—the wages and benefits—but also for the role work plays in cultivating healthy lifestyles, that is, in helping individuals achieve self-respect, feel happier, and set an example for younger generations. And the consensus on the centrality of work is near universal: Researchers Isabel Sawhill and Quentin Karpilow of the Brookings Institution—no bastion of conservatism— have identified a "work gap" that leaves poor families at a disadvantage in all of these areas. As Sawhill and Karpilow write, "some [poor] households lack an employed member, a majority lack two earners and a high proportion work very few hours even when the economy is operating at full employment."

Despite lots of high-minded rhetoric about the value of work, the conservative public policy agenda on work remains woefully underdeveloped. Historically, the focus has been on tying work requirements to welfare programs and, more recently, resisting the Obama administration's efforts to gut existing work requirements. This is all good. But given a still-sluggish economy and the relocation of many jobs away from areas where poor people live, work mandates alone—without appropriate plans to encourage and support the poor in their search for jobs—represent an insufficient response that, in its current form, just adds bureaucratic requirements to already bloated public programs.

Properly structured work incentives would build on what is already our largest welfare program, the Earned Income Tax Credit, which remains decidedly modest. For a single worker without children living at home, the EITC refunds less than $425 per year. Introducing and expanding similar wage supplements, even the short-lived "Making Work

Pay" tax credit included in the misbegotten 2009 stimulus package, would further encourage a life of work as preferable to welfare or life in the underground economy.

In the short term, conservatives should consider, and debate thoroughly, the merits of a variety of measures that encourage employers to create more entry-level jobs. These could include permitting employers to pay a sub-minimum "training" wage when they invest in developing the skills of the previously unemployed. They could also include relocation grants offered through the unemployment system to help people move away from pockets of high unemployment and to growing areas with a surplus of jobs.

20   Of particular interest should be reform of public programs whose structure discourages work. This might include allowing people to hang on to some benefits—including unemployment and a larger share of disability insurance payments—as they transition into the workforce. The disability system, in particular, should shift its focus to returning the disabled to work where possible, rather than cementing permanent dependence on the state.

In the longer term, Republicans may want to radically reorient the welfare system, away from a series of largely disconnected programs addressing segmented needs (food, disability, housing, medical care, and childcare) and toward a comprehensive, but less bureaucratic, wage supplement. In short, they should consider a negative income tax, designed to make work far more attractive. There are significant policy design challenges inherent in a negative income tax, and a poorly constructed one risks eliminating incentives to work altogether. Happily, there is no shortage of creative scholars who already have given significant thought to overcoming these challenges.

Of course, an emphasis on work alone is not enough. A truly conservative antipoverty agenda also must promote strong families. Married, two-income couples, even those earning only minimum wage, find it much easier to escape poverty, and most children who grow up with the example of hard work, thrift, and successful marriage can avoid becoming poor.

But many poor women face extensive barriers to marriage, ranging from the high proportion of men living in poverty who commit crimes and thereby end up in correctional facilities to the paucity of jobs for people with little formal education. Larger refundable child tax credits and even savings incentives for couples and singles of modest means would likewise relieve some of the financial pressure that can tear apart marriages and leave children without two parents.

Moreover, while marriage is the ideal, single parent households also must be recognized as family units that need support, as a child is far better off with a single competent mother or father than as a ward of the state. Efforts to expand counseling, classes, and even group homes for such parents and their children deserve consideration. A family values agenda would embrace and support existing families, even as it encouraged the formation of committed, loving marriages.

Conservatives also have a lot to say about the ways government itself often holds back the poor, for instance through the ever-growing regulatory state. Outdated union-protection laws like the Davis-Bacon Act, which requires union wages on many federal projects, reserve desirable jobs for union members. More generally, except where public health and safety are clearly at stake, government should play no role in deciding what professions individuals can pursue. 25

Occupational licensing may make sense for those doing open heart surgery or designing bridges, but a wide range of other jobs—hair dresser, teeth whitener, real estate salesperson, medical technician—that should be routes out of poverty are among the fields most protected by state licensing cartels. Where feasible, regulating bodies should replace the certification process, which locks out those without the time or resources to spend on classes, with on-the-job apprenticeship that allows trainees to earn a modest wage and enjoy the intrinsic benefits of work.

We should also take another look at government rules that bar those with a criminal record—a large percentage of adult men in poverty—from a host of government or government-licensed jobs. So long as there is no direct nexus between a crime and an ex-offender's desired career path, the government should not work to frustrate him. Drug abusers probably shouldn't be allowed to work as pharmacists, but neither should they face any special obstacle to becoming, say, plumbers. In all too many cases, they do.

The political left long has been able to outbid the right in its quest for the votes of the poor—and the votes of those concerned about the poor—mostly by offering programs aimed at relief. The right has failed to formulate a countervailing agenda of its own. As a result, in the fullness of time, much of the left's agenda has gone into force.

But the right can offer its own better vision for the relief of poverty. A conservative antipoverty agenda is one that offers both temporary relief and longer-term institutional changes, all aimed at holding out the possibility of steady employment and stable families. Republicans can advance a comprehensive strategy that meets people on their own terms and provides the combination of opportunity, incentive, and assistance necessary to move millions of fellow citizens toward lives of thrift, industry, and self-reliance.

Analyze

1. What "root causes" of poverty do Sanders and Lehrer see connected to the major social trends?
2. What is the "moral case" that Sanders and Lehrer say conservatives have made regarding poverty?
3. Why do the authors say that government regulations exacerbate the "significant misery, constant insecurity, and material deprivation" experienced by people in poverty?

Explore

1. Why do the authors say that now is the time for Republicans and the conservative movement to propose policies to ameliorate poverty in the U.S.? Do you agree? Explain.
2. Sanders and Lehrer argue that a conservative antipoverty agenda must "begin with work" and must "promote strong families." What policies and programs do they recommend? Research one of these policies or programs and write a research brief explaining it in more detail for legislators to consider.
3. Sanders and Lehrer argue that conservatives have failed to offer a countervailing antipoverty agenda to compete with the political left, so this article outlines ways to construct that agenda. Write a rhetorical analysis in which you assess how well this argument is constructed and suggest ways it could be more effective in motivating its target audience.

Muhammad Yunus
"Nobel Peace Prize Lecture"

Helping the poor escape poverty by providing them with financial education and loans to be paid back on terms that they can meet, economics professor Muhammad Yunus established Grameen Bank in Bangladesh in 1983. His model of eradicating poverty through micro-lending has been successfully replicated in over 100 countries. For his efforts, Yunus was awarded a Nobel Peace Prize in 2006. In the following transcript of his Nobel acceptance lecture (which you can also watch online), Yunus explains how peace is inextricably connected to poverty and how our assumptions about economics and human capabilities inform the ways in which we address poverty.

Do you agree with Yunus that "poverty is the absence of all human rights?"

Nobel Lecture, Oslo, December 10, 2006.
Your Majesties, Your Royal Highnesses, Honorable Members of the Norwegian Nobel Committee, Excellencies, Ladies and Gentlemen,

Grameen Bank and I are deeply honoured to receive this most prestigious of awards. We are thrilled and overwhelmed by this honour. Since the Nobel Peace Prize was announced, I have received endless messages from around the world, but what moves me most are the calls I get almost daily, from the borrowers of Grameen Bank in remote Bangladeshi villages, who just want to say how proud they are to have received this recognition.

Nine elected representatives of the 7 million borrowers-cum-owners of Grameen Bank have accompanied me all the way to Oslo to receive the prize. I express thanks on their behalf to the Norwegian Nobel Committee for choosing Grameen Bank for this year's Nobel Peace Prize. By giving their institution the most prestigious prize in the world, you give them unparalleled honour. Thanks to your prize, nine proud women from the villages of Bangladesh are at the ceremony today as Nobel laureates, giving an altogether new meaning to the Nobel Peace Prize.

All borrowers of Grameen Bank are celebrating this day as the greatest   5 day of their lives. They are gathering around the nearest television set in their villages all over Bangladesh, along with other villagers, to watch the proceedings of this ceremony.

This year's prize gives highest honour and dignity to the hundreds of millions of women all around the world who struggle every day to make a living and bring hope for a better life for their children. This is a historic moment for them.

Poverty Is a Threat to Peace
Ladies and Gentlemen:

By giving us this prize, the Norwegian Nobel Committee has given important support to the proposition that peace is inextricably linked to poverty. Poverty is a threat to peace.

World's income distribution gives a very telling story. Ninety-four percent of the world income goes to 40 percent of the population while sixty percent of people live on only 6 percent of world income. Half of the world population lives on two dollars a day. Over one billion people live on less than a dollar a day. This is no formula for peace.

10   The new millennium began with a great global dream. World leaders gathered at the United Nations in 2000 and adopted, among others, a historic goal to reduce poverty by half by 2015. Never in human history had such a bold goal been adopted by the entire world in one voice, one that specified time and size. But then came September 11 and the Iraq war, and suddenly the world became derailed from the pursuit of this dream, with the attention of world leaders shifting from the war on poverty to the war on terrorism. Till now over $530 billion has been spent on the war in Iraq by the USA alone.

I believe terrorism cannot be won over by military action. Terrorism must be condemned in the strongest language. We must stand solidly against it, and find all the means to end it. We must address the root causes of terrorism to end it for all time to come. I believe that putting resources into improving the lives of the poor people is a better strategy than spending it on guns.

Poverty Is Denial of All Human Rights

Peace should be understood in a human way—in a broad social, political and economic way. Peace is threatened by unjust economic, social and political order, absence of democracy, environmental degradation and absence of human rights.

Poverty is the absence of all human rights. The frustrations, hostility and anger generated by abject poverty cannot sustain peace in any society. For building stable peace we must find ways to provide opportunities for people to live decent lives.

The creation of opportunities for the majority of people—the poor—is at the heart of the work that we have dedicated ourselves to during the past 30 years.

Grameen Bank

15   I became involved in the poverty issue not as a policymaker or a researcher. I became involved because poverty was all around me, and I could not turn

away from it. In 1974, I found it difficult to teach elegant theories of economics in the university classroom, in the backdrop of a terrible famine in Bangladesh. Suddenly, I felt the emptiness of those theories in the face of crushing hunger and poverty. I wanted to do something immediate to help people around me, even if it was just one human being, to get through another day with a little more ease. That brought me face to face with poor people's struggle to find the tiniest amounts of money to support their efforts to eke out a living. I was shocked to discover a woman in the village, borrowing less than a dollar from the money-lender, on the condition that he would have the exclusive right to buy all she produces at the price he decides. This, to me, was a way of recruiting slave labor.

I decided to make a list of the victims of this money-lending "business" in the village next door to our campus.

When my list was done, it had the names of 42 victims who borrowed a total amount of US $27. I offered US $27 from my own pocket to get these victims out of the clutches of those money-lenders. The excitement that was created among the people by this small action got me further involved in it. If I could make so many people so happy with such a tiny amount of money, why not do more of it?

That is what I have been trying to do ever since. The first thing I did was to try to persuade the bank located in the campus to lend money to the poor. But that did not work. The bank said that the poor were not creditworthy. After all my efforts, over several months, failed I offered to become a guarantor for the loans to the poor. I was stunned by the result. The poor paid back their loans, on time, every time! But still I kept confronting difficulties in expanding the program through the existing banks. That was when I decided to create a separate bank for the poor, and in 1983, I finally succeeded in doing that. I named it Grameen Bank or Village bank.

Today, Grameen Bank gives loans to nearly 7.0 million poor people, 97 percent of whom are women, in 73,000 villages in Bangladesh. Grameen Bank gives collateral-free income generating, housing, student and micro-enterprise loans to the poor families and offers a host of attractive savings, pension funds and insurance products for its members. Since it introduced them in 1984, housing loans have been used to construct 640,000 houses. The legal ownership of these houses belongs to the women themselves. We focused on women because we found giving loans to women always brought more benefits to the family.

In a cumulative way the bank has given out loans totaling about US $6.0 20 billion. The repayment rate is 99%. Grameen Bank routinely makes profit.

Financially, it is self-reliant and has not taken donor money since 1995. Deposits and own resources of Grameen Bank today amount to 143 percent of all outstanding loans. According to Grameen Bank's internal survey, 58 percent of our borrowers have crossed the poverty line.

Grameen Bank was born as a tiny homegrown project run with the help of several of my students, all local girls and boys. Three of these students are still with me in Grameen Bank, after all these years, as its topmost executives. They are here today to receive this honour you give us.

This idea, which began in Jobra, a small village in Bangladesh, has spread around the world and there are now Grameen type programs in almost every country.

Second Generation

It is 30 years now since we began. We keep looking at the children of our borrowers to see what has been the impact of our work on their lives. The women who are our borrowers always gave topmost priority to the children. One of the Sixteen Decisions developed and followed by them was to send children to school. Grameen Bank encouraged them, and before long all the children were going to school. Many of these children made it to the top of their class. We wanted to celebrate that, so we introduced scholarships for talented students. Grameen Bank now gives 30,000 scholarships every year.

Many of the children went on to higher education to become doctors, engineers, college teachers and other professionals. We introduced student loans to make it easy for Grameen students to complete higher education. Now some of them have PhD's. There are 13,000 students on student loans. Over 7,000 students are now added to this number annually.

25   We are creating a completely new generation that will be well equipped to take their families way out of the reach of poverty. We want to make a break in the historical continuation of poverty.

Beggars Can Turn to Business

In Bangladesh 80 percent of the poor families have already been reached with microcredit. We are hoping that by 2010, 100 percent of the poor families will be reached.

Three years ago we started an exclusive programme focusing on the beggars. None of Grameen Bank's rules apply to them. Loans are interest-free; they can pay whatever amount they wish, whenever they wish. We gave them the idea to carry small merchandise such as snacks, toys or household items, when they went from house to house for begging. The idea worked. There are now 85,000 beggars in the program. About 5,000 of them have already stopped begging completely. Typical loan to a beggar is $12.

We encourage and support every conceivable intervention to help the poor fight out of poverty. We always advocate microcredit in addition to all other interventions, arguing that microcredit makes those interventions work better.

Information Technology for the Poor

Information and communication technology (ICT) is quickly changing the world, creating distanceless, borderless world of instantaneous communications. Increasingly, it is becoming less and less costly. I saw an opportunity for the poor people to change their lives if this technology could be brought to them to meet their needs.

As a first step to bring ICT to the poor we created a mobile phone company, Grameen Phone. We gave loans from Grameen Bank to the poor women to buy mobile phones to sell phone services in the villages. We saw the synergy between microcredit and ICT. 30

The phone business was a success and became a coveted enterprise for Grameen borrowers. Telephone-ladies quickly learned and innovated the ropes of the telephone business, and it has become the quickest way to get out of poverty and to earn social respectability. Today there are nearly 300,000 telephone ladies providing telephone service in all the villages of Bangladesh. Grameen Phone has more than 10 million subscribers, and is the largest mobile phone company in the country. Although the number of telephone-ladies is only a small fraction of the total number of subscribers, they generate 19 percent of the revenue of the company. Out of the nine board members who are attending this grand ceremony today 4 are telephone-ladies.

Grameen Phone is a joint-venture company owned by Telenor of Norway and Grameen Telecom of Bangladesh. Telenor owns 62 percent share of the company, Grameen Telecom owns 38 percent. Our vision was to ultimately convert this company into a social business by giving majority ownership to the poor women of Grameen Bank. We are working towards that goal. Someday Grameen Phone will become another example of a big enterprise owned by the poor.

Free Market Economy

Capitalism centers on the free market. It is claimed that the freer the market, the better is the result of capitalism in solving the questions of what, how, and for whom. It is also claimed that the individual search for personal gains brings collective optimal result.

I am in favor of strengthening the freedom of the market. At the same time, I am very unhappy about the conceptual restrictions imposed on the players in the market. This originates from the assumption that entrepreneurs are one-dimensional human beings, who are dedicated to one mission in their business lives—to maximize profit. This interpretation of capitalism insulates the entrepreneurs from all political, emotional, social, spiritual, environmental dimensions of their lives. This was done perhaps as a reasonable simplification, but it stripped away the very essentials of human life.

35   Human beings are a wonderful creation embodied with limitless human qualities and capabilities. Our theoretical constructs should make room for the blossoming of those qualities, not assume them away.

Many of the world's problems exist because of this restriction on the players of free-market. The world has not resolved the problem of crushing poverty that half of its population suffers. Healthcare remains out of the reach of the majority of the world population. The country with the richest and freest market fails to provide healthcare for one-fifth of its population.

We have remained so impressed by the success of the free-market that we never dared to express any doubt about our basic assumption. To make it worse, we worked extra hard to transform ourselves, as closely as possible, into the one-dimensional human beings as conceptualized in the theory, to allow smooth functioning of free market mechanism.

By defining "entrepreneur" in a broader way we can change the character of capitalism radically, and solve many of the unresolved social and economic problems within the scope of the free market. Let us suppose an entrepreneur, instead of having a single source of motivation (such as, maximizing profit), now has two sources of motivation, which are mutually exclusive, but equally compelling—a) maximization of profit and b) doing good to people and the world.

Each type of motivation will lead to a separate kind of business. Let us call the first type of business a profit-maximizing business, and the second type of business as social business.

Social business will be a new kind of business introduced in the market place with the objective of making a difference in the world. Investors in the social business could get back their investment, but will not take any dividend from the company. Profit would be ploughed back into the company to expand its outreach and improve the quality of its product or service. A social business will be a non-loss, non-dividend company.

Once social business is recognized in law, many existing companies will come forward to create social businesses in addition to their foundation activities. Many activists from the non-profit sector will also find this an attractive option. Unlike the non-profit sector where one needs to collect donations to keep activities going, a social business will be self-sustaining and create surplus for expansion since it is a non-loss enterprise. Social business will go into a new type of capital market of its own, to raise capital.

Young people all around the world, particularly in rich countries, will find the concept of social business very appealing since it will give them a challenge to make a difference by using their creative talent. Many young people today feel frustrated because they cannot see any worthy challenge, which excites them, within the present capitalist world. Socialism gave them a dream to fight for. Young people dream about creating a perfect world of their own.

Almost all social and economic problems of the world will be addressed through social businesses. The challenge is to innovate business models and apply them to produce desired social results cost-effectively and efficiently. Healthcare for the poor, financial services for the poor, information technology for the poor, education and training for the poor, marketing for the poor, renewable energy—these are all exciting areas for social businesses.

Social business is important because it addresses very vital concerns of mankind. It can change the lives of the bottom 60 percent of world population and help them to get out of poverty.

Grameen's Social Business

45   Even profit maximizing companies can be designed as social businesses by giving full or majority ownership to the poor. This constitutes a second type of social business. Grameen Bank falls under this category of social business.

The poor could get the shares of these companies as gifts by donors, or they could buy the shares with their own money. The borrowers with their own money buy Grameen Bank shares, which cannot be transferred to non-borrowers. A committed professional team does the day-to-day running of the bank.

Bilateral and multi-lateral donors could easily create this type of social business. When a donor gives a loan or a grant to build a bridge in the recipient country, it could create a "bridge company" owned by the local poor. A committed management company could be given the responsibility of running the company. Profit of the company will go to the local poor as dividend, and towards building more bridges. Many infrastructure projects, like roads, highways, airports, seaports, utility companies could all be built in this manner.

Grameen has created two social businesses of the first type. One is a yogurt factory, to produce fortified yogurt to bring nutrition to malnourished children, in a joint venture with Danone. It will continue to expand until all malnourished children of Bangladesh are reached with this yogurt. Another is a chain of eye-care hospitals. Each hospital will undertake 10,000 cataract surgeries per year at differentiated prices to the rich and the poor.

Social Stock Market

To connect investors with social businesses, we need to create social stock market where only the shares of social businesses will be traded. An investor will come to this stock-exchange with a clear intention of finding a social business, which has a mission of his liking. Anyone who wants to make money will go to the existing stock-market.

50   To enable a social stock-exchange to perform properly, we will need to create rating agencies, standardization of terminology, definitions, impact measurement tools, reporting formats, and new financial publications, such as, *The Social Wall Street Journal*. Business schools will offer courses and business management degrees on social businesses to train young

managers how to manage social business enterprises in the most efficient manner, and, most of all, to inspire them to become social business entrepreneurs themselves.

Role of Social Businesses in Globalization

I support globalization and believe it can bring more benefits to the poor than its alternative. But it must be the right kind of globalization. To me, globalization is like a hundred-lane highway criss-crossing the world. If it is a free-for-all highway, its lanes will be taken over by the giant trucks from powerful economies. Bangladeshi rickshaw will be thrown off the highway. In order to have a win-win globalization we must have traffic rules, traffic police, and traffic authority for this global highway. Rule of "strongest takes it all" must be replaced by rules that ensure that the poorest have a place and piece of the action, without being elbowed out by the strong. Globalization must not become financial imperialism.

Powerful multi-national social businesses can be created to retain the benefit of globalization for the poor people and poor countries. Social businesses will either bring ownership to the poor people, or keep the profit within the poor countries, since taking dividends will not be their objective. Direct foreign investment by foreign social businesses will be exciting news for recipient countries. Building strong economies in the poor countries by protecting their national interest from plundering companies will be a major area of interest for the social businesses.

We Create What We Want

We get what we want, or what we don't refuse. We accept the fact that we will always have poor people around us, and that poverty is part of human destiny. This is precisely why we continue to have poor people around us. If we firmly believe that poverty is unacceptable to us, and that it should not belong to a civilized society, we would have built appropriate institutions and policies to create a poverty-free world.

We wanted to go to the moon, so we went there. We achieve what we want to achieve. If we are not achieving something, it is because we have not put our minds to it. We create what we want.

What we want and how we get to it depends on our mindsets. It is extremely difficult to change mindsets once they are formed. We create the 55 world in accordance with our mindset. We need to invent ways to change our perspective continually and reconfigure our mindset quickly as new knowledge emerges. We can reconfigure our world if we can reconfigure our mindset.

We Can Put Poverty in the Museums

I believe that we can create a poverty-free world because poverty is not created by poor people. It has been created and sustained by the economic and social system that we have designed for ourselves; the institutions and concepts that make up that system; the policies that we pursue.

Poverty is created because we built our theoretical framework on assumptions which underestimate human capacity, by designing concepts, which are too narrow (such as concept of business, credit-worthiness, entrepreneurship, employment) or developing institutions, which remain half-done (such as financial institutions, where poor are left out). Poverty is caused by the failure at the conceptual level, rather than any lack of capability on the part of people.

I firmly believe that we can create a poverty-free world if we collectively believe in it. In a poverty-free world, the only place you would be able to see poverty is in the poverty museums. When school children take a tour of the poverty museums, they would be horrified to see the misery and indignity that some human beings had to go through. They would blame their forefathers for tolerating this inhuman condition, which existed for so long, for so many people.

A human being is born into this world fully equipped not only to take care of him or herself, but also to contribute to enlarging the well being of the world as a whole. Some get the chance to explore their potential to some degree, but many others never get any opportunity, during their lifetime, to unwrap the wonderful gift they were born with. They die unexplored and the world remains deprived of their creativity, and their contribution.

60   Grameen has given me an unshakeable faith in the creativity of human beings. This has led me to believe that human beings are not born to suffer the misery of hunger and poverty.

To me poor people are like bonsai trees. When you plant the best seed of the tallest tree in a flower-pot, you get a replica of the tallest tree, only inches tall. There is nothing wrong with the seed you planted, only the soil-base that is too inadequate. Poor people are bonsai people. There is nothing wrong in their seeds. Simply, society never gave them the base to grow on. All it needs to get the poor people out of poverty for us to create an enabling environment for them. Once the poor can unleash their energy and creativity, poverty will disappear very quickly.

Let us join hands to give every human being a fair chance to unleash their energy and creativity.

Ladies and Gentlemen,

Let me conclude by expressing my deep gratitude to the Norwegian Nobel Committee for recognizing that poor people, and especially poor women, have both the potential and the right to live a decent life, and that microcredit helps to unleash that potential.

I believe this honor that you give us will inspire many more bold initiatives around the world to make a historical breakthrough in ending global poverty.   65

Thank you very much.

Analyze

1. Yunus claims: "Poverty is a threat to peace." How does he support this claim?
2. How does Yunus define poverty?
3. How does Grameen Bank work? Consult outside sources if necessary.

Explore

1. Yunus imagines a world in which the only place you can see poverty is in a "poverty museum." Is the poverty museum concept a helpful visual? Sketch a room or exhibit in that museum.
2. Yunus says: "If we firmly believe that poverty is unacceptable to us, and that it should not belong to a civilized society, we would have built appropriate institutions and policies to create a poverty-free world. . . . We create what we want." According to this logic, we *want* poverty. Write a researched letter to Yunus responding to this idea.
3. Yunus argues that poor people have the same innate potential as everyone else. They simply weren't given the nourishment from society to grow to their full capacity. Poverty will disappear, he says, if we create an "enabling environment" for everyone. Do you agree? Write an essay in which you explain what it would take to create the kind of enabling environment Yunus envisions.

Sasha Abramsky
"New Help for the Poor:
Cash Grants, Through a Web Site"

A freelance journalist, Sasha Abramsky also serves as a senior fellow at Demos, a think tank focused on economic issues and lending citizens an "equal chance in our economy." He has also authored *The American Way of Poverty: How the Other Half Still Lives*, and his work has appeared in such publications as *The Nation, Slate, Salon*, and *New York Magazine*. In the following article from *The New Yorker*, Abramsky highlights how people are motivated to help others when they are able to personally connect to their specific needs and contribute to small-scale solutions.

Would you prefer to give to a specific person for a specific need as opposed to giving to an organization to support a broad cause?

In Vittorio De Sica's bleak, postwar Italian movie *The Bicycle Thief*, a man is humbled by a personal catastrophe involving a tiny amount of money: unemployed, he is given a chance at a job, but he is required to have a bike to travel to work sites. Antonio Ricci *does* have a battered old bike, but he is in the process of pawning it for food. Undaunted, his wife pawns the family linens instead. All is good until the bike is stolen, leaving Ricci to haunt the markets of Rome while trying to find it. The bicycle is worth about seven thousand lira—just a few dollars—but the loss is devastating; finally, out of options, Ricci makes an ill-fated decision to steal another man's bike in recompense for his own loss. The resulting public humiliation is one of cinema's most awesome, and moving, moments.

But what if the bicycle thief had had other options—like posting his tale on a Web site and soliciting donations for a new bike from strangers?

For almost two years, a Chicago not-for-profit corporation called Benevolent has highlighted the financial challenges of people referred to the site by community groups and nonprofits across the country. Users post a short description of their needs, as well as a Kickstarter-style video appeal to potential donors. Next to each posting is a dollar amount, usually in the several-hundred-dollar range. Donors can give all of the requested amount or a portion of it. Benevolent then sends the money, in the form of a grant, to the referring community group, which funds the client's needs.

Shavon Dossett, for instance, required a hundred and one dollars to take a North Carolina licensing exam after her nursing assistant's license expired. Without it, she couldn't work in the jobs for which she was trained and couldn't properly take care of her three children. "I did a short interview on an iPad," Dossett told me. "They interviewed me about who I am and what goals I was trying to accomplish. We put together the video and they posted it online. Within two weeks my needs were met." Once donors had sent in enough money, Benevolent gave a grant for that amount to Grace-Mar Services Inc., the nonprofit that had been working with Dossett. Grace-Mar then gave her the money. "I was able to take the state exam; I passed it," she said. "I'm working two jobs, I've got an interview with a local hospital—so everything is coming together."

Benevolent's rules are simple. It posts only the stories of clients referred   5
to Benevolent by trusted community groups. The people who post online requests have to be at least eighteen years old and low-income, and they can't seek money to pay off debts. Instead, they have to request one item that will allow them to pursue an opportunity: for instance, a security deposit for an apartment so that a family can get out of homelessness, or money to buy tools for a job, or cash for a laptop computer.

The model has its roots in recent academic research, collectively highlighted at the Experimental Approaches to the Study of Charitable Giving conference held in July of 2007, at Princeton University. The research shows that when people can personally identify with others in need, they respond far more generously than when they're presented with large-scale problems or abstract situations. Our brains like to be told a story—and it turns out that's as true for our interactions with charities as it is for our engagement with great novels.

Cash assistance for the poor has been controversial, with some critics arguing that it doesn't give people the tools they need to improve their situations in sustainable ways. But a set of recent studies of cash assistance for poor communities has found that it can be highly effective: research in Uganda indicated that small infusions of cash, donated as part of a World Bank-funded program, boosted recipients' earnings by forty percent, and increased the value of their business assets by more than fifty percent, on average; it also dramatically increased their consumption of staples such as food. Other research, looking at similar cash-infusion programs in Latin

America, Africa, and Asia, suggests that small cash donations can change a person's economic prospects more than any other single act, with the exception of specific health interventions.

Such findings probably would not have come as a surprise to the economist Milton Friedman. In the nineteen-sixties, Friedman advocated for a "basic income guarantee." Instead of giving poor people funds for specific purposes, he argued, the government should simply guarantee a baseline income level to all Americans, and watch as consumption and wealth expand. No less a conservative than Richard Nixon voiced his support for the plan. Ultimately, however, the plan fizzled: providing subsistence levels of welfare, with all sorts of strings attached, was one thing, but giving the poor unconditional grants to elevate them above the poverty line was seen as going too far.

Benevolent isn't the only site trying to use direct cash grants to help the poor. In 2008, GiveDirectly began allowing people to give cash grants to poor people in Kenya through cell phones. Kiva lets people lend small sums to people in need around the world, with donors choosing whom they will fund. Megan Kashner, Benevolent's founder and a longtime social worker, had been working with nonprofits in Chicago since the early nineteen-nineties, and kept hearing about clients' very specific needs that could not be met financially by those organizations. But what if clients could appeal directly to large numbers of potential donors? "I thought, 'We have the technology now,'" Kashner recalled. She had the idea to encourage people who were already looking to buy feel-good moments by matching them with clients in need. She believed that some clients' stories could even go viral on social-media sites. "People give higher amounts if they know who they're giving to and what it is they are giving for," she said. "People want to meet someone, know *why* the person needs help and *why* the help will make a difference."

10   And so, in 2011, Kashner and a team of volunteers set up Benevolent as a not-for-profit corporation and began developing the Web site. They concentrated on four communities: Chicago; Charlotte, North Carolina; Detroit; and Silicon Valley. Over time, community groups in other states began to send clients Benevolent's way. The site remains small: by late 2013, about a hundred and fifty clients had raised funds.

Last Christmas, Ronni Luther, a retired hairdresser from Royal Oak, Michigan, learned about Benevolent while watching television and decided to check out the site. She signed up for its e-mail blasts and started giving money. Sometimes her giving decisions are entirely random: "I just go 'eeny, meeny, miney, mo,' and that's the one I choose," she told me. Other times, she looks for elements of people's stories that remind her of her own life. "I was a single mother for years, so that goes to my heart," she said. "If I see a single mother in a homeless shelter, those are things I can relate to." In the past year, Luther estimated, she has given small donations—usually around twenty-five dollars—more than thirty times.

Kashner hopes Benevolent can eventually help thousands of people a year. But she's also aware of its limitations. After all, it works only if the clients are seen as "deserving," and if their stories trigger instant empathy from impulse givers. It works when the needs are small, and the solutions fairly easy to visualize—that is, when a small grant to one nonprofit can measurably change a person's life. It breaks down when the people in need are less easy to empathize with, the needs are more complex, or the proposed solutions are long-term or expensive. It also relies on a high level of trust. Without careful vetting of clients by the community groups that come to Benevolent, and without Benevolent having a good sense of the legitimacy of these groups, there's a real risk of fraud. Benevolent believes that it has done a good job monitoring this, but the larger the site becomes the harder it will be to screen all clients perfectly. As the site grows, meanwhile, some individuals' needs may go unmet as donors have more potential clients from whom they can choose.

Still, so far, users feel that Benevolent has given them a valuable opportunity to turn their lives around.

For Danielle King, a trained welder, the assistance meant that, after being homeless for many months, she and her teen-age son could afford the security deposit for an apartment in Westmont, Illinois, outside Chicago. She came up with half the required eleven hundred dollars; donors, responding to the story she posted on Benevolent using a pseudonym, came up with the other half. "They provided me the foundation so I could concentrate on other issues," King said. "That's what they did; they helped me get a foundation."

Analyze

1. What rhetorical purpose does the opening reference to the movie *The Bicycle Thief* serve? Is it effective?
2. How does the nonprofit Benevolent work?
3. What is controversial about cash assistance programs? Outline the different schools of thought on this.

Explore

1. Abramsky writes that "our brains like to be told a story." How does that apply to poverty and nonprofits?

2. Abramsky writes that sites like Benevolent only work if clients appear to be "deserving" to potential donors. Historically, societies have divided the poor into the deserving and the undeserving—those who seem worthy of public assistance and those who don't. In this case, private individuals get to make that call, giving or not, based on their own criteria. Write an essay in which you analyze this privatizing of assistance. Does this advance our ability to assist those in need, or could it in any way re-inscribe old biases?

3. Visit one of the sites mentioned in this article (e.g., Benevolent, Kiva .org, GiveDirectly, or a similar site) and do a rhetorical analysis of the appeals section of the site. Abramsky says such sites are most successful when the potential donors can "empathize" with the clients, which seems most likely if they tell simple stories about the difference a gift will make. Assess how the website is designed to produce empathy. How are the clients represented? Do they speak for themselves, or do others represent them? Is it the "sob story" frame Froomkin (chapter 5) mentions or something different—more complex, authentic, or sophisticated?

Phil Garrity
"Measuring the Immeasurable"

Phil Garrity evaluates the effectiveness of programs within Partners in Health, an organization that aims "to bring the benefits of modern science to those most in need of them and to serve as an antidote to despair" in the world's "poorest and sickest communities." In the following reflection, Garrity articulates how service to others is reciprocal and how intangible indicators are also important aspects of solving poverty.

Have you ever benefited from someone's "ministry of presence" to you, their just being with you in a time of need?

*P*hil Garrity, 25, joined the Partners In Health staff in Boston in 2011 after volunteering with Socios En Salud, PIH's sister organization in Peru. As program coordinator on the Monitoring, Evaluation, and Quality (MEQ) team, he helps measure and evaluate PIH programs to improve quality of care and demonstrate the success of the PIH model.

In August 2012, Garrity was unexpectedly diagnosed with osteosarcoma, an aggressive and rare bone cancer, and began an eight-month treatment program that included surgery and chemotherapy. As he transformed from a servant of the sick to a patient himself, he learned to value an under-appreciated aspect of service, which he terms "non-doing."

Garrity wrote the following reflection, which he read aloud to Partners In Health staff on May 15, 2013, the day his medical team declared him cancer-free, as a message of thanks for their accompaniment throughout his journey.

Over the past two years volunteering and working for PIH, I've been lucky enough to take part in a movement to integrate data-driven quality improvement into our operations. Much of my team's work involves distilling an often nebulous web of people and activities down into a conceptual framework that reflects what is actually happening on the ground. We map out work protocols and data flows, we select process and outcome indicators, we create systems to collect, analyze, and visualize the information— all to gauge three simple but key aspects of our programs: What are we doing? How well are we doing it? How can we make it better?

But without drowning in the details, I'll synthesize all this by saying that much of our work and my role here at PIH continues to place particular emphasis (as it rightly should) on an intrinsic part of serving the poor: the doing. My mind is often focused on what protocols our staff are implementing, how many home visits our community health workers have completed this month, how often our HIV patients have been seen in clinic. You may preoccupy yourself with such questions as how many letters have been sent, web pages designed, meetings scheduled, donors courted, supplies procured, services delivered, money raised. And, logically, we can't know what's being done unless we measure it. Because, as one MEQ site leader once remarked, "If it's not documented, it didn't happen."

But this is where we reach a dilemma. To simply measure the value and quality of our work by the numbers, the performance levels, or the concrete investments of time, energy, and resources seems to neglect another invaluable, but often hidden, dimension of this work: the non-doing. This concept may baffle those of us more accustomed to the rational side of life, for so much of our culture values and rewards the practical and pragmatic, the logical and analytical. The idea of "non-doing" is easily equated to "not doing anything"—nothing more than a futile exercise and utter waste of time. But allow me to reflect on a few personal experiences that have transformed this irrational concept into a mysterious truth, one that I've come to find resonates less with my mind and perhaps more with my spirit.

I'm drawn back to my time volunteering with a local nonprofit in Cusco, Peru, in the months preceding my internship with Socios En Salud. A few days each week, I'd help out at a nursing home for the destitute run by an order of kind yet stern nuns who led by rigid example and hardly ever by word. Feigning competence, I'd be handed a pot and ladle and I would feed the ancianos; handed a bottle of ointment, I'd rub it on their itchy legs; handed a pair of clippers, I'd trim their overgrown toenails—all of this often done in total silence, even lathering and shaving the old men's faces, eight of whom were blind. Their quiet gratitude for something so simple and seemingly trivial astounded me then and perhaps more so today as I look back and wonder what it all meant.

At the time, I was beginning to delve into questions that would serve me well in Lima and later in Boston: What were we really trying to achieve here? What were our goals and how close or far were we from reaching them? The long hours of just sitting with these old people, hearing their stories, tending to them in what small ways I could—it seemed nice enough, but was it doing anything of real value, at least as I understood it then? My mind would drift to hypotheticals somewhere beyond the confines of that small, quiet refuge. Shouldn't I be saving children from starvation, protecting refugees from mortal danger, pulling this country out of poverty and into the 21st century? After all, I had come here to rescue people from their lot, to save helpless victims from suffering and injustice. This place seemed so stagnant, these people so quiet and inert. What was I doing here?

Early one morning, we found a frail old man had fallen and broken his hip in the middle of the night. His groans and whimpers suggested he had been without pain relief for hours, and he needed to get to the hospital. We placed him on a wooden board, loaded him into the church's van, and were off. I rode alongside him, anxious yet keenly aware of my inability to do much of anything for the poor man. Once there, it pained me to see him relegated to a corner of a busy emergency room where he simply had to wait his turn to be seen. Hours went by and I sat near him, wallowing in the helplessness that I now shared with him. What could I do? I felt that I had failed to be the protector, the helper, the healer—not for an entire country, but even for this one feeble man.

Our driver, a seasoned caretaker from the nursing home, came in with   10 some bread and juice for the man, who silently accepted the gift and began nibbling away, partly concealed underneath the sheets draped over his stretcher. I sat and watched him intently with a mixture of exhaustion and pity as he littered himself with crumbs and peered out at me, eyes gleaming. It was then that something miraculous happened: the old man broke his bread roll in half and stretched out his hand toward mine. An acute sense of surprise and embarrassment came over me, and at first I refused his offer, insisting that he eat it, for surely he needed it more than I. But my feeble attempts to decline the gift were wholeheartedly dismissed as he pushed the bread into my hand, motioning me to eat. And so I did, me looking bewildered and humbled, he looking quite pleased to share his meal with a near stranger.

Moments like these continue to deepen my understanding of what it means to embrace the non-doing. It's come to mean being brave enough to disarm myself, to set aside my intellectual firepower and self-protective shields, and to enter into another's chaos—not to do for them, but to simply be with them. It takes courage to sit in that silence, often empty-handed, and humbly accept the lesson that that feeble man so beautifully demonstrated that day: that I am as much the patient as he is the healer. That he is not a broken machine idly waiting to be fixed by the "non-broken," the "privileged," the "fortunate" among us. I believe that those we intend to serve have bread to offer us every day—humble reminders that we are co-creators in the promotion of life, gentle invitations to discard our pity and crawl down into the pit with another. In these precious moments, we're able to see our shared vulnerability as humans and to simply open ourselves to it, perhaps without much of any real hope of fixing anything in that moment or hour or day.

Beyond all of the things we do to act in service for the poor—delivering medical supplies, building health systems, strengthening human capacity—I've come to believe that there is something far more powerful in simply being in service with those in need. We might consider this other dimension of our work a ministry of presence—one that underlies and encapsulates all of our tangible efforts to console, to palliate, to rebuild in the face of disease and distress. I would argue that this is our strategic advantage among those in the vast arena of development work: that we do not walk away when things appear impractical, unfeasible, or futile. We stay, to perhaps accept defeat again and again, if only to show the world that the people we serve are worth more than the steps they may gain or lose on their path to a more dignified life. That we ourselves are worth more than our successes or failures on our path to building a more just world.

I see more clearly now how all my dissecting questions obscured the real meaning in those quiet gestures at the nursing home. Our collective attempts to concretize an abstract world—to understand the mechanics of material privation, to design interventions and harness resources that achieve a positive and quantifiable effect on the lives of the poor—can create the illusion that fixing is our only aim, that we must constantly be doing if we are to succeed. We can believe that if we can't show progress, then none has been made. And so we easily fall into the trap of making systems and machines out of countries, communities, and individuals—broken devices that only we can fix.

But real solidarity, true compassion, as I've come to discover through lived experience these past eight months, is grounded in something far deeper than our displays of technical prowess or standard notions of progress. It evades our attempts to capture its value with metrics and analytics, and perhaps for good reason. I believe it's revealed through an earnest and humble kind of love, one that neither feigns strength nor fears weakness. It can simply sit with another in the silence, not feeling frantic to fill it with words or deeds. It has the courage to look into the darkness of our finitude—both of our bodies and of our ambitions—which we all face, not just the sick. It can trust in the value of non-doing, of simply being present.

15   And so I say all of this as a hopeful reminder for each of us to restore a balance between what we do and who we are, being careful to not forget the unconditional value of the latter. Because at our core we are radical love, we are goodness, we are justice—a core that cannot be marred or diluted by all the apathy, cynicism, and resistance the world might throw at it, a world of practicality that tries to convince us that our efforts to transform it will inevitably fall short, that our gestures of good will are in vain, that we have not done enough today. It is from this core of being that we are able to

infuse what we do with the goodness that we are—to make possible real healing, both visible and invisible, that often can't be measured.

I thank all of you for helping me to live out this truth and for being who you are, far beyond what you do.

Analyze

1. Describe the "doing" part of Garrity's work.
2. Describe the "non-doing" that Garrity now recognizes as critical to his work as well. What is another term he uses to describe this later in the essay?
3. What is the "something miraculous" that happens while Garrity waits with an old man with a broken hip in a Peruvian hospital?

Explore

1. Garrity explores the tension he feels between his expectations of "doing" with the reality that some of his work involves "non-doing." He writes of his work at a nursing home in Peru: "I had come here to rescue people from their lot, to save helpless victims from suffering and injustice. This place seemed so stagnant, these people so quiet and inert. What was I doing here?" Can you identify with Garrity's "drive to do"? Is that drive uniquely American? Male? White? Privileged? Youthful? What are the advantages or disadvantages of possessing that "drive to do"?
2. How does Garrity define and/or exemplify "real solidarity" and "true compassion"? Describe your own examples and observations of this.
3. Write a researched response to Garrity, either framed as a letter or blog post. Explain what does and does not resonate for you in his analysis of these two modes of serving and implementing solutions to problems like poverty. Is the intimate, relational non-doing of being with another human in need going to solve poverty? If you haven't ever done the type of one-on-one relational service Garrity describes, before writing, consider volunteering at a nursing home, correctional facility, or homeless center in a position that lets you get to know people personally so that you can understand the mode of non-doing Garrity describes.

David Bornstein et al.
"Solutions Journalism Network: Questions and Checklist"

David Bornstein is a journalist, author, and co-founder of Solutions Journalism Network, which aims to help journalists engage in "solutions journalism," reporting about responses to big social problems. He has authored books about developing social innovations and solving major social problems, including *How To Change the World, The Price of a Dream: The Story of the Grameen Bank*, and *Social Entrepreneurship: What Everyone Needs to Know*. He also co-authors the "Fixes" column in the "Opinionator" section of the *New York Times*, reporting on how people and organizations are working to solve major social problems. In the following list published on SolutionsJournalism.org, he offers 10 questions to guide journalists covering solutions-based stories.

In your own writing, do you tend to focus more on problems or solutions?

Here are 10 questions to ask yourself when writing a solutions-oriented story. Not every story will address all of these questions, and that's okay—but we hope this will inspire your thinking:

1. **Does the story explain the causes of a social problem?** A solution should be explained in the context of the problem it's trying to address. The causes of that problem should be documented in ways that make clear the opportunity for a solution to create leverage and impact.

2. **Does the story present an associated response to that problem?** The acid test; if the story doesn't describe a response, it's not solutions journalism.

3. **Does the story get into the problem solving and how-to details of implementation?** A great solutions story delves into the how-to's of problem solving, investigating questions like: What models are having success improving an educational outcome and how do they actually work?

4. **Is the problem solving process central to the narrative?** Solutions journalism, like all journalism, is about great story telling. It should include characters grappling with challenges, experimenting, succeeding, failing, learning. But the narrative is driven by the problem solving and the tension is located in the inherent difficulty in solving a problem.

5. **Does the story present evidence of results linked to the response?** Solutions journalism is about ideas—but like all good journalism, the determination of what works (or doesn't) and how is supported by solid data and evidence.

6. **Does the story explain the limitations of the response?** There is no such thing as a perfect solution to a social problem. Every response has caveats, limitations, and risks. Good solutions journalism does not shy away from imperfection.

7. **Does the story convey an insight or teachable lesson?** What makes solutions journalism compelling is the discovery—the journey that brings the reader or viewer to an insight about how the world works and, perhaps, how it could be made to work better.

8. **Does the story avoid reading like a puff piece?** Solutions journalism is expressly not about advocating for particular models, organizations or ideas. Journalists pursuing solutions stories are bringing their journalistic tools to bear on reporting, examining, and writing without a specific agenda.

9. **Does the story draw on sources who have a ground-level understanding, not just 30,000-foot expertise?** Beyond politicians and researchers from think tanks, solutions stories should consult and quote people who are working in the trenches and knowledgeable about the on-the ground realities of an issue.

10. **Does the story give greater attention to the response than to a leader/innovator/do-gooder?** We see a clear distinction between solutions journalism and what is often called "good news." "Good news" stories tend to celebrate individuals and inspirational acts. Solutions journalism is about ideas, how people are trying to make them work, and their observable effects.

Here's another way to think about solutions journalism—in a checklist format. Does your story do some of these?

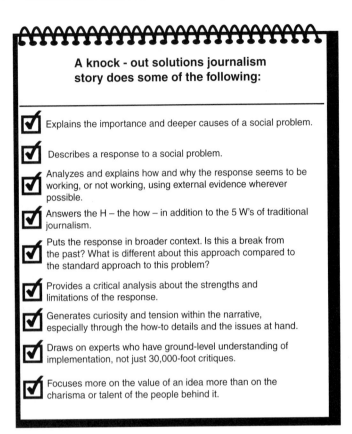

Figure 6.1

Analyze

1. What is the "acid test" to see if a story about a social problem counts as solutions journalism?
2. Solutions journalism avoids the "puff piece" frame. What is that and why should it be avoided?
3. Solutions journalism also avoids the "good news" frame. What is that and why should it be avoided?

Explore

1. Visit SolutionsJournalism.org. Do a rhetorical analysis of one of their stories as a solutions journalism model. Does it meet the criteria outlined in the questions and checklist?

2. Apply the solutions journalism frame to a reading in this book. Do a rhetorical analysis in which you identify ways in which it meets or does not meet the criteria outlined here.

3. Identify a news story about poverty from the past week. In what ways does it meet or not meet the criteria for solutions journalism? If it diverges from those criteria, explain how and whether it seems successful in its purpose.

Forging Connections

1. Several of the readings in this chapter (e.g., Abramsky, Banerjee and Duflo, Buffett, Garrity, Karlan and Appel, Theroux, Yunus) stress the importance of creating solutions informed by people who live in poverty. That could mean people with many resources spending significant time with those in poverty, or it could mean inviting people in poverty to participate directly in solutions. Research one antipoverty program, either governmental or private, and analyze the extent to which people in poverty helped to design and implement that program. For example, Yunus included the poor in the administration of Grameen Bank (and in his acceptance lecture for the Nobel Prize). What are the practical and ethical advantages and disadvantages of designing programs for the poor *with* the poor?

2. Karlan and Appel write, "Whether we like it or not, for most of us there's an element of social display mixed up in our motivations for giving." What do they mean? Would we be as generous if people didn't know how generous we were? Does it matter if social display motivates giving if it results in gifts that help the poor? Consult readings in this chapter (e.g., Abramsky, Bornstein et al., Buffett, Karlan and Appel, Sanders and Lehrer, Theroux) and outside research to help you write a persuasive argument in which you analyze the role of social display (by individuals, politicians, even countries) in designing and implementing solutions to poverty.

Looking Further

1. Banerjee and Duflo quote their exchange with a poor man in Morocco whom they notice has bought a TV instead of the food he just told them he needs. He replies: "Oh, but television is more important than food!" Compare and contrast this idea to other readings

(e.g., McMillan Cottom, Rector and Sheffield) that address the role of material goods. Can a television, and other materials of high social value, benefit the poor more than food?

2. Compassion often drives people to act when confronted with suffering. But can compassion cloud judgment? If we want to reduce poverty and relieve suffering, shouldn't we be as efficient and effective as possible? Readings in this book (e.g., Banerjee and Duflo, Buffett, Cole, Karlan and Appel, O'Connor, Theroux, Wright) show ways that our good intentions can go wrong. Policies meant to encourage work sometimes discourage it. Programs meant to feed the poor can lead them to eat less. Write a researched proposal argument in which you recommend an antipoverty policy or program for a local, national, or international organization. Temper your compassion with informed argument. Explain why the stakeholders in this community should support this policy or program at this time.

A Guide for Researching and Writing about Poverty/Privilege

Barbara Rockenbach and Aaron Ritzenberg[1]

Research-based writing lies at the heart of the mission of higher education: to discover, transform, and share ideas. As a college student, it is through writing and research that you become an active participant in an intellectual community. Doing research in college involves not only searching for information but also digesting, analyzing, and synthesizing what you find in order to create new knowledge. Your most successful efforts as a college writer will report on the latest and most important ideas in a field, as well as make new arguments and offer fresh insights.

It may seem daunting to be asked to contribute new ideas to a field in which you are a novice. After all, creating new knowledge seems to be in the realm of experts. In this guide, we offer strategies that demystify the research and writing process, breaking down some of the fundamental steps that scholars take when they do research and make arguments. You will see that contributing to scholarship involves strategies that can be learned and practiced.

Throughout this guide we imagine doing research and writing as engaging in a scholarly conversation. When you read academic writing, you will notice

[1]Barbara Rockenbach, director of Humanities & History Libraries, Columbia University. Aaron Ritzenberg, associate director of First-Year Writing, Columbia University.

that scholars cite studies that came before their own and allude to studies that may grow out of their research. When you think of research as engaging in a conversation, you quickly realize that scholarship always has a social aspect. Even if you like to find books in the darkest corners of the library, even if you like to draft your essays in deep solitude, you will always be aware of the voices that helped you form your ideas and the audience who will receive them. As if in conversation at a party, scholars mingle: They listen to others and share their most recent ideas, learning and teaching at the same time. Strong scholars, like good conversationalists, listen and speak with an open mind, letting their own thoughts evolve as they encounter new ideas.

You may be wondering, "What does it mean to have an open mind when I'm doing research? After all, aren't I supposed to find evidence that supports my thesis?" We will return to this question soon, but the quick answer is: To have an open mind when you're doing research means that you will be involved in the research process well before you have a thesis. We realize that this may be a big change from the way you think about research. The fact is, though, that scholars do research well before they know any of the arguments they will be making in their papers. Indeed, scholars do research even before they know what specific topic they will be addressing and what questions they will be asking.

When scholars do research, they may not know exactly what they are hunting for, but they have techniques that help them define projects, identify strong interlocutors, and ask important questions. This guide will help you move through the various kinds of research that you will need at the different stages of your project. If writing a paper involves orchestrating a conversation within a scholarly community, there are a number of important questions you will need to answer: How do I choose what to write about? How do I find a scholarly community? How do I orchestrate a conversation that involves this community? Whose voices should be most prominent? How do I enter the conversation? How do I use evidence to make a persuasive claim? How do I make sure that my claim is not just interesting but important?

GETTING STARTED

You have been asked to write a research paper. This might be your first research paper at the college level. Where do you start? The important thing when embarking on any kind of writing project that involves research is to find something that you are interested in learning more about. Writing and research are easier if you care about your topic. Your instructor may have given you a topic, but you can make that topic your own by finding something that appeals to you within the scope of the assignment.

Academic writing begins from a place of deep inquiry. When you are sincerely interested in a problem, researching can be a pleasure, since it will satisfy your own intellectual curiosity. More important, the intellectual problems that seem most difficult—the questions that appear to resist obvious answers—are the very problems that will often yield the most surprising and rewarding results.

PRESEARCHING TO GENERATE IDEAS

When faced with a research project, your first instinct might be to go to Google or Wikipedia, or even to a social media site. This is not a bad instinct. In fact, Google, Wikipedia, and social media can be great places to start. Using Google, Wikipedia, and social media to help you discover a topic is what we call "presearching"—it is what you do to warm up before the more rigorous work of academic research. Academic research and writing will require you to go beyond these sites to find resources that will make the work of researching and writing both easier and more appropriate to an academic context.

Google

Let's start with Google. You use Google because you know you are going to find a simple search interface that will produce many results. These results may not be completely relevant to your topic, but Google helps in the discovery phase of your work. For instance, let's say you are asked to write about the impact of poverty on children.

A Google search will produce articles from many diverse sources— magazines, government sites, and corporate reports among them. It's not a bad start. Use these results to begin to hone in on an issue you are interested in pursuing. A quick look through these results may yield a more focused issue such as how poverty affects the way children perform in school or make friends.

Wikipedia

A Wikipedia search on children and poverty will lead you to several articles that address both concepts. The great thing about Wikipedia is that it is an

| Google | impact of poverty on children | |

Web   News   Images   Videos   Shopping   More ▾   Search tools

About 59,000,000 results (0.47 seconds)

The Effects of Poverty - PracticalAction.org   ⓘ
[Ad] www.practicalaction.org/Poverty ▾ Practical Action ▾
Learn About the **Poverty Effects** on **Children** in Developing Countries.

Effects Of Poverty On Children - childrensdefense.org
[Ad] www.childrensdefense.org/ ▾ Children's Defense Fund ▾
State of America's **Children** 2014 **Children's** Defense Fund
Children's Defense Fund has 148 followers on Google+

How **Poverty** Affects **Children** - GrameenFoundation.org
[Ad] www.grameenfoundation.org/ ▾ Grameen Foundation ▾
Help provide the poor with loans that empower them to succeed.

Scholarly articles for **impact of poverty on children**
The **impact** of **poverty** on the mental health and ... - Aber - Cited by 148
The effects of **poverty** on **children** - Brooks-Gunn - Cited by 1624

Effects of Poverty, Hunger, and Homelessness on **Children** ...
https://www.apa.org/pi/.../**poverty**.as... ▾ American Psychological Association ▾
Where **child poverty** is concentrated, the **effects** of youth **poverty** regarding academic
achievement, psychosocial outcomes and physical health, the prevalence ...

Google   Results of a Google search for "impact of poverty on children."

easy way to gain access to a wealth of information about thousands of topics. However, it is crucial to realize that Wikipedia itself is not an authoritative source in a scholarly context. Even though you may see Wikipedia cited in mainstream newspapers and popular magazines, academic researchers do not consider Wikipedia a reliable source and do not cite it in their own research. Wikipedia itself says that "Wikipedia is not considered a credible source. . . . This is especially true considering that anyone can edit the information given at any time." For research papers in college, you should use Wikipedia only to find basic information about your topic and to point you toward scholarly sources. Wikipedia may be a great starting point for presearch, but it is not an adequate ending point for research. Use the references section at the bottom of a Wikipedia article to find other, more substantive and authoritative resources about your topic.

Using Social Media
Social media such as Facebook and Twitter can be useful in the presearch phase of your project, but you must start thinking about these tools in new ways. You may have a Facebook or Twitter account and use it to keep in touch with friends, family, and colleagues. These social networks are

Facebook Facebook page for the Institute for Research on Poverty.

valuable, and you may already use them to gather information to help you make decisions in your personal life and your workplace. Although social media are not generally useful to your academic research, both Facebook and Twitter have powerful search functions that can lead you to resources and help you refine your ideas.

After you log in to Facebook, use the "Search for people, places, and things" bar at the top of the page to begin. When you type search terms into this bar, Facebook will first search your own social network. To extend beyond your own network, try adding the word "research" after your search terms. For instance, a search on Facebook for "poverty research" will lead you to a Facebook page for the Institute for Research on Poverty. The posts on the page link to current news stories on poverty, describe similar research centers, and explore topics of interest in the field of poverty research. You can use these search results as a way to see part of the conversation about a particular topic. This is not necessarily the scholarly conversation we referred to at the start of this guide, but it is a social conversation that can still be useful in helping you determine what you want to focus on in the research process.

Twitter is an information network where users can post short messages (or "tweets"). Although many people use Twitter simply to update their friends ("I'm going to the mall" or "Can't believe it's snowing!"), more and

References [edit]

1. ^ "Convention on the Rights of the Child"[1] 📄 (1989) Office of the United Nations High Commissioner for Human Rights
2. ^ Childfund (2005) "Child and Poverty, Part I" Downloadable at 🔗
3. ^ *a b* "THE STATE OF THE WORLD'S CHILDREN... 20010" 📄
4. ^ Childfund (2005) "Understanding Children's Experience of Poverty: An Introduction to the DEV Framework" Downloadable at [2] 🔗
5. ^ Childhood Poverty Research and Policy Center (CHIP) (2005) "CHIP Briefing 1: Children and Poverty" [3] 🔗
6. ^ *a b c d* UNICEF (2006) "Children Living In Poverty" 📄
7. ^ Roelen, Keetie and Gassmann, Franziska (2008) "Measuring Child Poverty and Well-Being: a literature review" Maastricht Graduate School of Governance, Maastricht University (pdf available at the Munich Personal RePEc Archive) (MPRA) [4] 📄
8. ^ *a b* Citro and Michael (1995) "Introduction and overview"[5] 📄 in *Measuring Child Poverty and Well-Being: a literature review* National Academy Press, page 31 (downloadable from US Census site [6] 🔗)
9. ^ [World Bank http://devdata.worldbank.org/wdi2005/Section1_1_1.htm 🔗]
10. ^ [International Monetary Fund http://www.imf.org/external/np/sec/pr/2007/pr0773.htm 🔗]
11. ^ *a b* UNICEF (2005) "Child Poverty in Rich Countries 2005" 📄

Wikipedia List of references from a Wikipedia search on child poverty. Use these links to further your research.

more individuals and organizations use Twitter to comment on noteworthy events or link to interesting articles. You can use Twitter as a presearch tool because it aggregates links to sites, people in a field of research, and noteworthy sources. Communities, sometimes even scholarly communities, form around topics on Twitter. Users group posts together by using hashtags—words or phrases that follow the "#" sign. Users can respond to other users by using the @ sign followed by a user's Twitter name. When searching for specific individuals or organizations on Twitter, you search using their handle (such as @barackobama or @whitehouse). You will retrieve tweets that were created either by the person or organization, or tweets that mention the person or organization. When searching for a topic to find discussions, you search using the hashtag symbol, #. For instance, a search on #poverty will take you to tweets and threaded discussions on the topic of poverty that address such issues as unemployment, homelessness, hunger, and affordable healthcare.

There are two ways to search Twitter. You can use the search book in the upper right corner and enter either a @ or # search as described above. Once you retrieve results, you can search again by clicking on any words that are hyperlinked within your results, such as #antipoverty.

If you consider a hashtag (#) as an entry point into a community, you will begin to discover a conversation around topics. For instance, a search on Twitter for #poverty leads you to @povertynews, the handle for Spotlight on Poverty, a news aggregator for poverty coverage. Major news sources from around the world are also active in Twitter, so articles, videos, interviews, and other resources from the news media will be retrieved in a search. Evaluating information and sources found in social media is similar to the way you evaluate any information you encounter during the research process. And, as with Wikipedia and Google searches, this is just a starting point to help you get a sense of the spectrum of topics. This is no substitute for using library resources. Do not cite Facebook, Twitter, or Wikipedia in a research paper; use them to find more credible, authoritative sources. We will talk about evaluating sources in the sections that follow.

CREATE A CONCEPT MAP

Once you have settled on a topic that you find exciting and interesting, the next step is to generate search terms, or keywords, for effective searching. Keywords are the crucial terms or phrases that signal the content of any given source. Keywords are the building blocks of your search for information. We have already seen a few basic keywords such as "poverty" and "children." One way to generate keywords is to tell a friend or classmate what you are interested in. What words are you using to describe your research project? You may not have a fully formed idea or claim, but you have a vague sense of your interest. A concept map exercise can help you generate more keywords and, in many cases, narrow your topic to make it more manageable.

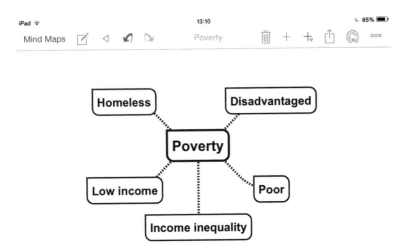

Concept Map   A concept map about poverty.

A concept map is a way to visualize the relationship between concepts or ideas. You can create a concept map on paper, or there are many free programs online that can help you do this (see, for instance, http://vue.tufts .edu or http://wisemapping.com). There are many concept-mapping applications available for mobile devices; the concept map here was created using the SimpleMind app.

Here is how you use a concept map. First, begin with a term like "poverty." Put that term in the first box. Then think of synonyms or related words to describe poverty such as "poor," "homeless," "low income," "disadvantaged," and "income inequality." This brainstorming process will help you develop keywords for searching. Notice that keywords can also be short phrases.

After some practice, you will discover that some phrases make for excellent keywords and others make for less effective search tools. The best keywords are precise enough to narrow your topic so that all of your results are relevant, but not so specific that you might miss helpful results. Concept maps created using apps such as SimpleMind allow you to use templates, embed hyperlinks, and attach notes, among other useful functions.

KEYWORD SEARCH

One of the hardest parts of writing is coming up with something to write about. Too often, we make the mistake of waiting until we have a fully formed idea before we start writing. The process of writing can actually help you discover what your idea is, and most important, what is interesting about that idea.

Keyword searches are most effective at the beginning stages of your research. They generally produce the most number of results and can help you determine how much has been written on your topic. Use keyword searches to retrieve a manageable number of results. What is manageable? This is a key question when beginning research. Our keyword search in Google on "children and poverty" produced almost three million results. The same search in JSTOR.org produced almost 200,000 results. These are not manageable results. Let's see how we can narrow our search.

Keyword searches in library resources or on Google are most effective if you employ a few search strategies that will focus your results.

1. Use quotation marks around a phrase and use AND when you are combining multiple keywords. We used this search construction:

   children AND poverty

The AND ensures that all your results will contain both the terms "children" and "poverty." Many search engines and databases will assume an AND search, meaning that if you type "children poverty," the search will automatically look for all terms. However, in some cases, the AND will not be assumed and "children poverty" will be treated as a phrase. Worse yet, sometimes the search automatically assumes an OR. That would mean that all your results would come back with either children or poverty. This will produce a large and mostly irrelevant set of results. Therefore, use AND whenever you want two or more words to appear in a result.

2. Using OR can be very effective when you want to use several terms to describe a concept such as:

   poverty OR poor OR homeless

A search on children and poverty can be broadened to include particular kinds of poverty. The following search casts a broader net because results will come back with children and either poverty, poor, or homeless:

   children AND (poverty OR poor OR homeless)

3. Use quotation marks when looking for a phrase. For instance, if you are looking for information on childhood development and poverty's impact on educational attainment, you can ensure that the search results will include all of these concepts and increase the relevance by using the following search construction:

> "childhood development" AND poverty AND "educational attainment"

This phrasing will return results that contain the word poverty and both the phrases "childhood development" and "educational attainment."

4. Use NOT to exclude terms that will make your search less relevant. You may find that a term keeps appearing in your search that is not useful. Try this:

> "poverty" NOT global

If you are interested in poverty in the U.S., getting a lot of results that discuss global poverty might be distracting. By excluding the keyword "global," you will retrieve far fewer sources and hopefully more relevant results.

RESEARCHABLE QUESTION

In a college research paper, it is important that you make an argument, not just offer a report. In high school, you might have found some success by merely listing or cataloging the data and information you found; you might have offered a series of findings to show your teacher that you investigated your topic. In college, however, your readers will not be interested in data or information merely for its own sake; your readers will want to know what you make of this data and why they should care.

In order to satisfy the requirements of a college paper, you will need to distinguish between a topic and a research question. You will likely begin with a topic, but it is only when you move from a topic to a question that your research will begin to feel motivated and purposeful. A topic refers only to the general subject area that you'll be investigating. A researchable question, on the other hand, points toward a specific problem in the subject area that you will be attempting to answer by making a claim about the evidence you examine.

"Children and poverty" is a topic, but not a researchable question. It is important that you ask yourself, "What aspect of the topic is most interesting to me?" It is even more important that you ask, "What aspect of the topic is it most important that I illuminate for my audience?" Ideally, your presearch phase of the project will yield questions about children and poverty that you would like to investigate.

A strong researchable question will not lead to an easy answer, but rather will lead you into a scholarly conversation in which there are many competing claims. For instance, the question "Which region of the U.S. has the highest childhood poverty rate?" is not a strong research question because there is only one correct answer and therefore no scholarly debate surrounding the topic. It is an interesting question, but it will not lead you into a scholarly conversation.

When you are interested in finding a scholarly debate, try using the words "why" and "how" rather than "what." Instead of leading to a definitive answer, the words "why" and "how" will often lead to complex, nuanced answers for which you will need to marshal evidence in order to be convincing. "Why is the childhood poverty rate in the South so much higher than in other regions of the U.S.?" is a question that has a number of complex and competing answers that might draw from a number of different disciplines (political science, history, economics, and geography, among others). If you can imagine scholars having an interesting debate about your researchable question, it is likely that you have picked a good one.

Once you have come up with an interesting researchable question, your first task as a researcher is to figure out how scholars are discussing your question. Many novice writers think that the first thing they should do when beginning a research project is to articulate an argument, then find sources that confirm their argument. This is not how experienced scholars work. Instead, strong writers know that they cannot possibly come up with a strong central argument until they have done sufficient research. So, instead of looking for sources that confirm a preliminary claim you might want to make, look for the scholarly conversation.

Looking at the scholarly conversation is a strong way to figure out if you've found a research question that is suitable in scope for the kind of paper you are writing. Put another way, reading the scholarly conversation can tell you if your research question is too broad or too narrow. Most novice writers begin with research questions that are overly broad. If your question is so broad that there are thousands of books and articles participating in the scholarly conversation, it's a good idea for you to focus your question so that you are asking something more specific. If, on the other hand, you are asking a research question that is so obscure that you cannot find a corresponding scholarly conversation, you will want to broaden the scope of your project by asking a slightly less specific question.

Keep in mind the metaphor of a conversation. If you walk into a room and people are talking about children and poverty, it would be out of place for you to begin immediately by making a huge, vague claim, such as "childhood poverty affects many life outcomes." It would be equally out of place for you to begin immediately by making an overly specific claim, such as "poverty makes it difficult for children to form lasting friendships, which later causes them to commit crimes." Rather, you would gauge the scope of the conversation and figure out what seems like a reasonable contribution.

Your contribution to the conversation, at this point, will likely be a focused research question. This is the question you take with you to the library. In the next section, we discuss how best to make use of the library. Later, we explore how to turn your research question into an argument for your essay.

YOUR CAMPUS LIBRARY

You have probably used libraries all your life, checking out books from your local public library and studying in your high school library. The difference between your previous library experiences and your college library experience is one of scale. Your college library has more "stuff." It may be real stuff like books, journals, and videos, or it may be virtual stuff, like online articles, e-books, and streaming videos. Your library pays a lot of money every year to buy or license content for you to use for your research. By extension, your tuition dollars are buying a lot of really good research material. Resorting to Google and Wikipedia means that you are not getting all you can out of your college experience.

Not only will your college library have a much larger collection, it will have a more up-to-date and relevant collection than your high school or community public library. Academic librarians spend considerable time acquiring research materials based on classes being taught at your institution. You may not know it, but librarians carefully monitor what courses are being taught each year and are constantly trying to find research materials appropriate to those courses and your professors' research interests. In many cases, you will find that the librarians know about your assignment and will already have ideas about the types of sources that will make you most successful.

Get to Know Your Librarians!

The most important thing to know during the research process is that there are people to help you. Although you may not yet be in the habit of going to the library, there are still many ways in which librarians and library staff can be helpful. Most libraries now have an e-mail or chat service set up so you can ask questions without even setting foot in the actual building. No question is too basic or too specific. It's a librarian's job to help you find answers, and all questions are welcome. The librarian can even help you discover the right question to ask given the task you are trying to complete.

Help can also come in the form of consultations. Librarians will often make appointments to meet one-on-one with you to offer in-depth help on a research paper or project. Chances are you will find a link on your library website for scheduling a consultation.

Among the many questions fielded by reference librarians, three stand out as the most often asked. Because librarians hear these questions with such regularity, we suggest that students ask these questions when they begin their research. You can go to the library and ask these questions in person, or you can ask vie e-mail or online chat.

1. How do I find a book relevant to my topic?   The answer to this question will vary from place to place, but the thing to remember is that finding a book can be either a physical or a virtual process. Your library will have books on shelves somewhere, and the complexity of how those shelves are organized and accessed depends on factors of size, number of libraries, and the system of organization your library uses. You will find books by using your library's online catalog and carefully noting the call number and location of a book.

Your library is also increasingly likely to offer electronic books or e-books. These books are discoverable in your library's online catalog as well. When looking at the location of a book, you will frequently see a link for e-book versions. You will not find an e-book in every search, but when

Online catalog   Library catalog search for books about social media.

you do, the advantage is that e-book content is searchable, making your job of finding relevant material in the book easier.

If you find one book on your topic, use it as a jumping-off point for finding more books or articles on that topic. Most books will have bibliographies either at the end of each chapter or the end of the book in which the author has compiled all the sources they used. Consult these bibliographies to find other materials on your topic. You can also return to the book's listing in your library's online catalog. Once you find the listing, look carefully at the record for links to subjects, topics, or similar sources. For instance, on the Northwestern Michigan College library catalog, individual listings include the following links: "Find more by this author," "Find more on this topic," and "Nearby items on shelf."

2. What sources can I use as evidence in my paper?   There are many types of resources out there to use as you orchestrate a scholarly conversation and support your paper's argument. Books, which we discussed earlier, are great sources if you can find them on your topic, but often your research question will be something that is either too new or too specific for a book to cover. Books are very good for historical questions and overviews of large topics. For current topics, you will want to explore articles from magazines, journals, and newspapers.

Magazines or periodicals (you will hear these terms used interchangeably) are published on a weekly or monthly schedule and contain articles of popular interest. These sources can cover broad topics like the news in magazines such as *Newsweek*, *Time*, and *U.S. News and World Report*. They can also be more focused for particular groups like farmers (*Dairy Farmer*) or photographers (*Creative Photography*). Articles in magazines or periodicals are by professional writers who may or may not be experts. Magazines typically are not considered scholarly and generally do not contain articles with bibliographies, endnotes, or footnotes. This does not mean they are not good sources for your research. In fact, there may be very good reasons to use a magazine article to help support your argument. Magazines capture the point of view of a particular group on a subject, like how farmers feel about government subsidies that incentivize them to produce crops that are exported and flood overseas markets. This point of view may offer support for your claim or an opposing viewpoint to counter. Additionally, magazines can also highlight aspects of a topic at a particular point in time. Comparing a *Newsweek* article from 1989 on farm subsidies to an article on the same topic in 2009 allows you to draw conclusions about the changing opinions on this topic over that 20-year period.

Journals are intended for a scholarly audience of researchers, specialists, or students of a particular field. Journals such as the *Journal of Poverty*, *International Social Work*, or the *Journal of Children & Poverty* are all examples of scholarly journals focused on a particular field or research topic. You may hear the term "peer-reviewed" or "refereed" in reference to scholarly journals. This means that the articles contained in a journal have been reviewed by a group of scholars in the same field before the article is published in the journal. This ensures that the research has been vetted by a group of peers before it is published. Articles from scholarly journals can help provide some authority to your argument. By citing experts in a field, you are bolstering your argument and entering into the scholarly conversation we talked about at the beginning of this guide.

Newspaper articles are found in newspapers that are generally published daily. There is a broad range of content in newspapers ranging from articles written by staff reporters, to editorials written by scholars, experts, and general readers, to reviews and commentary written by experts. Newspapers are published more frequently and locally than magazines or journals, making them excellent sources for very recent topics and events, as well as those with regional significance. Newspaper articles can provide you with a point of view from a particular part of the country or world (how Americans differ from Swedes in their opinions on the government's responsibility to reduce income inequality), or a strong opinion on a topic from an expert (a journalist writing an editorial on the reasons for poverty's lack of coverage in the media).

A good argument uses evidence from a variety of sources. Do not assume you have done a good job if your paper cites only newspaper articles. You need a broad range of sources to fill out your argument. Your instructor will provide you with guidelines about the number of sources you need, but it will be up to you to find a variety of sources. Finding two to three sources in each of the categories above will help you begin to build a strong argument.

3. Where should I look for articles on my topic?   The best way to locate journal, magazine, or newspaper articles is to use a database. A database is an online resource that organizes research material of a particular type or content area. For example, *PsycINFO* is a psychology database where you would look for journal articles (as well as other kinds of sources) in the discipline of psychology. Your library licenses or subscribes to databases on your behalf. Finding the right database for your topic will depend upon what is available at your college or university because every institution has a different set of resources. Many libraries will provide subject or research guides that can help you determine what database would be best for your topic. Look for these guides on your library website. Your library's website will have a way to search databases. Look for a section of the library website on databases, and look for a search box in that section. For instance, if you type "poverty" in a database search box, you may find that your library licenses a database called *Global Issues in Context*. A search for "history" in the database search box may yield *American History and Life* or *Historical Abstracts*. In most instances, your best bet is to ask a librarian which database or databases are most relevant to your research.

When using these databases that your library provides for you, you will know that you are starting to sufficiently narrow or broaden your topic when you begin to retrieve 30 to 50 sources during a search. This kind of narrow result field will rarely occur in Google, which is one of the reasons why using library databases is preferable to Google when doing academic research. Databases will help you determine when you have begun to ask a manageable question.

When you have gotten down to 30–50 sources in your result list, begin to look through those results to see what aspects of your topic are being written about. Are there lots of articles on homelessness, children, and low self-esteem? If so, that might be a topic worth investigating since there is a lot of information for you to read. This is when you begin to discover where your voice might add to the ongoing conversation on the topic.

USING EVIDENCE

The quality of the evidence and how you deploy the evidence are ultimately what will make your claims persuasive. You may think of evidence as what will help prove your claim. But if you look at any scholarly book or article, you will see that evidence can be used in a number of different ways. It can be used to provide readers with crucial background information. It can be used to tell readers what scholars have commonly thought about a topic (with which you may disagree). It can offer a theory that you use as a lens. It can offer a methodology or an approach that you would like to use. And finally, it can be used to back up the claim that you are making in your paper.

Novice researchers begin with a thesis and try to find all the evidence that will prove that their claim is valid or true. What if you come across evidence that doesn't help validate your claim? A novice researcher might decide not to take this complicating evidence into account. Indeed, when you come across complicating evidence, you might be tempted to pretend you never saw it! But rather than sweeping imperfect evidence under the rug, you should figure out how to use this evidence to complicate your own ideas.

The best scholarly conversations take into account a wide array of evidence, carefully considering all sides of a topic. As you probably know, often the most fruitful and productive conversations occur not just when you are talking to people who already agree with you, but when you are fully engaged with people who disagree with you.

Coming across unexpected, surprising, and contradictory evidence, then, is a good thing! It forces you to make a complex, nuanced argument and ultimately allows you to write a more persuasive paper.

Other Forms of Evidence

We've talked about finding evidence in books, magazines, journals, and newspapers. Here are a few other kinds of evidence you may want to use.

Interviews   Interviews can be a powerful form of evidence, especially if the person you are interviewing is an expert in the field that you're investigating. Interviewing can be intimidating, but it might help to know that many people (even experts) feel flattered when you ask them for an interview. Most scholars are deeply interested in spreading knowledge, so you should feel comfortable asking a scholar for his or her ideas. Even if the scholar doesn't know the specific answer to your question, he or she may be able to point you in the right direction.

Remember, of course, to be as courteous as possible when you are planning to interview someone. This means sending a polite e-mail that fully introduces yourself and your project before you begin asking questions. E-mail interviews may be convenient, but an in-person interview is best, since this allows for you and the interviewee to engage in a conversation that may take surprising and helpful turns.

It's a good idea to write down a number of questions before the interview. Don't just get facts (which you can easily get somewhere else). Ask the interviewee to speculate about your topic. Remember that "why" and "how" questions often yield more interesting answers than "what" questions.

If you do conduct an in-person interview, act professionally. Be on time, dress respectfully, and show sincere interest and gratitude. Bring something to record the interview. Many reporters still use a pen and a pad, since these feel unobtrusive and are very portable. Write down the interviewee's name, the date, and the location of the interview, and have your list of questions ready. Don't be afraid, of course, to veer from your questions. The best questions might be the follow-up ones that couldn't have occurred to you before the conversation began. You're likely to get the interviewee to talk freely and openly if you show real intellectual curiosity. If you're not a fast writer, it's certainly okay to ask the interviewee to pause for a moment while you take notes. Some people like to record their interviews. Just make sure that you ask permission if you choose to do this. It's always nice to send a brief thank-you note or e-mail after the interview. This would also be a good time to ask any brief follow-up questions.

Images   Because we live in a visual age, we tend to take images for granted. We see them in magazines, on TV, and on the Internet. We don't often think about them as critically as we think about words on a page. Yet, a critical look at an image can uncover helpful evidence for a claim. Use Google Image search or flickr.com to find images using the same keywords you used to find books and articles. Ask your instructor for guidance on how to properly cite and acknowledge the source of any images you wish to use. If you want to present your research outside of a classroom project (for example, publish it on a blog or share it at a community event), ask a research librarian for guidance on avoiding any potential copyright violations.

Multimedia   Like images, multimedia such as video, audio, and animations are increasingly easy to find on the Internet and can strengthen your claim. For instance, if you are researching children and poverty, you could find audio or video news clips illustrating the effects of school breakfast programs on educational performance. There are several audio and video search engines available such as Vimeo (vimeo.com) or Blinkx (blinkx .com), a search engine featuring audio and video from the BBC, Reuters, and the Associated Press, among others. As with images, ask a research librarian for guidance on how to properly cite and acknowledge the source of any multimedia you wish to use. If you want to present your research outside of a classroom project (for example, publish it on a blog or share it at a community event), ask a research librarian for guidance on avoiding any potential copyright violations.

EVALUATING SOURCES

A common problem in research isn't a lack of sources, but rather an overload of information. Information is more accessible than ever. How many times have you done an online search and asked yourself this question: "How do I know which information is good information?" Librarians can help. Evaluating online sources is more challenging than traditional sources because it is harder to make distinctions between good and bad online information than with print sources. It is easy to see that *Newsweek* magazine is not as scholarly as an academic journal, but everything online might look the same. But there are markers of credibility and authoritativeness when it comes to online information, and you can start to recognize them. We will provide a few tips here, but be sure to ask a librarian or your professor for more guidance whenever you are uncertain about the reliability of a source.

1. **Domain**: The domain of a site is the last part of its URL. The domain indicates the type of website. Noting the web address can tell you a lot. An "edu" site indicates that an educational organization created that content. This is no guarantee that the information is accurate, but it does suggest less bias than a "com" site, which will be commercial in nature with a motive to sell you something, including ideas.
2. **Date**: Most websites include a date somewhere on the page. This date might indicate a copyright date, the date something was posted, or the date the site was last updated. These dates tell you when the content on the site was last changed or reviewed. Older sites might be outdated or contain information that is no longer relevant.
3. **Author or editor**: Does the online content indicate an author or editor? Like print materials, authority comes from the creator of the content. It is now easier than ever to investigate an author's credentials. A general Google search may lead you to a Wikipedia entry on the author, a LinkedIn page, or even an online résumé. If an author is affiliated with an educational institution, try visiting the institution's website for more information.

MANAGING SOURCES

Now that you've found sources, you need to think about how you are going to keep track of them and prepare the bibliography that will accompany your paper. This is called "bibliographic citation management," and you will sometimes see references to bibliographic citation management on your library's website. Don't let this complicated phrase deter you—managing your citations from the start of your research will make your life much easier during the process and especially the night before your paper is due when you are compiling your bibliography.

EndNote and RefWorks

Chances are your college library provides software, such as EndNote and RefWorks, to help you manage citations. These are two commercially available citation-management software packages that are not freely available to you unless your library has paid for a license. EndNote and RefWorks enable you to organize your sources in personal libraries. These libraries help you manage your sources and create bibliographies. Both EndNote and RefWorks also enable you to insert endnotes and footnotes directly into a Microsoft Word document.

Zotero

If your library does not provide EndNote or RefWorks, a free software program called Zotero (Zotero.org) can help you manage your sources. Zotero helps you collect, organize, cite, and share your sources, and it lives right in your web browser where you do your research. As you are searching Google, your library catalog, or library database, Zotero enables you to add a book, article, or website to a personal library with one click. As you add items to your library, Zotero collects both the information you need for your bibliography and any full-text content. This means that the content of journal articles and e-books will be available to you right from your Zotero library.

To create a bibliography, simply select the items from your Zotero library you want to include, right click and select "Create Bibliography from Selected Items . . . ," and choose the citation style your instructor has asked you to use for the paper. To get started, go to Zotero.org and download Zotero for the browser of your choice.

Taking Notes

It is crucial that you take good, careful notes while you are doing your research. Not only is careful note-taking necessary to avoid plagiarism, careful note taking can help you think through your project while you are doing research.

Many researchers used to take notes on index cards, but most people now use computers. If you're using your computer, open a new document for each source that you are considering. The first step in taking notes is to make sure that you gather all the information you might need in your bibliography or works cited. If you are taking notes from a book, for instance, you'll need the author, title, place of publication, name of press, and year.

Be sure to check the style guide assigned by your instructor to make sure that you are gathering all the necessary information.

After you've recorded the bibliographic information, add one or two keywords that can help you sort this source. Next, write a one- or two-sentence summary of the source. Finally, have a section in your document that is reserved for specific places in the text that you might want to work with. When you write down a quote, remember to be extra careful that you are capturing the quote exactly as it is written—and that you enclose it in quotation marks. Do not use abbreviations or change the punctuation. Remember also to write down the exact page numbers from the source you are quoting. Being careful with small details at the beginning of your project can save you a lot of time in the long run.

WRITING ABOUT POVERTY/PRIVILEGE

In your writing, as in conversation, you should always be thinking about your audience. Although your most obvious audience is the instructor, most teachers will want you to write a paper that will be interesting and illuminating for other beginning scholars in the field. Many students are unsure of what kind of knowledge they can presume of their audience. A good rule of thumb is to write not only for your instructor but also for other students in your class and for other students in classes similar to yours. You can presume a reasonably informed audience that is curious but also skeptical.

Of course, it is crucial that you keep your instructor in mind. After all, your instructor will be giving you feedback and evaluating your paper. The best way to keep your instructor in mind while you are writing is to periodically reread the assignment while you are writing. Are you answering the assignment's prompt? Are you adhering to the assignment's guidelines? Are you fulfilling the assignment's purpose? If your answers to any of these questions are uncertain, it is a good idea to ask the instructor.

FROM RESEARCH QUESTION TO THESIS STATEMENT

Many students like to begin the writing process by writing an introduction. Novice writers often use early drafts of their introduction to guide the shape of their paper. Experienced scholars, however, continually return to their introduction, reshaping and revising as their thoughts evolve. After all, since writing is thinking, it is impossible to anticipate the full thoughts of your paper before you have written it. Many writers, in fact, only realize the actual argument they are making after they have written a draft or two of the paper. Make sure not to let your introduction trap your thinking. Think of your introduction as a guide that will help your readers down the path of discovery—a path you can only fully know after you have written your paper.

A strong introduction will welcome readers to the scholarly conversation. You will introduce your central interlocutors and pose the question or problem that you are all interested in resolving. Most introductions contain a thesis statement, which is a sentence or two that clearly states the main argument. Some introductions, you will notice, do not contain the argument, but merely contain the promise of a resolution to the intellectual problem.

Is Your Thesis an Argument?

So far, we have discussed a number of steps for you to take when you begin to write a research paper. We started by strategizing about ways to use presearch to find a topic and ask a researchable question, then we looked at ways to find a scholarly conversation by using your library's resources. Now we will discuss a crucial step in the writing process: coming up with a thesis.

Your thesis is the central claim of your paper—the main point that you would like to argue. You may make a number of claims throughout the paper; when you make a claim, you are offering a small argument, usually about a piece of evidence that you've found. Your thesis is your governing claim, the central argument of the whole paper. Sometimes it is difficult to know if you have written a proper thesis. Ask yourself, "Can a reasonable person disagree with my thesis statement?" If the answer is no, then you have likely written an observation rather than an argument. For instance, the statement "The U.S. childhood poverty rate is highest in the South" is not a thesis because it is a true fact. A reasonable person cannot disagree with this fact, so it is not an argument. The statement "The rate of childhood poverty is highest in the South because of the South's unique political climate" is a thesis because it is a debatable point. A reasonable person might disagree (by arguing, for instance, that "the unique economic conditions in southern states best explain the high rate of childhood poverty in the region"). Remember to keep returning to your thesis statement while you are writing. Not only will you be able to make sure that your writing remains on a clear path, but you will also be able to keep refining your thesis so that it becomes clearer and more precise.

Make sure, too, that your thesis is a point of persuasion rather than one of belief or taste. "Southern food tastes delicious" is certainly an argument you could make to a friend, but it is not an adequate thesis for an academic paper because there is no evidence that you could provide that might persuade a reader who doesn't already agree with you.

ORGANIZATION

In order for your paper to feel organized, readers should know where they are headed and have a reasonable idea of how they are going to get there. An introduction will offer a strong sense of organization if it:

- introduces your central intellectual problem and explains why it is important;
- suggests who will be involved in the scholarly conversation;
- indicates what kind of evidence you will be investigating; and
- offers a precise central argument.

Some readers describe well-organized papers as having a sense of flow. When readers praise a sense of flow, they mean that the argument moves easily from one sentence to the next and from one paragraph to the following. This allows a reader to follow your thoughts easily. When you begin writing a sentence, try using an idea, keyword, or phrase from the end of the previous sentence. The next sentence will then appear to have emerged smoothly from the previous one. This tip is especially important when you move between paragraphs. The beginning of a paragraph should feel like it has a clear relationship to the end of the previous paragraph.

Also keep in mind a sense of wholeness. A strong paragraph has a sense of flow and wholeness; not only will you allow your reader to trace your thoughts smoothly, but you will also ensure that your reader understands how all your thoughts are connected to a large, central idea. Ask yourself as you write a paragraph: What does this paragraph have to do with the central intellectual problem that I am investigating? If the relationship isn't clear to you, then your readers will probably be confused.

Novice writers often use the form of a five-paragraph essay. In this form, each paragraph offers an example that proves the validity of the central claim. The five-paragraph essay might have worked in high school since it meets the minimum requirement for making an argument with evidence.

You will quickly notice, however, that experienced writers do not use the five-paragraph format. Indeed, your college instructors will expect you to move beyond it. This is because a five-paragraph essay relies on static examples rather than fully engaging new evidence. A strong essay will grow in complexity and nuance as the writer brings in new evidence. Rather than thinking of an essay as something that offers many examples to back up the same static idea, think of it as the evolution of an idea that grows ever more complex and rich as the writer engages with scholars who view the idea from various angles.

INTEGRATING YOUR RESEARCH

As we have seen, doing research involves finding an intellectual community by looking for scholars who are thinking through similar problems and who may be in conversation with one another. When you write your paper, you will not be merely reporting what you found; you will be orchestrating the conversation that your research has uncovered. To orchestrate a conversation involves asking a few key questions: Whose voices should be most prominent? What is the relationship between one scholar's ideas and another scholar's ideas? How do these ideas contribute to the argument that your own paper is making? Is it important that your readers hear the exact words of the conversation, or can you give them the main ideas and important points of the conversation in your own words? Your answers to these questions will determine how you go about integrating your research into the paper.

Using evidence is a way of gaining authority. Even though you may not have known much about your topic before you started researching, the way you use evidence in your paper will allow you to establish a voice that is authoritative and trustworthy. You have three basic choices for ways to present information from a source: summarize, paraphrase, or quote. Let's discuss each one briefly.

Summary

You should summarize a source when the source provides helpful background information for your research. Summaries do not make strong evidence, but they can be helpful if you need to chart the intellectual terrain of your project. Summaries can be an efficient way of capturing the main ideas of a source. When you are summarizing, remember to be fully sympathetic to the writer's point of view. Put yourself in the scholar's shoes. If you later disagree with the scholar's methods or conclusions, your disagreement will be convincing because your reader will know that you have given the scholar a fair hearing. A summary that is clearly biased is not only inaccurate and ethically suspect, it will make your writing less convincing because readers will be suspicious of your rigor.

Let's say you come across the following quote that you'd like to summarize. Here's an excerpt from the web-based article "Subsidizing Starvation" by Maura O'Connor:

> Development experts argue that while U.S. exports may feed people cheaply in the short run, they have exacerbated poverty and food insecurity over time, and subsidies are largely to blame. "The support that U.S. rice producers receive is a big factor in why they are a big player in the global rice market and the leading source of imported rice in Haiti," said Marc Cohen, a senior researcher on humanitarian policy and climate change at Oxfam America. "If governments that preached trade liberalization in Geneva would practice it—and that includes reducing domestic support measures that affect trade—if everything was on a level playing field, that would be very helpful to Haiti."

Consider this summary:

> In "Subsidizing Starvation," Maura O'Connor says that international trade causes poverty and food insecurity. I agree that trade is harmful.

If you compare this summary to what O'Connor actually said, you will see that this summary is a biased, distorted version of the actual quote. O'Connor did not make a universal claim about whether trade is helpful or harmful. Rather, she explains why trade is harmful in one case under a specific set of circumstances.

Now let's look at another summary:

> O'Connor reports that while farm subsidies can help American growers and starving people abroad in the short run, they can harm long-term development efforts.

This is a much stronger summary than the previous example. The writer shortens O'Connor's original language, but she is fair to the writer's original meaning and intent.

Paraphrase

Paraphrasing involves putting a source's ideas into your own words. It's a good idea to paraphrase if you think you can state the idea more clearly or directly than the original source does. Remember that if you paraphrase, you need to put the entire idea into your own words. It is not enough for you to change one or two words. Indeed, if you only change a few words, you may put yourself at risk of plagiarizing.

Let's look at how we might paraphrase the O'Connor selection that we've been discussing. Consider this paraphrase:

> Experts in the field claim that subsidies are at fault in making poverty and food insecurity worse over time, even if American trade products might be a low-cost way to quickly reduce starvation (O'Connor).

You will notice that the writer simply replaced some of O'Connor's original language with synonyms. Even with the parenthetical citation, this is unacceptable paraphrasing. Indeed, this is a form of plagiarism, because the writer suggests that the language is his or her own, when it is in fact an only slightly modified version of O'Connor's own phrasing.

Let's see how we might paraphrase O'Connor in an academically honest way:

> Because exports of American goods can flood international economies, farm subsidies that incentivize American growers to produce and profit from excess crops can actually increase starvation and poverty abroad (O'Connor).

Here the writer has taken O'Connor's message but has used his or her own language to describe what O'Connor originally wrote. The writer offers O'Connor's ideas with fresh syntax and new vocabulary, and the writer is sure to give O'Connor credit for the idea in a parenthetical citation.

Quotation

The best way to show that you are in conversation with scholars is to quote them. Quoting involves capturing the exact wording and punctuation of a passage. Quotations make for powerful evidence, especially in humanities papers. If you come across evidence that you think will be helpful in your project, you should quote it. You might be tempted to quote only those passages that seem to agree with the claim you are making. But remember to write down the quotes of scholars who might not seem to agree with you. These are precisely the thoughts that will help you build a powerful scholarly conversation. Working with fresh ideas that you might not agree with can help you revise your claim to make it even more persuasive, since it will force you to take into account potential counterarguments. When your readers see that you are grappling with an intellectual problem from all sides and that you are giving all interlocutors a fair voice, they are more likely to be persuaded by your argument.

To make sure that you are properly integrating sources into your paper, remember the acronym ICE, which stands for Introduce, Cite, and Explain. Let's imagine that you have found an idea that you'd like to incorporate into your paper investigating the effects of domestic farm subsidies on food exports to developing countries. We'll use a quote from David Harvey's *A Brief History of Neoliberalism* as an example. On page 7, you find the following quote that you would like to use: "The assumption that individual freedoms are guaranteed by freedom of the market and of trade is a cardinal feature of neoliberal thinking, and it has long dominated the US stance towards the rest of the world."

The first thing you need to do is **introduce** the quote (the "I" in ICE). To introduce a quote, provide context so that your readers know where it is coming from and integrate it into your own sentence. Here are some examples of how you might do this:

> In his book *A Brief History of Neoliberalism*, David Harvey writes . . .
> One expert on the relationship between economics and politics claims . . .
> Professor of anthropology David Harvey explains that . . .
> In a recent book by Harvey, he contends . . .

Notice that each of these introduces the quote in such a way that readers are likely to recognize it as an authoritative source.

The next step is to **cite** the quote (the "C" in ICE). Here is where you indicate the origin of the quotation so that your readers can easily look up the original source. Citing is a two-step process that varies slightly depending on the citation style that you're using. We offer an example using MLA style. The first step involves indicating the author and page number in the body of your essay. Here is an example of a parenthetical citation that gives the author and page number after the quote and before the period that ends the sentence:

> One expert on the relationship between economics and politics claims that neoliberal thinking has "long dominated the US stance towards the rest of the world" (Harvey 7).

Note that if it is already clear to readers which author you are quoting, you need only give the page number:

> In *A Brief History of Neoliberalism*, David Harvey contends that neoliberal thinking has "long dominated the US stance towards the rest of the world" (7).

The second step of citing the quote is providing proper information in the works cited or bibliography of your paper. This list should include the complete bibliographical information of all the sources you have cited. An essay that includes the quote by David Harvey should also include the following entry in the works cited:

> Harvey, David. *A Brief History of Neoliberalism*. New York: Oxford UP, 2005. Print.

Finally, the most crucial part of integrating a quote is **explaining** it (the "E" in ICE). This is often overlooked, but a strong explanation is the most important step in involving yourself in the scholarly conversation. Here is where you will explain how you interpret the source you are citing, what aspect of the quote is most important for your readers to understand, and how the source pertains to your own project. For example:

> David Harvey writes, "The assumption that individual freedoms are guaranteed by freedom of the market and of trade is a cardinal

feature of neoliberal thinking, and it has long dominated the US stance towards the rest of the world" (7). As Harvey explains, neoliberalism suggests that free markets do not limit personal freedom but actually lead to free individuals.

Or:

David Harvey writes, "The assumption that individual freedoms are guaranteed by freedom of the market and of trade is a cardinal feature of neoliberal thinking, and it has long dominated the US stance towards the rest of the world" (7). For Harvey, before we understand the role of the United States in global politics, we must first understand the philosophy that binds personal freedom with market freedom.

Novice writers are sometimes tempted to end a paragraph with a quote that they feel is especially compelling or clear. But remember that you should never leave a quote to speak for itself (even if you love it). After all, as the orchestrator of this scholarly conversation, you need to make sure that readers are receiving exactly what you would like them to receive from each quote. Notice in the above examples that the first explanation suggests that the writer quoting Harvey is centrally concerned with neoliberal philosophy, whereas the second explanation suggests that the writer is centrally concerned with U.S. politics. The explanation, in other words, is the crucial link between your source and the main idea of your paper.

AVOIDING PLAGIARISM

Scholarly conversations are what drive knowledge in the world. Scholars using each other's ideas in open, honest ways form the bedrock of our intellectual communities and ensure that our contributions to the world of thought are important. It is crucial, then, that all writers do their part in maintaining the integrity and trustworthiness of scholarly conversations. It is crucial that you never claim someone else's ideas as your own and that you are always extra careful to give the proper credit to someone else's thoughts. This is what we call responsible scholarship.

The best way to avoid plagiarism is to plan ahead and keep careful notes as you read your sources. Remember the advice (above) on Zotero and taking notes: Find the way that works best for you to keep track of what ideas are your own and what ideas come directly from the sources you are reading. Most acts of plagiarism are accidental. It is easy when you are drafting a paper to lose track of where a quote or idea came from; if you plan ahead, this won't happen. Here are a few tips for making sure that confusion doesn't happen to you:

1. Know what needs to be cited. You do not need to cite what is considered common knowledge, such as facts (the day Lincoln was born), concepts (the Earth orbits the Sun), or events (the day Martin Luther King was shot). You do need to cite the ideas and words of others from the sources you are using in your paper.
2. Be conservative. If you are not sure whether you should cite something, either ask your instructor or a librarian, or cite it. It is better to cite something you don't have to than not cite something you should.
3. Direct quotations from your sources need to be cited, as well as anytime you paraphrase ideas or words from sources.
4. Finally, extensive citation not only helps you avoid plagiarism, but it also boosts your credibility and enables your readers to trace your scholarship.

CITATION STYLES

It is crucial that you adhere to the standards of a single citation style when you write your paper. The most common styles are MLA (Modern Language Association, generally used in the humanities), APA (American Psychological Association, generally used in the social sciences), and Chicago (*Chicago Manual of Style*). If you are not sure which style to use, you should ask your instructor. Each style has its own guidelines regarding the format of a paper. While proper formatting within a given style may seem arbitrary, there are important reasons behind the guidelines of each style. For instance, while MLA citations tend to emphasize author's names, APA citations tend to emphasize the dates of publications. This distinction makes sense, especially given that MLA standards are usually followed by departments in the humanities and APA standards are usually followed by departments in the social sciences. While papers in the humanities value original thinking about arguments and texts that are canonical and often old, papers in the social sciences tend to value arguments that take into account the most current thought and the latest research.

There are a number of helpful guidebooks that will tell you all the rules you need to know in order to follow the standards for various citation styles. If your instructor hasn't pointed you to a specific guidebook, try the following online resources:

Purdue Online Writing Lab: owl.english.purdue.edu/

Internet Public Library: www.ipl.org/div/farq/netciteFARQ.html

Modern Language Association (for MLA style): www.mla.org/style

American Psychological Association (for APA style): www.apastyle.org/

The Chicago Manual of Style Online: www.chicagomanualofstyle.org/tools_citationguide.html

Olivia Cogan

April 9, 2014

Involving Parents in Education:

Suggested Improvements for the Upward Bound Program

Education has long held a position as the "great equalizer" within society. In theory, we depend on education as a force that will level the social playing field for people of all socioeconomic backgrounds and ethnicities. In practice, however, we face the stark reality that education, especially higher education, remains out of reach for a large sector of the American population, particularly those born into poverty. These children face obstacles such as an inability to pay application fees and tuition, inadequate academic preparation, and a lack of knowledge within the realm of higher education (Tierney and Hagedorn 1). Despite these obstacles, we tend to agree that these children would most directly benefit from a postsecondary education that would provide them with an opportunity to earn a sustainable living. Summoning scholars and practitioners to expose and wrestle with the root causes of poverty, the Joseph Rowntree Foundation specifically challenges researchers to examine "the most effective methods of increasing involvement and support for the education of children among their parents or guardians." In this essay, I begin to answer this question, arguing that integrating familial involvement programming into the national Upward Bound Program will likely increase students' propensities to pursue higher education.

In 1965, the U.S. Department of Education introduced the Upward Bound Program, seeking to "reduce the gaps in college access and completion among student populations differing by race/ethnicity, socioeconomic status, and disability while increasing the educational attainment of all" (Cahalan and Thomas 1). Since its outset in 1965, Upward Bound has operated to achieve the ultimate goal of narrowing the social-achievement gap by enhancing access to postsecondary education for low-income and potentially first-generation college students. Upward Bound exists as a series of after-school and summer classes that offer mentoring, counseling, work-study opportunities, and tutoring in core subjects. The program's services are available to 13–19-year-old students who display a need for academic support and who come from low-income backgrounds and are potentially first-generation college students. Although Upward Bound has increased college enrollment rates for low-income students, research suggests that it could take additional steps to enhance its effectiveness.

Many obstacles impede students' access to higher education. Students growing up in poverty most often live in underfunded school districts, where technology and other resources are scarce (DNLee). Students living in impoverished areas also often experience health-related hardships including environmental hazards and an inability to access healthcare to treat the effects of these (Gammon). Students' families often further complicate higher education achievement. Overstressed, overworked, and inexperienced parents are less able to help their children to the degree they need to in order to compensate for these obstacles. Also, parents without personal experience in higher education lack important knowledge about completing basic admissions procedures, navigating college applications, making connections between career goals and education requirements, and financing tuition charges. The latter phenomenon is especially problematic as low-income students are often the prey of for-profit schools that offer loans with especially steep, financially crippling interest rates (Wright). Additionally, many scholars agree that parents who did not attend college themselves tend to defer decision-making regarding their children's educational careers and entrust school officials with their children's placements in courses. Consequently, college discussions and decisions transpire separately from the student's home life. Finally, first-generation college students often—though certainly not always—experience a lack of support and even discouragement from their families. As Carmen Tym and her colleagues explain, "while going to college may be seen as a rite of passage for any student, it marks a significant separation from the past for those who are the first in their families to do so" (5). Many students also endure criticism as they redirect their time from fulfilling family responsibilities to pursuing academic aspirations. Thus, first-generation college students face great struggles in their journeys toward higher education in terms of support from their families.

Although some families of potentially first-generation college students hinder students' educational well-being, research indicates that family involvement is the most crucial nonacademic factor in a first-generation student's path toward postsecondary education (Dottin, Steen, and Samuel 68). Specifically, Tierney and Hagedorn conclude that "a majority of the research indicated that students performed better and had higher levels of motivation when they were raised in homes characterized by supportive and demanding parents who were involved in schools and encouraged and expected academic success" (195). Many other studies indicate a strong link between parental involvement and student educational achievement, even during early childhood (Duncan and Magnuson). In essence, schooling and educational advancement programs should be directly linked to students' home environments.

In accordance with Tierney's findings, I advocate that low-income parents with minimal higher education should take an active role within their children's academic endeavors. Consequently, enhancing parental involvement at home would constitute a logical first step. In particular, both parents and students would benefit if parents involved themselves in their children's college exploration and selection processes (Garcia 87–88). In particular, they should volunteer to visit college campuses and discuss college options early in their children's high school careers. In turn, this would allow parents with no college experience to become more comfortable with their children's transition to higher education.

Additionally, research shows that direct parent-to-school communication is beneficial (Engberg and Allen). Accordingly, Upward Bound could create a webpage that would allow parents to track their children's progress within the program if they have Internet access. This web connection would also serve as a medium in which parents could raise questions and voice any concerns regarding their children's academic careers within Upward Bound.

In addition to increased parental involvement in their children's educational endeavors at home, the students would benefit if Upward Bound worked to inform parents about the necessary steps for applying to and financing higher education. Studies indicate that parents with minimal education are far less knowledgeable about the college admissions and enrollment process, including details about required testing and prerequisite courses, applications, deadlines, and scholarship options and procedures (Tierney and Hagedorn 205). Upward Bound could organize, for instance, "workshops on financial aid, college requirements and information to help students excel in school" (Garcia 24). For parents who don't have college experience, Upward Bound could become an important mediator in this process.

Furthermore, parents may benefit from general guidance on raising a high school-aged student. In particular, Stahl concedes that "a key understanding for the teachers to keep in mind is that even though they . . . deal with students of a certain age every day and every school year, this may be the first time that the parents are experiencing a child of that

Cogan   6

age" (3). Consequently, it could be beneficial for programs like Upward Bound to provide knowledgeable advisors who could work to instruct parents in addition to the program participants themselves. This proposal corresponds with the strategies that Stuart Greene and Joyce Long have successfully devised within their program based in South Bend, Indiana called "No Parent Left Behind," which seeks to nourish trusting, reciprocal relationships between parents and educators. In accordance with their mission, Upward Bound should place a particular emphasis on helping "families become informed agents in their children's education" (Ferlazzo).

In addition to making a conscious effort to educate the students' parents, Upward Bound should encourage parents to attend regular meeting times for parent-teacher conferences. In particular, Stahl illustrates direct correlations between conferences for parents and the students' academic successes; thus, he asserts that the planned meetings "[create] continuity between the two dominant spheres of influence in the child's life, home, and school" (7). In essence, the meetings would incentivize parents to invest in their children's educations and, in turn, serve as an additional motivator for the students to perform well academically. Despite the potential benefits, however, some might argue that conferences would create unnecessary demands on the parents in that they "might require transportation, childcare arrangements, and job flexibility" (Tierney and Hagedorn 205). Although I concede that the parent-teacher meetings would

Cogan   7

pose an additional strain on parents' time and income, I still contend that this sort of involvement serves as a crucial factor in students' academic successes and progression.

Finally, along with the establishment of parent-teacher conferences, Upward Bound could coordinate meetings between parents with no postsecondary education who have children who earned a bachelor's degree and parents with potentially first-generation college students. For example, Anat Gofen finds that "families who broke through can mentor other families with school-aged children and guide them about how to invest their nonmaterial resources such as discussions of future plans, explicitly expressing expectations, decision making that prioritizes schooling, and building motivations" (117). Thus, this type of guidance can equip mentee families with the knowledge they need to act as effective axes of support for students in their quests for higher education.

All too often, children born into low-income families become trapped within the cycle of poverty as they venture toward adulthood. Consequently, we look to education as the solution that could end this vicious cycle. Unfortunately, potentially first-generation college students from low-income families face the greatest struggles in accessing higher education. In turn, the U.S. Department of Education has taken significant steps to make postsecondary education more accessible to youth from low-income families with its introduction of the Upward Bound Program, and creating family involvement programs could narrow the

Cogan   8

college accessibility gap even further. With the implementation of these strategies, we could come closer to tackling
inequality in access to education and thus equip underpriv-
ileged youth with the skills they need to break through the
cycle of poverty.

References

Cahalan, Margaret W., and Thomas R. Curtin. *A Profile
of the Upward Bound Program: 2001–2002.*
Washington, D.C.: U.S. Dept. of Education, 2004.

DNLee. "If I Were a Wealthy White Suburbanite." The
Urban Scientist. *Scientific American*, Dec. 13, 2011.
Web. March 15, 2014.

Dottin, Erskine S., Daris L. Steen, and Denise Samuel.
*Bringing Out the Best in Human Effectiveness:
Lessons for Educators from an Upward Bound
Project.* Lanham, MD: University of America, 2004.

Duncan, Greg J., and Katherine Magnuson. "The Long
Reach of Early Childhood Poverty." *Pathways*, Winter
2011. Web. March 17, 2014.

Engberg, MarkAllen, Daniel. "Uncontrolled Destinies:
Improving Opportunity for Low-Income Students
in American Higher Education." *Research In Higher
Education* 52.8 (2011): 786–807. *Professional
Development Collection.* Web. March 27, 2014.

Ferlazzo, Larry. "No Parent Left Behind." *Engaging
Parents in School.* N.p., 16 Apr. 2010. Web.
March 28, 2014.

Gammon, Crystal, and Environmental Health News.
"Pollution, Poverty and People of Color: Asthma and

the Inner City." *Scientific American*, June 20, 2012. Web. April 1, 2014.

Garcia, Diana Michelle. "Experiences of Upward Bound Alumni: Influence of Upward Bound on Student Persistence." Thesis. Ed. Edmund W. Lee. California State University–Sacramento, 2009.

Gofen, Anat. "Family Capital: How First-Generation Higher Education Students Break the Intergenerational Cycle." *Family Relations* 58.1 (2009): 104–120.

Gullatt, Yvette, and Wendy Jan. "How Do Precollegiate Academic Outreach Programs Impact College-Going among Underrepresented Students?" *The Pathways to College Network* (2003): 57–66.

"100 Questions: Identifying Research Priorities for Poverty Prevention and Reduction." Joseph Rowntree Foundation, n.d. Web. April 3, 2014.

Stahl, Jeff D. "Parental Involvement in Education." Jeffdstahl.com, n.d. Web. March 18, 2014.

Tierney, William G., and Linda Serra Hagedorn. *Increasing Access to College: Extending Possibilities for All Students*. Albany, NY: State University of New York, 2002.

Tym, Carmen, Robin McMillion, Sandra Barone, and Jeff Webster. *First-Generation College Students: A Literature Review*. Research and Analytical Services, Texas Guaranteed Student Loan Corporation. 2004. Web. March 14, 2014.

Wright, Kai. "Young, Black and Buried in Debt: How For-Profit Colleges Prey on African-American Ambition." *Salon.com*. June 9, 2013. Web. April 5, 2014.

credits

Chapter 1: Definitions: What Is Poverty?

Chapter opener photo - Library of Congress, Prints & Photographs Division, FSA/
OWI Collection, [reproduction number, e.g., LC-USF34-9058-C].

Page 3 Iceland, John. "Early Views of Poverty in America" from *Poverty in America:
A Handbook* by John Iceland. © 2013, the Regents of the University of California.
Reprinted by permission.

Page 15 Ehrenreich, Barbara. "How We Cured 'The Culture of Poverty,' Not Poverty
Itself" by Barbara Ehrenreich. © 2012 by Barbara Ehrenreich. Used by permission.
All rights reserved.

Page 19 "Penury Portrait: The Consensus on Raising People out of Poverty Is Relatively
Recent" from *The Economist*, July 27, 2013. © *The Economist* Newspaper Limited,
London 2013. Reprinted by permission.

Page 23 Offenheiser, Ray. "Poverty at Home" from *Politico*, April 2, 2013, and online
at oxfamamerica.org. Reprinted by permission of Oxfam America.

Page 26 Adair, Vivyan. "Reclaiming the Promise of Higher Education: Poor Single
Mothers in Academe." Testimony to the U.S. Senate Committee on Finance,
September 21, 2010. Used by permission of Vivyan Adair.

Page 32 Kaufmann, Greg. "U.S. Poverty: By the Numbers" from "This Week in
Poverty: The Older Americans Act and U.S. Seniors" by Greg Kaufmann.
Reprinted with permission from the June 21, 2013, issue of *The Nation*. Portions
can be accessed at http://www.thenation.com.

Page 33 Addy, Sophia, Will Engelhardt, and Curtis Skinner. Basic Facts About Low-
income Children, Figure 1, "Children by Family Income, 2011." © National
Center for Children in Poverty (www.nccp.org). Used by permission.

Page 34 U.S. Census Bureau, "Definition and Resources for Poverty," http://www
.census.gov/hhes/www/poverty/methods/definitions.html, accessed July 14, 2014.

Page 42 Measure of America. "About Human Development," online at
measureofamerica.org. Designed by Humantific and reprinted by permission
of Measure of America, a project of the Social Science Research Council.

Page 49 Rector, Robert, and Rachel Sheffield. Excerpted from "Air Conditioning,
Cable TV, and an Xbox: What Is Poverty in the United States Today?" from the
Heritage Foundation, Backgrounder #2575 on Poverty and Inequality, July 19,
2011. Used by permission.

Page 52 Haveman, Robert. "What Does It Mean to Be Poor in a Rich Society?" from *Focus*, Institute for Research on Poverty. © 2009 by the Board of Regents of the University of Wisconsin. Reprinted by permission.

Page 65 Kenny, Charles. "In Praise of Slums" from *Foreign Policy*, Aug. 13, 2012. Republished with permission of *Foreign Policy*. Permission conveyed through Copyright Clearance Center, Inc.

Chapter 2: Causes: Why Are People Poor?

Chapter opener photo courtesy of the Children's Aid Society Archive, New York City.

Page 74 Haskins, Ron, and Isabel Sawhill. "Perspectives on Poverty" from *Creating an Opportunity Society* by Ron Haskins and Isabel Sawhill. © 2009, the Brookings Institution. Reprinted by permission of Brookings Institution Press.

Page 98 Burd-Sharps, Sarah, and Kristen Lewis. "Inequality: Shifting the Spotlight from Wall Street to Your Street" appeared in the *Huffington Post*, July 9, 2013, and online at Oxfam America. Reprinted by permission of the authors.

Page 102 Sessions, Jeff. "Memo on FY14 Budget Process." Senate Memo, Feb. 11, 2013.

Page 106 Wright, Kai. "Young, Black, and Buried in Debt: How For-Profit Colleges Prey on African-American Ambition" from *Salon*, June 9, 2013. This article first appeared in Salon.com, at http://www.Salon.com. An online version remains in the Salon archives. Reprinted with permission.

Page 114 Alexander, Michelle. "The New Jim Crow: How the War on Drugs Gave Birth to a Permanent American Undercaste" appeared in *Race, Poverty & the Environment*, Vol. 17, No. 1, 20th Anniversary Issue (Spring 2010). Reprinted by permission of the author.

Page 120 DuBois, Joshua. "The Fight for Black Men" from *Newsweek*, June 19, 2013. Reprinted by permission of the author.

Page 136 NPR. " 'Life, Death And Politics': Treating Chicago's Uninsured," *Fresh Air*, June 15, 2011. Fresh Air is produced by WHYY, Inc. and distributed by NPR. Used by permission of WHYY, Inc.

Page 138 Ansell, David. Excerpts from *County: Life, Death and Politics at Chicago's Public Hospital* by David Ansell. © 2011. Used by permission of the Susan Schulman Literary Agency LLC on behalf of the author.

Page 147 Joseph Rowntree Foundation. "100 Questions about Poverty: Identifying Research Priorities for Poverty Prevention and Reduction" from http://www.jrf .org.uk/publications/100-questions-about-poverty and reproduced by permission of the Joseph Rowntree Foundation.

Chapter 3: Consequences: Who Is Poor?

Chapter opener photo - © Kevin Carter/Sygma/Corbis.

Page 159 Thompson, Gabriel. "Could You Survive on $2 a Day?" Originally published at *Mother Jones* and reproduced by the Economic Hardship Reporting Project. Reprinted by permission.

Page 167 Bauer, Mary, and Mónica Ramírez. From "Injustice on Our Plates: Immigrant Women in the U.S. Food Industry." © 2010 Southern Poverty Law Center. Reprinted by permission of the Southern Poverty Law Center.

Page 171 Feeding America, "Map the Meal Gap," 2013. Used by permission.

Page 175 Potts, Monica. "Pressing on the Upward Way" from *The American Prospect*, June 12, 2012. Used with the permission of *The American Prospect*, prospect.org.

Page 192 Sanders, Bernie. "Poverty in America: A Death Sentence." *Spotlight on Poverty and Opportunity.*

Page 195 Livingston, Sonja. "Shame" from *Ghostbread* by Sonja Livingston, published by the University of Georgia Press. © 2009 by Sonja Livingston. Reprinted by permission of the publisher.

Page 197 Sullivan-Hackley, Laura. "Speech Pathology: The Deflowering of an Accent" was first published in *Kalliope* 21, No. 3: 39. Reprinted by permission of the author.

Page 199 Alexie, Sherman. "Why Chicken Means So Much to Me" from *The Absolutely True Diary of a Part-Time Indian* by Sherman Alexie. © 2007 by Sherman Alexie. By permission of Little, Brown and Company. All rights reserved.

Page 205 Gammon, Crystal. "Pollution, Poverty, and People of Color: Asthma and the Inner City" from *Environmental Health News*, June 19, 2012, www.EHN.org. Reprinted by permission of *Environmental Health N*ews.

Page 213 Shriver, Maria. "The Female Face of Poverty" as first published in *The Atlantic.* © 2014, The Atlantic Media Co. All rights reserved. Distributed by Tribune Content Agency, LLC.

Page 217 Duncan, Greg J., and Katherine Magnuson. "The Long Reach of Early Childhood Poverty" originally published in *Pathways Magazine*, Winter 2011. Reprinted by permission of the authors and *Pathways Magazine.*

Page 219 Gornick, Janet C. and Markus Jäntti. Figure from "Child Poverty in Upper-Income Countries: Lessons from the Luxembourg Income Study," from *Child Welfare to Child Well-Being*, 2010, pp 339–368. Copyright © 2010, Springer Science+Business Media B.V. With kind permission from Springer Science and Business Media.

Page 227 Blunt, Roger R., and Paul D. Monroe Jr. "We Have a Wealth Gap, and Military Is Poorer for It," published in *Stars and Stripes*, April 15, 2013, and online at oxfamamerica.org. Reprinted by permission of Oxfam America.

Page 231 O'Connor, Maura. "Subsidizing Starvation" from *Foreign Policy*, Jan. 11, 2013. Republished with permission of *Foreign Policy*. Permission conveyed through Copyright Clearance Center, Inc.

Chapter 4: Privilege: Who Isn't Poor?

Chapter opener photo - Library of Congress, Prints & Photographs Division, FSA/OWI Collection, [reproduction number, e.g., LC-USZ62-45985].

Page 245 Martin, Courtney. "Moving Past Acknowledging Privilege" from *The American Prospect*, April 18, 2011. Used with the permission of *The American Prospect*, prospect.org.

Page 249 Cole, Teju. "The White Savior Industrial Complex," originally published in *The Atlantic.* © 2012 by Teju Cole. Used by permission of the Wylie Agency LLC.

Page 258 Marks, Gene. "If I Were a Poor Black Kid" from *Forbes*, Dec. 12, 2011. © 2011 Forbes. All rights reserved. Used by permission.

Page 262 DNLee. "If I Were a Wealthy White Suburbanite" from *Scientific American*, Dec. 13, 2011. © 2011 *Scientific American*, a division of Nature America, Inc. Reprinted by permission.

Page 266 Cottom, Tressie McMillan. "Why Do Poor People 'Waste' Money on Luxury Goods?" from *Talking Points Memo*, Nov. 1, 2013. Reprinted by permission of the author.

Page 272 Webb, James. "Diversity and the Myth of White Privilege" from the *Wall Street Journal*, July 22, 2010. © 2010, Dow Jones & Company. Used by permission.

Page 276 Serwer, Adam. "Webb and 'White Privilege'" from *The American Prospect*, July 26, 2010. Used with the permission of *The American Prospect*, prospect.org.

Page 279 "The Rich Are Different from You and Me" from *The Economist*, July 31, 2010. © The Economist Newspaper Limited, London 2010. Used by permission.

Page 282 Zurcher, Anthony. "'Affluenza Defence': Rich, Privileged, and Unaccountable" from *BBC News*, *Echo Chambers*, Dec. 13, 2013. Used with permission.

Chapter 5: Rhetoric: How Do the Media Represent Poverty?

Chapter opener photo - Time & Life Pictures/Getty Images.

Page 289 Kuper, Simon. "Poverty's Poor Show in the Media" from the *Financial Times*, March 29, 2013. © Financial Times Limited 2013. All rights reserved. Reprinted by permission.

Page 293 Froomkin, Dan. "It Can't Happen Here: Why Is There Still So Little Coverage of Americans Who Are Struggling with Poverty?" from *Nieman Reports*, Winter 2013. Reprinted by permission of the Nieman Foundation for Journalism at Harvard.

Page 299 Brennan, Emily. "Reporting Poverty: Interview with Katherine Boo," originally published in *Guernica*, Sept. 4, 2012. Reprinted by permission of the author.

Page 307 Solnit, Rebecca. "When the Media Is the Disaster: Covering Haiti," published in the *Huffington Post*, Jan. 21, 2010. © 2010 by Rebecca Solnit. Used by permission of the Hill Nadell Literary Agency.

Page 315 King, Noel. "American Presidents and the Rhetoric of Poverty" from American Public Media's *Marketplace*. © 2014. Used with permission. All rights reserved.

Page 318 Mehta, Nazneen. "Opposing Images: 'Third World Women' and 'Welfare Queens'" from *Women's Policy Journal of Harvard*, 2010. © 2010 by the President and Fellows of Harvard College. Reprinted by permission.

Page 324 Olson, Miriam Meltzer, et al. "Picture This: Images and Realities in Welfare to Work" from *Affilia: Journal of Women in Social Work*, 15 (2), 329–344 (Summer 2000). Reprinted by permission of SAGE Publications.

Page 337 United Nations Development Programme. "There Are 8 Things Maria Wants to See Happen by 2015" and "The UN Has Picked a Group of People to Eliminate World Poverty," posters for "Teams to End Poverty" campaign. Used by permission of the United Nations Development Programme.

Chapter 6: Solutions: What Should We Do about Poverty?

Chapter opener photo - Surplus Commodities: School Lunch Programs (Library ID: 53227(1771)).

Page 346 Karlan, Dean S., and Jacob Appel. "Introduction: The Monks and the Fish" from *More than Good Intentions: How a New Economics Is Helping to Solve Global Poverty* by Dean S. Karlan and Jacob Appel. © 2011 by Dean S. Karlan and Jacob Appel. Used by permission of Dutton, a division of Penguin Group (USA) LLC.

Page 360 Buffett, Peter. "The Charitable-Industrial Complex" from the *New York Times*, July 26, 2013. © 2013, the New York Times Company. Reprinted by permission.

Page 363 Theroux, Paul. "Africa's Aid Mess" from *Barron's*, Nov. 30, 2013. © 2013, Dow Jones & Company. Reprinted by permission.

index